Food Security

UNU World Institute for Development Economics Research (UNU-WIDER) was established by the United Nations University as its first research and training centre and started work in Helsinki, Finland in 1985. The purpose of the institute is to undertake applied research and policy analysis on structural changes affecting developing and transitional economies, to provide a forum for the advocacy of policies leading to robust, equitable, and environmentally sustainable growth, and to promote capacity strengthening and training in the field of economic and social policymaking. Its work is carried out by staff researchers and visiting scholars in Helsinki and via networks of collaborating scholars and institutions around the world.

World Institute for Development Economics Research (UNU-WIDER) Katajanokanlaituri 6 B, FIN-00160 Helsinki, Finland. www.wider.unu.edu

Food and Agriculture Organization of the United Nations leads international efforts to defeat hunger. Serving both developed and developing countries, FAO acts as a neutral forum where all nations meet as equals to negotiate agreements and debate policy. FAO is also a source of knowledge and information. FAO helps developing countries and countries in transition modernize and improve agriculture, forestry, and fisheries practices and ensure good nutrition for all. Since its founding in 1945, FAO has focused special attention on developing rural areas, home to 70 per cent of the world's poor and hungry people. FAO's activities comprise four main areas:

- Putting information within reach
- Sharing policy expertise
- Providing a meeting place for nations
- Bringing knowledge to the field.

Indian Council of Social Science Research (ICSSR), established in 1969 promotes social science research in India. ICSSR supports twenty-seven research institutes in India engaged in multi-disciplinary research. ICSSR is the nodal agency for implementing the social science component of the Cultural Exchange Programmes (CEPs) signed between the Government of India and other countries, and with foreign counterparts outside CEPs, for activities like the exchange of scholars, joint seminars, and research projects. ICSSR is a member of the International Social Science Council (ISSC)—Paris, the Association of Asian Social Science Research Council (AASSREC), Science Council of Asia—Japan, and the International Federation of Social Sciences Organizations (IFSSO). Collaborative ties have also been established with UNU-WIDER and the Organization for Economic Cooperation and Development (OECD).

Food Security

Indicators, Measurement, and the Impact of Trade Openness

Edited by
Basudeb Guha-Khasnobis, Shabd S. Acharya, and Benjamin Davis

UNU-WIDER Studies in Development Economics

OXFORD
UNIVERSITY PRESS

OXFORD
UNIVERSITY PRESS

Great Clarendon Street, Oxford OX2 6DP

Oxford University Press is a department of the University of Oxford.
It furthers the University's objective of excellence in research, scholarship,
and education by publishing worldwide in

Oxford New York

Auckland Cape Town Dar es Salaam Hong Kong Karachi
Kuala Lumpur Madrid Melbourne Mexico City Nairobi
New Delhi Shanghai Taipei Toronto

With offices in

Argentina Austria Brazil Chile Czech Republic France Greece
Guatemala Hungary Italy Japan Poland Portugal Singapore
South Korea Switzerland Thailand Turkey Ukraine Vietnam

Published in the United States
by Oxford University Press Inc., New York

First published 2007

British Library Cataloguing in Publication Data
Data available

Library of Congress Cataloging in Publication Data
Data available

Typeset by SPI Publisher Services, Pondicherry, India
Printed in Great Britain
on acid-free paper by
Biddles Ltd., King's Lynn, Norfolk

ISBN 978–0–19–923655–8

10 9 8 7 6 5 4 3 2 1

Foreword

As many as 2.8 million children and 300,000 women die needlessly every year because of malnutrition in developing countries. Despite the enormity of the problem, and even though reducing hunger is one of the Millennium Development Goals (MDGs), hunger and food security receive less attention than poverty reduction from both a policy and research perspective. The lack of action in the fight against hunger may have arisen from a belief that success in poverty reduction, resulting from market-driven economic development, would automatically take care of the problem of hunger. However, this thinking does not take into account three points: first, poverty reduction takes time, while the hungry need immediate relief; second, the means to feed everyone are readily and cheaply available; and third, hunger is as much a cause as an effect of poverty. Unless action is taken to reduce hunger directly, progress in cutting poverty will be slow. Moreover, a substantial and sustainable reduction in hunger will greatly improve the chances of meeting, not only the MDGs related to poverty reduction, but also those related to education, child mortality, maternal health, and disease.

This volume brings together a major collection of studies focusing on some under-researched areas of food security both at the national as well as household and individual levels. The studies arise from a two-year project entitled 'Hunger and Food Security', undertaken by UNU-WIDER in collaboration with the Indian Council of Social Science Research and the Food and Agriculture Organization of the United Nations.

The studies point out that high growth rates in some developing countries may make headlines, but they are not consonant with rates at which nutrition status is improving (if at all). This calls for more efficiently *targeted* interventions by the state. Women's status matters tremendously for child-health, hence gender issues require more attention. At the macro level, freer agricultural trade tends to increase import dependence for food for some countries. At the micro level, it raises the risk exposure of small farmers, which has a negative impact on their nutrition status.

The target audience for this volume is broad, encompassing staff from international organizations and policymakers interested in policy-relevant results on malnutrition, targeting, and measuring the impact of trade liberalization, through to researchers from various disciplines linked with development.

Anthony Shorrocks
Director, UNU-WIDER

Acknowledgements

This volume is the result of a joint project meeting between UNU-WIDER and the Indian Council of Social Science Research (ICSSR), with research contributions from the Food and Agriculture Organization of the United Nations (FAO). The editors are grateful to Adam Swallow, Publications Assistant at UNU-WIDER, for his invaluable support in preparing the manuscript, and also wish to thank Liisa Roponen for her help. UNU-WIDER thanks the ICSSR for its financial inputs, and the Institute of Development Studies (IDS–Jaipur) for hosting the first project workshop in March 2005.

UNU-WIDER acknowledges the financial contributions to the research programme by the governments of Denmark (Royal Ministry of Foreign Affairs), Finland (Ministry for Foreign Affairs), Norway (Royal Ministry of Foreign Affairs), Sweden (Swedish International Development Cooperation Agency—Sida) and the United Kingdom (Department for International Development—DfID).

Contents

Part II Trade Openness, the WTO, and Food Security

List of Figures

List of Tables

List of Acronyms and Abbreviations

AAY	*Antodaya Anna Yojana* (grain scheme for the poorest of the poor)
ADB	Asian Development Bank
AFDC	aid to families with dependent children
AGOA	African Growth and Opportunity Act
ALSMS	Albania Living Standard Measurement Survey (2002)
AMS	aggregate measures of support
AoA	Agreement on Agriculture (WTO)
BLNS	Botswana, Lesotho, Namibia, and Swaziland
BMI	body mass index
BPL	below poverty line
BRAC	Building Resources Across Communities (formerly Bangladesh Rural Advancement Committee)
CAADP	Comprehensive Africa Agriculture Development Programme (NEPAD)
CAP	common agricultural policy
CAQ	consumption adequacy question
CEGIS	Center for Environmental and Geographic Information Services (Dhaka)
COMESA	Common Market of East and Southern Africa
CUTS	Centre for International Trade, Economics and Environment (Jaipur)
CV	coefficient of variation
DES	dietary energy supply
DFID	Department for International Development
DPAP	Drought Prone Area Programme (India)
EAC	East African Community
EAS	Employment Assurance Scheme
EBA	Everything But Arms
EER	estimated energy requirement
EU	European Union
FAO	Food and Agriculture Organization of the United Nations
FBS	food balance sheets

FCI	Food Corporation of India
FCT	food composition table
FEI	food energy intake
FGT	Foster, Greer, Thorbecke
FIC	food import capacity
FIVIMS	Food Insecurity and Vulnerability Information and Mapping Systems
G20	Group of 20 developing countries
GATT	General Agreement on Tariffs and Trade
GDP	gross domestic product
GMOs	genetically modified organisms
GOI	Government of India
HDI	human development index
ICDS	integrated child development services programme
ICMR	Indian Council of Medical Research
ICSSR	Indian Council of Social Science Research
IFLS3	Indonesia Family Life Survey (2000)
IFPRI	International Food Policy Research Institute
INSTAT	Institute of Statistics (in both Albania and Madagascar)
ITDG	Intermediate Technologies Development Group
ITF	International Task Force (on Commodity Risk Management)
JGSY	*Jawahar Gram Samriddhi Yojana*
JRY	*Jawahar Rozhar Yojana*
LDCs	least developed countries
LSMS	Living Standards Measurement Surveys (World Bank)
MDGs	Millennium Development Goals
MDM	Mid-day Meal scheme (National Programme for Nutritional Support to Primary Education)
MFA	multi-fibre arrangement
MFN	most favoured-nation
MHS	Madagascar Household Survey (2001)
MSSRF	M. S. Swaminathan Research Foundation
NEPAD	New Partnership for Africa's Development
NFIDC	net food importing developing countries
NGOs	non-governmental organizations
NIEs	newly industrialized economies
NLSMS	Nepal Living Standard Measurement Survey (1995/96)
NREG	National Rural Employment Guarantee

NREGA	National Rural Employment Guarantee Act
NREP	National Rural Employment Programme
NSAPs	national social assistance programmes
NSSO	National Sample Survey Organization (India)
NTB	non-tariff barriers
OBCs	other backward classes (India)
ODI	Overseas Development Institute (London)
OECD	Organization for Economics Cooperation and Development
PDS	public distribution system
PIHS	Pakistan Integrated Household Survey
PPP	purchasing power parity
PWP	public works programmes
QRs	quantitative restrictions
RDA	recommended dietary allowance
RLEGP	Rural Landless Employment Guarantee Programme
RNF	rural non-farm
SACU	Southern African Customs Union (comprising Botswana, Lesotho, Namibia South Africa, and Swaziland)
SADC	Southern African Development Community
SAP	Structural Adjustment Programmes
SC/ST	scheduled castes/scheduled tribes
SGRY	*Sampoorna Grameen Rozgar Yojana* (rural umbrella employment programme)
SOW-VU	Stichting Onderzoek Wereldvoedsel-voorziening van de Vrije Universiteit (Centre for World Food Studies, Amsterdam)
SPS	sanitary and phytosanitary measures
SSA	Sub-Saharan Africa
SSM	special safeguard mechanism
STE	state trading enterprises
TBT	technical barriers to trade
ToT	terms of trade
TPDS	targeted public distribution system
TRIPS	Trade-Related aspects of Intellectual Property Rights
TRQ	tariff rate quota
UNCTAD	United Nations Conference on Trade and Development
UNDP	United Nations Development Programme
UNU-WIDER	World Institute for Development Economics Research of the United Nations University

UR	Uruguay Round
USDA	United States Department of Agriculture
VAR	Vector Autoregression
VLSS	Vietnamese Living Standard Surveys
WFC	World Food Conference (1974)
WFS	World Food Summit (1996)
WHO	World Health Organization
WTO	World Trade Organization

Notes on Contributors

Shabd S. Acharya is currently Honorary Professor at the Institute of Development Studies, Jaipur (India). He is also Vice President of National Academy of Agricultural Sciences and President of Agricultural Economics Research Association of India since 2003. He has published extensively in the areas of agricultural economics, agricultural marketing, and agricultural development and policy.

Mehmet Arda retired in 2006 from UNCTAD as the Head of its Commodities Branch. Currently, he is Associate Professor at Galatasaray University in Istanbul. His work focuses on globalization, the trading system, value chains, and market structures—particularly of agricultural products—as well as sustainable development, and poverty reduction. Economic and commercial diplomacy, the economy of Turkey, and national and international policies are also covered.

Kathleen Beegle is a senior economist in the Development Research Group of the World Bank. Her research interests include the socioeconomic impact of economic shocks and HIV/AIDS on households, and child schooling and labour. She completed her PhD in Economics at Michigan State University.

Calogero Carletto is a senior economist in the Development Research Group of the World Bank. His research interests include poverty, food security, and migration. He holds a PhD in Agricultural and Resource Economics from the University of California at Berkeley.

Ramesh Chand is currently Indian Council of Agricultural Research National Professor at the National Centre for Agricultural Economics and Policy Research, New Delhi. He has earlier worked at the Institute of Economic Growth, Delhi, and the Punjab Agricultural University, Ludhiana. At present he researches trade liberalization, the WTO and Asian agriculture, food policy, and development economics.

Andrew Charman is a director of Sustainable Livelihood Consultants. He is a development economist and has specialized in the field of food security and small farmer agricultural development. Working extensively throughout Southern African as a consultant and development practitioner, his research interests are agricultural policy and development practice, with a particular interest in improving market access for smallholders.

Benjamin Davis is an economist with the Agricultural Development Economics Division of the FAO. His research focuses on the interplay between off farm activities, migration, food security and rural development. He holds a Masters in Public Policy and a PhD in Agricultural and Resource Economics from the University of California at Berkeley.

Indranil Dutta is a lecturer in the Department of Economics, University of Sheffield. He received his PhD from University of California, Riverside, and was previously a research fellow at UNU-WIDER, Helsinki. His research interests are in development economics and welfare economics and in particular measurement issues related to poverty and inequality.

Samuel K. Gayi is Senior Economic Affairs Officer, Office of the Special Coordinator for Africa, UNCTAD, Geneva. He has researched and published on a range of development issues of relevance to the least developed countries and Africa, including, trade diversification, financial sector reforms, WTO/trade issues, structural adjustment and poverty reduction, commodities, external debt/HIPC Initiative, FDI and ODA.

Nilabja Ghosh has a PhD in Economics from the Indian Statistical Institute. She taught at university level for several years in Calcutta before moving to the Institute of Economic Growth (IEG) where, at present, she is Associate Professor. Her areas of work include agriculture and rural development.

Basudeb Guha-Khasnobis is a Senior Research Fellow at UNU-WIDER. He holds a PhD in Economics from the University of Rochester and his research interests are international economics, development economics, emerging market finance, informal labour markets, and food security. He is the editor (with Ravi Kanbur and Elinor Ostrom) of *Linking the Formal and Informal Economy: Concepts and Policies* (Oxford University Press, 2006).

Craig Gundersen is an associate professor in the Department of Human Development and Family Studies and a Cooperating Member of the Department of Economics at Iowa State University. His research agenda includes, among other topics, analyses of food insecurity in the US and Zimbabwe, the effect of food assistance programmes on various outcomes in the US, and the well-being of orphans in Zimbabwe.

Gautam Hazarika received his PhD in Economics at the University of Rochester. He is presently an assistant professor of economics at the University of Texas at Brownsville where he researches a variety of topics in development economics. He has published in such journals as the *American Journal of Agricultural Economics* and the *Journal of Development Studies*.

Michael Herrmann works as economic researcher and policy analyst with UNCTAD, Division for Africa, Least Developed Countries and Special Programmes (ALDC). He specializes in least developed countries and co-authors UNCTAD's Least Developed Countries Reports. His research interests include economic growth, structural change, trade, investment, employment and poverty.

James Hodge is a partner in the competition and regulatory economics practice of Genesis Analytics. An economist who has specialized in the areas of trade and public utilities regulation, he was formerly a senior lecturer in the Department of Economics, UCT. He has advised the Africa Group, SADC, and the South African government on multilateral and bilateral trade negotiations, and his research interests are trade bargaining and imperfect competition markets.

Marco Knowles is a socio-economist working with the FAO, and has also worked with the World Food Programme, International Fund for Agricultural Development, and the Netherlands Development Organization. His main research interests include vulnerability and food security analysis to support national-level programming. He has worked in Latin America, Africa, and Asia, and in particular in Bhutan.

Christian Romer Løvendal is an Economist with the Agriculture and Development Economics Division of FAO. He has previously served as Head of Section for the Ministry of Foreign Affairs in Denmark and as Food Security Advisor for the European Commission in Bangladesh. His research interests include food security, vulnerability and power structures and negotiations.

J. V. Meenakshi is currently with HarvestPlus and is based at IFPRI. She obtained her PhD in Agricultural Economics from Cornell University and has taught for several years at the Delhi School of Economics. She has worked and published in the areas of: poverty and welfare, health and nutrition in developing countries, impact assessment of nutrition programmes, safety nets, and agricultural markets.

Mauro Migotto is finishing his PhD thesis on a Bayesian approach to poverty mapping at the University of Reading, and is currently a consultant with the OECD in Paris. His research interests include food security, poverty and nutrition measurement and information systems, statistics for development and statistical capacity building, and agricultural development.

Vasco Molini is a Post-Doctoral researcher at the Centre for World Food Studies in Amsterdam. He has a PhD in development economics from the University of Florence. His main research interests are income distribution and poverty reduction policies in developing countries.

George Rapsomanikis holds a PhD in Agricultural Economics from the University of Reading, and is an economist in the Trade and Policy Service of the FAO Trade and Markets Division. His research focuses on issues related to commodity market analysis, international trade, market structure, and time series econometric modelling and his journal, book and conference contributions are mainly on the econometric modelling of agricultural markets, food demand, and international trade.

Alexander Sarris holds a PhD in economics from the Massachusetts Institute of Technology. He is Director of the Trade and Markets Division of the FAO, and is also Professor in the Department of Economics, University of Athens (currently on leave). His current research interests include; commodity market and price analysis; agricultural development and policy, and; applied international trade policy.

Brinda Viswanathan obtained her PhD in Development Policy from the Indira Gandhi Institute for Development Research, Mumbai. At present she is a faculty at the Madras School of Economics and teaches courses in quantitative economics. Her research interest is in the area of poverty and well-being and has published on nutrition, health, and female employment focusing on India.

1

Introduction

Basudeb Guha-Khasnobis, Shabd S. Acharya, and Benjamin Davis

Global hunger is severe. Nearly 30 per cent of the world's population is currently suffering from one or more forms of malnutrition, including inadequate caloric consumption, protein deficiency, poor dietary quality, and inadequate concentrations of protein and micronutrients. Worldwide approximately 840 million people are undernourished or chronically food insecure, and as many as 2.8 million children and 300,000 women die needlessly every year because of malnutrition in developing countries. The situation is particularly grave in Sub-Saharan Africa and South Asia.

While lack of sustained economic growth is an important determinant of hunger, the persistence of hunger also feeds back to limit economic growth. Many years of empirical evidence point to the negative impact of hunger and malnutrition on labour productivity, health, and education, which ultimately leads to lower levels of overall economic growth. Hunger is thus as much a cause as an effect of poverty. Good nutrition is increasingly understood as an investment in human capital that raises output as well as the returns on investments in education and health care. Taken together, these findings provide powerful evidence that public spending in reducing hunger is an investment with high returns and should constitute a top priority for developing countries.

A number of recent global initiatives has sought to put a spotlight on the problem of persistence of world hunger. The 1996 World Food Summit (WFS), which brought together all member countries of the United Nations, set the goal of halving the number of hungry people in the world by 2015. This goal means moving from the estimated 818 million hungry in 1990–2 (benchmark period for the WFS) to 410 million by 2015. The UN Millennium Declaration in 2000 set the Millennium Development Goals (MDGs), the first of which is to halve poverty and hunger by 2015.

Despite these efforts, in many parts of the world trends are either worsening over time, or progress is too slow to meet the targets. According to data from the FAO (2005), if each of the developing regions continues to reduce hunger at the current pace, only South America and the Caribbean will reach the MDG target of cutting the proportion of hungry people by half. None will reach the more ambitious WFS goal of halving the number of hungry people. Further, as detailed by the FAO (2005), hunger and malnutrition are major causes of the deprivation and suffering targeted by all of the other MDGs. Without rapid progress in reducing hunger, achieving other MDGs related to poverty reduction, education, child mortality, maternal health, and disease will be difficult, if not impossible.

Surprisingly, despite the scale of human suffering brought about by malnutrition, the fight against world hunger receives far less attention than the fight against poverty from bilateral and multilateral donors and lending agencies. Given the influence of these institutions in the determination of national policy agenda of the least developed countries, poverty plays a much more prominent role in policy documents, particularly those that form part of the process of conditionality, such as the Poverty Reduction Strategy Papers (PRSP).

One important by-product of the lack of attention to food security is that the issue is relatively understudied compared to poverty. This book is the product of a two-year joint initiative by the United Nations University—World Institute for Development Economics Research (UNU-WIDER) and the Indian Council for Social Science Research (ICSSR), in collaboration with the Food and Agriculture Organization of the United Nations (FAO), to explore topics in hunger and food security and address these holes in the literature. A diverse group of researchers representing international organizations and research centres as well as academic institutions from both developing and developed countries met twice in a workshop setting to discuss a range of issues related to hunger and food security.

The book brings together a significant collection of studies arising from the project, focusing on some of the relatively under-researched areas including;

- attempts to improve measurement tools,
- the applications of existing tools for empirical analysis using household data, and
- the impact of freer trade—especially, the World Trade Organization's (WTO) Agreement on Agriculture (AoA) on national food security.

Our motivation for the selection of chapters is to provide a technical, yet eclectic, collection which will be of use to researchers in a number of disciplines linked with development, and, a wider audience interested in the same. Food security at the household and individual levels tends to lend itself to rigorous econometric work. It is also the level at which existing measurement tools are debated and scrutinized. We contribute to this area in the first section. Food security at the national or aggregate level forms the subject matter of the second part of the book, and our aim there is to examine the implications of perhaps the most relevant recent development in that area—freer trade in agriculture under the WTO regime.

Overall, we view food security and hunger against the backdrop of a combination of economic reforms in a growing number of developing countries and the global move towards freer trade, particularly in agriculture. This is reflected in our choice of country case studies in the first part, and the entire thrust of Part II.

Part I: Issues in Measurement and the Quantitative Analysis of Food Security

Measurement issues are important because we are constantly forced to ask ourselves if the available measures are adequate for accurate assessments of food insecurity across regions and over time. In fact, the search for better measures is a top research priority for the broader concept of human well-being, hunger being one dimension of it. Part I of this collection covers measurement and quantitative methods in food security analysis and policy. The seven chapters in this section fall into two groups. The first three deal with innovations in the development and use of food security indicators. This includes proposals for a new set of household food security measures and a framework for analysing vulnerability to food security, as well as an empirical evaluation of the use of subjective or 'self-perception' indicators of household food security. The second set of chapters is more heavily empirical, with country or region specific studies of different aspects of food security indicators, using currently available measures. These include changes in food security during an economic boom in Vietnam, changing regional patterns of under nutrition and the efficacy of targeted interventions in India, and the intra household dimensions of food security in Pakistan.

Concepts of food insecurity and hunger used to be linked to clinical signs of malnutrition. With the advent of more sensitive indicators of food insecurity and hunger that are poverty-driven and not limited to clinical definitions, countries are exploring the development and use of qualitative food security measures. The information from these methods also provides a concept of food security that is well understood by policymakers. A major advantage is that qualitative measures incorporate as essential elements the perceptions of food insecurity and hunger by the people most affected. Thus, many view these qualitative methods as more direct measures of food insecurity than other proxy measures.

Chapter 2 tackles the practical issue of measuring food security by carrying out an empirical evaluation of the use of self assessment indicators of household food security. The evidence on the external validity of self assessment indicators is scarce, especially using representative household surveys. The aim of the chapter is to compare information on self-perceived food consumption adequacy from the subjective modules of household surveys with standard quantitative indicators, namely calorie consumption, dietary diversity and anthropometry. Datasets from four countries are analysed: Albania, Indonesia, Madagascar, and Nepal. The chapter uses simple descriptive statistics, correlation coefficients, contingency tables, and multivariate regression to show that the self assessment indicator is at best poorly correlated with standard quantitative indicators. One may therefore assert that while self assessment food adequacy indicators may provide insight on certain dimensions of food insecurity, they are too blunt an indicator for food insecurity targeting. An effort towards developing improved self assessment food security modules that are contextually sensitive should go hand in hand with research into how to improve household survey data for food security measurement along other dimensions of the phenomenon, particularly calorie consumption.

A new indicator for measuring food insecurity at the household level is proposed in Chapter 3. Taking food security self assessment data from the national survey administered by the United States Department of Agriculture, it reports a calculation of alternative indices along the lines of a well established poverty measure. These alternative indices gauge the depth and severity, in addition to the incidence, of food insecurity—in this case—in the United States. Along with providing a richer picture of food insecurity in the United States, these measures demonstrate that the ordering of various demographic categories differs depending on the choice of measure. In some cases the new measures are in agreement (in terms of ordering different subgroups according to overall food insecurity) with the head count ratio. In such instance, considering a broader set of measures then indicates the robustness of the results. However, in other cases orderings of the different subgroups differ depending on whether one uses just the head count measure of food insecurity or if one uses the measures that reflect the depth and severity, in addition to the incidence, of food insecurity. In such cases just relying on the head count ratio, may provide a misleading picture. In either case, therefore, it helps to use a broader set of aggregate measures of food insecurity.

While traditional food security analysis offers an ex post view on who the food insecure are and why they are food insecure, considering food insecurity from a vulnerability perspective provides a dynamic and forward-looking way of analysing causes and, more importantly, developing options for reducing food insecurity. Chapter 4 provides a framework for analysing vulnerability to food insecurity. Such an approach can help improve policy responses to food insecurity. This chapter seeks to expand a standard food security analytical framework by including risks and the ability to manage these at different levels in order to reduce the probability of being food insecure in the future. It looks at how different shocks can impact availability, access and utilization and uses a twin-track approach to identify policy options for reducing vulnerability.

We then move onto a set of empirical case studies of three Asian countries. The data used in these chapters are based on household surveys. Using data from the Pakistan Integrated Household Survey, Chapter 5 measures the effect of women's intra-household position on their children's food security status, and, by extension, provides a test between the unitary and bargaining models of the household. The chapter finds that the relative standing of the mother compared to her husband, as measured by differential educational attainment, as well as her access to cash income, indeed is positively associated with improved nutritional status of her children. Further, the mother's relative standing is also associated with less spending on adult related goods. Taken together, these results suggest that the bargaining model of the household is more appropriate, and that policy initiatives which seek to improve child nutritional status should focus in part on improving the relative bargaining power of women in Pakistani households through access to education.

There are complex and at times counterintuitive changing regional patterns of undernutrition in India during the 1980s and 1990s. The trend in poverty over this period has been the centre of an extensive debate among researchers in India, while trends in food security have remained comparatively understudied. Using a caloric minimum to measure undernutrition which takes into account the demographic composition of the household, Chapter 6 documents an apparent increase in the prevalence of undernutrition over time in rural India. In contrast, in urban areas average intakes have surpassed that in rural India in most states, while the prevalence of undernutrition has remained unchanged or has declined. Caloric income elasticities are large and significant, especially among the poor, and, surprisingly, declining caloric intakes in rural areas has been accompanied by some dietary diversification. Overall, in comparison with other developing nations, in India the prevalence of undernutrition is high and the level of dietary diversification is low. Also, the changes in the rates of undernourishment, as measured in this chapter, are not in harmony with the changes in poverty rates. This reiterates our basic motivation for undertaking the project—over-reliance on poverty indicators, to the exclusion of direct food security indicators, can be misleading.

Chapter 7 examines the case of Vietnam, which experienced an unprecedented economic boom during the 1990s, with annual economic growth rates of over 7 per cent. While there is a large literature documenting significant poverty reduction during this decade, the trend in food security remains relatively understudied. Using nationally representative household surveys for 1993 and 1998, Molini compares changes between years in a number of food security indicators, including dietary composition and caloric consumption, focusing on differences across the welfare distribution and by regions. The chapter finds that while over this period average caloric intake increased in Vietnam, the intensity varied by income level and region. Poor households living generally in rural areas increased calorie consumption while wealthier households preferred to trade quantity for an improvement in quality. The chapter presents evidence of the substitution of items poor in micronutrients (rice and cereals) with higher quality foods like fruits, vegetables, fish, and meat. Poor households, however, while increasing the amount of calories consumed, still lack important micronutrients. Calculating parametric and non parametric estimates of the income elasticity of calories, the chapter confirms the standard result that income elasticity decreases with household level of wealth. However, the chapter also finds that, during this period of high economic growth, the income elasticity of calories decreased over time across the wealth distribution. Overall, along with economic growth and reductions in the incidence of poverty, food security improved in Vietnam during the 1990s. Big differences, however, still remain across the wealth distribution. We shall note in a subsequent chapter that an added dimension of worry is that poor Vietnamese households are more vulnerable to market risks that come with more trade openness. This may further worsen the relative nutrition status of the poorer sections.

The current process of structural adjustment and globalization across the developing world may provide benefit to many, but will also leave many others worse off. The 'losers' are likely to be people who are unskilled, physically and economically too weak to compete and geographically disadvantaged. Growth alone cannot correct the human specificities related to gender, geography, social class or disease. Many believe that mainstream strategies need to be accompanied by direct attempts to eliminate deprivation. India is a prime example. While pursuing economic reforms vigorously, India's political system is also struggling to achieve a consensus for eliminating povertyinduced food insecurity through approaches and instruments that would be consistent with its macroeconomic policies. Chapter 8 reviews the experience of India in changing the orientation of food-security strategies towards new and innovative methods. It traces the evolution of the 'public works programme' and examines its merits and concerns. An empirical study of the rural public works programme in four states is conducted, first, to determine whether a linkage exists between a public work programme and food insecurity, and second, to measure whether the programme indeed succeeds in seeking out households likely to be food insecure and further to highlight who among the food insecure the programme possibly passes over.

Part II: Trade Openness, the WTO, and Food Security

The second theme focuses on the relationship between globalization, trade, and food security. The six chapters in this section address the impact on food security of one of the main sources of current economic change throughout the world—globalization—as well as the institutional construct attempting to manage this process of change—the WTO. This process of change is analysed from a variety of perspectives and covering a wide range of regions and countries across the globe. These dimensions include the impact of agricultural support measures in developed countries on food security in developing countries; the relationship between commodity price and agricultural income instability in selected countries; targeted approaches of combating poverty in India, the impact of WTO negotiations on food safety and government policy in Africa; and globalization and food retailing in Latin America.

Chapter 9 focuses on the extent to which commodity price volatility affects the income and vulnerability to food insecurity of producer households in developing countries. It is argued that the key elements are household production diversification patterns and the degree of exposure to markets. The chapter estimates income uncertainty deriving from price and production volatility under different scenarios of exposure to the international and the domestic markets shocks for a number of stylized household types in Ghana, Peru, and Vietnam. The results indicate that market and non market uncertainties significantly affect the variability of agricultural income of households in these countries, and especially households that are specialized in few commodities. However, almost all of their income variability is due to domestic factors. Wider exposure to international markets would increase the income variability of producers that have been subjected to domestic market stabilization policies in Ghana and Vietnam, while it would decrease income variability in the case of Peru.

The controversial issue of the linkages between agricultural support measures in developed countries and food security in developing countries is the subject matter of Chapter 10. The chapter argues that these agricultural support measures place downward pressure on agricultural wages in developing countries. The least developed countries may derive considerable gains from multilateral trade liberalization provided that developed countries eliminate unnecessary non-tariff barriers to trade, and that international donors assist developing countries in meeting the remaining non-tariff barriers, as well helping them strengthen their domestic production capabilities.

Chapter 11 focuses on the implications of WTO agricultural negotiations on the agricultural and food security policy of South African Development Community (SADC) countries. The chapter documents how changes in food security policy since the Uruguay Round, including trade liberalization, and the subsequent food crisis of 2001–3 have impacted the negotiating strategy of these countries. It provides an assessment of the potential impact of the proposed tariff and subsidy reduction modalities on government policymaking. The chapter concludes that the proposed modalities in the current round are unlikely to restrict SADC policies to enhance and assure food availability, access, and security. Moreover, the low levels of domestic support and high bound tariffs ensure that agreed reductions would still leave SADC countries with sufficient policy space to pursue food security and agricultural development policy.

The impact of the WTO on agriculture and food security among the countries of South Asia is taken up in Chapter 12. It takes an empirical look at the impact of trade liberalization on food security, centering attention on changes in agricultural trade, dependence on food imports, trade orientation and agricultural growth before and after WTO. One finds that trade liberalization led to increased dependence on imports in order to meet the demand for food in the region in general. This is due in part to the inability of domestic production to compete with cheap imports; a major factor of which is continuing subsides in OECD countries. The chapter argues for increased domestic capacity for food production, given the low levels of per capita income in the region. Chapter 13 addresses these issues for Sub-Saharan Africa. It examines the state of food security from 1990 to 2002, within the context of the WTO AoA, and suggests a policy framework for improving food security in the region. Changes in the food security situation following the Uruguay Round are identifiable, but these changes are not due to the AoA but instead country specific factors, particularly the state of the agricultural sector. The chapter argues that under the current rules there is some policy leeway for Sub-Saharan Africa countries to enhance food security, and the chapter advocates for a self sufficient strategy to addressing food insecurity, at least until protectionism in the developed world is reduced.

Chapter 14 deals with the impact of globalization on food retailing. Specifically, the chapter analyses the growth of the importance of supermarkets in the food marketing chain in Latin America, focusing particularly on the impact on food security. The phenomenon of spectacular growth in supermarkets in developing countries has been extensively documented in recent years. Supermarkets have not only changed the retail end of the food chain, but also generated very significant changes in the organization of production and delivery of food to the point of sale. The chapter's contribution is the focus on food security, which is usually overlooked in the supermarket debate. It finds that for urban consumers, the food safety of those with access to supermarkets appears to have improved, and for some food commodities, particularly bulk products, a reduction in prices has also been observed, improving access to food for those with access to supermarkets. From the perspective of producers, while the growth of supermarkets has opened up unprecedented opportunities for some, mostly larger farmers, it has generated negative impacts on small producers who are unable to meet the stringent requirements of supermarket chains and other modern food supply channels.

Concluding Remarks

This collection seeks to cover a range of issues that cuts across a wide ranging audience. Within measurement tools, we also address *ex ante* food insecurity by discussing its main elements and hope to have taken a step towards creating a possible *vulnerability index*. We present three selected empirical case studies on India, Pakistan, and Vietnam, based on household data. In the case of Pakistan the role of women in ensuring food security for children is brought to the fore. An empirical model relating the status of women to children's health is proposed and tested, with the hope that it will provoke others to refine our model (to develop better measures of women's status), and also encourage similar exercises for other countries. The studies on India (Chapter 6) and Vietnam (in Chapters 7 and 9) present inter-temporal comparisons of the state of undernutrition. Both these countries have out-performed others in their development cohort in terms of overall growth rates. But while the nutritional status of the population shows an improvement over time in Vietnam, it shows a worsening in India, particularly for the rural poor. It seems to imply that the challenges of reforms and globalization—in protecting the wellbeing of the poor—may be different for large (India) and small (Vietnam) countries in important ways. What does India need to do in order to make changes in rural nutritional standards commensurate with its high growth rate? This issue, among with others pertaining to globalization, is taken up in Chapter 8. The trickle-down effects of recent spectacular growth rates, globalization, and economic reforms in India are dubious. It is clear that large sections of the population in different states are untouched by these recent developments. Fortunately, there are efforts on the part of the government (goaded mainly by civil society groups) to implement poverty alleviation measures which target the poor (and food insecure) *directly*. We examined the efficacy of these programmes in India, and hope that similar evaluations will be made of, for example, public works programmes, in other developing nations, particularly in Africa.

The liberalization of trade in agriculture is one of the most contentious issues in WTO negotiations. The welfare impacts of OECD's farm subsidies on developing countries depend on whether they are net exporters or net importers of protected products as well as on the bilateral trade patterns. With few exceptions, the import dependence of developing countries has risen in the past decade and half. We examine the implications of the WTO's AoA on food security in several developing regions. In the case of South Asia we would add the caveat that not all of the changes in import dependence patterns can be attributed to the WTO—we do not yet have enough time series evidence to establish causality. Thus, the South Asian numbers are measures of *association*.

In the final chapter of the volume we switch gear—moving from the rural populace and agricultural sector to an essentially city phenomenon, supermarkets. Established food chains of developed countries, opening shop in developing countries, is an emerging trait of globalization. What are its possible implications for the availability of quality food for the urban poor? We feel this issue needs further research attention.

There are other dimensions to the problem of food security, such as human rights, the right to food movements in different societies, gender concerns, and food aid policy, which are not covered in this volume. However, these issues were addressed in the overall research project and the interested reader is invited to visit the UNU-WIDER website (www.wider.unu.edu) for further details. UNU-WIDER has also extended the project to a second phase, entitled 'Gender and Food Security', with the aim of focusing on the role of women in providing intra household food security. It is currently under implementation.

Reference

FAO (2005). *The State of Food Insecurity in the World, 2005*. Rome: FAO.

Part I

Issues in Measurement and the Quantitative Analysis of Food Security

2

Measuring Food Security Using Respondents' Perception of Food Consumption Adequacy

Mauro Migotto, Benjamin Davis, Calogero Carletto, and Kathleen Beegle

2.1 Introduction

The 1996 World Food Summit (WFS) brought to centre-stage in the development debate the issue of hunger and food insecurity as both cause and effect of poverty and slow growth. In the wake of this new push, reducing hunger and food insecurity also became one of the Millennium Development Goals (MDGs), bringing with it the necessity for individual countries to measure progress in achieving the proposed targets.

The conceptualization of food security has evolved over time, partly preceding and partly paralleling similar evolutions in poverty. Since the World Food Conference (WFC) of 1974, food security paradigms have shifted from the global and national level to the household and individual level; from a 'food first' to a 'livelihood' perspective and from objective indicators to subjective perceptions (Maxwell 1996). In this chapter, we focus on the last of these issues, which is directly related to the increasing demand for rigorous measurement methods and to the debate over qualitative versus quantitative indicators.

Measuring and assessing food insecurity have proved to be challenging and daunting tasks for researchers and practitioners, a point carefully noted by

The authors would like to acknowledge, without implying, both the Albanian Institute of Statistics and the World Bank for providing data access, the FAO and the World Bank for funding part of this work, and Basudeb Guha-Khasnobis and participants at seminars in Jaipur, India and Helsinki, Finland, for comments. We are also grateful to Carlo Azzarri for helping with the data and for valuable comments. The views expressed are those of the authors, and any errors and omission are theirs.

Webb *et al.* (2006). Traditionally, a divide has persisted between objective-quantitative methods versus subjective-qualitative techniques for the measurement of poverty and food insecurity. More recently, these two types of measures and methods have been increasingly viewed as complementary, and it has become evident that a suite of indicators is necessary to capture the multifaceted nature of food security. In response, an increasing number of quantitative surveys now collect subjective-type information. Despite these methodological advances and the availability of better quality data, empirical evidence on the reliability and validity of the various subjective indicators in use remains scant. Even though much work has been done on alternative indicators, and the literature on subjective poverty lines is growing, relatively less progress has been made in terms of externally validating self-assessment indicators of food security that use representative household surveys. Towards this end, the use of household surveys containing both objective and subjective information on the same household potentially provides a valuable workbench for this type of validation.

Most examples of validation are found in the poverty literature, as can be seen in Pradhan and Ravallion (2000), Ravallion and Lokshin (1999), Lokshin *et al.* (2003), and Carletto and Zezza (2006). Pradhan and Ravallion (2000) and Lokshin *et al.* (2003), using multivariate regression analyses, take the subjective perception of food consumption adequacy questions to construct a money matrix subjective poverty line, which is then compared to the standard objective poverty line. In terms of food security, Hamilton *et al.* (1997) compare the US subjective food security index to a variety of alternative indicators. Coates *et al.* (2003) do the same for a prototype index in Bangladesh, as well as cite other studies in developing countries. More recently, a special issue of the *Journal of Nutrition* (2006, volume 136) contains a series of papers on the use of USA-food insecurity measures applied to developing countries, some comparing 'experience-based' measures with more standard quantitative indicators, such as expenditure (see for example Melgar-Quinonez *et al.* 2006).

Our initial intention was to validate self-assessment indicators with respect to some standard quantitative indicators normally used as benchmarks available within the same household survey. This approach was based implicitly on the assumption that the non-subjective measure itself is a more direct and accurate measure of the 'true' food security status. In that sense, the objective measure would serve as the benchmark, or gold standard measure, something that approximates 'the true' food security status of households. Various standard measures (including consumption, poverty, anthropometry, and other socioeconomic variables) have all been used as such benchmarks (Frongillo and Nanama 2006); in practice, per capita calorie consumption is often utilized as the main benchmark measure. However, this approach to validating subjective measures is problematic when the benchmarks themselves are problematic, for example if calorie consumption is measured with error or systematically misreported among households. Moreover, if food security is a multidimensional phenomenon and cannot be captured by a single indicator, testing alternative indicators against a single benchmark is not a definitive critique of the indicator tested. As a result, this chapter may appear to ask more questions than it answers, and the main objective is thus to contribute to these debates. Building on the analysis of four household surveys, we offer some recommendations on future research aimed at integrating objective and subjective indicators in household surveys. Thus, while the focus is comparing subjective measures to traditional objective measures, in fact, we are comparing two different dimensions of an overall construct, rather than validating whether a proxy indicator for food security accurately predicts the underlying concept we are trying to measure.

The chapter is structured as follows. The next section reviews the concept of food security and the search for alternative indicators. Section 2.3 briefly describes the datasets, and 2.4 presents the empirical results. The final section provides a discussion of the results and concludes.

2.2 Measuring Food Security

The most frequently cited definition of food security is still the one that was proposed almost two decades ago by the World Bank (1986: 1), which defines food security as 'access by all people at all times to sufficient food for an active and healthy life'. The operationalization of this concept presents many challenges. Measurements and assessment methodologies and methods can differ considerably, even within the boundaries of the qualitative and quantitative traditions. Food security, as with poverty, is a cross-cutting, complex and multifaceted phenomenon. The food security literature spans a wide range of disciplines, including anthropology, nutrition, sociology, economics, geography, public health, and epidemiology (Chung *et al.* 1997).

Conceptually, food security is generally broken down into four different components—availability, access, utilization, and vulnerability—each capturing different, but overlapping, dimensions of the phenomenon. As discussed above, there is a consensus that no single indicator can capture all aspects of food insecurity while also providing policymakers with relevant and timely information in a cost-effective manner. For this reason, efforts have been put into finding easy to implement and reliable alternative indicators which complement each other.

Following FAO (2003a), we identify five general types of methods/indicators. The first indicator can be labelled *undernourishment*, a measure commonly identified with the Food and Agriculture Organization of the United Nations (FAO). This FAO method begins with an estimate of the per capita dietary food energy supply, derived from aggregate food supply data. Assumptions regarding the distribution of this supply across households are made on the basis of income or consumption distribution, or other available data. The proportion of the undernourished in the total population is then defined as that part of the distribution lying below a minimum energy requirement level (Naiken 2003). The FAO measure is useful for comparisons across countries and over time.

A second group of indicators, which can be termed *food intake*, measures the amount of food actually consumed at the individual or household level. Indicators at the individual level can be obtained directly by measuring actual food intake through a number of techniques. Food intake surveys, however, are relatively rare, given its cost considerations. Instead, food consumption is usually measured indirectly through household surveys. Household surveys in general, and multipurpose household surveys in particular, are aimed at assessing living standards, not just food security. Although they are time-, resource-, and skill-intensive, they are now regularly implemented in many countries. Household-level data can be used to construct a number of measures of food insecurity, including food energy deficiency and poor diet quality and diversity.

The third approach to the assessment of dietary deficiencies is to measure *food utilization* through nutritional status. Anthropometric measures of children under age five are regularly collected in random sample surveys in many countries. Anthropometric measures, as outcome measures, are well suited for monitoring and evaluating interventions, and can be collected with socioeconomic information in order to analyse the determinants of malnutrition. Anthropometric attainment, however, is a nonspecific indicator, because it is the result not only of food intake, but also of factors such as sanitation, health and childcare practices. Since nutritional status is an individual-level indicator, it has distinct advantages. For example, it does not mask food insecurity in seemingly food secure households when intrahousehold allocation rules result in unequal distribution of food resources. This is a problem for both objective and subjective measures, where, for example, one household member responds (e.g. the head) perhaps on basis his/her response on his/her own situation. However, as nutritional status is only available for young children, it has limited power in describing food security for the broad population.

Fourth, food availability is of little use if households or individuals do not have enough financial or productive resources to acquire food. The fourth group of indicators revolves around the concept of *access* to food and can be proxied by wealth status, measured by total consumption, expenditures or income. Access-to-food indicators, and in particular income, have served as the main food security indicator in many countries. The link between access and a given wealth proxy breaks down when local markets are not functioning, as in the case of war or disaster, for example.

Finally, the last approach revolves around the concept that even if households are not currently undernourished, they may be at risk or vulnerable to future deprivation. *Vulnerability* is an inherently dynamic concept which expresses *ex-ante* vulnerability and *ex-post* outcomes. Because it is an expression of a 'future state of the world' which, by definition, we do not know *a priori*, vulnerability is, in itself, difficult to measure (Dercon 2001). Vulnerability is often gauged through qualitative or 'self-assessment' indicators of food insecurity, capturing dimensions which are difficult to isolate with traditional quantitative measures, especially in the absence of panel data. Households may regard themselves as hungry, even if there are no recognizable signs of undernutrition. Further, even if households are not currently undernourished, they may have a significant probability, or well-founded fear, of future deprivation. Other measures of vulnerability to food deprivation also drawn from household surveys include the share of income spent on food and various coping-strategy indexes.

In terms of self-assessment indicators, the United States government pioneered the approach of assessing household food security on the basis of a score derived from 18 questions on food-related behaviours and conditions that are known to be associated with food deprivation (Kennedy 2003). A number of developing countries have successfully implemented similar methodologies (see, for example, Nord *et al.* 2002). This type of survey has been piloted extensively in Brazil (Segall Corrêa *et al.* 2003), and a module has recently been included in that country's biannual national income survey. It also recently formed the centrepiece of a large food security study in Yemen and has been tested and applied in Bangladesh (Coates *et al.* 2003). Reduced forms of these subjective modules are found in many recent standard national household surveys, such as the World Bank's Living Standards Measurement Surveys (LSMS), and focus on respondents' perceived assessment of individual or household food security situation. One of the questions most commonly asked is called the *consumption adequacy question* (CAQ), and is generally worded as follows: 'Concerning your food consumption, which of the following is true?' Answers are generally coded as: (i) more than adequate; (ii) just adequate, and (iii) less than adequate. This question, common to all the selected surveys, is the focus of our analysis.

2.3 The Data

We analyse four household surveys to estimate household calorie consumption and total expenditure/consumption, dietary diversity and anthropometry, which are compared with the answers to the subjective food

Table 2.1. Percentage of food insecure households, using a variety of indicators

	Perception of food adequacy (% of 'less than adequate' answers)			Poverty headcount	Below caloric threshold	FAO measure
	National	Urban	Rural	National	National	National
Nepal	51	36	52	42	na	26
Madagascar	52	45	55	70	35	37
Albania	52	51	53	25	17	6
Indonesia*-household	10	7	13	16	na	6
Indonesia-children	9	6	10	na	na	na

Note: * The Indonesia survey asked the CAQ for the whole household as well as just for the corresponding children.

Source: Own calculations; FAO (2003b and 2004); Prennushi (1999); World Bank and INSTAT (2003); Strauss *et al.* (2004).

CAQ.[1] The surveys are: the Nepal 1995/96 Living Standard Measurement Survey (NLSMS); the 2000 Indonesia Family Life Survey (IFLS3); the Albania 2002 LSMS (ALSMS) and the 2001 Madagascar Household Survey (MHS).[2] Only for Albania were we able to construct all five variables. For Nepal we were limited to dietary diversity and the subjective indicators. For Madagascar, household calorie consumption, total expenditure and dietary diversity were constructed, as well as the subjective indicator. For Indonesia, only the subjective and anthropometric indicators were available. An interesting feature of the Indonesia survey is that it asked the CAQ for the whole household as well as just for the children of the household.

2.4 The Results

2.4.1 *Perception of Food Adequacy*

Subjective indicators were included in all four household surveys, and the distribution of responses across countries can be seen in Table 2.1. In all cases, with the exception of Indonesia, approximately 50 per cent of those surveyed considered their food consumption (and in the case of Madagascar, food expenses) less than adequate. The incidence of subjective food insecurity is many times smaller in Indonesia, around 10 per cent, which allows us to make our first point. Subjective indicators, as defined here, are not comparable across countries. It is extremely unlikely that the real (though unknown) incidence of food insecurity in Madagascar is the same as Albania, a country

[1] Appendix 2.1 describes the datasets in more detail. Appendix 2.2 presents the methodology used, and the problems encountered, in constructing household caloric availability/consumption.

[2] Details on each survey, as well as details on the process by which calorie consumption was constructed for each country can be found in the Appendices and in Migotto *et al.* (2005).

Table 2.2. Percentages of households above/below the caloric norm and median caloric consumption per capita per day—Albania

	National (*n* = 3,456)	Urban (*n* = 1,899)	Rural (*n* = 1,557)	Coastal (*n* = 955)	Central (*n* = 954)	Mountain (*n* = 971)	Tirana (*n* = 575)
Caloric threshold							
Below (%)	17.3	21.8	13.4	17.7	15.0	15.0	26.3
Median kcal per capita	2,912	2,673	3,131	2,863	3,007	2,992	2,567
Poverty*							
Moderate (%)	25.4	19.5	29.6	20.6	25.6	44.5	17.8
Extreme (%)	4.7	4.1	5.2	3.6	4.6	10.8	2.3
Subjective							
Not adequate (%)	52.3	50.8	53.4	44.7	56.2	55.9	54.2

Note: *Extreme poverty headcount index is based on a food poverty line, or the cost of obtaining a minimum amount of calories. Moderate poverty headcount is based on the food poverty line plus essential nonfood items.

Source: ALSMS, own calculations; World Bank and INSTAT (2003); Azzarri *et al.* (2006).

with much higher per capita GDP, much lower incidence of poverty, and lower incidence of food insecurity according to the caloric threshold and FAO indicators.

A small percentage of households stated that they had more than sufficient food consumption/expenses—2 per cent in Nepal, 3 per cent in Madagascar and Albania, and 17 per cent in Indonesia. It is not clear how respondents interpret this question. Also, in all four countries, the percentage of households stating that they had sufficient food consumption is higher in rural than in urban areas, although the difference is slight in Albania.[3]

2.4.2 *Caloric Availability*

How do the results for subjective measures of food insecurity compare to the other indicators? We first compare the subjective indicators with calorie consumption for Albania and Madagascar, the countries where the latter indicator is available.[4] Median per capita daily calorie consumption and the percentage of households below the caloric norm are given in Table 2.2

[3] In the case of Madagascar, the subjective question refers to food expenses, and not to food consumption, and we are unclear on how respondents interpreted the question. If the question is interpreted as referring only to purchased foods, then we might expect a downward bias in the percentage of households reporting less than adequate consumption, increasing in size as we move from urban to rural areas, as food purchases and calories from food purchases are higher in urban areas.

[4] Results are presented only for households whose estimated per capita per day calorie consumption lies in the range of 1,000 to 6,000 kcal. The sample size has thus been reduced from 5,075 to 4,558 for Madagascar (90 per cent of the full sample) and from 3,599 to 3,456 for Albania (96 per cent). Although point estimates are different with reduced samples, the overall results of the analysis—in particular the correlation with the subjective measure—do not change significantly.

for Albania as a whole and at the urban/rural and regional level. Although the national median value of 2,912 is plausible when compared to the FAO figure of 2940 (FAO 2003b), the results are somewhat counter intuitive and contrary to the incidence of poverty in Albania. Approximately 17 per cent of the Albanian population is found to be below the caloric threshold level. Calorie consumption is greater and a higher percentage of households are above the threshold in rural areas. Tirana has the lowest median calorie consumption, and the lowest share of households above the threshold (less than 75 per cent) of all regions, while the other regions are all roughly similar. In terms of the headcount index of poverty, Tirana has the lowest incidence of poverty, while the mountain region has an incidence 2 to 3 times higher. For the coastal region, the incidence of poverty and the percentage of households below the caloric threshold are roughly similar. Similar results are evident with Madagascar, as we shall see shortly.

The finding of higher calorie consumption in rural areas does not sit well with the common finding of higher poverty in rural areas, such as we find for Albania. There could be various reasons behind these results. First, because of heavier physical activities, rural people on average may consume more calories which are cheaper relative to the calories consumed by the urban population. In addition, or alternatively, there may be a systematic misreporting in rural or urban areas, or both, or overestimated consumption of home production in rural areas. Finally, there may be some kind of systematic nonsampling errors.

There is also a parallel here with the debate on poverty lines, namely the difference between the food energy intake (FEI) method and the cost of basic needs (CBN) method. It is not uncommon for poverty analyses based on the FEI method, where separate poverty lines are calculated, to indicate higher poverty rates in urban than in rural areas. At a given level of income, urban households tend to consume fewer, but more expensive, calories (Tarp *et al.* 2002). Therefore, higher calorie consumption in rural areas is not an uncommon result, and has been found in other similar empirical studies (Hoddinott and Yohannes 2002; Skoufias 2001).

Despite these difficulties, while we do not estimate the income elasticity of calories, we find a positive correlation coefficient of 0.53 between per capita calorie consumption and per capita real total consumption in Albania.

Going back to Table 2.1, contrary to the calorie consumption results, according to which rural areas have a significantly higher median, a marginally higher share of rural households (53 to 51 per cent) perceived their food consumption as inadequate. Despite these contradictory results, on average, some correlation between the two indicators is evident. The higher the per capita total consumption and the per capita calorie consumption, the more likely it is that a household reported adequate food consumption, as can be seen in Table 2.3.

Table 2.3. Real per capita total consumption and daily per capita caloric consumption by subjective food adequacy answer—Albania

	More than/just adequate (n = 1,706)	Less than adequate (n = 1,872)
Real per capita total consumption (New Leks)		
Median	7,963	5,877
Mean	9,261	6,566
	(n = 1,622)	(n = 1,813)
Daily per capita caloric consumption (Kcals)		
Median	3,042	2,833
Mean	3,157	2,944

Source: ALSMS, own calculations.

However, this relationship holds only on average. Although the contingency table (Table 2.4) is significant at the conventional confidence levels, it shows that calorie consumption and subjective perceptions do not classify the same households as food insecure. More than half of the 83 per cent of households above the caloric threshold felt that their food consumption was less than adequate. About 58 per cent below the threshold felt the same way.

Similar results emerge for Madagascar. Using the figures based on the 30-day recall, overall median per capita calorie consumption is 2,274 kcal, which is roughly approximate to the 2,080 kcal estimated by the FAO method (FAO 2004).[5] As for Albania, median calorie consumption is higher in rural areas than in semi-urban areas, and in semi-urban areas greater than in urban areas (Table 2.5). Per capita calorie consumption and real per capita food and total expenditure (consumption aggregates) are positively correlated, with a correlation coefficient of 0.58 for food expenditure and 0.38 for total expenditure.

Table 2.4. Contingency table between per capita caloric availability and subjective food adequacy—Albania

	Above caloric threshold	Below caloric threshold	Totals	χ^2 : 7.546
Food expenditure more than/just adequate	1,370	248	1,618	Design-based
	(40)	(7)	(47)	F: 4.337
	(48)	(42)		P: 0.0379
Food expenditure less than adequate	1,473	343	1,816	Un-corrected Cramer's
	(43)	(10)	(52)	V: 0.0682
	(52)	(58)		
Totals	2,843	591	3,434	
	(83)	(17)	(100)	
	(100)	(100)		

Source: ALSMS, own calculations.

[5] Using the 7-day recall we obtain a slightly lower median, closer to the FAO estimate.

Table 2.5. Percentage of households below the caloric norm and median caloric consumption per capita, per day, by location—Madagascar

	National (n = 4,558)	Urban + Semi-urban (n = 2,753)	Rural (n = 1,773)
Caloric threshold			
Below (%)	32.4	37.2	30.8
Median kcal per capita	2, 274	2, 158	2, 317
Poverty			
Moderate (%)	69.6	44.1	77.1
Subjective			
Not adequate (%)	52.5	45.6	54.8

Source: MHS, own calculations; Rakutomehefa *et al.* (2002).

Also in the case of Madagascar there is an evident correlation between the subjective measure, on one side, and the calorie and total consumption measures, on the other side. The higher the per capita total consumption and the per capita calorie consumption, the more likely is that a household reported adequate food consumption, as it can be seen in Table 2.6.

Once again, however, this is true only on average. The correlation coefficient between subjective food adequacy and calories is only 0.1, while the correlation with total consumption is 0.23. While statistically significant, from the contingency table (not shown) just over half of the 68 per cent of households above the caloric threshold felt that they had less than adequate

Table 2.6. Real per capita total consumption and daily per capita caloric consumption by subjective food adequacy answer—Madagascar

	More than/just adequate	Less than adequate
Real per capita total consumption monthly (Malagasy Franc)		
Median	850,759	547,233
Mean	1,347,280	757,999
	(n = 2,561)	(n = 2477)
Daily per capita caloric consumption (Kcals)		
National	(n = 2,336)	(n = 2,190)
Median	2,425	2,140
Mean	2,640	2,463
Urban	(n = 928)	(n = 731)
Median	2,250	1,982
Mean	2,438	2,247
Semi-Urban	(n = 594)	(n = 500)
Median	2,248	2,210
Mean	2,535	2,410
Rural	(n = 814)	(n = 959)
Median	2,501	2,165
Mean	2,696	2,498

Source: MHS, own calculations.

food expenditures. Similarly, approximately 45 per cent of the households below the caloric threshold considered that they had adequate food expenditures. Again, these two measures do not classify the same households as food insecure.

2.4.3 *Dietary Diversity*

In her review of the literature, Ruel (2002) finds that while there is no consensus in terms of conceptualizing or measuring dietary diversity, various measures of dietary diversity have been positively associated with nutrition adequacy, child growth, per capita consumption and energy availability. In its simplest form, dietary diversity can be defined as the number of different foods or food groups consumed over a given reference period (Hoddinott 1999a, 1999b; Hoddinott and Yohannes 2002). For Albania, Madagascar, and Nepal, we tested the subjective variable against four different diversity scores:

(i) Simple count of foods (as listed in the questionnaire);
(ii) Simple count of food groups (as listed in the questionnaire);
(iii) Simpson Index, given by $1 - \sum \Pi_i^2$; and
(iv) Shannon Index, given by $- \sum \Pi_i \log(\Pi_i)$.

where Π_i is the calorie share of food i ($i = 1, 2 \ldots$). If only one food item was consumed, the last two indexes would be zero, so variety increases with the index value, thus establishing a continuum between a 'diverse' and a 'non-diverse' diet. We present results only for the simple count of foods, as none of the indexes tested outperformed the others, and dietary diversity—however measured—are found to be poorly correlated with subjective food adequacy in all countries analysed.

Figure 2.1 shows that, for Albania, on average, as we move from the first to the fifth dietary diversity quintile, the percentage of households reporting less than adequate food consumption declines. These trends are similar nationally as well as separately between urban and rural households. The decrease, however, is not monotonic and the correlation coefficient is in fact quite low (0.15). Similar results are found for Madagascar, with a correlation coefficient of (0.16).[6]

2.4.4 *Anthropometry*

Anthropometric indicators were calculated for Albania and Indonesia. Two anthropometric indices (z-scores) were calculated—wasting and underweight—and compared to the subjective food adequacy answers. In

[6] Note that a diversity index for Madagascar computed using only food purchases (to better compare with the subjective question) was also tested, but the results were similar.

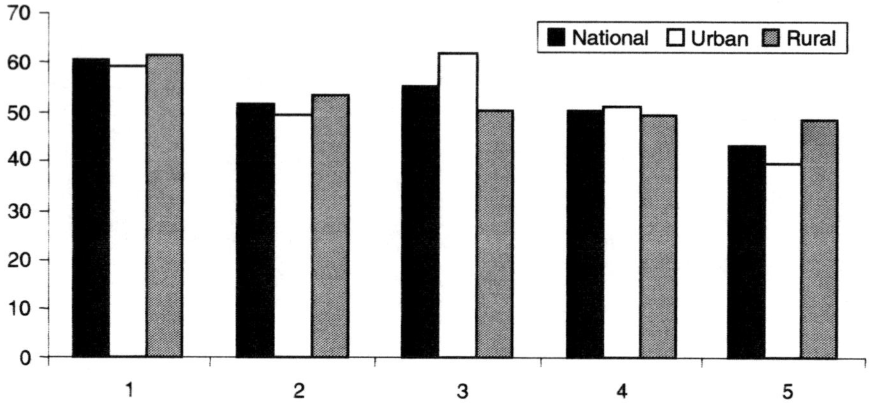

Figure 2.1. Food adequacy answers (percentage of 'less than adequate') by simple food count quintiles and location-Albania

Source: ALSMS, own calculations.

Albania, approximately 13 per cent of children were underweight, and 8 per cent wasted, with higher percentages in rural areas in both cases (16 versus 9 per cent, and 9 versus 8 per cent). In comparing with the subjective indicator, we find no correlation for both indices, and contingency tables are statistically insignificant (not shown).[7]

Indonesia at the national level has a higher incidence of underweight children (25 per cent) than Albania, but a similar prevalence of wasted children. For both indicators the percentages are similar across urban and rural areas. The Indonesia survey also collected data on child subjective food adequacy, which in theory is more likely to be correlated with the anthropometric measures.[8] However, all matrices are statistically insignificant, with little evident correlation (not shown).

2.4.5 *Multivariate Regression*

If subjective food adequacy (as defined here) is only weakly correlated with calorie consumption and with dietary diversity, and not at all with anthropometry, what is behind the subjective indicator? Does it reflect real perceptions of households regarding food insecurity, or is it too vague or blunt an indicator? Is it too subjective to lead to valid comparisons among households?

[7] As one would expect, similar results have been found for stunting. Results for stunting are not shown because stunting reflects long-term processes, which are less likely to be related to current food consumption. Note that these figures are not identical to those reported in World Bank and INSTAT (2003) because neither the age group nor flagging criteria are the same.

[8] The age range here is between 3 and 59 months.

One way to explore further the relationship across indicators is to use multivariate regressions to determine which socioeconomic characteristics are associated with perceptions of subjective food adequacy. We model the relation as a probit, where a positive coefficient of a given explanatory variable can be interpreted as being associated with a higher probability of food adequacy.[9]

Two models are estimated. The second model is identical to the first except for the use of per capita food expenditures in lieu of per capita calorie consumption to see whether subjective answers are more responsive to food expenditure than to calories, but also because the food CAQ for Madagascar asked about food expenses, not consumption.

We start by simply regressing the CAQ response on per capita calorie consumption (and food expenditure) to quantify how much of the variability of respondent's perception is explained by our objective indicators. In the case of Albania, even though the binary model is statistically significant and the marginal effect fairly high, including only per capita calorie consumption explains very little (1 per cent) of the variation of the subjective indicator. The same applies to per capita food expenditure (6 per cent). This confirms our earlier discussion: per capita calorie consumption has little overlap with subjective perceptions and much remains to be explained of the variability of our dependent variable.

More formally, the full model can be expressed as:

$$\begin{aligned}\text{CAQ} = \alpha + \beta_1\text{C} + \beta_2\text{D} + \beta_3\text{A} + \beta_4\text{NF} + \beta_5\text{Z} + \beta_6\text{M} + \beta_7\text{O} + \beta_8\text{R} \\ + \beta_9\text{E} + \beta_{10}\text{G} + \beta_{11}\text{RD} + \beta_{12}\text{S} + \varepsilon\end{aligned}$$

where:

C refers to the log of per capita calories per day or to the log of per capita food expenditure (two separate, identical models);[10]

D refers to a dietary diversity index;

Following Morris *et al.* (2000), A refers to a household asset index, including both agricultural and non agricultural assets;

NF refers to the share of nonfood items in total consumption;

Z refers to a vector of household characteristics including household size, dependency ratio, gender, age of the household head, pension status, gender of the respondent and age composition of the household;

M refers to migration variables;

[9] We also estimated ordered probit models (i.e. including all three categories of the subjective question), but results (not shown here) are similar to those of the standard probit.

[10] Anthropometry has not been included due to the reduced number of observations.

O refers to occupation of the household head (skilled versus unskilled) and to whether the household head is employed;

R refers to the religion of the head of the household;

E refers to education;

G refers to a series of geographical location variables;

RD refers to relative deprivation, that is, a household's wealth position relative to other households in a given geographical area, which is calculated following Stark and Taylor (1989). For Albania, the reference community is the village, which is feasible given access to census data. For Madagascar, the reference community is the province, the lowest possible level of disaggregation;[11] and

S refers to other subjective variables.

The results for the two full models can be found in Table 2.7 for Albania and Table 2.8 for Madagascar.

Once we add the full specification, the log of per capita calories becomes statistically insignificant. However, adding the remaining variables explains a larger part (36 per cent) of the variation in food adequacy perception. When per capita calorie consumption is replaced by per capita food expenditure, the model produces similar results. However, unlike per capita calories, per capita food expenditure remains statistically significant. This makes sense, as discussed earlier, given the tradeoff between calories and food quality as income increases.

Just as interesting is the role of the different types of variables in explaining perceptions of food adequacy in Albania. First, dietary diversity is highly correlated to subjective food adequacy. However, the dietary diversity index becomes insignificant when per capita calories are substituted with per capita food expenditure. This suggests that the dietary diversity index may convey similar information as food expenditure, and in fact the two are collinear, with a high coefficient of correlation (0.6). Second, a number of wealth indicators are associated with perceptions of greater food adequacy. These include the share of nonfood items in total consumption, ownership of assets and higher wage/skilled occupations. Greater levels of human capital, in the form of average years of education among adults in the household, are also associated with a higher probability of food adequacy. Third, differences in household size and gender and age composition do not appear to influence perceptions of food adequacy. However, in the case of Albania, at equal levels of calorie/food consumption, being a female respondent, a widow(er), or a pensioner is associated with a greater probability of food inadequacy.

[11] See Carletto *et al.* (2005) for a detailed description of the construction of this variable in the case of Albania.

Table 2.7. Probit of perception of food adequacy—Albania
Dependent variable (0 = less than adequate; 1 = more than/just adequate)

	Calorie consumption		Food expenditures	
	Coefficient	Robust *z* statistics	Coefficient	Robust *z* statistics
Per capita kcal/food expenditure				
Log of per capita calories per day	0.179	(1.53)		
Log of per capita food expenditure			0.340	(3.05)***
Dietary diversity				
Simpson Index of dietary diversity	1.386	(3.20)***	0.707	(1.62)
Wealth				
Household asset index	0.088	(2.73)***	0.074	(2.26)**
Share of nonfood items in total consumption	0.008	(2.96)***	0.011	(3.68)***
Household composition				
Household size	0.053	(1.18)	0.072	(1.60)
Age of HH head	0.002	(0.69)	0.002	(0.58)
HH head is female	0.125	(1.04)	0.135	(1.13)
Dependency ratio	0.060	(0.34)	0.055	(0.32)
Respondent is female	−0.106	(1.69)*	−0.099	(1.58)
HH head is divorced	−0.030	(0.08)	−0.046	(0.12)
HH head is widow(er)	−0.215	(1.66)*	−0.226	(1.75)*
HH head is single	−0.137	(0.82)	−0.159	(0.95)
HH member(s) received a pension or other assistance during the past 12 m	−0.148	(1.96)*	−0.153	(2.03)**
No. of HH members 0–14 yrs of age	−0.062	(1.25)	−0.063	(1.25)
No. of HH members 15–34 yrs of age	−0.049	(1.11)	−0.053	(1.20)
No. of HH members 35–59 yrs of age	−0.044	(0.80)	−0.047	(0.86)
Migration/remittances				
HH has permanent migrants in Italy	−0.024	(0.24)	−0.023	(0.22)
HH has permanent migrants in Greece	−0.351	(2.58)***	−0.353	(2.58)***
Occupation				
HH head in skilled occupation	−0.260	(2.01)**	−0.257	(1.99)**
Unemployed HH head, dummy	−0.063	(0.49)	−0.051	(0.40)
Health				
HH head suffers from chronic illness, dummy	−0.023	(0.34)	−0.026	(0.38)
Religion				
HH head is Catholic	0.638	(2.60)***	0.633	(2.62)***
HH head is Orthodox	−0.318	(1.37)	−0.347	(1.52)
HH head is Muslim	−0.033	(0.16)	−0.052	(0.26)
Education				
Average HH years of education	0.025	(2.02)**	0.021	(1.65)*
Location				
Urban	−0.242	(2.29)**	−0.229	(2.21)**
Central region (coastal region excluded)	−0.444	(4.02)***	−0.423	(3.79)***
Mountain region	0.104	(0.84)	0.111	(0.90)
Tirana region	−0.456	(3.55)***	−0.467	(3.61)***
Relative wealth				
Relative deprivation index	−0.117	(0.95)	−0.110	(0.91)
Subjective				
Satisfaction with current situation	0.483	(8.64)***	0.479	(8.57)***
Concern in providing family with basic needs in next 12 m	0.111	(2.61)***	0.111	(2.59)***
Ten-step wealth ladder	0.294	(9.04)***	0.282	(8.58)***
General situation past 3 years	0.369	(8.43)***	0.367	(8.35)***
HH head rates health condition with respect to one year ago as better (than worse/same)	−0.116	(1.79)*	−0.117	(1.81)*
Constant	−6.175	(5.19)***	−7.054	(6.84)***
Observations	3351		3351	
Log Likelihood	−1484.99		−1479.61	
chi2	908.10		908.15	
Pseudo-R2	0.36		0.36	

Note: *significant at 10%; ** significant at 5%; *** significant at 1%.

Table 2.8. Probit of perception of food adequacy—Madagascar
Dependent variable (0 = less than adequate; 1 = more than/just adequate)

	Calorie consumption		Food expenditures	
	Coefficient	Robust *z* statistics	Coefficient	Robust *z* statistics
Per capita kcal/food expenditure				
Log of per capita kcal per day, 30-day recall	0.049	(0.69)		
Log of per capita food expenditure			0.196	(3.01)***
Dietary diversity				
Simple count of foods consumed, monthly recall	0.001	(0.25)	−0.004	(1.11)
Wealth				
Household asset index	−0.001	(0.06)	−0.000	(0.01)
Share of nonfood items in total consumption	0.005	(2.44)**	0.008	(3.73)***
Household composition				
Household size	−0.040	(0.48)	−0.069	(0.87)
Age of HH head	−0.002	(0.50)	−0.000	(0.10)
HH head is female	−0.102	(1.29)	−0.122	(1.67)*
Dependency ratio	−0.185	(0.98)	−0.153	(0.88)
HH head is divorced	0.017	(0.09)	0.054	(0.31)
HH head is widow(er)	0.187	(1.69)*	0.234	(2.28)**
HH head is single	0.045	(0.37)	0.012	(0.10)
HH head entitled to pension	−0.019	(0.24)	−0.041	(0.55)
No. of HH members 0–14 yrs of age	0.025	(0.31)	0.061	(0.78)
No. of HH members 15–34 yrs of age	0.050	(0.57)	0.096	(1.16)
No. of HH members 35–59 yrs of age	−0.022	(0.28)	−0.007	(0.10)
Migration				
No. of temporary migrants: absent more than 1 month	−0.008	(0.22)	0.005	(0.16)
Housing				
Log of house surface (area)	0.089	(2.50)**	0.079	(2.39)**
Occupation				
HH head in skilled occupation	0.022	(0.27)	0.057	(0.72)
HH head is unemployed, ILO definition	0.051	(0.50)	0.109	(1.13)
Member of HH with non-agric enterprise	0.119	(2.08)**	0.096	(1.77)*
Health				
HH head suffered from disease/wound	0.066	(0.77)	0.105	(1.28)
HH head had medical attention	0.104	(0.92)	0.005	(0.04)
Religion (excl. traditional)				
HH head is Catholic	−0.06	(0.76)	−0.094	(1.27)
HH head is Protestant	0.013	(0.16)	−0.016	(0.21)
HH head is Muslim	−0.177	(0.96)	−0.199	(1.12)
HH head is of another religion	−0.03	(0.27)	−0.041	(0.39)
Education				
Highest diploma obtained by HH head	0.04	(2.93)***	0.038	(2.89)***
HH head has never studied	0.031	(0.44)	0.003	(0.04)
Location				
Urban	0.039	(0.40)	−0.143	(1.27)
Semi urban	0.067	(0.95)	−0.015	(0.22)
Fianarantsoa Province (excl. Antananarivo)	−0.399	(4.18)***	−0.28	(2.82)***
Toamasina Province	−0.423	(4.42)***	−0.325	(3.31)***
Mahajanga Province	0.057	(0.60)	0.099	(1.06)
Toliara Province	−0.196	(2.04)**	−0.184	(2.06)**
Antsiranana Province	0.045	(0.44)	0.081	(0.85)
Relative wealth				
Relative Deprivation Index	−0.000	(3.89)***	−0.000	(1.39)
Subjective				
Household's budget compared to last year	0.285	(8.30)***	0.272	(8.38)***
Current standard of living	0.748	(21.59)***	0.740	(22.73)***
Constant	−2.949	(4.48)***	−5.221	(5.39)***
Observations	3543		3952	
Log Likelihood	−1832.58		−2046.43	
chi2	1246.48		1384.32	
Pseudo-R2	0.25		0.25	

Note: * significant at 10%; ** significant at 5%; *** significant at 1%.

Fourth, food adequacy is highly correlated with other subjective perceptions.[12] Households that are satisfied with their general current situation, who are little concerned about providing the family with food and other basic needs for the future, who do not perceive themselves as poor and who think that life has improved during the previous three years have a higher probability of considering their food consumption adequate. This suggests that perceptions of food consumption are influenced not only by the current situation (however the question was formulated), but also by changing status over time ('relative' food security) and the perspectives for the future (vulnerability). If this is the case, then we should not be surprised that little correlation is found with *current* caloric adequacy. However, the statistical significance of other subjective answers may be simply capturing 'attitudinal characteristics' (Carletto and Zezza 2006; Lokshin *et al.* 2003) rather than relative food insecurity and vulnerability. In other words, if a person is pessimistic about the present situation, it is likely that he/she is pessimistic also about the past and the future.

The probit models for Madagascar tell a similar story, albeit with some notable exceptions. Dietary diversity, occupation (except having a member of the household owning a non-agricultural enterprise), household asset score, religion and migration are statistically insignificant in both models. Household composition and characteristics still have little influence. However, the share of nonfood in total consumption and greater levels of human capital are also associated with a higher food adequacy. Furthermore, relative deprivation is statistically significant, suggesting that perceptions of food adequacy are influenced by relative wealth status. The poorer a given household is in comparison to a reference group, the higher the probability of perceived food inadequacy.

Also in the case of Madagascar, other subjective perceptions count. Those households whose budget has improved compared to the year before the interview and those who think that they are currently among the wealthy/wealthier households, have a higher perception of food adequacy. This makes eminent sense given the importance of relative wealth as measured by total per capita consumption.

2.5 Discussion and Conclusions

The objective of this chapter was to compare measures of self-perceived food consumption from household survey data with standard quantitative indicators of food security, namely calorie consumption, dietary diversity and

[12] We should not infer a causal effect of the other subjective variables on subjective food adequacy, when in fact it is just as possible that perceptions of food adequacy influence these other subjective variables.

anthropometry. To that end, the study has analysed data from four large-scale household surveys which collected information on these subjective measures as well as the more traditional indicators of food security.

The simple descriptive analysis presented suggests that, overall, calorie consumption, dietary diversity and anthropometry are at best weakly correlated to subjective perceptions of food consumption. 'Subjective' and 'objective' indicators do not classify the same households as food (in)secure. The weak correlations are similar to those found in other studies. Hamilton *et al.* (1997) find only a weak correlation between income and the US food security measure, with correlation coefficients ranging from −0.12 to −0.33, depending on the definition of income utilized. Coates *et al.* (2003) find in a small sample in Bangladesh somewhat higher correlation coefficients (0.42−0.44), though they find particularly low correlation with calorie consumption. Both of these food security indicators were far more sophisticated than the CAQ utilized in our study, and were the result of extensive field testing.

The lack of correlation between anthropometry and perceptions is not surprising, at least for underweight. Anthropometric indicators reflect not only food consumption, but also care practices, health and other environmental factors. More surprising is the lack of correlation between wasting and perceptions, especially the (weakly) negative correlation found between wasting and subjective children's food consumption adequacy in Indonesia. Coates *et al.* (2003) find a similar lack of association between anthropometric measures and the subjective indicator in Bangladesh.

From the multivariate analysis, dietary diversity appears to be more correlated with subjective perceptions than calories or anthropometry, at least for Albania. This corresponds to conventional wisdom on the relationship between food consumption, calories and wealth. As households become wealthier, instead of maximizing calories, they improve the quality of consumption (substituting better types of the same foods or expanding the diversity of foods eaten) and the type of consumption, such as eating out more often. This implies small marginal changes in caloric intake as incomes increase, but a large change in the composition of the diet and in the cost of each calorie. Hoddinott and Yohannes (2002), in their cross country study, find that as households diversify their diets, they increase the consumption of relatively prestigious nonstaple foods rather than increase the variety of consumption within the group of staples. Note, however, that dietary diversity is not interchangeable with dietary quality, but is instead only one component (Ruel 2002).

The multivariate results for Albania show that the responses to the food adequacy question depend on a variety of household level and wealth characteristics. This confirms the earlier work of Pradhan and Ravallion (2000) for Nepal and Lokshin *et al.* (2003) for Madagascar, who perform similar regressions, albeit with a different objective. Also, both of these studies find that relative income or, more generally, the relative position in society, influence reported perceptions. In Madagascar, Lokshin *et al.* (2003) find that households living in population clusters with a high mean income are more likely to perceive their food consumption expenditure as less adequate compared to an average household, and that higher intra-cluster inequality negatively affects perceptions of food consumption adequacy. We find similar results for both Madagascar and Albania.

We take their analysis a step further, however, and we find for Madagascar that households that are poorer compared to their neighbours (relative deprivation)—holding household and community level wealth constant—have a lower perception of food adequacy. Finally, if the household's economic situation has worsened in the past—holding wealth constant—the household is much more likely to have a lower perception as well. These two results together suggest that the food adequacy questions may be capturing relative food adequacy, in comparison with neighbours, and respondent's perception of changing status over time. As such, they would reveal perceptions of vulnerability and would denote something quite different from standard quantitative measures. Our multivariate regressions show that perceptions of food adequacy are highly correlated with perception of relative and absolute wealth, both in the past and in the present. Therefore, not surprising is the finding of a weak (or, lack of) correlation with *current* food security and wealth as measured by quantitative indicators, which cannot capture vulnerability. On the other hand, we have suggested that the correlation among subjective indicators may be due also to 'attitudinal characteristics' and not to relative food insecurity and/or to vulnerability. Panel data would be needed to control for fixed individual effects and thus to determine whether perceptions are determined by vulnerability.

Finally, the measure of perception of food adequacy that we have been analysing in this chapter is alarmingly simple when compared to the US food security index or to standard calorie consumption measures. While the relative imprecision of the CAQ compared to the more sophisticated US-type subjective food index may be sufficient for academic studies, this imprecision translates into missing food insecure households, when it concerns targeting food security interventions. While subjective food adequacy indicators may provide insight on the vulnerability and/or relative dimension of food insecurity, the CAQ is a too blunt and ambiguous indicator for directly mapping food insecurity.

Of course, a limiting factor in this study is the implicit assumption that our quantitative measures of food security are, in some sense, reliable benchmarks. As noted in the introduction, subjective measures might actually perform well despite the findings in this study, to the extent that the traditional quantitative benchmarks for food security are flawed and inaccurate measures of actual food security. That is, not finding a strong correlation is not necessarily an indictment of subjective measures. Thus, an effort towards developing subjective food security modules should go hand in hand with research into how to improve household survey data for food security measurement along other dimensions of the phenomenon, particularly calorie consumption. The recent trend in a number of countries such as Brazil, Yemen, and Bangladesh to redesign a food security index based on local conditions and notions of food consumption is an important step forward, and should be encouraged in other countries carrying out LSMS-type household surveys.

This surely is not an easy task. The US food security module is the product of several years of methodological advances and of field testing. It measures the sufficiency of household food through food-related behaviours as directly experienced by people. One of its main drawbacks is that, while its *internal* validity and consistency have been extensively tested (at the population level, not at the level of an individual household), its *external* validity has not (Bickel *et al.* 2000). One important recent exception is provided by Frongillo and Nanama (2006), who successfully assessed the validity of their experienced-based food insecurity measure by examining its reliability and by comparing it with economic status, dietary, and anthropometric measures and with a measure created by an observer who rated the households' food insecurity. This is an encouraging result and, together with our results, suggests that 'easy shortcuts' in the form of CAQ do not serve their intended purpose. The inclusion of a contextually sensitive module similar to that of the US into household surveys in developing countries, reflecting also future vulnerability, thus provides an excellent opportunity to validate externally 'subjective' indicators, both at the population level and at the level of the individual household.

Appendix 2.1 Description of the Data Sets

The Nepal 1995/96 LSMS has a food consumption module which includes food purchases and home consumption, plus a question on the annual value of foods in kind received. The recall period for purchases and home consumption is one month, the 'typical month consumption' over the previous year. A total of 65 items were listed, including general categories (other cereals, etc.), of which only 46 could be converted into calories, plus meals taken outside home and miscellaneous food expenditure (for which only expenditure was reported). The subjective module contains two questions on food consumption. The first is worded as described in section 2.2 with a month recall, and the second was asked to those who answered that their food consumption was less than adequate for the family's needs, and was formulated as follows: 'Do you consider that you, or any member of your family, eats too little food to live a healthy and active life? (yes/no)'. Calorie consumption and dietary diversity were computed, although numerous problems were encountered in the construction of the calorie consumption variable, and thus we considered it unreliable. Anthropometry was not computed because the age variable was not deemed reliable.

In the 2001 Madagascar (MHS) questionnaire, information on food consumption was split among various modules: (a) the food expenditure section contained only food purchases and a question on the annual value of foods in kind received. There are two recall periods for food purchases, 7-day recall and monthly recall, the latter intended to account for seasonality factors. The food list contains 66 items, including general categories, of which 62 were convertible into calories; (b) meals eaten outside (7-day recall; only expenditures reported); (c) food wage (annual recall; only values reported); (d) self-consumption from non-agricultural enterprises (annual recall; same food items as the food expenditure section; only values reported); (e) livestock self-consumption (number of animals slaughtered for self-consumption during the year, with a generic list of 10 animals, including general categories); (f) self-consumed harvest (69 convertible food items, annual quantities). The subjective question was formulated as following: Your expenses related to food: (1) are below your household's needs; (2) are on average compared to your household's needs; (3) exceed your household's real needs. Calorie consumption and dietary diversity were computed. Anthropometric data were not collected.

The Albania 2002 LSMS included a food diary that was left in the household by the interviewer during the first visit for the household to compile, and then collected during the second visit. Upon collection, interviewers checked the entries (with the help of a checklist provided at the end of the booklet) and corrected them as appropriate with the help of the most knowledgeable person in the household. The diary consisted of a three-part section, one for each of 14 days, for the recording of (1) food products purchased daily; (2) non-purchased food products consumed by the household (e.g. from own production or payments in kind); (3) food eaten outside the home (e.g. at work, in restaurants); and a checklist for use by the interviewer with a list of the 14 main food products consumed in Albania. A specific column was provided to the interviewers to record the 'reference period' for bulk purchases of food. Whenever unusually large quantities of a specific item were recorded, the interviewer asked the household—upon collecting the diary—to specify the expected period over which the said quantity would be consumed to allow for ex-post adjustments of the purchased quantities. In addition, interviewers were instructed to check, for the 14 main food staples in the checklist, whether any consumption of the item had been recorded in the diary. Whenever an item had not been recorded, the interviewer would ask the respondent to report whether the item (a) had not been used in the 14-day period, or (b) had been consumed but the household had forgotten to record its consumption, or else (c) had been consumed by the household drawing on stocks purchased or produced outside the 14-day period. If the inclusion of an item had simply been forgotten, the interviewer would then fill the appropriate section of the diary by asking the household to recall the details of that consumption. If the household reported consuming an item purchased before the beginning of the 14 day period, then information on the frequency of purchase, quantity, unit of measure and value of the purchase were recorded in the columns provided to this end in the checklist. The diary listed over 180 items, including general categories and composite dishes. The subjective food adequacy question referred to the 'current level of food consumption of the family'. Household calorie consumption, dietary diversity, and anthropometric indicators were all computed.

In Indonesia, the 2000 IFLS3 is the third wave of a panel survey (see Strauss *et al.* 2004). Only anthropometric indicators were calculated for this study because the items in the food expenditure section were too aggregated to allow for calculation of calories. The interesting feature of the IFLS3 is the inclusion of two subjective food adequacy questions. The first is the same as in the other surveys, and has a one month recall. The second is the same as the first but refers specifically to children in the household, also with one month recall.

Appendix 2.2 Methodology and Assumptions in Estimating Caloric Availability and Adequacy

While each survey differs in how information is collected, in estimating calorie consumption we followed a standard procedure, which can be divided in the following steps.

(1) All reported quantities are converted into grams.

(2) Quantities expressed in units/pieces and in wrong units of measurement (e.g. litres of maize etc.) are converted into quantities (see step 3). For some food items, such as eggs or bananas, units are directly converted into grams, using some 'standard' weight per unit. Information on unit weights comes from secondary sources or, more frequently, from the USDA nutrition database (see below).

(3) Unit values for each food item are computed as reported expenditure divided by grams, so as to obtain costs per gram. Unit values are computed for both market purchases and home consumption. However, the former are normally used. Medians of unit values for each food item and each administrative unit are then computed. Indicator variables are created to see how many unit values per food item there are for each administrative unit. This allows us to see on how many observations the medians have been computed for each food item and each administrative level. Quantities expressed in wrong units of measurement or in difficult-to-convert units are imputed by dividing reported expenditure by a median unit value. The choice of which median to use is done on the basis of the number of observations and on the distribution/range of medians, following the general rule of using the median at the lowest possible administrative level. As a rule of thumb, if the median at some administrative level was computed on less than five observations, the next administrative level was used. However, the choice was ultimately dependent on the distribution of the medians. Imputation was done for all food sources (purchases, home consumption and in kind). Price data were available only for Albania. When available and when plausible, prices were used to impute quantities.

(4) Food items not convertible into calories (because calorie-less or because there were no observations on quantities, and thus on unit values) and irrelevant items for

household's diet (e.g. alcoholic beverages, for which there were no observations on quantities and unit values anyway) were dropped. The items dropped were not important in households' consumption, so we are confident that excluding them does not significantly affect estimates.

(5) Once all quantities and expenditures are converted into grams, grams per capita per day are computed for each food item. Quantities per capita are used for the trimming of outliers (reimputing implausibly high values). The trimming is done for each food item, by source of food (purchases, home consumption, in kind, etc.) and by location (urban/rural). The trimming is done in two steps. First, outliers are re-imputed by dividing expenditure by median unit values, following the same procedure as in step 3. If the imputation does not work (i.e. there are still outliers or imputed quantities are implausibly low/high), extreme values are 'squeezed' to the 90th–99th percentile of the (weighed) per capita distribution, depending on the magnitude of the values in the upper tail of the distribution. The choice of which percentile to use was done on a case-by-case basis, also using common knowledge on human nutrition. For example, if the per capita distribution for rice shows that in rural areas the 90th percentile is 600 g per capita per day and the 95th is 1,000 g, the 90th is chosen (i.e. if the imputation does not work, those observations above the 600 g are assigned the value of 600 g per capita per day). As a rule of thumb, the lowest percentile used is the 90th, even if it is an outlier/too high value itself. This was a problem especially for staples in rural Nepal and Madagascar, where one could find that half of the observations or those above the upper inter-quartile range were simply too high (for instance, a 75th percentile of 800 g-1 kg of cereals per capita per day). This partly explains the higher calorie consumption found in rural areas, but only partly, because it may well be the case that if a household reported exaggerated quantities for many food items, this household would still be an outlier even after trimming of all items.

(6) Reported values on meals/foods eaten outside, miscellaneous food expenditure and other not-well-specified expenditures/values are converted into calories assuming that the cost per calorie is higher, equal or lower than the cost per calorie of food purchased, depending on the type of expenditure or value. Calories were therefore imputed using the general formula: kcal = Ekcal*exp*s/totexp, where *Ekcal* is total calories from food purchases, *exp* is expenditure for the calories to be imputed, *totexp* is total household expenditure on food purchases and *s* is the adjusting factor. For meals eaten outside we assumed that the cost per calorie is 20 per cent higher—a conservative assumption. Outliers in resulting calories were trimmed, using the derived distribution of calories per capita per day (e.g. if observations above the 90th–99th percentiles were higher than, say, 3,000 kcal per capita per day, outliers were squeezed to the 90th-99th percentile). In the case of Madagascar we used the median cost per calorie at the rural/urban province level, because there were too few observations at lower administrative levels.

(7) Grams are converted into calories (using food composition tables) and total household calorie consumption is compared to the household-specific caloric norm.

Table 2A.1 Daily caloric requirements by age and sex

Age	Male	Female
0	649	600
1	948	851
2	1129	1035
3	1252	1145
4	1360	1231
5	1467	1320
6	1350	1225
7	1450	1325
8	1550	1450
9	1675	1575
10	1825	1700
11	2000	1825
12	2175	1925
13	2350	2025
14	2550	2075
15	2700	2125
16	2825	2125
17	2900	2125
18–29	2794	2322
30–59	2678	2200
≥ 60	2255	2000

We used age- and sex-specific caloric requirements taken from the 2001 FAO/UNU/WHO (2001) expert consultation interim report on human energy requirements. The high side of light physical activity is assumed for all (1.6*BMR), and the requirement used is that corresponding to the mean of the weight/requirement range for appropriate age and sex groups Table 2A.1 shows the daily caloric requirements used.[13]

The food composition tables (FCTs) used were:

(1) For Nepal, the 'Nutrient Contents in Nepalese Foods' (Ministry of Agriculture of Nepal, Nutrition Programme Section, Kathmandu 1994).
(2) For Madagascar, the 'Food Composition Table for Use in Africa' (Source: FAO, personal communication)
(3) For Albania, the 'Slovak Food Composition Table' (ALIMENTA database. Source: FAO and Food Research Institute of Slovakia 2000).

The FCTs listed were complemented by the USDA Nutrition Database ('Composition of Foods Raw, Processed and Prepared', US Department of Agriculture, National Nutrient Database for Standard Reference, Release 16, January 2004).

[13] We also calculated household caloric adequacy by using the universal cut off of 2,100 kcal per capita per day. Even though estimates are clearly different depending on which cut-off is used, final results (i.e. correlation with the subjective indicator) do not change significantly (results not shown here).

Additional Assumptions and Methodology for Calorie Conversion for Madagascar

The 2001 MHS questionnaire was particularly problematic for calculating calories. Information on food consumption was split among various modules.

The questionnaire includes also a section on transfers in and out of the household, to members and non-members of the household, including food. The question on food transfers asked to estimate the value of food received and given out during the year prior to the interview. Since the food expenditure section contains also a column on food in kind received, broken down by food item, we disregarded the sections on transfers. This is not a problem also because there were relatively few households that reported values for transfers (less than 200).

For imputing calories from food wage and from self-consumption from non-agricultural enterprises (most of which were trading enterprises and hotels/restaurants), we assumed that the cost per calorie is 20 per cent less than the cost per calorie from market purchases.

For the livestock self-consumption section, we used FAO data on dressed (eviscerated) carcass weight—grams per animal—excluding offal and slaughter fats (complemented with USDA data on some offal) and dressed carcass weight as percentage of live weight (for animals for which there are data). An average calorie value was then used for meat and offal/fats. However, data were not available for all animals and calories are therefore a rough approximation (especially for offal and fats, where calories values for liver have been used—when available—when not, 100 kcal/100 g have been used because values for kidney and liver—the only offal found in the FCTs—of various animals range around 100). This probably means under-estimating calories, because we do not account for fat. On the other hand, this is probably counter-balanced by the likely over-estimation of the offal/fats weight and that derived from not accounting for wastage. The source and magnitude of biases are not known. However, given the relatively low number of households that reported self-consumption of livestock, it is unlikely that estimates for calories from livestock have seriously biased overall estimates.

General Problems in the Calculation of Household Caloric Availability

The calculation of household caloric availability presented formidable challenges. The main problems encountered included:

- *Units of measurement.* Some food items are expressed in the wrong unit of measurement because of data entry mistakes (e.g. litres of rice) and some are expressed in undefined units. In such cases, quantities have to be imputed using unit values. Besides the usual problem of unit values not being the same thing as prices because contaminated by quality differences, unit values have at times a too wide range and/or there are too few observations. As a result, imputation is often unsatisfactory. This is true also for some frequently consumed items for which there are many observations. Having prices is not necessarily better than using unit values, if collected prices are biased. For example, in the case of Albania, for some items, the price range is dubious, with items costing up to 20 times more in different areas. Furthermore, for some items, prices are expressed in units, without specifying the weight (e.g. bread), in which case the weight has to be estimated combining unit values and prices.

- *Vague food items.* Many food items are too vaguely specified (e.g. pastry cook, baking, frozen sweets, etc.). Together with dubious imputing of quantities and misreported quantity values, giving a calorie content is sometimes more a guess than an accurate estimation.
- *Imputing quantities from values.* When only expenditure is available, quantities (or directly calories) have to be imputed. This is especially a problem when respondents are asked to report the annual value of a particular item received in kind or the food wage, as in the case of Nepal and Madagascar.
- *Unavailable and/or inadequate FCTs.* Nepal was the only country for which a FCT was available to us. For the rest, we had to resort to other FCTs and nutrition databases (see above for details). Even when a FCT is available, some food items are not reported or, being the foods listed in the questionnaire quite vague (e.g. bread, without specifying which type) and foods listed in the FCT more specific (i.e. different varieties), some average caloric content is to be used, unless prior information on local diets is available (which was not to us).
- *Different recall periods for different sections.* This was a problem especially for Madagascar and for calculating calories for in kind food for Madagascar and Nepal.
- *Misreported quantities and/or values.* This is especially the case for Nepal and, more generally, for staples, with some implausibly high quantities per capita.

We are conscious of the fact that the assumptions made to impute calories when only expenditure or values are available (and especially when they are annual values) can create serious biases. For these reasons we calculated calorie consumption including and excluding these components. For Nepal, we calculated calorie consumption including and excluding in kind food received and meals eaten outside/miscellaneous food expenditure in turn, thus producing four different estimates. Given the relatively small importance of these components, estimates were close to each other. For Madagascar, we differentiated between calories derived from food purchases and total calories (computed using all components), and between recall periods (7-day and 30-day recall). For Albania, we computed calories including and excluding meals/foods eaten outside. In all cases, the basic results presented in the chapter (especially the correlation with the subjective question) are not significantly affected by the inclusion/exclusion of these components.

References

Azzarri, C., C. Carletto, B. Davis, and A. Zezza (2006). 'Monitoring Poverty without Consumption Data: An Application Using the Albania Panel Survey'. *Eastern European Economics*, 44 (1).

Bickel, G., M. Nord, C. Price, W. Hamilton, and J. Cook (2000). 'Guide to Measuring Household Food Security'. Washington, DC: Office of Analysis, Nutrition and Evaluation, Food and Nutrition Service, US Department of Agriculture.

Carletto, G., and A. Zezza (2006). 'Being Poor, Feeling Poorer: Combining Objective and Subjective Measures of Welfare in Albania'. *Journal of Development Studies*, 42: 739–60.

Carletto, G., B. Davis, and M. Stampini (2005). 'Familiar Faces, Familiar Places: The Role of Family Networks and Previous Experience for Albanian Migrants'. ESA Working Paper 05–03. Rome: FAO.

CDC (2002). 'EpiInfo 2002. Revision 2'. Atlanta: Department of Health and Human Services.

Chung, K., L. Haddad, J. Ramakrishna, and F. Riely (1997). 'Alternative Approaches to Locating the Food Insecure: Qualitative and Quantitative Evidence from South India'. Discussion Paper 22. Washington, DC: Food Consumption and Nutrition Division, IFPRI.

Coates, J., P. Webb, and R. Houser (2003). 'Measuring Food Insecurity: Going Beyond Indicators of Income and Anthropometry'. Food and Nutrition Technical Assistance Project. Washington, DC: Academy for Educational Development.

Dercon, S. (2001). 'Assessing Vulnerability'. Oxford: Oxford University. Mimeo.

FAO/UNU/WHO (2001). 'Expert Consultation on Energy in Human Nutrition. Interim Report'. Rome: FAO. Mimeo.

FAO (2003a). *Measurement and Assessment of Food Deprivation and Undernutrition. Proceedings of the International Scientific Symposium, Rome, 26–28 June 2002*. Rome: FAO.

—— (2003b). *The State of Food Insecurity in the World 2003*. Rome: FAO.

—— (2004). *The State of Food Insecurity in the World 2004*. Rome: FAO.

Frongillo, E. A., and S. Nanama (2006). 'Development and Validation of an Experience-Based Measure of Household Food Insecurity within and across Seasons in Northern Burkina Faso'. *Journal of Nutrition*, 136: 1409S–1419S.

Hamilton, W. L., J. Cook, W. W. Thompson, L. F. Buron, E. A. Frongillo, C. M. Olson, and C. A. Wehler (1997). 'Household Food Security in the United States in 1995, Technical Report of the Food Security Measurement Project'. Alexandria: US Department of Agriculture.

Hoddinott, J. (1999a). 'Choosing Outcome Indicators of Household Food Security'. IFPRI Technical Guide 7. Washington, DC: IFPRI.

—— (1999b). 'Operationalizing Household Food Security in Development Projects: An Introduction'. IFPRI Technical Guide 1. Washington, DC: IFPRI.

Hoddinott, J., and Y. Yohannes (2002). 'Dietary Diversity as a Food Security Indicator'. FCND Discussion Paper 136. Washington, DC: IFPRI.

Kennedy, E. (2003). 'Qualitative Measures of Food Insecurity and Hunger', in *Measurement and Assessment of Food Deprivation and Undernutrition. Proceedings of the International Scientific Symposium, Rome, 26–8 June 2002*. Rome: FAO, 165–84.

Lokshin, M., N. Umapathi, and S. Paternostro (2003). 'Robustness of Subjective Welfare Analysis in a Poor Developing Country: Madagascar 2001'. Washington, DC: World Bank. Mimeo.

Maxwell, S. (1996). 'Food Security: A Post-Modern Perspective'. *Food Policy*, 21 (2): 155–70.

Melgar-Quinonez, H. R., A. C. Zubieta, B. MkNelly, A. Nteziyaremye, M. F. D. Gerardo, and C. Dunford (2006). 'Household Food Insecurity and Food Expenditure in Bolivia, Burkina Faso, and the Philippines'. *Journal of Nutrition*, 136: 1431S–1437S.

Migotto, M., B. Davis, C. Carletto, and K. Beegle (2005). 'Measuring Food Security Using Respondents' Perception of Food Consumption Adequacy'. ESA Working Paper 05–10. Rome: FAO.

Morris, S. S., C. Carletto, J. Hoddinott, and J. M. Christiansen (2000). 'Validity of Rapid Estimates of Household Wealth and Income for Health Surveys in Rural Africa', *Journal of Epidemiology and Community Health*, 54 (12): 0–6.

Naiken, L. (2003). 'FAO Methodology for Estimating the Prevalence of Undernourishment', *Measurement and Assessment of Food Deprivation and Undernutrition. Proceedings of the International Scientific Symposium, Rome, 26–28 June 2002*. Rome: FAO, 7–42.

Nord, M., A. K. Satpathy, N. Raj, P. Webb, and R. Houser (2002). 'Comparing Household Survey-Based Measures of Food Insecurity across Countries: Case Studies in India, Uganda and Bangladesh'. Discussion Paper 7. Boston: Friedman School of Nutrition Science and Policy, Tufts University.

Pradhan, M., and M. Ravallion (2000). 'Measuring Poverty using Qualitative Perceptions of Consumption Adequacy'. *The Review of Economics and Statistics*, 82 (3): 462–71.

Prennushi, G. (1999). 'Nepal: Poverty at the Turn of the Twenty-First Century. Main Report and Background Studies'. Report IDP 174, South Asia Region Internal Discussion Paper. Washington, DC: World Bank.

Rakutomehefa P., M. Razakamanansoa, and M. Romani (2002). 'Madagascar Poverty Profile 2001: Technical Report'. INSTAT Technical Report. Antananarivo, Madagascar: INSTAT.

Ravallion, M., and M. Lokshin (1999). 'Subjective Economic Welfare'. WB Policy Research Working Paper 2106. Washington, DC: World Bank.

Ruel, M. T. (2002). 'Is Dietary Diversity an Indicator of Food Security or Dietary Quality? A Review of Measurement Issues and Research Needs'. FCND Discussion Paper 140. Washington, DC: IFPRI.

Segall Corrêa, A., R. Pérez Escamilla, L. Kurdian Maranha, and F. Archanjo Sampaio (2003). 'Relatório técnico. Acompanhamento e avaliação da segurança alimentar de famílias brasileiras: validação de metodologia e de instrumento de coleta de informação'. UNICAMP, Faculdade de Ciências Médicas, Departamento de Medicina Preventiva e Social, August.

Skoufias, E. (2001). 'Changes in Regional Inequality and Social Welfare in Indonesia from 1996 to 1999'. *Journal of International Development*, 13 (1): 7391.

Stark, O., and J. E. Taylor (1989). 'Relative Deprivation and International Migration'. *Demography*, 26 (1): 1–14.

Strauss, J., K. Beegle, B. Sikoki, A. Dwiyanto, Y. Herawati and F. Witoelar (2004). 'The Third Wave of the Indonesia Family Life Survey (IFLS): Overview and Field Report'. WR–144/1–NIA/NICHD, RAND.

Tarp, F., K. Simler, C. Matusse, R. Heltberg, and G. Dava (2002). 'The Robustness of Poverty Profiles Reconsidered'. FCND Discussion Paper 124. Washington, DC: IFPRI.

Webb, P., J. Coates, E. A. Frongillo, B. L. Rogers, A. Swindale, and P. Bilinsky (2006). 'Measuring Household Food Insecurity: Why It's So Important and Yet So Difficult to Do'. *Journal of Nutrition*, 136: 1404S–1408S.

World Bank (1986). *Poverty and Hunger: Issues and Options for Food Security in Developing Countries*. Washington, DC: World Bank.

World Bank and INSTAT (2003). 'Albania: Poverty during Growth. A Poverty Profile of Albania'. Background paper for the World Bank Poverty Assessment. Washington, DC and Tirana: World Bank and Albanian Institute of Statistics (INSTAT). Mimeo.

3

Measures of Food Insecurity at the Household Level

Indranil Dutta and Craig Gundersen

3.1 Introduction

The extent of hunger and food insecurity in a country is an important indicator of standard of living (Anand and Harris 1990). The Food and Agriculture Organization of the United Nations (FAO 2003) estimates around 800 million people worldwide to be food insecure and they are not limited to the developing world. Using a different definition of food insecurity, the US Department of Agriculture (USDA) has found that approximately one-in-eight persons in the United States are food insecure (Nord *et al.* 2004). However, the simple head count aggregation rules, as followed by USDA and FAO, though easy to calculate, can be seriously misleading. In the spirit of well established poverty measures such as Sen (1976) and Foster, Greer, and Thorbecke (1984), we propose here aggregation rules to measure food insecurity that go beyond simple head count ratios.

Measuring food inseucurity at the individual/household level rather than the national level differs from the more traditional approach of identifying food insecurity as the inadequacy of aggregate supply of and acessibility to food (Busch and Lacy 1984; FAO 2003). Given the weaknesses of the supply side approach to food insecurity (Reutlinger 1989; Drèze and Sen 1989), several different methods have been put forward including measuring variables (e.g. household income, height to weight ratios) generally thought

This chapter would not have been feasible without the substantive input and encouragement from Prasanta Pattanaik from the very begining. To him we are most grateful for all his help. Further, we would also like to thank Bejamin Davis, R. Radhakrishan, Adam Swallow, and the participants of the Conference on Hunger and Food Security (2005) in Jaipur, India for comments on earlier drafts. Financial support from the Economic Research Service of the US Department of Agriculture (Co-operative Agreement Number 43-3AEM-6-890066) for Dutta is gratefully acknowledged. The usual disclaimer applies.

to be correlated with food insecurity (see Reutlinger 1985; Maxwell and Frankenberger 1992; FAO 2003). Recently, however, dissatisfaction with these measures has led to the use of direct measures of food insecurity (e.g. Maxwell 1995; Maxwell *et al.* 1999; Wolfe and Frongillo 2001) such as household food consumption data (based on recalls) and qualitative measures. In this chapter we focus on the measure food insecurity in the US which is directly based on subjective household survey questionnaires.

Our interest in the US food insecurity measure stems mainly from two reasons. First, any direct measures of food insecurity requires a comprehensive set of questions on food consumption; this has been collected in the US Current Population Survey (CPS). Several questions (described in Table 3.1 below) reflecting varying degrees of food insufficiency are asked and the qualitative nature of the questions do capture, at least to certain extent the level of food insecurity through individuals' perceptions of their food situation. Second, although there has been quite a few studies in the US on food insecurity, households are generally classified into just a few categories such as food secure, food insecure without hunger, or food insecure with hunger (Andrews *et al.* 2001). Under such classification, much of the information contained in the multiple questions is not utilized. The presence of multiple questions allows us to apply new methodology, based on existing poverty measures, which would be better able to capture aggregate food insecurity. In other words, our interest is on the aggregation aspect of a measure of food insecurity rather the identification of the households that are food insecure. We implicitly assume that using some indicator[1] we are properly able to identify households that suffer from food insecurity. Exactly how we should combine the amount of food insecurity suffered by each household to form a societal measure of food insecurity is the object of this chapter. Although this chapter examines food insecurity in the US, the methodology that we use can equally be applied for developing countries.

It has been argued strongly that aggregate measures of food deprivation should take in to account aspects of inequality within food insecure households (Sen 1981; Foster and Leathers 1999). We would like our aggregate measure of food insecurity to distinguish households experiencing slight reductions in food intake from households suffering from more severe levels of hunger. This distinction is important since we surely do not want to treat both the households at a similar level in terms of policy intervention. The aggregation rules we propose gives a higher weight to the more food deprived household and provides a single food insecurity index. Obviously we will have different food insecurity indices depending upon the different weighting procedure used. This type of aggregation rules have been used by

[1] This indicator may be direct consumption of food by households, anthropometirc measures or, as is the case in this paper, subjective measures.

Vecchi and Coppolla (2003); Fujii (2004); and Jha (2004) in other contexts related to food deprivation. Vecchi and Coppola (2003) and Jha (2004) had used the aggregation rule proposed by Foster *et al.* (1984) to measure severity of undernutrition in terms of calorie deficiency while Fujii (2004) uses the same aggregation rule to measure malnutrition using standardized heights and weights. Compared to these papers, here we have proposed broader set of rules that take includes rank based aggregation measures (Sen 1976) along with the Foster *et al.* (1984) measures to calculate food insecurity in the US. We also discuss the theoretical issues associated with these measures especially in the context of its application to subjective measures of food insecurity as is the case with the US food insecurity data that we have. Taking a step further, using these aggregation rules, we test whether food insecurity measures are statistically significantly different among different demographic categories.

In this chapter we begin with a brief description of the qualitative approach and our design of a theoretical framework that allows us to incorporate more information from food insecurity instruments with multiple questions. We then consider an empirical application of this framework. With the indices established in the theoretical framework, we calculate the extent of food insecurity and the extent of food insecurity with hunger in the US in 1998. To do so, we use the 18-item Core Food Security Module (CFSM) which is on numerous surveys including the CPS. In addition to comparing results for all households, we further consider how the indices differ by various demographic categories.

3.2 Basic Framework

3.2.1 *A Qualitative Approach*

In the US, where the extent of hunger and food insecurity is much less severe than in the developing world, insufficient demand for food rather than the supply of food is the reason for food insecurity. As a consequence, aggregate food supplies in a particular region are not used as a measure of food insecurity. The income-based (indirect) measure of food insecurity at the household level is also not effective because some poor households do not suffer from food insecurity and, conversely, many households above the poverty line do suffer from food insecurity.

In a qualitative approach to food insecurity, developed in US, food insecurity is treated as a latent variable (such as IQ) and hence subjective questions related to the food intake of the household are used to elicit that information. Depending on their response to the set of questions, each houshold in then given a food insecurity index that is calculated using multivariate analysis (see Hamilton *et al.* 1997). More affirmative responses to food inadequacy questions represent higher degrees of food insecurity. The household food insecurity index varies between zero and some upper bound with higher numbers indicating greater food insecurity. Once each household is given a food insecurity index, the next step is to formulate an aggregate measure of food insecurity.

Instead of a single food insecurity index, in the official statistics households are classified as food secure, food insecure without hunger, or food insecure with hunger (Andrews *et al.* 2001). Hence, households (with children) are classified as food insecure without hunger if they respond affirmatively to more than three and less than seven (out of 18) questions and households are classified as food insecure with hunger if they respond affirmatively to eight or more questions. Through this classification system, the possible richness of the measure is not fully utilized. Consider two households, one responding affirmatively to eight questions and one responding affirmatively to eighteen questions. Both are treated as food insecure with hunger yet, as Sen (1976) has eloquently argued in the context of poverty measurement, such differences in the degree of deprivation are important and should be reflected in the indices we construct. Just plain distinguishing the households in terms of severity of food insecurity, however, is not very helpful since it simply partitions the set of food insecure households in to coarse sets and does not provide a unified index of food insecurity. While this kind of partitioning may be helpful for policy targeting purposes, in the sense that one knows exactly which group within the food insecure should be given first priority, one can still argue that a unified index which takes the severity of food insecurity in to account within the coarse sets will lead to a better understanding of various policy relevant issues.

3.2.2 *Notation and Concepts*

Let $N = \{1, \ldots, n\}$ denote the set of all households under consideration, n being the total number of households in the set. For all $i \in N$, let s_i denote the *food indicator* (FI) for household i where a higher value of s_i indicates a more unfavourable food situation for household i. We assume that, for every $i \in N$, s_i lies in the interval $[0, z]$, where the value 0 denotes the complete absence of any unfavourable circumstance relating to food and z denotes the most unfavourable situation with respect to food. What one would consider the most unfavourable or least unfavourable food situation will generally depend on the specific context and the judgement of the assessor. In a study in Ghana, Maxwell *et al.* (1999) defines the least unfavourable response as a response of 'once a week' to 'Because food is not enough, or money to buy food is not enough, in the past month, how often have you had to rely on less preferred and less expensive foods.' The most unfavourable response is a response of 'every day' to 'Because food is not enough, or money to buy food is not enough, in the past month, how often have you had to skip whole days without eating?' In the US, Nord *et al.* (2004) has an affirmative response to 'Our family worried food would run out before we got more money to buy more because we were running out of money for food' as the least unfavourable food situation and an affirmative response to 'The children did not eat for a whole day because there wasn't enough money for food' as the most unfavourable food situation.

Let e $(1 > e \geq 0)$ be the benchmark such that a household i is considered food insecure if and only if $s_i > e$. Note that it is possible to set $e = 0$. However, this will constitute a very stringent criterion for a household to be considered food secure (as we will see later, a benchmark, that is widely used in the US, for judging whether a household is food insecure does not set e at 0). We can now define the notions of a *food insecurity index* and a *normalized food insecurity index* for a household. For every household i, the *food insecurity index* (FII) for i is defined to be 0 if $s_i \leq e$ and it is defined to be $(s_i - e)$ if $s_i > e$. The FII of a household provides us with a measure of the extent to which the household is food insecure; it is clearly analogous to the notion of an individual's 'shortfall' from the poverty line, used in the literature on poverty measurement. We get the *normalized food insecurity index* (NFII) for a household when we normalize the FII by dividing it by $(z - e)$. Thus, the normalized food insecurity index for household i, to be denoted by d_i, is given by

$$d_i = \begin{cases} \frac{s_i - e}{z - e} & \text{if} \quad s_i > e \\ 0 & \text{if} \quad s_i \leq e \end{cases}. \tag{3.1}$$

Let d denote the degree of food insecurity suffered by the group, N, of all households. We assume that d is a (real valued) function of $d_1, \ldots, d_n$. We shall call such a function a rule for aggregating household food insecurity levels, or, simply an aggregation rule. Thus, an *aggregation rule* is a function $D : [0,1]^n \longrightarrow R^n$. We write

$$d = D(d_1, \ldots, d_n). \tag{3.2}$$

3.2.3 *The Form of the Aggregation Rule* D

What form should one assume for the function D that aggregates the food insecurity levels, $d_1, \ldots, d_n$, of the households to arrive at the index, d, of social food insecurity? The properties of similar rules for aggregating deprivation levels have been discussed extensively in the literature on income poverty. Some of the familiar properties that one may wish to impose on D are:

Normalization: For all $(d_1, \ldots, d_n) \in [0, 1]^n$, [if $d_i = 0$ for all $i \in N$, then $d = 0$] and [if $d_i = 1$ for all $i \in N$, then $d = 1$].

Anonymity: For all $(d_1, \ldots, d_n)$, $(d'_1, \ldots, d'_n) \in [0, 1]^n$, and, for all $i, j \in N$, if $[d_i = d'_j]$, $[d_j = d'_i]$ and [for all $t \in N - \{i, j\}$, $d_t = d'_t$], then $d = d'$.

Monotonicity: For all $(d_1, \ldots, d_n)$, $(d'_1, \ldots, d'_n) \in [0, 1]^n$, if $[d_i \geq d'_i$ for all $i \in N]$ and $[d_i > d_i$ for some $i \in N]$, then $d > d'$, where $d = D(d_1, \ldots, d_n)$ and $d' = D(d'_1, \ldots, d'_n)$.

Transfer: For all $(d_1, \ldots, d_n)$, $(d'_1, \ldots, d'_n) \in [0, 1]^n$, and all distinct $i, j \in N$, if $[($for all $p \in N - \{i, j\}$, $d_p = d'_p)$ and $(d_i > d_j > 0$ and, for some $\delta > 0$, $d'_i = d_i + \delta$ and $d'_j = d_j - \delta > 0)$ and (for all $p, q \in N$, $d_p \geq d_q$ if and only if $d'_p \geq d'_q)]$, then $d' > d$.

Normalization, which requires that d be 0 when the *NFII* is 0 for all households and d should be 1 when the *NFII* is 1 for all households, is an innocuous property. Its justification lies in the convenience it ensures. Anonymity requires that, other things remaining the same, if the *NFII* of two households are interchanged, then the food insecurity index for the society remains unaffected. Thus, anonymity demands that the households be treated by the aggregation rule in a symmetric fashion. In a framework based on the aggregation of individual deprivation levels, symmetric treatment of individuals is a compelling property. However, in our framework, where D aggregates the *NFII*'s of households to arrive at the measure of overall food insecurity for N, the symmetric treatment of the households is a much less compelling property, given the possibility that the households may differ in their sizes. Monotonicity requires that, other things remaining the same, an increase in the *NFII* of a household leads to a rise in the value of the food insecurity index of the society as a whole. The transfer property is the counterpart of a similar property in the literature on poverty measurement (see, for example, Sen 1976). Suppose, to start with, two households i and j suffer from food insecurity but the food insecurity of i is greater than the food insecurity of j. Now suppose the *NFII* of i increases by δ, and, simultaneously, the *NFII* of j decreases by δ, while the *NFII* of every other household, the set of food-insecure households, and the ranking of the food-insecure households all remain unchanged. Then the transfer property stipulates that the food insecurity of the set, N, of all households must increase.

In this chapter we use four different aggregation rules for the function D. Let N' denote the set of all food insecure households (i.e. the set of all households such that $s_i > e$) and let $\#N'$ be denoted by n'. Name the households in N' as $r(1), \ldots, r(n')$ such that $d_{r(1)} \leq d_{r(2)} \leq \cdots \leq d_{r(n')}$. The rank $l(i)$ of each household, i, in N' is defined to be v, where $i = r(v)$.[2] The four food insecurity measures we use are: (i) the head count, denoted by d^H; (ii) the food insecurity gap, denoted by d^G; (iii) the squared food insecurity gap, denoted by d^{SG}; and

[2] Later, we empirically analyse the extent of food insecurity with hunger in the United States using various measures. In that context, we shall consider different groups of households, such as the set of all households without children and the set of all households with children, and so on. It is clear that, N, N', n, n', and the rank number of a household have to be interpreted with reference to the specific set of households under consideration.

the (iv) 'Sen' food insecurity measure, denoted by d^{SN}. The four measures are given by:

$$d^H = \frac{n'}{n}, \quad (3.3)$$

$$d^G = \frac{\sum_{i=1}^{n} d_i}{n}, \quad (3.4)$$

$$d^{SG} = \frac{\sum_{i=1}^{n} (d_i)^2}{n} \quad (3.5)$$

and

$$d^{SN} = \frac{\sum_{i=1}^{n'} l(i) d_i}{n(n'+1)}. \quad (3.6)$$

The first three indices are members of a class of measures discussed by Foster *et al.* (1984) and defined by (3.7) below:

$$d^{\alpha} = \frac{\sum_{i=1}^{n} d_i (d_i)^{\alpha}}{n}, \quad (3.7)$$

where α is a given positive number. When $\alpha = 0$, d^{α} defines the head count measure; when $\alpha = 1$, d^{α} defines the food insecurity gap; and when $\alpha = 2$, d^{α} defines the squared food insecurity gap.

The Sen food insecurity measure ranks the households in an ascending order, starting with rank 1 for the household with the lowest food insecurity. These rank numbers are then used as weights to aggregate the household insecurity levels into an overall index. Thus, the household with the highest food insecurity gets the highest weight in the aggregate index. One of the problems with the Sen food insecurity measure is that, if the food insecurity of a household increases, with the rank of the household remaining unchanged, the Sen index would still attribute the same weight to the household. In the squared food insecurity index, the weight of a household in the aggregate increases as the food insecurity of the household increases. Both these indices take into account the inequality in terms of food deprivation within the food insecure households.[3] If the inequality gets worse, this measures will also register an increase in food insecurity. The currently used measures of aggregate food insecurity do not follow this property.

The table below shows which of the four properties, normalization, anonymity, monotonicity, and transfer sensitivity, are satisfied by each of the measures mentioned above. ✓ in the appropriate place indicates that the

[3] More specifically, the Sen index measures the gini coefficient of inequality in terms of food deprivation within the food insecure households, whereas the squared food insecurity gap measures the coefficient of variation.

measure satisfies the relevant property, while the absence of ✓ indicates that the measure does not satisfy the relevant property.

	Normalization	Anonymity	Monotonicity	Transfer
d^H	✓	✓		
d^G	✓	✓	✓	
d^{SC}	✓	✓	✓	✓
d^{SN}	✓	✓	✓	✓

3.3 An Application of the Theoretical Framework

We now apply our theoretical framework to the measurement of food insecurity in the United States. We first discuss in a little more detail how food insecurity is measured in the US followed by a discussion of the data used for our analysis.

3.3.1 *The Core Food Security Module*

The CFSM contains eighteen questions that provide detailed information about the experiences of household members as it pertains to a household's inability to meet basic food needs due to financial constraints. A household's responses to these questions are used to categorize the household as (a) food secure, (b) food insecure without hunger, or (c) food insecure with hunger. The CFSM has been included in numerous national surveys, including the CPS, the Survey of Program Dynamics, the Panel Study of Income Dynamics, the National Food Stamp Program Survey, and in surveys at a sub-national level. The results from the CPS are used to derive the official measure of food insecurity and hunger in the US. The CFSM built on previous research into various food security measurement issues (e.g. Briefel and Woteki 1992; Radimer *et al.* 1990) and was established by the US Department of Agriculture and the US Department of Health and Human Services.

The eighteen questions used in the CFSM are listed in Table 3.1. Each question is designed to capture some aspect of food insecurity and, for some questions, the frequency with which that particular aspect of food insecurity manifests itself. The questions in Table 3.1 are listed in ascending order of food inadequacy. Examples of questions include 'I worried whether our food would run out before we got money to buy more' (the least severe question); 'Did you or the other adults in your household ever cut the size of your meals or skip meals because there wasn't enough money for food?'; 'Were you ever hungry but did not eat because you couldn't afford enough food'; and 'Did a

Table 3.1. The 1998 household food insecurity scale by the number of affirmative responses in the core food security module of the current population survey

Households with children		Households without children		Food Security Question Associated with the Modal Number of Affirmative Responses
Number of affirmative responses	Food Indicator (FI)	Number of affirmative responses	Food Indicator (FI)	
1	1.30	1	1.72	Worried food would run out
2	2.56	2	3.10	Food bought did not last
3	3.41	3	4.23	Respondent not eat balanced meals
4	4.14			Child fed few, low-cost foods
5	4.81	4	5.24	Adult cut/skip meals
6	5.43			Child not fed balanced meals
7	6.02	5	6.16	Respondent eat less than should
8	6.61	6	7.07	Adult skip meals, 3+ months
9	7.18			Child not eating enough
10	7.74	7	8.00	Respondent hungry but did not eat
11	8.28	8	8.98	Respondent lost weight
12	8.79			Child meal size cut
13	9.31	9	10.15	Adult not eat for whole day
14	9.84			Child hungry
15	10.42	10	11.05	Adult not eat for whole day, 3+ months
16	11.13			Child skipped meal
17	12.16			Child skipped meal, 3+ months
18	13.03			Child not eat for whole day

child in the household ever not eat for a full day because you couldn't afford enough food?' (the most severe question).

For many of the questions, the response can be of more than two types. Consider, for example, the following question in Table 3.1: 'How often did [the adults in this household not eat for a whole day]—almost every month, some months but not every month, in only one or two months, or never?' There are four different responses to this question. However, for every question, irrespective of whether it admits two or more than two possible responses, the responses are converted into a binary format (1 or 0) by following certain rules. (For a discussion of these rules, see Hamilton *et al.* 1997). A value of 1 indicates that the aspect of food deprivation that the question seeks to capture is present in the household (i.e. an 'affirmative response') and 0 indicates the absence of that aspect of food insecurity (i.e. a 'negative response').

Based on households' responses to the eighteen questions, an FI is assigned to each household. This assignment is done as follows. The affirmative and negative responses to the eighteen-item questionnaire are converted into a single indicator by the Rasch scoring method. The underlying assumption of the Rasch method is that the probability that a household will answer a question affirmatively relative to answering it negatively (that is the odds ratio), follows a logistic distribution, the parameters of which depend on the household's food insecurity level and the level of severity of the question. Using a maximum likelihood estimation based on the overall response pattern of households to all the questions, one can then derive each household's level of insecurity (or Rasch score) which is shown to depend on the number of questions the household answers affirmatively. The FI for a household can be expressed as a one-to-one mapping to its Rasch score. Note that by this rule, the FI for a household depends on the particular sample under consideration; the FI is not assigned exogenously.[4]

Using the 1998 CPS (discussed below), the FI ranges from 0 (no affirmative responses) to 13.026 (18 affirmative responses) for households with children and from 0 to 11.052 (10 affirmative responses) for households without children.[5] Along with a list of the questions in ascending order of severity, Table 3.1 displays the FI associated with the number of a household's affirmative responses (m). While we do not list the item severities in Table 3.1, there is a connection between the questions and the FI for the modal household. In terms of Table 3.1, the modal household responding affirmatively to m items will have responded affirmatively to the mth question but negatively to the $(m+1)$th question and each subsequent question. Thus, for the modal household, the most severe affirmative response corresponds with the question listed in the final column.

In the 1998 CPS, a household is defined as food insecure if they respond affirmatively to three or more questions. For households with children, this means that any household with an FI of more than 2.56 is food insecure and any household without children with an FSI of more than 3.10 is food insecure. In other words, $e = 2.56$ for households with children and $e = 3.10$ for households without children. A household with children is defined as food insecure with hunger if they answer affirmatively to 8 or more questions (i.e. $e = 6.61$) and a household without children is defined as food insecure with hunger if they answer affirmatively to 6 or more questions (i.e. $e = 7.07$).

At this time we return to a discussion of the property of anonymity as it pertains to the method of measuring food insecurity at the household rather than individual level. All four of the food insecurity indices we use in this paper satisfy anonymity. With the CFSM, we do not have information regarding individual levels of food insecurity rather we only observe household level. This is problematic as the following example illustrates. Consider a society of 100 households, where households 1 through 50 have 20 members each and households 51 through 100 have 2 members each. To start with, assume that each of the first fifty households has a normalized FII of, say, 0.2 and

[4] The Rasch score converts categorical variable in to continuous variables. It does this by assuming that probability that a household will answer a question affirmatively follows a logistic distribution.

[5] Eight of the 18 questions in the CFSM refer to the food insecurity status of children and these questions are therefore not asked of households without children.

each of the other households has a normalized FII of 0.8. Suppose D yields a social food insecurity index of 0.6 in this situation. Then symmetry will require that, in another situation, where each of the first fifty households has a food insecurity index of 0.8 and each of the other households has a food insecurity index of 0.2, the social food insecurity index must be 0.6. Yet, this would seem unreasonable, since, intuitively, it would seem that in the second situation a much larger fraction of the total number of individuals suffer from food insecurity.

One solution to this problem can be to assume that: (i) aggregate food insecurity is a function of the food insecurity levels of all the individuals in the society (rather than being a function of the food insecurity levels of the households); and (ii) every individual in a household suffers from a degree of food insecurity which is the same as the degree of food insecurity of the household as a whole. Assumption (ii) however, does not seem to be a reasonable assumption if we use the FII for the households. This is because, in the construction of the FII for the different households, there is no presumption that all individuals in a given household suffer from the same degree of food insecurity. This important intra-household difference will be neglected if one assumes that all individuals within a household suffer from the degree of food insecurity specified by the FII for the household as a whole.

It may seem that the ideal procedure would be to measure the degree of food insecurity of each individual in each household and then to aggregate the food insecurity indices of all the individuals to arrive at the overall social food insecurity level. We do not have such data for individuals, but, even if such data were available, the appropriateness of this procedure will depend on what we are seeking to measure through the food insecurity index for the society. The food insecurity index, constructed in this fashion, will reflect the deprivation that the individuals suffer themselves. However, it will not reflect the 'external diseconomy' that the children of a household may suffer by watching their parents suffer from hunger, although the children themselves may not be hungry. Nor would it be able to distinguish between the deprivations of two mothers, both of whom have to go hungry but only one of whom has to see the hunger of her children as well.

In any case, the CFSM does not give us information about individuals. Thus, one has two options. One can aggregate the food insecurity indices for the households, ignoring the size differences between the different households. Alternatively, one can assume that the food insecurity index for any given household measures the extent of food insecurity of each individual belonging to the household; one can then aggregate these individual food insecurity levels to arrive at the social food insecurity. Each of these two procedures involves conceptual problems. In the case of the second option, the construction of the food insecurity measure is designed to portray household rather than individual food insecurity.[6] Thus, to assign the household-level food insecurity measure to each individual would be ascribing information to the measure that it was not designed to portray. Hence, we have chosen to use the first option and aggregate the food insecurity indices for the households. In the process, we are ignoring household size. (We are breaking the analyses down by whether or not children are present so household size is controlled for to some extent.) While household size is one determinant of food insecurity, its effect in multivariate settings is generally either insignificant or small in magnitude in comparison to other factors. (See, e.g., Dunifon and Kowaleski-Jones 2003; Gundersen *et al.* 2003; Ribar and Hamrick 2003.)

3.3.2 *Data*

We use data from the CFSM in the Food Security Supplement that has been fielded with the CPS each year since 1995. The CPS is administered to a sample of approximately 50,000 households each month. The Food Security Supplement used in this paper was collected in August 1998 and refers to the twelve months previous to the survey. We apply weights in our analysis such that the CPS is representative of the nation as a whole.

3.4 Empirical Analysis

In this section we discuss the empirical findings of our paper. Tables 3.2 and 3.3 contain the food insecurity rates under the four measures discussed above (the headcount, the food insecurity gap, the squared food insecurity gap, and the Sen food insecurity measure). In Table 3.2, the results are for households with children and, in Table 3.3, the results are for households without children. Tables 3.4 and 3.5 contain the rates of food insecurity with hunger for households with children and households without children respectively. One important reason for separating out households with children and without children is that the scale of FI is different in each of these categories. In each table, we list food insecurity under the different measures for all households and we also break these into various demographic characteristics of note. We find that food insecurity is statistically significantly different from zero for all the demographic categories in these tables.[7] For expositional reason, we multiply all our food insecurity measures by 100 in what follows.

[6] The only exception is for households with one individual. There, of course, the household and the individual are the same.

[7] To calculate the standard errors, which are required to test for significance, we have used the methods provided in Kakwani (1993) for the Foster *et al.* (1984) class of measures; for the Sen (1976) class of measures we have used bootstrap methods (see Osberg and Xu 2001).

Table 3.2. The extent of food insecurity for households with children in 1998

	Head Count	Food Insecurity Gap	Squared Food Insecurity Gap	Sen Food Insecurity Measure
All households	14.19 (0.27)	3.73 (0.09)	1.39 (0.05)	5.03 (0.12)
Income of household, per cent of poverty line				
≤100	19.21 (0.54)	5.54 (0.19)	2.24 (0.11)	7.44 (0.25)
>100 and ≤200	22.10 (0.69)	5.57 (0.21)	1.98 (0.11)	7.48 (0.30)
>200	7.07 (0.32)	1.57 (0.09)	0.52 (0.04)	2.13 (0.12)
Education of household head				
Less than high school education	28.95 (0.91)	7.99 (0.32)	3.09 (0.18)	10.70 (0.42)
High school graduate	15.91 (0.49)	3.95 (0.15)	1.40 (0.08)	5.32 (0.20)
At least some college education	9.04 (0.30)	2.41 (0.10)	0.92 (0.05)	3.26 (0.13)
Homeownership status				
Homeowners	8.62 (0.26)	2.07 (0.08)	0.72 (0.04)	2.81 (0.11)
Renters	26.25 (0.60)	7.30 (0.21)	2.84 (0.12)	9.80 (0.29)
Race-ethnicity of household head				
Non-Hispanic White	10.47 (0.28)	2.72 (0.08)	1.03 (0.05)	3.70 (0.12)
Non-Hispanic Black	25.91 (0.96)	7.00 (0.32)	2.68 (0.18)	9.44 (0.44)
Hispanic	24.39 (0.98)	6.52 (0.32)	2.40 (0.18)	8.62 (0.41)
Non-Hispanic Other	15.50 (1.25)	3.70 (0.35)	1.17 (0.015)	4.85 (0.45)
Household composition				
Wife and husband	9.04 (0.26)	2.13 (0.07)	0.70 (0.03)	2.85 (0.10)
Single person	26.27 (0.62)	7.46 (0.22)	3.00 (0.13)	10.08 (0.30)
Households with child(ren) under age 6	14.92 (0.41)	3.68 (0.12)	1.24 (0.06)	4.88 (0.16)

Notes: The standard errors are in parentheses. The standard errors for the Headcount, the Food Insecurity Gap and the Squared Food Insecurity Gap have been calculated using the methods in Kakwani (1993). The standard errors for the Sen Food Insecurity Measure have been calculated using the bootstrap method.

3.4.1 *Food Insecurity for Households with Children*

As seen in Table 3.2, for households with children, the head count measure of food insecurity is 14.19, the food insecurity gap is 3.73, the squared food insecurity gap is 1.39, and the Sen food insecurity measure is 5.03. The results for the various demographic categories are generally as expected. Households with characteristics associated with higher poverty rates also have higher food insecurity under all the measures. For example, the head count is 28.95 and the squared food insecurity gap is 3.09 for households headed by someone with less than a high school education while the figures are 9.04 and 0.92 for households headed by someone with at least some college education. The only surprise is for the breakdown of households by poverty status. Under the head count measure, food insecurity rates are actually higher among households with incomes between 100 and 200 per cent of the poverty line than among households with incomes below the poverty line. For the better-off households, the head count is 22.10 and for households below the poverty line it is 19.21. This finding, though, is reversed when we use the squared food insecurity gap where the figures are 1.98 and 2.24.[8] One conclusion from this is that while the incidence of food insecurity may be higher in these slightly better-off households, the depth of food insecurity is worse in the poor households. The finding of higher food insecurity rates for households above the poverty line is also consistent with studies showing that current income is not always a good predictor of food insecurity (e.g. Gundersen and Gruber 2001). With the exception of income, the ordering of categories is robust to choice of food insecurity measure. For example, homeowners have lower food insecurity levels than renters across all four measures—8.62 versus 26.25 for the head count, 2.07 versus 7.30 for the food insecurity gap, 0.72 versus 2.84 for the squared food insecurity gap, and 2.81 versus 9.80 for the Sen food insecurity measure.

Our wider array of food insecurity measures enables us to comment on previous work on how parents protect their children, especially the youngest children, from food insecurity (Nord and Bickel 2001). We find that food insecurity rates are higher for families with children under the age of 6—14.92 versus 14.19. However, we find that the squared food insecurity gap for households with children under 6 are lower than for all households with children, 1.24 versus 1.39. Thus, it may be that households with small children are more likely to prevent their children from suffering from more severe food insecurity but not from more mild levels of food insecurity.

3.4.2 *Food Insecurity for Households without Children*

In Table 3.3 we present the results for households without children. The head count measure for all households in this category is 6.95, the food insecurity gap is 2.79, the squared food insecurity gap is 1.57, and the Sen food insecurity measure is 3.76. The breakdown of results by categories presents further evidence as to the insights that can be drawn when we move beyond the simple head count of food insecure households. For all common demographic categories, the percentage of food insecure households is substantially higher for households with children in comparison to households without children. As an example, in non-Hispanic white households with children, the head count measure is 10.47 and in non-Hispanic white households without children, it is 5.38. This ordering often changes when we look at our other measures, especially the squared food insecurity gap which gives more weight to those suffering from higher levels of food insecurity. Considering again, households headed by a non-Hispanic white person with children, the squared food insecurity gap is 1.03 whereas it is 1.20 for households without

[8] In this and all succeeding discussions of differences, unless otherwise noted, we only consider differences significant at the 95 per cent confidence level.

Table 3.3. The extent of food insecurity for households without children in 1998

	Head Count	Food Insecurity Gap	Squared Food Insecurity Gap	Sen Food Insecurity Measure
All households	6.95 (0.15)	2.79 (0.07)	1.57 (0.61)	3.76 (0.93)
Income of household, per cent of poverty line				
≤100	13.62 (0.46)	5.96 (0.25)	3.64 (0.19)	8.04 (0.32)
>100 and ≤200	10.80 (0.42)	4.12 (0.19)	2.21 (0.14)	5.54 (0.25)
>200	4.17 (0.16)	1.58 (0.07)	0.83 (0.05)	2.11 (0.10)
Education of household head				
Less than high school education	12.72 (0.45)	4.90 (0.22)	2.78 (0.17)	6.71 (0.28)
High school graduate	6.92 (0.26)	2.78 (0.12)	1.54 (0.09)	3.72 (0.16)
At least some college education	4.87 (0.18)	2.03 (0.09)	1.16 (0.06)	2.71 (0.12)
Homeownership status				
Homeowners	3.82 (0.13)	1.39 (0.06)	0.73 (0.04)	1.88 (0.08)
Renters	13.71 (0.35)	5.82 (0.18)	3.40 (0.14)	7.80 (0.24)
Race-ethnicity of household head				
Non-Hispanic White	5.38 (0.14)	2.14 (0.07)	1.20 (0.05)	2.88 (0.09)
Non-Hispanic Black	15.53 (0.69)	6.67 (0.36)	3.97 (0.28)	8.96 (0.47)
Hispanic	15.05 (0.92)	5.69 (0.43)	3.08 (0.31)	7.71 (0.58)
Non-Hispanic Other	9.86 (0.92)	3.70 (0.42)	2.02 (0.31)	5.03 (0.57)
Household composition				
Wife and husband	3.07 (0.15)	1.04 (0.06)	0.52 (0.04)	1.41 (0.09)
Single person	9.94 (0.23)	4.14 (0.11)	2.39 (0.09)	5.55 (0.15)
Presence of elderly persons				
Households with elderly persons	4.60 (0.20)	1.57 (0.08)	0.78 (0.06)	2.13 (0.11)
Households without elderly persons	8.26 (0.20)	3.47 (0.10)	2.02 (0.07)	4.65 (0.13)

Notes: The standard errors are in parentheses. The standard errors for the Headcount, the Food Insecurity Gap and the Squared Food Insecurity Gap have been calculated using the methods in Kakwani (1993). The standard errors for the Sen Food Insecurity Measure have been calculated using the bootstrap method.

children. Or, for example, renters with children have a head count of 26.25 and renters without children have a head count of 13.71 but for the squared food insecurity gap, the figures are 2.84 and 3.40.

3.4.3 *Food Insecurity with Hunger*

In Tables 3.4 and 3.5, we present our results for food insecurity with hunger. As in Tables 3.2 and 3.3, these are broken down by whether households have children and broken down further by various demographic categories. By definition, the rates of food insecurity with hunger will be lower than the rates of food insecurity because all households suffering from food insecurity with hunger also suffer from food insecurity but the converse is not true. In Table 3.4, the extent of food insecurity with hunger is presented for households with children. The head count measure for all households in this category is 2.55, the food insecurity gap is 0.69, the squared food insecurity gap is 0.28, and the Sen food insecurity measure is 0.95. Across all categories, the ordering is the same for all food insecurity measures. For example, high-school graduates have higher levels of food insecurity than

Table 3.4. The extent of food insecurity with hunger for households with children in 1998

Variable	Head Count	Food Insecurity Gap	Squared Food Insecurity Gap	Sen Food Insecurity Measure
All households	2.55 (0.12)	0.69 (0.04)	0.28 (0.03)	0.95 (0.06)
Income of household, per cent of poverty line				
≤100	4.41 (0.28)	1.24 (0.10)	0.54 (0.07)	1.71 (0.14)
>100 and ≤200	3.44 (0.30)	0.88 (0.09)	0.33 (0.05)	1.20 (0.13)
>200	0.79 (0.11)	0.23 (0.04)	0.09 (0.02)	0.31 (0.05)
Education of household head				
Less than high school education	5.61 (0.46)	1.56 (0.16)	0.69 (0.11)	2.17 (0.23)
High school graduate	2.51 (0.21)	0.63 (0.07)	0.24 (0.04)	0.86 (0.09)
At least some college education	1.73 (0.14)	0.48 (0.05)	0.20 (0.03)	0.65 (0.06)
Homeownership status				
Homeowners	1.20 (0.10)	0.32 (0.03)	0.13 (0.02)	0.44 (0.05)
Renters	5.46 (0.31)	1.49 (0.11)	0.63 (0.07)	2.05 (0.15)
Race-ethnicity of household head				
Non-Hispanic White	1.97 (0.13)	0.54 (0.04)	0.21 (0.02)	0.73 (0.06)
Non-Hispanic Black	5.10 (0.48)	1.39 (0.16)	0.57 (0.10)	1.88 (0.23)
Hispanic	3.74 (0.43)	1.06 (0.16)	0.52 (0.12)	1.50 (0.23)
Non-Hispanic Other	1.89 (0.47)	0.34 (0.10)	0.09 (0.03)	0.44 (0.13)
Household composition				
Wife and husband	1.09 (0.10)	0.27 (0.03)	0.09 (0.01)	0.36 (0.04)
Single person	5.97 (0.33)	1.68 (0.12)	0.73 (0.08)	2.32 (0.17)
Households with child(ren) under age 6	2.04 (0.16)	0.48 (0.05)	0.18 (0.03)	0.66 (0.07)

Notes: The standard errors are in parentheses. The standard errors for the Headcount, the Food Insecurity Gap and the Squared Food Insecurity Gap have been calculated using the methods in Kakwani (1993). The standard errors for the Sen Food Insecurity Measure have been calculated using the bootstrap method.

households headed by someone with at least some college education. In two instances, however, the differences are statistically significant for the head count, food insecurity gap, and the Sen food insecurity measure but not for the squared food insecurity gap. This happens in comparisons of high school graduates with households headed by someone with at least some college education and in comparisons of non-Hispanic blacks with Hispanics. In the latter comparison, the head count measure for households headed by a non-Hispanic black person is 5.10 and it is 3.74 for families headed by a black person. But for the squared food insecurity gap the figures are 0.57 and 0.52 and this difference is not statistically significant.

In Table 3.5, we present the food insecurity with hunger measures for households without children. The head count measure for all households in this category is 1.74, the food insecurity gap is 0.93, the squared food insecurity gap is 0.66, and the Sen food insecurity measure is 1.22. As occurred to a lesser extent in the food insecurity measure, the food insecurity with hunger measures are lower for households without children in comparison to households with children when one examines the head count measure but are higher when one examines many of the more sensitive measures. As an example, in households with children the food insecurity with hunger head

Table 3.5. The extent of food insecurity with hunger for households without children in the United States in 1998

Variable	Head Count	Food Insecurity Gap	Squared Food Insecurity Gap	Sen Food Insecurity Measure
All households	1.74 (0.08)	0.93 (0.05)	0.66 (0.04)	1.22 (0.06)
Income of household, per cent of poverty line				
≤100	4.14 (0.27)	2.42 (0.18)	1.81 (0.16)	3.11 (0.22)
>100 and ≤200	2.71 (0.25)	1.52 (0.16)	1.09 (0.14)	1.95 (0.20)
>200	0.91 (0.77)	0.44 (0.04)	0.29 (0.04)	0.58 (0.06)
Education of household head				
Less than high school education	3.10 (0.23)	1.73 (0.15)	1.27 (0.13)	2.25 (0.18)
High school graduate	1.61 (0.13)	0.85 (0.08)	0.60 (0.07)	1.12 (0.10)
At least some college education	1.32 (0.09)	0.69 (0.06)	0.48 (0.05)	0.90 (0.07)
Homeownership status				
Homeowners	0.77 (0.06)	0.39 (0.04)	0.27 (0.03)	0.51 (0.05)
Renters	3.84 (0.20)	2.10 (0.12)	0.82 (0.11)	2.74 (0.16)
Race-ethnicity of household head				
Non-Hispanic White	1.31 (0.07)	0.70 (0.04)	0.49 (0.04)	0.91 (0.05)
Non-Hispanic Black	4.32 (0.39)	2.49 (0.25)	1.84 (0.22)	3.21 (0.32)
Hispanic	3.61 (0.48)	1.75 (0.27)	1.15 (0.23)	2.28 (0.35)
Non-Hispanic Other	2.28 (0.46)	1.18 (0.28)	0.83 (0.25)	1.54 (0.37)
Household composition:				
Wife and husband	0.55 (0.06)	0.26 (0.04)	0.17 (0.03)	0.35 (0.05)
Single person	2.66 (0.12)	1.45 (0.08)	1.03 (0.07)	1.89 (0.10)
Presence of elderly persons:				
Households with elderly persons	0.77 (0.08)	0.38 (0.05)	0.25 (0.04)	0.50 (0.06)
Households without elderly persons	2.28 (0.11)	1.24 (0.07)	0.88 (0.06)	1.62 (0.08)

Notes: The standard errors are in parentheses. The standard errors for the Headcount, the Food Insecurity Gap and the Squared Food Insecurity Gap have been calculated using the methods in Kakwani (1993). The standard errors for the Sen Food Insecurity Measure have been calculated using the bootstrap method.

count measure is 1.97 in households headed by a non-Hispanic white person and is 1.31 in households without children and headed by a non-Hispanic white person. For the food insecurity gap, however, the order is reversed, with figures of 0.54 and 0.70.

3.5 Conclusions

We moved beyond the simple head count measure of food insecurity in this paper and proposed three measures of food insecurity, along the lines of new poverty measures (Zheng, 1991) and explained the desirable properties of these measures that are not present in the head count measure. We then applied these food insecurity measures to the official statistics used to derive the extent of food insecurity in the United States.

Our intention is not to demonstrate whether one particular measure is better than others. Instead, by adapting aggregation rules based on the poverty measure to the context of food security, we were able capture the depth and intensity of food insecurity in a better way than what has been acheived previously. In some cases, as discussed above, we found that the new measures are in agreement (in terms of ordering different subgroups according to overall food insecurity) with the head count ratio. In such instance, considering a broader set of measures then indicates the robustness of the results. However, in other cases we found that orderings of the different subgroups differ depending on whether one uses just the head count measure of food insecurity or if one uses measures we use that also reflect the depth and severity of food insecurity. In such cases just relying on the head count ratio, may provide a misleading picture. In either case, therefore, it helps to use a broader set of aggregate measures of food insecurity.

Building on the work of this chapter, there are many directions for future research. First, in the US, other data sets could be used besides the CPS to examine what new insights are possible when multiple food insecurity measures are used. Second, these food insecurity measures could be applied to household-based food security measures in developing countries. Given the greater depth of food insecurity in comparison to the US, food insecurity measures that incorporate the depth and severity along with the prevalence of food insecurity would seem to be especially important. Third, in this paper we have created food insecurity measures based on two sets of income poverty measures—the Foster, Greer, and Thorbecke and the Sen measures. More generally, there are numerous other income poverty measures that may be justifiable as food insecurity measures. Finally, we have examined the aggregate food insecurity measure by aggregating the standard food insecurity index (which is based on the Rasch score) for each household. Deriving the household food insecurity from the Rasch score, however, may not be wholly satisfactory since it does not account for the ordinal nature of the data at the household level properly. It would be interesting to see how the results change when we use different measures of household food insecurity.

References

Anand, S., and C. J. Harris (1990). 'Food and Standard of Living: An Analysis Based on Sri Lankan Data', in J. P. Drèze and A. K. Sen (eds), *The Political Economy of Hunger*, vol. 1. Oxford: Clarendon Press, 297–350.

Andrews, M., M. Nord, G. Bickel, and S. Carlson (2001). 'Household Food Security in the United States, 1999', US Department of Agriculture, Economic Research Service, Food and Nutrition Research Report, 11–12. Washington, DC. www.ers.usda.gov/publications/fanrr8/fanrr8.pdf

Briefel, R., and C. Woteki (1992). 'Development of Food Sufficiency Questions for the Third National Health and Nutrition Examination Survey', *Journal of Nutrition Education*, 24: 24S–28S.

Busch, L., and W. Lacy (1984). 'What Does Food Security Mean?' in L. Busch and W. Lacy (eds), *Food Security in the United States*, 1–10. West View Press, Boulder, Colorado.

Drèze, J., and A. Sen (1989). *Hunger and Public Action*. Oxford: Clarendon Press.

Dunifon, R., and L. Kowaleski-Jones (2003). 'The Influences of Participation in the National School Lunch Program and Food Insecurity on Child Well-Being'. *Social Service Review*, 77(1): 72–92.

Foster, J., J. Greer, and E. Thorbecke (1984). 'Notes and Comments: A Class of Decomposable Poverty Measures'. *Econometrica*, 52: 761–765.

Foster, P., and H. D. Leathers (1999). *The World Food Problem*. Lynne Rienner Publishers, Boulder, Colorado.

FAO (2003). 'The State of Food Insecurity in the World'. www.fao.org/SOF/sofi/index_en.htm.

Fujji, T. (2004). 'Micro-Level Estimation of Child Malnutrition Indicators and Its Application in Cambodia'. Working Paper, University of California, Berkeley.

Gundersen, C., and J. Gruber (2001). 'The Dynamic Determinants of Food Insufficiency' , in M. Andrews and M. Prell (eds), *Second Food Security Measurement and Research Conference*, volume II: Papers, US Department of Agriculture, Economic Research Service, Food and Nutrition Research Report, 11–2, 92–110. Washington, DC. www.ers.usda.gov/publications/fanrr11-2/fanrr11-2g.pdf

Gundersen, C., L. Weinreb, C. Wehler, and D. Hosmer (2003). 'Homelessness and Food Insecurity'. *Journal of Housing Economics*, 12(3): 250–72.

Hamilton, W., J. Cook, W. Thompson, L. Buron, E. Frongillo, C. Olson, and C. Wehler (1997). 'Household Food Security in the United States in 1995: Summary Report of the Food Security Measurement Project'. US Dept of Agriculture, Food and Consumer Service, Office of Analysis and Evaluation. Alexandria, Virginia.

Jha, R. (2004). 'Calorie Deficiency in Rural India in the Last Three Quinquennial Rounds of the NSS', in M. Bhattacharya, R. Smyth, and M. Vicziany (eds), *South Asia in the Era of Globalization: Trade Industrialization and Welfare*. Nova Science Publishers, New York.

Kakwani, N. (1993). 'Statistical Inference in the Measurement of Poverty'. *Review of Economics and Statistics*, 75: 632–9.

Maxwell, D. (1995). 'Alternative Food Security Strategy: A Household Analysis of Urban Agriculture in Kampala'. *World Development*, 23: 1669–81.

Maxwell, D., C. Ahiadeke, C. Levin, M. Armar-Klemesu, S. Zakariah, and G. Lamptey (1999). 'Alternative Food-Security Indicators: Revisiting the Frequency and Severity of 'Coping Strategies'. *Food Policy*, 24: 411–29.

Maxwell, S., and T. Frankenberger (1992). 'Household Food Security: Concepts, Indicators, Measurements. A Technical Review'. UNICEF and IFAD, New York and Rome.

Nord, M., and G. Bickel (2001). 'Problems with Estimating the Prevalence of Child Hunger', in M. Andrews and M. Prell (eds), *Second Food Security Measurement and Research Conference*, volume II: papers, US Department of Agriculture, Economic Research Service, Food and Nutrition Research Report, 11–2. Washington, DC: 31–49. www.ers.usda.gov/publications/fanrr11-2/fanrr11-2c.pdf

Nord, M., M. Andrews, and S. Carlson (2004). 'Household Food Security in the United States, 2003'. Washington, DC: US Department of Agriculture, Economic Research Service, Food Assistance and Nutrition Research Report 42.

Osberg, L. and K. Xu (2001). 'International Comparison of Poverty Intensity: Index Decomposition and Bootstrap Inference'. *Journal of Human Resources*, 35: 51–81.
Radimer, K., C. Olson, and C. Campbell (1990). 'Development of Indicators to Assess Hunger'. *Journal of Nutrition*, 120: 1544–8.
Ribar, D., and K. Hamrick (2003). 'Dynamics of Poverty and Food Sufficiency'. US Department of Agriculture, Economic Research Service, Food Assistance and Nutrition Research Report 33. Washington, DC.
Sen, A. (1976). 'Poverty: An Ordinal Approach to Measurement'. *Econometrica*, 44: 219–31.
Sen, A. (1981). *Poverty and Famines: An Essay on Entitlements*. Clarendon Press, Oxford.
Vecchi, G., and M. Coppola (2003). 'Nutrition and Growth in Italy, 1861–1911. What Macroeconomic Data Hide'. Working Paper, Universidad Carlos III de Madrid.
Wolfe, W., and E. Frongillo (2001). 'Building Household Food-Security Measurement Tools from the Ground Up'. *Food and Nutrition Bulletin*, 22: 5–12.
Zheng, B. (1997). 'Aggregate Poverty Measures'. *Journal of Economic Surveys*, 11: 123–62.

4

Tomorrow's Hunger: A Framework for Analysing Vulnerability to Food Security

Christian Romer Løvendal and Marco Knowles

4.1 Introduction

The Millennium Development and World Food Summit Goals (MDGs, WFS) of halving the number/share of undernourished by 2015 are fast approaching, but progress towards them is slow. The number fell only by a total of nine million over the last decade and, more worryingly, four million people were added per year in the second part of the decade, wiping out earlier achievements. Recent figures suggest that 815 million are undernourished (FAO 2004). While no comparative estimate exists on the number of vulnerable people, several studies related to income or consumption poverty point out that the number of vulnerable people is much larger.

Reducing vulnerability is a prerequisite for addressing global and national food security targets. This is because policies and interventions seeking to reduce the number of undernourished or the prevalence of underweight children under 5 years of age will be more effective if based on a forward-looking analysis: Who are those most likely to be food insecure *in the future*, why are likely they to be or to become so and what instruments exist for influencing this probability.

Frameworks for integrating longer-term vulnerability into food security analysis are largely absent (Haddad and Frankenberger 2003; Webb and Rogers 2003) and most existing vulnerability analyses, often applied in the context of

Seniority of authorship is equally shared. The authors wish to thank Genevieve Coullet, Marijke Drysdale, Margarita Flores, Yasmeen Khwaja, Francesca Matalucci, Naoki Minamiguchi, Frank Mischler, Mark Smulders, Jim Tefft, Alberto Zezza, participants in the UNU-WIDER seminars in Jaipur, India and Helsinki, Finland, and especially Benjamin Davis, for their comments on earlier draft versions of this paper. The views expressed are those of the authors, and any errors and omission are theirs.

early warning information systems, focus on transitory risks.[1] Less emphasis is placed on identifying and analysing the potential longer-term food security impact of risks, which require a set of interventions different from humanitarian responses.

While some existing food security frameworks (Smith *et al.* 2000; Commission on the Nutrition Challenges 1999; FIVIMS 2000) identify a range of multisectoral food security risks, these often assume a direct causal relationship between risks and food security outcomes and are static. Risks are treated as exogenous, thus putting aside the range of risk management strategies that are used for attenuating the impact risks have on food security.

Over the last five years, frameworks for analysing vulnerability to negative social welfare outcomes in general (Holzmann and Jørgensen 2000), and specifically income and consumption poverty (Mansuri and Healy 2001; Dercon 2001a), have been developed. These frameworks are geared towards identifying those who are likely to have an income below a certain threshold and as such are helpful in analysing the access dimension of food security, but less so when it comes to the availability and utilization dimensions. There are, of course, strong linkages between poverty and food insecurity, but the causes and consequences of each are different (Webb and Rogers 2003).

This chapter seeks to fill this analytical gap by providing a framework for understanding who is likely to be food insecure in the future and why this is so, with the overall aim of improving the ability to address vulnerability before it manifests itself as food insecurity.

The chapter is structured in the following way: section 4.2 clarifies conceptual issues and presents an expanded food security framework for understanding vulnerability. Section 4.3 explains the role that present conditions play in determining vulnerability. The risk side is analysed in section 4.4, while risk management is addressed in section 4.5, where instruments for reducing vulnerability are also presented. In these two latter sections, results of the preliminary application of the framework are presented. Finally, section 4.6 presents the main conclusions of the study.

4.2 Concepts of Food Security and Vulnerability

4.2.1 *What are Food Insecurity and Vulnerability?*

Following a number of international summits since the World Food Conference in 1974 and based on work over several decades, the definition of food security is today generally agreed upon. The WFS in 1996 captured earlier work by adopting that *food security exists when all people at all times, have physical and*

[1] Examples of these include Save the Children's Household Economy Approach and WFP's Standard Analytical Framework.

economic access to sufficient, safe and nutritious food to meet their dietary needs and food preferences for an active and healthy life (FAO 1996). This definition integrates access to food, stability, availability of nutritionally adequate food and the biological utilization of food.

Food availability refers to the physical presence of food at various levels from household to national level, be it from own production or through markets. *Food access* refers to the ability to obtain an appropriate and nutritious diet and is in particular linked to resources at the household level. *Biological utilization* relates to individual level food security and is the ability of the human body to effectively convert food into energy.

The 'at all times' and *stability* dimensions point to the need for understanding current as well as likely future status at different points in time. Thus, a framework for analysing food security must capture the temporal dynamics of food security.

The concept of vulnerability is used with different connotations. A fundamental difference exists between *vulnerability as defencelessness vis-à-vis a harmful event* (for example, vulnerability to drought) and *vulnerability to a specific negative outcome, following a harmful event* (for example vulnerability to food insecurity).

Much of the disaster management literature uses vulnerability with reference to a natural hazard (Alwang *et al.* 2001) while the food security literature, and more recently part of the social risk management and poverty literature (Mansuri and Healy 2001; Dercon 2001a; Holzmann and Jørgensen 2000; World Bank 2000), defines vulnerability in terms of an unfavourable future outcome. This dichotomy is, to some extent, driven by the underlying policy questions that are sought to be addressed. Humanitarian aid and disaster management tend to focus on short-term responses targeted at people who require relief assistance following a natural hazard, these being the vulnerable. Looking at vulnerability relative to a social welfare outcome, on the other hand, is concerned with guaranteeing a minimum welfare threshold in terms of food security, through short as well as longer-term measures.

We define vulnerability relative to the negative outcome of food insecurity. Thus, vulnerability refers to people's propensity to fall, or stay, below this food security threshold within a certain timeframe.

The terms 'vulnerability' and 'food insecurity' are often used interchangeably. This matters less when focusing on short-term unstable conditions, where there is little or no difference between those being food insecure today or tomorrow. However, over longer periods of time, people move in and out of food insecurity. Thus, while vulnerability refers to the ex ante probability of falling or remaining below a specific threshold, food insecurity is the current or ex post measure relative to the threshold.

Because vulnerability is linked to the uncertainty of events, everyone is vulnerable to food insecurity, but some more so than others. Vulnerability

Table 4.1. Poverty dynamics due to consumption shocks in KwaZulu-Natal, South Africa

	1998	
	Nonpoor	*Poor*
1993		
Nonpoor	48% never poor	24% became poor
Poor	10% got out of poverty	18% stayed poor

Source: Adapted from Carter and May (2001).

can be thought of as a continuum. The higher the probability of becoming food insecure, the more vulnerable one is. While 'the vulnerable' in praxis are often implicitly understood to be those with a probability of becoming food insecure above a certain predetermined threshold, no standard exists that defines this threshold.[2] For the purpose of this chapter we assume that a cut-off point exists and so the term vulnerable refers to people below such predetermined threshold.

4.2.2 *Why the Little Difference Matters*

Expanding the analysis of food security to include risks and risk management, and focusing on vulnerability is important for several reasons.

First, numerous studies on poverty dynamics suggest that people move in and out of poverty. Summing up 13 panel data studies, Baulch and Hoddinott (2000) show that the share of the population being poor at times is often much larger that the share being always poor, and in some cases several times larger. If vulnerable is understood as the probability of experiencing at least one period of poverty in a given period, while 3 per cent in Pakistan comparing 1986 and 1991 were always poor, 55.3 per cent were sometimes poor making 58.3 per cent vulnerable. Following the same definition of vulnerability, Pritchett *et al.* (2000) shows that in Indonesia at the level of current poverty of 20 per cent, another 10–30 per cent of the population face a high probability of falling below the poverty line.

Table 4.1, based on per capita consumption expenditures from KwaZulu-Natal in South Africa in 1993 and 1998, gives an example of how people moved in and out of consumption poverty. Eighteen per cent of households were poor in both periods, while 48 per cent were nonpoor in both time periods; 10 per cent of households got ahead and 24 per cent fell into poverty. The implication of all this is that basing interventions on a snapshot at a given time will most likely miss a large part of the picture.

[2] To illustrate, Tesliuc and Lindert (2002) use a 50 per cent probability as the cut-off point implying that being vulnerable means facing a higher probability of being food insecure than being food secure.

Table 4.2. Present and future food security

		Expected future food security status	
		Food secure	*Food insecure*
Present food	*Food secure*	Food secure	Potentially food insecure
security status	*Food insecure*	Potentially food secure	Chronically food insecure
Vulnerable/nonvulnerable		*Nonvulnerable*	*Vulnerable*

Source: Compiled by the authors.

Second, the food insecure and vulnerable are not homogenous groups. Some are chronically food insecure, others transitorily so and others again food insecure on a seasonal basis—and for different reasons. These are important distinctions since the causes of, and policy measures, for addressing transitory food insecurity may be different from those associated with chronic food insecurity (Barrett and Sahn 2001).

Third, the presence of risks influences livelihood choices. High risk adversity can lead to income earning strategies with low variability but often also low mean returns. Reducing the potential impact of shocks, for example, through provision of social benefits under certain conditions, allows households to make productivity enhancing-investments perceived riskier.

Finally, vulnerability analysis identifies ex ante as well as ex post interventions, thus partly shifting the focus of interventions from addressing an already manifested negative outcome (coping) to addressing problems before they actually arise (prevention or mitigation).

4.2.3 *A Framework for Analysing Vulnerability to Food Insecurity*

Being food insecure today does not necessarily imply vulnerability. Chronically food insecure people live below the food security threshold today. Potentially food insecure people are 'living on the edge'. Although they are not food insecure today, they face a high probability of becoming so (see Table 4.2).[3]

Figure 4.1 presents a causality framework for identifying the factors determining the probability of negative food security outcomes in the future. The probability of becoming food insecure at a future point in time is determined by present conditions, the risks potentially occurring within a period defined and the capacity to manage these.

Vulnerability is determined by a cumulative chain of events through time. What happened yesterday is reflected in today's status and what happens

[3] Dercon (2001a, 2001b) makes a further categorization of the potentially vulnerable into those who are potentially insecure following an unexpected shock, those who are potentially following cyclical/seasonal shocks and those who are potentially food insecure due to negative trends for example negative changes over time in key food security factors.

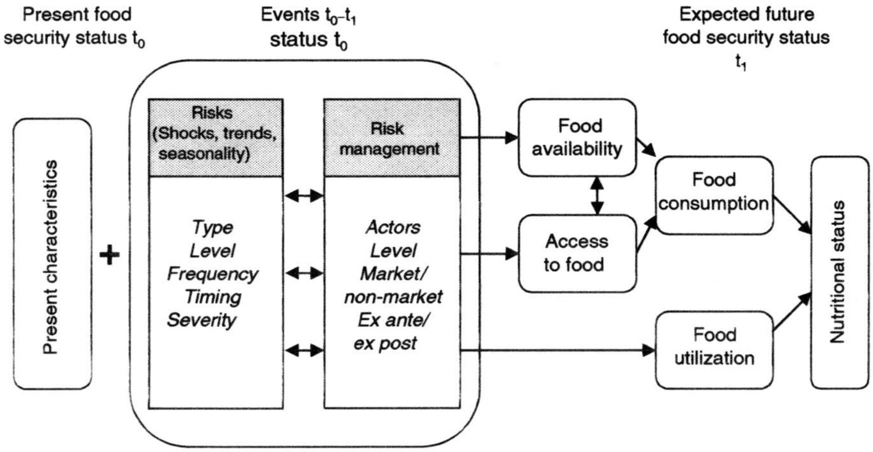

Figure 4.1. A framework for analysing vulnerability to future food insecurity
Source: Compiled by the authors.

today influences tomorrow's status and so forth. As well as connections through time, there is an interrelationship between risk management instruments at different levels (global, national, community, household, and individual). For instance, the presence of a functioning state-sponsored safety-net programme lowers the need for individual insurance against economic or health shocks. There can also be crowding-in effects, if risk management instruments at one level create an environment that stimulates activities at other levels. In 1998, the government of Bangladesh accelerated trade liberalization policies by removing rice import tariffs, minimizing government open-market price sales, and speeding up customs procedures. This encouraged the private sector to play an important role in guaranteeing national food availability through private sector imports during the major 1998 floods (del Ninno *et al.* 2001).

4.2.4 *Measuring Vulnerability*

Although not the focus of this chapter, we here briefly discuss what should be measured in relation to vulnerability to food insecurity and ways in which it is being measured.[4]

There is no unique approach to measuring vulnerability to food security (FAO 2002). The challenge is both to choose an outcome measure, given the multi-dimensionality of food security, and to select an approach of measuring vulnerability.

[4] For a detailed treatment of the subject, see Dercon (2001b).

In terms of choice of food security dimension to be measured, one option is to select food availability and focus on predicting supply shortages through forecast of seasonal variations in food production through crop, drought, and flood monitoring. This can include longer-term food production scenarios focusing on specific risks, such as environmental changes. As food availability usually is related to the national or sub-national level, the question addressed by such measure is whether, at the aggregated level, there is sufficient food available to meet aggregate demand. The weakness by using availability as outcome is that it ignores that in most cases, food is not distributed or accessed equally. Second, food availability is often not necessarily the binding constraint to achieving food security at the household level.

Another option is to measure the probability of households falling under a specific consumption threshold as a measure of access to food (based on the cost of minimum daily energy requirements), in line with many of the studies related to vulnerability to poverty (see below). However, such measure ignores for example the question of adequacy of diets.

A third option is to measure the probability of a negative nutritional outcome such as underweight, wasting or stunting of children under five or adults with a body mass index (BMI) below 18.5. This encompasses all dimensions of food security, including food utilization, but also picks-up other factors as well, such has health and care practices (a well-fed child can be wasted due to diarrhoea). Another issue is that anthropometric indicators record both acute (wasting) and chronic malnutrition (stunting) or a combination of both (underweight) and thus include also a 'historical' path of food security and thus are not stochastic.

Regardless of the choice of the dependent variable and in line with the proposed framework, measurement of vulnerability to food insecurity must be based on information about assets, existing food security status, livelihoods, idiosyncratic and covariant risks faced and options available for managing these.

Different approaches exist to measuring vulnerability and consensus lacks on how it is best done. Amongst the simpler measures are different indices, based on a selection of variables such as household characteristics, risks (e.g. probability of droughts, floods and other shocks) and risk management characteristics (e.g. access to markets). Variables are aggregated through various weighting schemes ranging from simple aggregation of normalized data to the use of more sophisticated statistical methods such as principle components analysis or factor analysis. This allow for areas or households to be ranked according to their degree of vulnerability. While such indices are simple and much used to generate, for example, vulnerability maps, they do not, however, attempt to predict any future outcome and thus do not measure vulnerability as per our definition.

An example of a simple access-based measure is how much 'buffer' there is in current income for accommodating increasing food expenditures. Vulnerability is thus the probability of food expenditures as a share of total expenditures raise above a certain level (Engel coefficient) and vulnerable households are thus those whose income is within a certain percentage above the poverty line.

More sophisticated approaches generally fall into three categories, either based on low expected social welfare outcomes, low expected utility caused by risk, or welfare losses due to exposure to uninsured risk (for a comprehensive overview, see Hoddinott and Quisumbing 2003).

The expected welfare outcome approach, which comes closest to measuring vulnerability as defined here, seeks to infer the distribution of possible food security outcomes from the error process in cross-section regression models and establish the probability that a household falls under a given threshold within a specified timeframe given different idiosyncratic risk events. Its immediate appeal is its direct correspondence to the ex-post outcome, e.g. food security (for specific applications on poverty, see e.g. Pritchett *et al.* 2000; Vakis *et al.* 2004).

Another strain of work follows a utilitarian approach, measuring vulnerability as the difference between the utility a household would derive from consuming some particular bundle with certainty and the household's expected utility of consumption under exposure to risk, allowing a distinction between covariant and idiosyncratic risk. The third, less frequently applied approach differs from the others in the sense that it is backwards looking, measuring to what extend an unmanaged shock resulted in a welfare loss.

A range of studies and econometric applications of the approaches exists (for a comparison, see e.g. Lingon and Schechter 2004). Common to all are a range of econometric challenges and the assumption of stationarity in the sense that events and behaviours are sufficient to predict the future. All of above approaches have significant data requirements both in terms of variables and observation sets. As the aforementioned study notes 'it's hard to avoid the conclusion that if all one has is cross-sectional data, one shouldn't bother even trying to estimate vulnerability, but rather stick with poverty measures instead'.

4.3 Understanding Present Conditions

Present conditions play a role in determining which risks threaten food security and how effectively these can be managed. Of relevance to vulnerability is food security status, asset portfolio, the livelihood-related activities people are engaged in (e.g., food production, income generation, and healthcare practices) and the context within which people are embedded.

4.3.1 *Food Security Status*

Present food security status can indicate how far people have to climb or fall before their food security status changes. Although major falls into food insecurity or jumps out of food insecurity are possible, those who are well above the minimum threshold and those who are well below the threshold are less likely to cross this within a short timespan. For those living close to the minimum threshold, even a small push can make them change status.

Present food-security status also has important intertemporal effects. Undernourished mothers are more likely to give birth to children with low birth weight, while malnourished children tend to have lower educational attainments and reduce income earning potential.

4.3.2 *Livelihood Assets and Activities*

The livelihood activities that people pursue are based on the quantity and quality of assets that they have access to. Assets can be of various types (social, financial, physical, natural, and human) and be privately or publicly held. Assets are important to risk management as tools for smoothening consumption. Different households have different levels of access to assets, influencing their ability to prevent, mitigate, or cope with shocks.

The types of risks that form a threat to people's food security is also a function of their livelihoods. For example, communities relying on access to forests will be more affected by policy reform affecting forest access or forest depletion than urban-area rickshaw drivers.

The characteristics of assets which contribute to determining risk management capacities include the security of access and use; the rate and volatility of returns and their ability to maintain value during crisis; the ease with which assets can be liquidated or traded; and the absence of markets.

4.3.3 *Policies, Institutions, Organizations*

The access to assets, the use thereof and the expected returns to these are influenced by the policy, the institutional and the organizational environment within which people are embedded. Policies provide a framework that constrains or supports the role played by institutions or organizations. Institutions refer to the 'rules of the game' which include established sets of rules, legislation, norms and patterns of behaviour. They determine the context within which organizations operate; the activities that can legitimately be undertaken; the relationships within organizations; and relationships between organizations and the public. Institutions can be formal (include laws, constitution, treaties, regulations, and established rights at international, national, and sub-national levels) and informal (e.g. gender relations or caste).

Organizations are the 'players' or service delivery structures in private, public and civil society spheres at different levels. They include political bodies (political parties, a city council, a regulatory agency); economic bodies (firms, trade unions, co-operatives) and social bodies (churches, clubs, associations). These players have specific objectives based on, inter alia, self-interests, political power, ideology, perceptions of risks, and their impacts and resources. If food security is not high on the agenda, neither will managing risks to reduce vulnerability.

4.4 Understanding Threats to Food Security: The Risk Side

Risks are events, trends, and structural factors that threaten food supplies, access, or utilization. This section looks at the defining characteristics of risks to determine how they are best managed.

4.4.1 *Characteristics of Risks*

The defining characteristics of risks are *type, level, frequency, timing*, and *severity*. These determine the potential impacts on food security of a specific risk, including which dimension(s) they affect.

TYPE

The types of risks that are perceived as impinging on future food security depend on the food security model adopted. Until the early 1980s, food security used to be associated with national food stocks and production, and consequently economic, environmental and natural risks were considered as the predominant threats to food security through their impact on national/subnational food availability. Along with the increased acknowledgement of the importance of other dimensions of food security, a wider range of risks has become relevant when analysing vulnerability.

Risks can be clustered into various categories, including political risks, social risks, economic risks, health risks, natural risks, environmental risks and lifecycle related risks.

Different types of risks affect different people in different ways. While an economic shock in the form of a collapse in grain prices may be beneficial to net food buying urban or rural households at least in the short run, the impact on food surplus producing rural households will be negative.

LEVEL

Risks affect different levels, be it individual/household (micro), community/regional (meso), national (macro) or global/regional (supra-macro).

Meso, macro and supra-macro level risks, also referred to as covariant risks, have low inter-household variance and affect groups of households, livelihoods, or even entire nations. Political, social, economic, health, natural, and environmental risks often fall in this category. Micro-level risks, also referred to as idiosyncratic risks, have high inter-household variance. Lifecycle related risks fall in this category. The extent to which a risk is covariant or idiosyncratic largely depends on the causes of the risk—ill health can be an individual risk, or it can be covariate if the cause is a pandemic such as HIV/AIDS (World Bank 2000; Murdoch 1999).

FREQUENCY AND TIMING

Risks can be transitory, trend-related or structural. *Transitory* risks 'come and go' and include unpredictable events as well as cyclical/seasonal events, which can be more predictable. *Trends*, such as falling economic growth or declining agricultural yields, refer to the movement of variables over time. *Structural* risks are associated with longterm conditions that are rooted in the social, economic or political fabric. Examples of these include discrimination against ethnic groups, or on the basis of gender or risks related to poor working conditions. Although unexpected transitory risks are more eye-catching, structural or regularly occurring transitory risks often have a greater role in determining people's vulnerability by gradually but continuously wearing away risk management capacities (Tesiluc and Lindert 2002; Devereux 2001).

The timing of negative events matters. Ability to manage risks differs seasonally, through life and within economic cycles. A single idiosyncratic shock may suffice to tumble an individual into food insecurity during times of hardship, while it could be easily handled during more buoyant times. This is especially relevant in the case of concatenated risks, striking with short intervals between them, or compounded risks, striking simultaneously, because they place a greater strain on risk management capacities. The 2001–2 drought in Southern Africa was less severe in terms of lack of rainfall than the 1991–2 drought but had far harsher consequences since it was compounded by political instability, an economic downturn, poor governance and HIV/AIDS (Heitzmann *et al.* 2002; Baulch and Hoddinott 2000; Ellis 2002).

SEVERITY

Negative events differ in strength or intensity (Holzmann and Jørgensen 2000). The severity of a flood is characterized by its coverage, duration, deviation from standard water levels or the number of people affected, while the severity of an economic shock may be measured by its duration, deviation from trend levels or sectors affected. The greater the severity of a risk, the greater the capacities required for managing it.

4.4.2 *Types and Levels of Risks and Links to Food Security*

Table 4.3 provides an overview of the main risk types and their potential impact on the different dimensions of food security. For simplicity, risks have been associated with the main level of occurrence, but it is recognized that some risks are relevant to several levels.

At the global and regional level, key threats to food security relate in particular to two factors. Macro-economic shocks, transmitted via flows of capital or goods, affect access to food through their impact on income and wealth of households and, together with global climate changes, can reduce food availability through changes in production incentives, increasing fluctuations and regional variance.

The main threats to food security at *national level* are political, economic, and natural risks. In 2003–4, almost a third of all food emergencies (35) were caused by present or past conflicts, half of them caused by natural shocks, two caused by economic shocks and the remaining by a mix of causes. The causes of national level food emergencies have shifted over the last decade, with food emergencies caused by conflict or economic shocks growing from 15 per cent to 35 per cent (FAO 2004). These risks are often highly co-variant and influence food availability by their impact on food production, import/export and the pressure they put on food stocks. These risks can also increase transaction costs or isolate entire parts of countries, either because of damages to infrastructure or because of lack of security in specific areas. On the access side, most risks work through the pressure they put on real income, stemming from the erosion of purchasing power and reduction in agricultural income, amplified by the absence of alternative income generating opportunities. Both the political and economic risks can erode the ability of the national governments—in some cases not even in existence—to provide national health care. Finally, earthquakes and floods and other natural shocks can result in increased water-borne diseases, negatively affecting food utilization.

Apart from some of the above risks that may have particular sub-national effects, natural, environment, health, and social related threats are the key risks affecting *groups of households or communities*. At this level, natural risks cause in particular higher variability in production as well as increased production costs related to higher losses, irrigation, treatment of infections and insecticides. Pending on the stock levels and the ability of traders to bring in food from other (non-) affected areas, this may or may not interrupt food supplies or lead to price increases. The key environmental risks are trends rather than shocks. They affect mean production negatively, in the case of declining soil fertility through lower yields but also through increased unit production costs. This limits the profitability of farming and the opportunities to earn income from other natural resource based activities. On the health

Table 4.3. Key risks and potential impact on food security

Types of risks	Availability	Access	Utilization
Supra-macro (global, regional)			
Economic risks Financial crisis, trade-related shocks	• Reduced import capacity • Changes in production incentives	• Reduced income and wealth • Reduced economic growth	• Falling public health expenditures
Natural risks Global climate changes	• Falling productivity of cropland	• Increased income variability • Increased pressure on resources for livelihood adaptation	• Increase in waterborne diseases
Macro (national)			
Political risks Civil strife, war	• Lower production • Increased transaction costs • Breakdown in agricultural support system	• Reduced purchasing power (price, income)	• Breakdown of health-care system
Economic risks Growth collapse, fiscal or monetary crisis	• Food stock depletion • Reduced import capacity • Changes in production incentives • Falling public expenditures to support agricultural production, rural development	• Reduced purchasing power (price, income) • Reduced wealth	• Breakdown of health-care system
Natural risks Earthquakes, floods, droughts, desertification	• Lower production • Reduced livestock holdings • Pressure on food stocks	• Reduced income (agricultural, non-farm) • Reduced wealth • Reduced economic growth	• Reduced access to clean drinking water • Increase in waterborne diseases
Meso (community)			
Political risks Civil strife, war	• Lower production • Increased transaction costs • Breakdown in agricultural support system		• Breakdown of health-care system
Natural risks Landslides, rainfall, high winds, pest attacks, livestock diseases	• Lower production • Increased pressure on natural resources • Increased year to year fluctuations and regional variance	• Reduced income (agricultural, non-farm) • Reduced purchasing power • Reduced wealth (livestock)	• Reduced access to clean drinking water • Increase in waterborne diseases

Meso (community)			
Environmental risks Deforestation, declining soil fertility	• Increased production costs		
Health risks Epidemics, HIV/AIDS, poor water and sanitation	• Lower food production	• Loss of working days (reduced income) • Increased non-food expenditures	• Reduced uptake of macro- and micronutrients • Exhaustion of health care systems leading to less treatment
Social risks Discrimination of access to common resources, social exclusion, loss of patronage	• Lower livestock production	• Reduced income diversification opportunities • Exclusion from informal insurance	
Micro (household)			
Health risks Illness, disability, injury	• Lower own production	• Reduced income • Increased health costs • Reduced asset holdings (selling off) • Increased indebtedness	• Reduced uptake of macro- and micronutrients • Poor food utilization
Lifecycle related risks Old age, death, dowry	• Lower own production	• Reduced income • Increased health costs • Increased non-food expenditures • Reduced asset holdings • Increased indebtedness	
Social risks Inequitable intra-household food distribution		• Discriminatory access to food by certain household members (women or children)	• Transfer of malnourishment to children
Economic risks Unemployment, harvest failure	• Less own production	• Reduced income earned • Reduced asset holdings • Increased indebtedness	

Source: Adapted from World Bank (2000).

side, the risk of epidemics, and increasingly HIV/AIDS, increase vulnerability. WHO (2002) ranked unsafe water supply, sanitation and hygiene the third most important risk leading to poor health and death in 2000. In developing countries, the main burden of such risks falls on children, increasing their immediate food insecurity. However, these health-related risks also increase vulnerability by reducing educational achievements because of higher absence and lower cognitive capacity due to poor nutritional status. Health risks imply loss of labour time either periodically or permanently, meaning lower income and less food access, reduced ability to absorb both macro- and micronutrients, and in cases where a large part of a community is affected, reduced food production locally. Social risks relate to the lack of access to common resources and informal networks in times of difficulties, leading to lower income earnings and seclusion from drawing on community resources.

At the *household level*, risks (health, lifecycle related, social, and economic) primarily affect the access to food and food utilization. For households based on subsistence farming without alternative income source or no access to markets, such shocks can also reduce food availability. Lifecycle events, such as funerals or weddings, often imply significant extra expenditures, reducing the resources available for food purchase. Similarly, illnesses, disability and injuries involve additional expenditures, but also reduce labour supply and income and can lead to poor food utilization. Economic risks can reduce the access to food through the loss of income, either as a result of unemployment, or because income-generating activities, be it farming, small trade or manufacturing, fail.

While some of these risks relate to the household per se, members of households are also faced with individual risks. In addition to lifecycle events, a set of risks relates to individual food access. Sufficient aggregated access to food at household level does not imply that all individual household members access food in proportion to their needs. Discrimination on the basis of gender or age can make individuals vulnerable, even if their household on an aggregate basis is not.

4.4.3 *Assessing Food Security Risks in Northwest Bangladesh*

An initial version of the framework being described in this chapter was applied for analysing vulnerability to food insecurity in Fulchhari and Saghatta *upazillas*, which are two flood-prone *upazillas* in Gaibandha district, in Northwest Bangladesh. The analysis draws mainly on qualitative data from a vulnerability assessment (CEGIS 2005) and a local-level institutional assessment (ITDG 2005) carried out in late 2004.[5] Data was collected for these studies through

[5] These assessment studies are part of a technical cooperation project between FAO and the Government of Bangladesh, with the objective of strengthening the disaster preparedness capacity in the agricultural sector.

literature reviews, key informant interviews, consultations with government officials, representatives of NGOs and groups with agriculturally based livelihoods.[6]

TYPE AND LEVEL

Recurrent floods are the major risk to food security that households with agriculturally based livelihoods are exposed to in Saghatta and Fulchhari *upazillas*. Cyclones, droughts and pest infestations are other important risks, but these are far less threatening to food security and wellbeing compared to floods. Eighty per cent of households in these *upazillas* are engaged in agriculturally based activities and so floods have a high degree of inter-household co-variance.

SEVERITY AND TIMING

The severity of a flood and its impact on agriculturally based livelihoods is dependant on the depth, duration, timing, debris deposits and velocity of the flooding. The depth of flooding determines which assets are at peril and influences the duration of floods (the deeper the floods, the longer the flood waters take to recede). The duration determines for how long crops are covered in water and/or delays in land preparation and sowing. Also, floods with a long duration facilitate the spread of water-borne diseases. Large amounts of debris such as sand and stones damage agricultural land and imply high labour investments for removing these. Finally, high velocity floods cause greater land erosion and damages to infrastructure.

The timing of a flood is critical—an early rise of a flood can cause damages to the harvesting of the winter (*boro*) crop between April and May. A fifteen-day delay in the onset of a flood compared to the normal period of onset retards the sowing of the monsoon season (*aman*) rice.

FREQUENCY

Floods in Saghatta and Fulchhari occur every year mainly between June and October with variable severity. Under conditions of 'normal' flooding, likely to occur every two years, around 80 per cent of Fulchhari and Saghatta *upazillas* are inundated with between 30 cm to 180 cm. Floods take from two to seven months to recede, depending on elevation levels and the depth of the flooding. As a consequence of climate change and environmental degradation the frequency and severity of these floods are expected to increase, with deeper and more prolonged floods.

[6] A total of 60 Government of Bangladesh officials and NGO workers were consulted together with 168 men and women with agriculturally based livelihoods.

Households with agriculturally based livelihoods in the areas are involved in small-scale farming, livestock rearing, fishing and agricultural and non-agricultural wage labour, all of which are affected by floods. Floods damage standing crops, delay sowing, wash away fish from fish ponds, drown livestock, reduce the availability of animal feed, spread animal diseases and stall wage-labour. During particularly severe flooding, the combination of reduction in local food production and damages to transport and market infrastructure limits local food availability. Floods also damage latrines and cause the contamination of drinking water, which leads to the spread of intestinal diseases, thus undermining households' food utilization capacities (CEGIS 2005).

4.5 Dealing with Threats to Food Security: The Risk Management Side

Individuals, households, and communities are not passive victims of negative events, but seek to reduce vulnerability through risk management.[7] The effectiveness of risk management instruments depends partly on their suitability *vis-à-vis* the specific risks. Hence, identifying and analysing the instruments that are available for managing risks is an integral step in understanding people's degree of vulnerability and the causes of this. In the following sections, the characteristics of risk management instruments are analysed to understand their potential effectiveness in relation to ensuring food security.

4.5.1 *Characteristics of Risk Management*

Features of risk management instruments that need to be considered include their level, the actors involved, whether they are market or non-market based and whether they are ex ante or ex post.

LEVELS AND ACTORS

Risks can be managed at different levels, be it at the individual, household, community, (sub-)national or global level and at different levels simultaneous. Effectively managing risks requires the ability to share the burden either across time or between affected and non-affected people.

Instruments available at one level are often embedded in, and/or related to, instruments at other levels. Suppose that an effective way for managing a

[7] The ability to recover or resist being effected by an adversity is also termed resilience. However, to stress that options to influence future food insecurity include both ex post response capacity (ability to cope) as well as ex ante preventive or mitigating actions altering the characteristics of the risk itself (sometimes termed resistance), the term 'risk management' is used here.

given idiosyncratic risk is through access to credit. Although the immediate response is at the individual level (taking a loan), the framework for providing financial services and the required financial resources need to be in place at the macro level. Thus, effective risk management can involve several levels simultaneously.

When it is not possible to spread the costs of risk management over time, risks that are covariant can be more difficult to manage locally as micro- and meso level support mechanisms are simultaneously affected. Thus, macrolevel interventions, which can draw from a wider pool of unaffected resources, are often better suited for managing covariate risks. Similarly, recurring or severe risks may require transfers beyond micro- and meso level capacities, requiring interventions at macro levels where actors can draw from a wider pool of resources (Gaiha and Imai 2003; Heitzmann *et al.* 2002; Baulch and Hoddinott 2000).

The levels at which risks are managed are associated with specific risk management *actors*. Some of these actors operate at more than one level or switch between levels depending on the circumstances.

As the manifestation of food security ultimately is individual, any risk not managed by other actors falls back on individuals and households. These are mainly involved in managing risks related to food access and utilization, and in the absence of functioning markets, also availability.[8] The degree of influence over household assets and income vary between household members, resulting in different degrees of vulnerability within a household. In times of food shortages, for example, women are often the first to reduce their own food consumption and redistribute part of their share of food to other household members. While this may reduce the impact of a shock on particular members of a household, this is at the cost of other members' food security (Murdoch 1995; Dercon 2002; Siegel and Alwang 1999).

The role of *community-based organizations* (CBOs) in managing risks, especially in the absence of formal safety nets, is well documented and related to all dimensions of food security. The 'Susu' schemes in West Africa, mutual support arrangements reinforced through celebration and rituals in South Asian countries, and burial societies in Andean countries are just some examples. CBOs assist households in mitigating and coping with risks and are sometimes used as vehicles for larger programmes sponsored by macro-level actors. Some CBOs also play a role in strategies aimed at preventing risks, for example through co-sponsoring local initiatives to develop infrastructure. Where traditional practices and norms are sources of risks, community based organizations can also be used for changing these (Marsh 2003).

[8] If functioning food markets exist, few vulnerable households, given their size, are likely to influence aggregate food availability, even if production for auto-consumption is an important livelihood strategy.

The functioning of CBOs depends on the presence of social capital within communities and on principles of reciprocity. These solidarity bonds may be unevenly distributed and poorer households may be unable to reciprocate or to afford the ex ante investments (in social assets) required to benefit from these. As a result, some community members receive more support than others and some groups are excluded on the basis of ethnicity, caste, sex or socioeconomic status. The consequences can be that risk management instruments serve the interests of the more influential community elites and/or marginalize the less powerful (Marsh 2003; Mattingly 2002).

Private sector institutions are involved in risk management in numerous ways in the search for business opportunities. Traders often play a key role in ensuring national and local food availability in times of production shortfall, both directly and as providers of credit against harvests, labour, etc. Traders also facilitate the availability of agricultural inputs, sometimes based on credit. Banks and insurance companies sometimes provide credit and savings facilities as well as insurance to compensate for income losses.

Through their control over macroeconomic, structural and sector policies, early warning systems and their possible efforts to complement community and private sector efforts, national governments play a central important role in managing threats to food security through policies and budgetary allocations and by providing the legislative framework for risk management efforts of other actors. These functions are supported by international institutions, UN agencies, bilateral donors, etc. through their provision of resources, technical guidance, and global frameworks and facilities to manage risks that are beyond the national-level capacity.

MARKET/NON-MARKET-BASED INSTRUMENTS

Formal risk management instruments can be market or non-market-based. Market-based mechanisms relate mainly to mitigating or coping to ensure stable access to food. Market-based mechanisms rely on functioning market institutions and are motivated by profits. However, often, rural poor are not seen as profitable clients by bankers or insurance firms for a range of reasons, including moral hazard problems, information asymmetries, chronic poverty, lack of collateral, high transaction costs and weak contract enforcing environments. This has meant that formal market-based insurance, credit and savings instruments in rural areas of developing countries have largely failed to emerge (Devereux 2001; Heitzmann *et al.* 2002; Holzmann and Jørgensen 2000), and thus the task of providing such services are often left with governments and/or CBOs.

PREVENTING/MITIGATING/COPING

Risk management instruments can be implemented, before, during or after risks materialize and can be categorized as ex-ante (prevention and mitigation) and ex-post (coping) instruments. The same risk can often be addressed at different points in time. For instance, floods can be managed ex ante by building embankments to avoid inundation of agricultural land and by providing crop and livestock insurance that is accessible to farmers with low incomes. Alternatively, or in combination with these ex-ante instruments, floods can be managed ex-post by distributing food aid and inputs for rehabilitating agriculture.

Prevention instruments aim at reducing the probability of a shock or negative event taking place. Mitigation instruments seek to reduce the impact of a negative event by providing compensation for risk-generated losses. Risk preparedness efforts are ex ante measures seeking to ensure effective ex-post responses.

Ex-post instruments, also referred to as coping mechanisms, are reactive and put to work only once risks materialize. In relation to food security, they aim at relieving immediate food needs. Changes in livelihood strategies, such as migration in search of work elsewhere, do not necessarily imply negative repercussions on future risk management capacities. On the other hand, distress sales of assets, borrowing at high interest rates, reducing consumption or withdrawing children from school are examples of ex-post instruments that relieve immediate food needs at the expense of future risk management capacities. Hence, although such strategies may reduce food insecurity, they increase vulnerability, even if the degree of exposure to risks remains constant.

Some empirical studies suggest that ex-ante instruments can be more effective than ex-post instruments in managing risks. An analysis by Vakis *et al.* (2004) on the impact of the coffee crisis in Nicaragua on rural households shows that ex-ante strategies were more effective in allowing households to insulate themselves from the shock than ex-post strategies. Similarly, using data on poverty rates in Zimbabwe, Owens *et al.* (2004) suggest that ex-ante instruments would have been more effective than ex post instruments in controlling the impact of the 1994–5 drought in terms of poverty levels.

4.5.2 *Instruments for Managing Threats to the Availability, Access, and Utilization of Food*

In the following we look at the main instruments for managing threats related to the availability, access, and utilization of food.

The choice of instruments is specific to the natural, political, social and economic conditions of a country or region and to the risks faced. It is also specific to the group of vulnerable targeted, given that risks, but also risk management instruments, can have different impacts on different groups. Some risk management instruments reduce vulnerability for some groups, but increase it for other groups. One example of this is a currency devaluation that increases domestic prices of food and tradables, benefiting farmers producing surpluses of tradable products, but negatively affecting producers of non-tradables, such as subsistence farmers or unskilled landless labourers (FAO 1997).

Following recent work in FAO on how best to reduce hunger in a sustainable manner, this chapter uses the twin-track approach to analyse different instruments for risk management. The approach builds on the premise that sustainable reductions in hunger require two sets of interventions: (i) sustainable agricultural and rural development aimed at supporting and enhancing the livelihoods of the poorest and most vulnerable groups and (ii) targeted interventions and programmes to enhance immediate and direct access to food and nutrition by the most needy (FAO 2003).

The first track includes mainly ex ante measures. These include prevention instruments for removing structural risks and for creating the conditions that allow households to mitigate risks. The second track mainly addresses food insecurity through ex-post instruments. As post-shock environment also are pre-shock environment in a dynamic chain of events, some track II instruments, aimed at addressing immediate food needs, can also be used for reducing vulnerability in the future. The main mechanism for this is to support households in avoiding meeting current food needs by exhausting capacities to manage future risks.

Table 4.4 presents an overview of key instruments available for managing risks related to food security. Most of the different measures are well known and so are not described in detail. As with risks, the instruments have been linked to the food security dimension they foremost address. However, given the links between the different dimensions of food security, some of the instruments affect more than one dimension.

INSTRUMENTS FOR MANAGING RISKS RELATED TO FOOD AVAILABILITY

Instruments for stabilizing food availability must aim at ensuring the supply of nutritionally adequate food. This stability can be achieved through domestic production, domestic food stocks changes and concessional/non-concessional food imports. Empirical research indicates that among these instruments, improved food productivity and non-concessional imports are more useful in dampening volatility in food availability than concessional imports (Barrett 2001).

Improving food production and its handling comprises measures that concern agricultural sector development (FAO 1997). Instruments for improving national production include investments in irrigation, research into drought/pest resistant varieties and encouraging farm level adoption of new technologies. These also include the provision of effective agricultural extension services addressing longer-term food production issues as well as

Table 4.4. Instruments for managing risks related to the availability, access, and utilization of food

	Availability	Access	Utilization
Track 1: Improving long-term food security			
Prevention	• Stable macro environment • Trade promotion • Develop market and storage infrastructure • Improve input and output markets • Improve natural resource management • Increase productivity and production capacity • Improve sustainable and diversified production • Reduce production variability • Improve agricultural research • Raise investment in agriculture	• Increase productivity of income generating activities • Promote rural development and farm/non-farm linkages • Empower women and other marginalized groups • Promote and protect needs of children • Promote access to education	• Promote preventive health practices • Enforce food safety regulations and institutions • Increase immunization • Water and sanitation infrastructure
Mitigation	• Improve agricultural extension services • Facilitate diversification • Establish buffer stocks	• Livelihoods diversification • Promote insurance and savings	• Provision of health services
Track 2: Addressing immediate food requirements			
Coping	• Market facilitation (transport, information) • Food aid • Facilitate food imports	• Social safety nets, including cash transfers, food subsidies, work fare programmes • Migration • Consumption smoothening • Asset sales • Formal/Informal credit • School feeding	• Disease control • Immunization • Water and sanitation

Source: Adapted from World Bank (2001) and FAO (2003).

rehabilitating agricultural activities after shocks affecting production. The ability to diversify or change production will vary between livelihoods and wealth group, pending on risk adversity.

A range of instruments relate to the capacity of the market to respond to supply fluctuations. This includes efforts to improve the longer-term performance of input/output markets through infrastructural development aimed at increasing spatial market integration and the development of information systems to increase market transparency and allow a more efficient spread of supply shocks. Early warning systems, providing weather, crop or price forecasts are ways of bridging information asymmetries between actors. Such systems also provide contingency planners a basis for estimating the extent of risks and preparing effective responses (Von Braun *et al.* 1992; Buchanan-Smith and Davies 1995; Mattingly 2002).

Commercial imports—by the public or private sector—play a crucial role in stabilizing food availability in low and middle income developing countries, but foreign exchange constrains can limit the capacity to use this instrument (Barrett 2001). An alternative is to maintain buffer stocks, either public, private or community based, to assist in spreading out the impact of local, regional, or national harvest failures or in seasonally cut off areas.

INSTRUMENTS FOR MANAGING RISKS RELATED TO FOOD ACCESS

Instruments for managing access to food aim at ensuring that households are able to meet food consumption needs. This requires instruments that stabilize households' purchasing power/consumption ability through asset management and by stabilizing income flows and/or stabilizing food prices. This is in particular achieved through financial instruments, diversifying income and livelihood activities, increasing the returns to livelihood activities, asset sales, and safety net programmes.

Formal and informal insurance, savings and consumption credit are financial instruments used for smoothening consumption. However, informal community-based insurance mechanisms relying on limited pools of participants may default when confronted with a covariate shock. Alternatively, savings involve investing income surpluses in private assets (e.g. livestock, food stocks, jewellery, and cash) with the intention of using these to gain access to food in times of need. The extent to which the invested assets maintain, or even increase, their value over time is critical in determining their effectiveness as risk management instruments (Zeller *et al.* 1997).

In the absence of formal credit services, households obtain consumption credit through informal mechanisms such as friends and family. However, among the poor, lending capacities may be limited, especially *vis-à-vis* meso and macro level shocks, when a large proportion of households are facing disruptions to income flows. Credit restrictions drive interest rates up, and so households can be forced to take out expensive loans undermining their longer-term asset accumulation and increasing their vulnerability.

Income diversification can also be used for mitigating risks. To be effective in increasing stability of income and access to food, a household's set of income sources must have low covariance for each given risk. Unfortunately, a characteristic of developing countries is that most income-generating opportunities available to rural households are highly covariant for specific risks because income-earning opportunities depend on a limited set of mainly agriculturally based activities. Economic development beyond the agricultural sector can thus be used as an instrument for increasing the effectiveness of livelihood diversification (Swift 1989; Ellis 1998; Baulch and Hoddinott 2000), including improving farm/non farm linkages. Changing or diversifying livelihoods is also used for ex-post coping, for example through migration, to find additional sources of income, or in more desperate stages forcibly as a consequence of asset sales (Ellis 1998; Devereux 2001).

When households are faced with falling access to food, they may decide to tradeoff short-term consumption needs against longer-term viability by selling their assets, reducing expenditures on nonfood items or shifting to lower-cost diets. Instruments that have lower long-term costs, such as food rationing, are adopted first, whereas instruments with higher long-term costs and low reversibility, for example selling the family's plough, are adopted later (Corbett 1988). The effectiveness of distress sales of assets will depend on the price behaviour of the asset in question. With highly covariant risks, asset prices tend to rise and fall widely if many households want to buy and/or sell similar goods at the same time (Murdoch 1999; Holzmann and Jørgensen 2000).

Safety net programmes, such as public employment programmes, food subsidies and school feeding, transferring assets to households, be it cash, food or other commodities, can be used to maintain a minimum nutritionally adequate food consumption level and at the same time help to avoid households eroding their asset base. In non-emergency contexts, safety nets can also be used to reduce risk adversity and encourage diversification into more risky activities with higher returns (Drèze 1990; Sinha and Lipton 1999; Devereux 2001).

Until the 1980s, many governments kept large quantities of food reserves that were used to stabilize food prices in the event of hikes in food prices. These were the target of much criticism because of the expenses of storage and effects on producers' incentives. Despite criticism, government food-stock policies still play an important role in many developing countries. Another less well-tested ex-post instrument involves using variable import tariffs to dampen the effect of rises in international food prices on domestic prices (Barrett and Sahn 2001).

INSTRUMENTS FOR MANAGING RISKS RELATED TO UTILIZATION OF FOOD

Risk management instruments related to proper food utilization evolve around protecting health status of individuals. The main instruments are concerned with improving nutrition and healthcare practices, health service delivery, ensuring access to safe water and sanitation, but also with protection of food quality and safety.

Promotion of good nutritional practices, including safe food handling and the awareness of balanced diets, together with simple information on how to avoid or treat basic diseases like diarrhoea, all assist in preventing diseases. Such activities are often a part of community-based nutrition programmes or larger health sector programmes and can include campaigns for national immunization and better sanitary habits.

Access to health services is the key to mitigating disease-related risks to food security. Unfortunately, resources devoted to healthcare in developing countries are low, despite these countries having often larger health problems (Schieber and Maeda 1999). This can be a particular problem when dealing with highly covariant health risks, stretching resources to or beyond the limit when treatments are costly, as has been the case with HIV/AIDS. Furthermore, poorer people have less access to health service than richer people. In a review of eight developing country studies of inequality in the health sector, Makinen *et al.* (2000) conclude that access to health care services was unequally distributed to the advantage of richer, partly caused by their higher health expenditure, but also because of better access to publicly subsidized health care services.

Finally, controlling risks related to food safety for consumers requires both national and international regulation to guide national food production as well as ensure standards for internationally traded food. Moreover, it requires food control systems and programmes at national and local levels monitoring processes from primary production to final consumption. While export industries in developing countries are pressed to implement food standards in compliance with their target markets, incentives for tight control of food standards in the local markets are often weaker.

4.5.3 *Assessing Flood Management in Northwest Bangladesh*

As explained, floods in Saghatta and Fulchhari destabilize food access, availability and utilization. Thus, it is necessary to assess the risk management instruments that are in place for protecting all three dimensions of food security.

AVAILABILITY

The Government of Bangladesh has taken important measures for stabilizing food availability at national and sub-national levels through ex-ante measures. National production has been stabilized through agricultural and investment programmes that expanded cultivation of irrigated winter (*boro*) rice crop and reduced the country's dependence on the flood-susceptible monsoon (*aman*) rice crop (del Ninno *et al.* 2003). Additional measures that stabilize national production are the large infrastructural projects for flood protection through which embankments have been built for protecting agricultural land from floods. However, as seen in Saghatta and Fulchhari during the floods of 2004, these embankments are subject to breeching because of increasing flood levels and poor maintenance (CEGIS 2005). Investments made in the construction of bridges and road networks facilitate food distribution at sub-national levels, unless flooding is especially deep.

The Government runs an extensive public food distribution system with local storage depots in most *upazillas* of the country, including in Fulchhari and Saghatta, which serve as buffer stocks for the Government's short-term food based relief interventions.

While private sector imports of rice were permitted in 1994, additional steps towards trade liberalization were taken in early 1998 to encourage private sector imports. The measures included removing rice import tariffs, minimizing government open-market price sales, and speeding up customs procedures. These proved to be an important risk management instrument for guaranteeing food availability and avoiding hikes in food prices by facilitating grain trade. As a result, rice prices did not rise beyond import-parity levels during the extensive 1998 floods (del Ninno *et al.* 2003).

ACCESS

Since households in Saghatta and Fulchhari are aware of the high probability of seasonal flooding, they are involved in a mixture of ex-ante risk management strategies. These include growing more seedlings to replace likely losses, using floating seed beds, delaying planting of crops until flood waters recede, building houses on stilts and storing seeds, livestock and valuable assets above expected flood levels. Although households are engaged in a variety of income generating activities, this provides low protection against income variability because the large majority of these are agriculturally based and similarly susceptible to floods. During more buoyant times, households save part of their harvest and income as a buffer against declines in income flows. Some savings are kept in the form of livestock and poultry, even if these risk loosing their value during floods due to the spread of animal diseases or insufficient fodder (CEGIS 2005).

The key ministries responsible for the agricultural sector, Ministry of Agriculture and Ministry of Fisheries and Livestock have, until recently, provided little attention on assisting households in managing floods ex ante. The main involvement of the Ministry of Agriculture in ex-ante activities is through the participation of extension officers in Disaster Management Committees at national, district, *upazila* and union levels (focusing in particular on contingency planning) and involvement in providing early warning information and crop forecasts. The main focus of the Ministry of Agriculture and Ministry of Fisheries and Livestock, in collaboration with NGOs, is on ex-post activities which include providing households affected by natural disasters with basic inputs such as seeds, seedlings and fish stock to rehabilitate income-generating activities (ITDG 2005; Young 2000).

The Government of Bangladesh recognizes the importance of increasing the productivity of crop, fishing and livestock and poultry-rearing activities in order to increase incomes which would provide households with additional resources to protect food security. The measures envisaged by the government include intensifying cereal production and diversifying into high value non-cereal crops such as vegetables and fruits, with a specific focus on agro-ecologically disadvantaged regions, including flood-prone areas. Likewise, measures are envisaged for increasing the productivity of inland fishing, livestock and poultry rearing activities through species improvements, better husbandry practices and support services (GoB 2004). Although the measures described can lead to increases in incomes, their impact on reducing vulnerability depends on whether these activities are also susceptible to floods.

Even though the National Strategy for Accelerated Poverty reduction (GoB 2004) recognizes the importance of diversifying income generating activities into rural non-farm (RNF) activities, it notes that these are closely linked with the agricultural sector. Thus, even if RNF activities are developed, their productivity may fall when the agricultural sector slumps during floods.

Following the 1998 flood, the Government, with the support of international agencies and donors, provided needy households with food and/or cash transfers for ensuring their access to food. These transfers were well targeted to needy households but they were small relative to the needs of these households. Flood-exposed households from the bottom-two income quintiles received monthly transfers worth only 3.4 per cent of monthly expenditure and only marginally increased food consumption (del Ninno *et al.* 2003). Part of this may be related to targeting. Because of exclusionary processes at the community level, the most marginalized groups sometimes do not have access to the organizations responsible for local food aid distributions (CEGIS 2005).

In the absence of adequate public mechanisms to protect access to food during floods, households in Fulchhari and Saghatta resort to coping strategies that undermine food security in the future in order to address their immediate food security needs. They re-distribute their expenditures from non-food to food items and take out loans from formal and informal credit mechanisms in times of crisis (CEGIS 2005; del Ninno *et al.* 2003). In 1998, informal borrowing was the major risk management instrument used by households during the first three months of the flood. Debts rose to an average of 1.5 months of typical consumption compared with only a small percentage of monthly consumption about eight months before the flood, with interest rates ranging between 21 per cent and 67 per cent. It was estimated that nationwide total private borrowing reached US$1–1.5 billion, compared to about US$0.6 billion of total annual loan disbursement by the two largest micro-credit providers, Grameen Bank and BRAC (del Ninno *et al.* 2003). As a proportion of the private borrowing, government transfers for safeguarding food access were also of limited importance, at around one-sixth to one-eighth the size of the average households borrowing. Fifteen months after the 1998 floods, Bangladesh's poorest households were still repaying their debts taking during the floods, negatively affecting the ability to withstand new floods.

Another study on floods in Bangladesh (Stevens undated) shows that households with high loan burdens and those that had borrowed from money lenders had slower rates in recovery of nutritional status than households with lower loan burdens who had borrowed from others sources (banks, neighbours).

Transport constraints during flooding mean that access to markets is problematic. Small farmers' earnings on asset sales fall, since they often rely on middlemen, with whom they have little negotiating power and who are able to underpay their products (CEGIS 2005).

UTILIZATION

Flood-proof sanitation facilities for preventing health and environmental contamination are largely absent in the two *upazillas*. As a consequence, floods cause the overflow of pit latrines, which pose a high health risk since they contaminate surface and drinking water. This is compounded by insufficient knowledge among rural people of health and hygiene, as well as lack of access to dry fuel-wood for boiling water (Kazi and Rahman 1999). As a consequence, during floods, health deteriorates and food utilization declines. Immediately after the 1998 floods, 9.6 per cent of individuals in affected areas had diarrhoea and 4.7 per cent were affected by respiratory diseases (del Ninno *et al.* 2003). To address these deteriorations in health during and after floods, the government and aid agencies provide medical treatment in health centres and through mobile clinics and medical supplies, oral re-hydration salts and water purification tablets. However, during widespread floods, the large scale of impure drinking water means that this is difficult to address through purification and so more attention is placed on mitigating the effects of diarrhoea by distributing oral re-hydration salts than on preventing its spread. After floods recede, training is provided on rehabilitating tube-wells (Young 2000).

4.5.4 *Opportunities for Reducing Vulnerability*

Risk management instruments available for stabilizing national-level food availability are largely suitable for stabilizing food availability at a national-level, even in the face of widespread floods. However, because of the disruption that floods cause to transport infrastructure, when floods are especially severe, the combined impact of falls in local food production and constraints in transport of food across the country, including Fulchhari and Saghatta *upazillas*, can lead to declines in local availability and local increases in prices.

Existing instruments for stabilizing households' food access in the face of floods are largely insufficient. Macro-level ex-ante instruments are limited and ex-ante household-level instruments are unable to stabilize food access given the co-variant impact of floods. Informal savings are low and subject to losses in value and households' portfolios of livelihood activities are covariant with floods.

Ex-post instruments partially protect access in crises. However, household borrowing from informal lenders at high interest rates comprises a risk to future food access. Although government food distributions contribute to reducing asset deprivation, their extent and coverage is limited and so the protective role of these instruments is limited. Utilization is being protected through ex-post interventions by governments, donors and NGOs but ensuring the complete coverage of this assistance to all households suffering from water-borne diseases is difficult.

The co-variance and frequency of floods and characteristics of available instruments indicates that households with agriculturally based livelihoods in Saghatta and Fulchhari will continue to be vulnerable food insecurity. The vulnerability of these households could be reduced through ex-ante instruments that prevent flooding of agricultural areas and the spread of water-borne diseases; mitigate the impact of floods on food production and income generating activities; and improve national capacities to respond to floods. Ex-post instruments that avoid households compromising their longer-term food security in order to maintain their short-run access to food are also required.

4.6 Conclusion

Improving food security requires an understanding not just of who is food insecure today and why they are so, but also of who is likely to be food insecure in the future and why so. Basing interventions on ex-post measures of food security will likely miss important parts of the food security picture, both in terms of who the future food insecure are (targeting), why they are so (causes) and what can be done about it (policy options).

Analysing vulnerability offers a dynamic, forward-looking way of understanding food security dynamics, calling for explicit attention to risks and the options for managing these so as to improve future food security.

Managing risks goes beyond assisting those affected by a particular shock in addressing their immediate food needs. A range of options are available for addressing longer-term food security through sustainable agricultural and rural development, aiming at preventing or mitigating risk.

Risk factors will continue to threaten food security and cause vulnerability. Increasing incidences of HIV/AIDS, continuing civil conflicts and political instability, increasing severe weather events and adverse consequences of globalization are some of the risks likely to cause vulnerability in the coming years (Devereux 2001). Clearly, dealing with such risks through an effective mix of ex post and ex ante interventions will be essential in moving towards achieving the global food security targets.

References

Alwang, J., P. B. Siegel, and S. L. Jørgensen (2001). 'Vulnerability: a View from Different Disciplines'. Social Protection Discussion Paper 115. Washington, DC: World Bank.

Barrett, C. (2001). 'Does Food aid Stabilize Food Availability?'. *Economic Development and Cultural Change,* 39 (2): 335–49.

Barrett, C. B., and D. E. Sahn (2001). 'Food Policy in Crisis Management'. Food Policy Toolkit Draft Report. Washington, DC: World Bank.

Baulch, B., and J. Hoddinott (2000). 'Economic Mobility and Poverty Dynamics in Developing Countries'. *Journal of Development Studies,* 36 (6): 1–24.

Buchanan-Smith, M., and S. Davies (1995). *Famine Early Warning and Response: the Missing Link.* London: Intermediate Technology Publications.

Carter, M. R., and J. May (2001). 'One Kind of Freedom: Poverty Dynamics in Post-Apartheid South Africa'. *World Development,* 29 (12): 1987–2006.

Commission on the Nutrition Challenges of the 21st Century (2000) 'Ending Malnutrition by 2020: An Agenda for Change in the Millennium'. Final report to the ACC/SCN by the Commission on the Nutrition Challenges of the 21st Century. *Food and Nutrition Bulletin Supplement,* 21 (3).

Corbett, J. (1988). 'Famine and Household Coping Strategies'. *World Development,* 16 (9): 1099–112.

CEGIS. (2005). 'Study on physical and environmental context, vulnerable groups profiling and institutional analysis'. Dhaka: Center for Environmental and Geographic Information Services (CEGIS).

del Ninno, C., P. A. Dorosh, and L. C. Smith (2003). 'Public Policy, Food Markets and Household Coping Strategies in Bangladesh: Lessons from the 1998 Floods'. FCND Discussion Paper 156 Washington, DC: IFPRI.

——— ——— ——— D. K. Roy (2001). 'The 1998 Floods in Bangladesh: Disaster Impacts, Household Coping Strategies and Response'. Research Report 122. Washington, DC: IFPRI.

Dercon, S. (2001a). 'Assessing Vulnerability to Poverty'. Oxford: Oxford University. A paper prepared for DFID (August).

——— (ed.) (2001b). *Insurance against Poverty*. Oxford: Oxford University Press for UNU-WIDER.

——— (2002). 'Income Risk, Coping Strategies and Safety Nets'. *World Bank Research Observer*, 17 (2): 141–66.

Devereux, S. (2001). 'Livelihood Insecurity and Social Protection: a Re-emerging Issue in Rural Development'. *Development Policy Review*, 19 (4): 507–19.

Drèze, J. (1990). 'Famine Prevention in India', in J. Drèze and A. Sen (eds), *The Political Economy of Hunger: Hunger and Public Action*, vol. 2. Oxford: Clarendon Press for UNU–WIDER.

Ellis, F. (1998). 'Survey Article: Household Strategies and Rural Livelihood Diversification'. *Journal of Development Studies*, 35 (1): 1–38.

——— (2002). 'Human Vulnerability and Food Insecurity: Policy Implications'. Forum for Food Security in Southern Africa Theme Paper. London: ODI.

FAO (1996). 'World Food Summit: Rome Declaration on World Food Security and WFS Plan of Action'. World Food Summit document. Rome. FAO/WHO.

——— (1997). 'Implications of Economic Policy for Food Security: A Training Manual'. Training Materials for Agricultural Planning, 40. Rome: FAO.

——— (2000). *The State of Food Insecurity in the World, 2000*. Rome: FAO.

——— (2002). 'Proceedings: Measurement and Assessment of Food Deprivation and Undernutrition'. International Scientific Symposium, 26–28 June. Rome: FAO. Available at: www.fao.org/DOCREP/005/Y4249E/Y4249E00.HTMInternational

——— (2003). 'Anti-Hunger Programme. A Twin-Track Approach to Hunger Reduction: Priorities for National and International Action'. Rome: FAO.

——— (2004). 'The State of Food Insecurity in the World 2004: Monitoring Progress towards the World Food Summit and Millennium Development Goals'. Rome: FAO.

FIVIMS (2000). 'Guidelines for National FIVIMS: Background and Principles'. IAWG Guidelines Series 1. Rome: FAO.

Gaiha, R., and K. Imai (2003). 'Vulnerability, Shocks and Persistence of Poverty: Estimates for Semi-Arid Rural South India'. Royal Economic Society Annual Conference Paper 111. Nottingham.

Government of Bangladesh. (2004). 'National Strategy for Accelerated Poverty Reduction'. Dhaka: General Economics Division (GED).

Haddad, L., and T. Frankenberger (2003). 'Integrating Relief and Development to Accelerate Reductions in Food Insecurity in Shock-Prone Areas'. Occasional Paper 2. Washington, DC: USAID Office for Food for Peace.

Heitzmann, K., R. S. Canagarajah, and P. B. Siegel (2002). 'Guidelines for Assessing the Sources of Risk and Vulnerability'. Social Protection Discussion Paper 0218. Washington, DC: World Bank.

Hoddinott, J., and A. Quisumbing (2003). 'Methods for Microeconometric Risk and Vulnerability Assessments'. Social Protection Discussion Paper 0324. Washington, DC: World Bank.

Holzmann, R., and S. Jørgensen (2000).'Social Risk Management: A New Conceptual Framework for Social Protection and Beyond'. Social Protection Discussion Paper 0006. Washington, DC: World Bank.

ITDG. (2005). 'Participatory training needs assessment relevant to disaster risk management in flood and drought prone areas'. Dhaka: Intermediate Technologies Development Group—Bangladesh (ITDG).

Kazi, N. M. and M. M. Rahman. (1999). 'Sanitation strategies for flood-prone areas'. *25th WEDC Conference: Integrated development for water supply and sanitation.* Addis Ababa.

Ligon, E., and L. Schechter (2004). 'Evaluating Different Approaches to Estimating Vulnerabilty'. Social Protection Discussion Paper 0410. Washington, DC: World Bank.

Makinen, M., H. Waters, M. Rauch, N. Almagambetova, R. Bitran, L. Gilson, D. McIntyre, S. Pannarunothai, A. L. Prieto, G. Ubilla, and S. Ram (2000). 'Inequalities in Healthcare Use and Expenditures: Empirical Data from Eight Developing Countries and Countries in Transition'. *Bulletin of the World Health Organization,* 78 (1): 55–65. Geneva: WHO.

Mansuri, G., and A. Healy (2001). 'Vulnerability Prediction in Rural Pakistan'. Washington, DC: World Bank. Mimeo.

Mansuri, G., and A. Healy (2001). 'Vulnerability Prediction in Rural Pakistan'. Washington, DC: World Bank. Mimeo.

Marsh, R. (2003). 'Working with Local Institutions to Support Sustainable Livelihoods'. Rome: FAO.

Mattingly, S. (2002). 'Summary Paper on Best Practices in Disaster Mitigation'. Regional Workshop on Practices in Disaster Mitigation, 24–26 September, Bali.

Murdoch, J. (1995). 'Income Smoothing and Consumption Smoothing'. *Journal of Economic Perspectives,* 9 (3):103–14.

—— (1999). 'Between the State and the Market: Can Informal Insurance Patch the Safety Net?'. *The World Bank Research Observer,* 19 (2): 187–207.

Owens, T., J. Hoddinott, and B. Kinsey (2004). 'Ex Ante Actions and Ex Post Responses to Drought Shocks: Evidence and Simulations from Zimbabwe'. *World Development,* 31 (7): 1239–56.

Schieber, G., and K. Maeda (1999). 'Healthcare Financing and Delivery in Developing Countries'. *Health Affairs,* 18 (3): 193–205.

Siegel, S. P., and J. Alwang (1999). 'An Asset-based Approach to Social Risk Management: a Conceptual Framework'. Social Protection Discussion Paper Series 9926. Washington, DC: World Bank.

Sinha, S., and M. Lipton (1999). 'Damaging Fluctuations, Risk and Poverty: A Review'. Background paper for the World Development Report 2001/01. Brighton: Poverty Research Unit, University of Sussex.

Smith, L., A. E. Obeid, and H. Jensen (2000). 'The Geography and Causes of Food Insecurity in Developing Countries'. *Agricultural Economics,* 22 (2): 199–215.

Stevens, E. (undated). 'Lessons learnt from the 1998 Bangladesh floods'. Save the Children Fund UK. Available at: www.ennonline.net/fex/11/fa19.html

Swift, J. (1989). 'Why Are Rural People Vulnerable to Famine?'. *IDS Bulletin,* 20 (2): 8–15.

Tesliuc, E. D., and K. Lindert (2002). 'Vulnerability: A Quantitative and Qualitative Assessment'. Guatemala Poverty Assessment Program. Washington, DC: World Bank.
UNDP (2004). *Reducing Disaster Risk: A Challenge for Development*. New York: Bureau for Crisis Prevention and Recovery, UNDP.
Vakis, R., D. Kruger, and A. D. Mason (2004). 'Shocks and Coffee: Lessons from Nicaragua'. Social Protection Discussion Paper Series 0415. Washington, DC: World Bank.
Von Braun, J., H. Bouis, S. Kumar, and R. Pandya-Lorch (1992). *Improving Food Security of the Poor: Concept, Policy and Programs*. Washington, DC: IFPRI.
Webb, P., and B. Rogers (2003). 'Addressing the "In" in Food Insecurity'. Occasional Paper 1. Washington, DC: USAID Office of Food for Peace.
World Bank (nd). 'The Contribution of Social Protection to the Millennium Development Goals'. Washington, DC: World Bank.
—— (2000). *World Development Report 2000/01: Attacking Poverty*. Washington, DC: World Bank.
Young, R. and Associates. (2000). 'Bangladesh: 1998 Flood Appeal and Independent Evaluation'. Dhaka: Disasters Emergency Committee.
Zeller, M., G. Schreider, J. von Braun, and F. Heidues (1997). 'Rural Finance for Food Security for the Poor: Implications for Research and Policy'. Food Review 4. Washington, DC: IFPRI.

5

Women's Status and Children's Food Security in Pakistan

Basudeb Guha-Khasnobis and Gautam Hazarika

5.1 Introduction

This chapter examines the effect of women's intra-household status relative to men upon children's food security in Pakistan. Food security, defined as access to sufficient food for an active and healthy life, is pivotal to early childhood development. Children's food security is, thus, a factor in economic growth since well-developed children are more productive as adults. Yet, malnutrition afflicts about a third of pre-school aged children in less developed countries. It is associated with over half of worldwide child mortality (Pelletier *et al.* 1995). South Asia has the world's highest rate of child malnutrition, with 49.3 per cent of its 0 to 5 year old children underweight (Smith and Haddad 2000), this despite the fact that South Asia fares better than, for example, Sub-Saharan Africa by a number of measures of economic development. It has been argued that this—the so called South Asian Enigma—is due in part to the particularly low status of women in South Asia (e.g. Smith *et al.* 2004). Therefore, by examining the effect of women's status upon children's food security in a South Asian nation, namely, Pakistan, this chapter hopes to contribute to a topical area of study in development economics.

There are some studies relating child health to socio-economic factors in Pakistan. Arshad M. Mahmood (2002) examines data from the Demographic and Health Survey in Pakistan in 1991 and finds that the rise in parental education, improvements in the quality of water supply, and motivation of mothers to utilize health services for pre and postnatal care are key factors that determine infant mortality in Pakistan. Naushin Mahmood (2002) uses the Fertility and Family Planning Survey of 1996–7 and finds that an enhanced role of Pakistani women in household decisionmaking has the desired effect on fertility reduction and the overall achievement of gender-equality.

Inquiry into the effect of women's intra-household status relative to children's food security is also the means of testing between two competing views of households. While economists have traditionally considered the household a monolithic unit, this 'unitary' model has lately been yielding to the view that a household's allocation decisions instead result from bargaining between its members. The unitary model, attributed to Becker (1965, 1981), typically assumes that, subject to a budget constraint, the household combines its labour with market inputs to produce a composite consumption good that is distributed among its members according to a single set of household preferences. It follows that improvement in women's status may not affect intra-household distribution. Collective models of intra-household allocation, on the other hand, often view intra-household distribution as the outcome of Nash Bargaining between members, so that allocations to a member (and her constituency) are dependent on her bargaining power. Thus, the models predict that improvement in women's status shall increase allocations to women and children. It is necessary to test between these competing views of households since mistaken adherence to the unitary model may reduce the efficacy of policy (Haddad *et al.* 1997). For instance, public transfers to benefit children may be less effective if the particular adult recipient is not wholly solicitous about children.

There is now much empirical support of bargaining models of intra-household allocation. For example, Schultz (1990) finds that a woman's unearned income in Thailand has a more pronounced positive effect upon her fertility and consumption of leisure than the unearned income of her spouse, such income being taken to measure intra-household bargaining power. Similarly, Thomas (1990) discovers that family health outcomes in Brazil, such as child survival probabilities, are improved much more by increases in mothers' than fathers' unearned income. Hoddinott and Haddad (1995) find that an increase in the share of household income earned by women in Côte d'Ivoire raises the proportion of the household budget expended on food and reduces the budget shares of alcohol and cigarettes. Handa (1996) uncovers evidence from Jamaica that the presence in a household of a female decisionmaker generally increases the share of the household budget allocated to child and family goods. Lundberg *et al.* (1997), in an examination of a late 1970s policy change in the UK that transferred a substantial child allowance to wives, find that this resulted in greater expenditures on women's and children's clothing relative to men's clothing. Pitt and Khandker (1998), in a study of microcredit programmes in Bangladesh, determine that household consumption expenditure increased by 18 *taka* for every 100 *taka* borrowed by women, as opposed to an increase of only 11 *taka* for every 100 *taka* borrowed by men. Similarly, Levin *et al.* (1999), in a study of urban households in Ghana, find that women allocate a larger share of their income towards meeting their children's and their own basic needs despite earning less than men. Thomas, Contreras, and Frankenberg (2002) learn that child health in Java is influenced by the relative asset positions of parents at the time of their marriage, pre-marital assets being taken to measure intra-household bargaining power. In their examination of US data, Rubalcava and Thomas (2002) find that a woman's options outside her marriage, as proxied by the generosity of aid to families with dependent children (AFDC) benefits in her state of residence, appear to influence her bargaining power with consequences for intra-household resource allocation. Lastly, using assets at the time of marriage as measures of bargaining power, Quisumbing and Maluccio (2003) reject the unitary model of the household in data from Bangladesh, Ethiopia, Indonesia, and South Africa.

It is clear, therefore, that tests of the unitary model against collective models of households have consisted of the investigation of links between, on the one hand, plausible measures of household members' bargaining power and, on the other, either household demand for certain goods and services, such as health care and food, or the consequences thereof, such as children's health outcomes. Quisumbing and Maluccio (2003) aptly note it is imperative that the tests employ exogenous measures of bargaining power. Accordingly, Hoddinott's and Haddad's (1995) measure of women's bargaining power as the share of household income earned by women may not be suitable since earned or labour income reflects time allocation decisions that may be the outcomes of bargaining. In other words, the share of household income earned by women may be correlated with the unobserved aspects of bargaining power that make up part of the error term in a regression of household expenditure patterns against women's income share. Other tests have adopted the intra-household distribution of unearned income (e.g. Schultz 1990), or of the ownership of inherited or pre-marital assets (e.g. Thomas *et al.* 2002), as their measure of bargaining power. While it is more likely to be exogenous than earned income, unearned income too may be endogenous if it derives from assets accumulated by the means of earned income. Neither are inherited or pre-marital assets unambiguously exogenous. For instance, if parents follow the compensatory strategy of bequeathing more to less able children, and ability is correlated with post-marital bargaining power, inherited assets shall be endogenous. Marriage market selection poses difficulties as well. For example, a study that finds a positive relation between mother's schooling and children's educational outcomes would be wrong in concluding that this owes to the increased resources for children's education being wrested from the household budget by means of the greater bargaining power of a more educated mother, if the children's favourable educational outcomes are due instead to the father's unobserved taste for educated children, the very taste that drove him to take an educated wife (Foster 2002). Only measures of bargaining power related to state supplied resources such as the child allowance in the UK investigated by Lundberg *et al.* (1997) are likely to be unambiguously exogenous. Such natural experiments are, however, rare. This study must therefore adopt measures of the relative status of women that are not indisputably exogenous.

Following Smith *et al.* (2004), the measures chosen are: an indicator of whether a woman is working for cash income, her age at first marriage, the per cent age difference between a woman and her spouse, and the difference between their years of education. Following Schultz (1990) and Thomas (1990), women's intra-household status is in addition measured by the unearned income from remittances accruing to a household's women. It is acceded that none of these five measures is unambiguously exogenous. A woman's decision to work for cash income may, in fact, be the outcome of bargaining. A woman's age at first marriage, the per cent age difference between herself and her spouse, and the difference between their years of education may be endogenous because of marriage market selection. Income from remittances too might be endogenous if, for example, a neglected woman in an unequal marriage were more likely to receive material assistance from her natal family.

Children's food security is assessed by anthropometric measures of nutrition, as well as by means of the examination of household expenditures. Data from the 1991 Pakistan Integrated Household Survey (PIHS) yield a measure of evidence of a positive relation between women's intra-household status and children's food security.

5.2 Data and Empirical Methodology

The study's empirical analyses are performed upon data from the PIHS, conducted by the World Bank and the Federal Bureau of Statistics of Pakistan in 1991 as part of the Living Standards Measurement Survey (LSMS) series of the Human Resources Division of the World Bank. The survey covered 4,800 households in 300 communities divided equally between rural and urban areas. The data are rich in personal, household, and community descriptors. These readily permit computation of the aforementioned measures of women's intra-household status, namely, an indicator of whether a woman is working for cash income, her age at first marriage, the per cent age difference between the woman and her spouse, the difference between their years of education, and the income from remittances received by a household's women.

In the parlance of bargaining models, a woman's earned income is positively related to her reservation or threshold utility, that is, to her options outside marriage. Hence, minimum resource allocations to her must increase in her earned income. Further, a woman who works outside her home may, from wider social contact, build extra-familial support networks as well as become exposed to progressive norms of behaviour. She may thus turn more assertive at home. A woman's age at first marriage is considered linked to her status since the earlier a woman marries, the less likely she is to complete schooling and embark upon an income earning career. Further, Pakistani women often enter a cloistered world upon marriage (the phrase 'char divari' or 'four walls' has been used to describe the circumscribed world of married women in Pakistan) and so it is conceivable that a woman who marries young will have had fewer opportunities to forge external support networks. The age difference between a woman and her spouse too may be relevant to her bargaining power. It is likely that the larger[1] the age difference, the higher the woman's status. Since it is plausible that a given age difference is less consequential the older the couple, the variable is calculated as the difference between the ages of a woman and her spouse expressed as a percentage of her spouse's age. Similarly, since education pertains to earning capacity and, hence, to options outside marriage, it is likely that the larger the difference between the educational attainments of a woman and her spouse, the higher her status and bargaining power. Finally, unearned income from remittances accruing to a household's women is considered related to their intra-household bargaining power. Since the income is unearned, it is less likely to be the outcome of bargaining than earned income, and as it is received by women, it is possible they have more control over its allocation. Kishor (2000) considers measures of women's bargaining power to be of three types: those that give direct evidence of such power, such as an index of women's participation in household decisionmaking; those that are sources of such power, such as employment and income; and those that characterize the setting or background of the power, such as the age and education differences between spouses. By this taxonomy, the first two and the fifth of this study's measures of women's status are 'source' indicators, whereas the third and fourth measures are 'setting' indicators.

The empirical strategy is twofold. First, the relation between women's status and children's food security is examined by the means of regressions of 0 to 5-year old children's height-for-age, weight-for-height, and weight-for-age anthropometric nutritional Z-scores, against a variety of explanatory variables including measures of women's status. The height-for-age Z-score, which measures 'stunting', is a gauge of children's long-term nutritional status. The weight-for-height Z-score, which measures 'wasting', is a gauge of children's shorter-term nutritional status. The weight-for-age Z-score, a combination of weight-for-height and height-for-age and the most common measure of

[1] Given that wives are typically younger than their husbands, 'larger' mostly translates as 'less negative'.

children's nutritional status, is used to assess if a child is underweight. The regression equations may be specified as:

$$haz = \alpha_1.Mawork + \alpha_2.Agemar + \alpha_3.Agediff + \alpha_4.Educdiff + \alpha_5.Remitinc + X'\beta_1 + e_1, \quad (5.1)$$

$$whz = \gamma_1.Mawork + \gamma_2.Agemar + \gamma_3.Agediff + \gamma_4.Educdiff + \gamma_5.Remitinc + X'\beta_2 + e_2. \quad (5.2)$$

and

$$waz = \delta_1.Mawork + \delta_2.Agemar + \delta_3.Agediff + \delta_4.Educdiff + \delta_5.Remitinc + X'\beta_3 + e_3, \quad (5.3)$$

where *haz*, *whz*, and *waz* denote, respectively, a child's height-for-age, weight-for-height, and weight-for-age anthropometric Z-scores, *Mawork* is an indicator of whether the child's mother worked for wages in the preceding twelve months or currently operates a household enterprise, *Agemar* is the mother's age at first marriage, *Agediff* is the age difference between the mother and child's father expressed as a percentage of the father's age, *Educdiff* is the difference between their years of formal education, *Remitinc* is the sum of remittances received in the past 12 months by the women in the child's household, *X* is a vector of other plausible correlates of children's anthropometric nutritional status, and e_i, $i = 1, 2, 3$, the error terms, signify unobserved random influences. (5.1), (5.2), and (5.3) may be estimated by OLS. The finding that the estimated coefficients of the five measures of women's status are positive and the variables significant would yield the conclusion that women's bargaining power and children's food security in Pakistan are positively related. Note, given that sampling in Living Standards Measurement Surveys is clustered, it is likely that multiple children are sampled from the very same cluster or village and, hence, probable that there is intra-cluster correlation in the regression errors, e_i, $i = 1, 2, 3$. Adjustment of the OLS generated standard errors is, therefore, necessary.

Next, household budgets are scrutinized to identify expenditure items that are plausibly related to children's food security. It may be argued, for example, that since mainly children consume milk, household spending on milk is positively related to children's food security. The difficulty, however, is that milk is not consumed exclusively by children. Indeed, it is near impossible to pick food items consumed solely by children in LDC household budgetary data. On the other hand, goods consumed solely by adults, such as tobacco, adult clothing, and adult footwear, are readily identified. Hence, why not draw inferences about children's food security from budget shares devoted to adult goods? *Ceteris paribus*, an increase in household budget shares devoted to goods consumed exclusively by adults ought to decrease children's food security. This argument draws upon the logic employed by Deaton (1989) in his study of intra-household gender discrimination. Hence, women's status may be inferred to be positively related to children's food security if improvement in women's status causes reduction in household budget shares devoted to adult goods. This may be tested via the augmented Working-Leser specification for Engel curves,

$$w = \alpha + \beta.\log(x/n) + \gamma.\log n + \lambda_1.(n04/n) + \lambda_2.(n59/n) + \lambda_3.(n1014/n) + \mu_1.Mawork + \mu_2.Agemar + \mu_3.Agediff + \mu_4.Educdiff + \mu_5.Remitinc + Z'\pi + u, \quad (5.4)$$

estimable by OLS, where w is the share of a household's budget devoted to the easily identified adult goods of tobacco, adult clothing, and adult footwear, x is total household expenditure, n is household size, *n04*, *n59*, and *n1014* denote, respectively, the number of the household's children in the age groups 0–4, 5–9, and 10–14, the first four measures of women's status now pertain to the male household head's spouse, Z is a vector of other plausible correlates of the share of the household's budget devoted to adult goods, and u is the regression error. The finding that the estimated coefficients of the measures of women's status are negative and the variables significant may be considered evidence of a positive relation between women's status and children's food security in Pakistan.

Since Equations (5.1)–(5.3) are to be estimated upon data wherein the unit of observation is a child, whereas Equation (5.4) is to be estimated upon data wherein the unit of observation is a household, two separate samples, termed for the remainder of the paper as the 'anthropometrics sample' and the 'adult goods sample', are extracted from the PIHS. The anthropometrics sample consists of 3,718 children. Table 5.1 presents the sample mean values of the relevant variables. The adult goods sample consists of 3,745 households. Table 5.2 presents the sample mean values of the pertinent variables.

Approximately half of the children included in the anthropometrics sample are male. The average age among these 0–5-year-olds is near 2 years and 4 months. About 54.8 per cent of the children are from rural households. Approximately 14.5 per cent of the children sampled have mothers who either worked for wages in the preceding 12 months or currently operate household enterprises. The average age at first marriage among mothers was about 17.5 years. On average, mothers have about 2.9 fewer years of schooling than fathers. Moreover, they are on average about 14.7 per cent younger than the children's fathers. Average annual income from remittances per household is about 254.9 rupees of which about 88.4 rupees accrue to women.

Slightly more than half of the households included in the adult goods sample are rural. On average, households in the sample spend about 7.4 per cent of their budgets upon the three adult goods of tobacco, adult clothing, and

Table 5.1. Sample means: anthropometrics sample ($n = 3{,}718$)

Variable	Sample mean
Dependent variables	
Height-for-age Z-score (*haz*)	−1.87
Weight-for-height Z-score (*whz*)	−0.40
Weight-for-age Z-score (*waz*)	−1.37
Child attributes	
Child is male	0.50
Child's age in years	2.26
Father's years of schooling	4.12
Father's age in years	35.61
Mother's age in years	29.83
Household attributes	
Natural log of household per capita annual expenditure	8.15
Actual household per capita annual expenditure in rupees (Rs.)	3463.38
Natural log of household size	2.19
Actual household size	8.94
Household net worth in thousands of Rs.	227.76
Remittances received in past 12 months by household in Rs.	254.95
Household has no unshared source of drinking water	0.12
Household has no drainage	0.86
Household uses a community latrine	0.03
Household has no garbage disposal	0.64
Distance to closest medical facility in km	3.19
Multi-generational household	0.53
Rural household	0.55
Resident of Punjab Province	0.52
Resident of Sind Province	0.23
Resident of NWF Province	0.18
Key variables	
Child's mother worked for cash income in past 12 months	0.15
Age in years at first marriage of child's mother	17.45
Mother's years of schooling less father's years of schooling	−2.89
Per cent age difference between mother and father	−14.72
Remittances received in past 12 months by household women in Rs.	88.42

adult footwear. About 16 per cent of the wives[2] of household heads either worked for wages in the preceding 12 months or currently operate household enterprises. The average age at first marriage among these women was about 17.5 years. They have on average about 2.4 fewer years of schooling than their husbands. Further, they are on average about 14.3 per cent younger than their husbands. Average annual income from remittances per household is about 318.5 rupees of which about 128 rupees accrue to women.

5.3 Empirical Findings

Table 5.3 presents estimates of Equations (5.1)–(5.3). Boys in Pakistan appear significantly less nourished than girls by the weight-for-age anthropometric

[2] In the event a household head has multiple wives, the eldest is considered the reference wife.

Table 5.2. Sample means: adult goods sample (n = 3,745)

Variable	Sample mean
Dependent variable	
Percentage of household budget expended upon adult goods	7.40
Household attributes	
Natural log of household per capita annual expenditure	8.29
Actual household per capita annual expenditure in rupees (Rs.)	3983.83
Natural log of household size	1.94
Actual household size	6.96
Percentage of household in 0–4 age group	14.98
Percentage of household in 5–9 age group	15.78
Percentage of household in 10–14 age group	11.90
Household head's years of schooling	3.50
Household head's age in years	45.78
Age in years of wife of household head	39.08
Household net worth in thousands of rupees (Rs.)	232.27
Remittances received in past 12 months by household in Rs.	318.52
Multi-generational household	0.42
Rural household	0.52
Resident of Punjab Province	0.53
Resident of Sind Province	0.27
Resident of NWF Province	0.14
Key variables	
Wife of household head worked for cash income in past 12 months	0.16
Age in years at first marriage of wife of household head	17.50
Difference in years of schooling between wife and household head	−2.43
Per cent age difference between wife and household head	−14.26
Remittances received in past 12 months by household women in Rs.	128.04

nutritional measure, that is, boys seem more likely to be underweight. This is consistent with the findings of, e.g., Das Gupta (1987), that the male–female calorie intake ratio was less than one in the 0–1 age group in rural Punjab, India, and Walker and Ryan (1990), that more boys than girls of preschool (1–6) and school age (7–12) were poorly nourished on a standard of weight-for-age in six Southern Indian villages. Older children appear significantly less nourished by all three nutritional standards. Children's nutrition by the height-for-age measure increases in paternal education. Nutrition by the height-for-age and weight-for-age measures increases in household per capita annual expenditure. Since children's anthropometric nutritional status depends not only upon the ingestion of nutrients but also upon household sanitation and the availability of health care, the regressors include measures of sanitation as well as the distance in kilometres to the nearest medical facility. It appears households without their own latrine have less nourished children by the weight-for-height and weight-for-age standards.

Maternal status as measured by women's earning of cash income is significantly positively related to children's nutrition by the weight-for-height and weight-for-age standards. Maternal status as measured by the difference

Table 5.3. Determinants of 0–5-year-old children's anthropometric nutritional status: OLS estimates

Variable	Coefficients		
	haz stunted	*whz* wasted	*waz* underweight
Constant	−3.96*** (−5.06)	0.46 (0.22)	−2.09 (−1.51)
Child attributes			
Child is male	−0.08 (−1.01)	−0.25 (−1.27)	−0.29** (−2.34)
Child's age in years	−0.17*** (−5.42)	−0.16*** (−2.72)	−0.11*** (−2.60)
Father's years of schooling	0.12*** (6.34)	−0.01 (−0.31)	0.04 (1.54)
Father's age in years	−0.001 (−0.07)	0.10 (0.71)	0.09 (0.90)
Mother's age in years	0.04 (1.50)	−0.13 (−0.77)	−0.10 (−0.81)
Household attributes			
Natural log of household per capita annual expenditure	0.21*** (2.75)	0.05 (0.28)	0.21* (1.86)
Natural log of household size	−0.05 (−0.36)	0.17 (0.55)	0.03 (0.15)
Household net worth in thousands of Rs.	−0.00 (−0.59)	0.00 (0.57)	0.00 (0.18)
Remittances received in past 12 months by household in Rs.	0.00 (0.10)	−0.00 (−1.19)	−0.00 (−0.82)
Household has no unshared source of drinking water	−0.04 (−0.20)	0.24 (0.61)	0.08 (0.40)
Household has no drainage	−0.07 (−0.49)	−0.04 (−0.14)	−0.08 (−0.37)
Household uses a community latrine	0.23 (1.50)	−0.66*** (−2.73)	−0.29* (−1.74)
Household has no garbage disposal	−0.06 (−0.55)	−0.07 (−0.29)	−0.11 (−0.64)
Distance to closest medical facility in km	0.002 (0.37)	−0.005 (−0.62)	−0.002 (−0.33)
Multi-generational household	−0.12 (−1.09)	−0.06 (−0.20)	−0.11 (−0.61)
Rural household	−0.14 (−1.01)	0.18 (0.62)	−0.03 (−0.18)
Resident of Punjab Province	0.32 (1.49)	−0.38 (−1.02)	−0.13 (−0.47)
Resident of Sind Province	−0.09 (−0.30)	0.19 (0.37)	0.00 (0.00)
Resident of NWF Province	0.09 (0.35)	0.34 (0.75)	0.13 (0.47)
Child's mother worked for cash income in past 12 months	−0.01 (−0.05)	0.68* (1.72)	0.46* (1.70)
Age in years at first marriage of child's mother	−0.02 (−1.48)	0.00 (0.00)	−0.01 (−0.58)
Mother's years of schooling less father's years of schooling	0.07*** (3.98)	0.03 (0.91)	0.04* (1.89)
Per cent age difference between mother and father	−0.002 (−0.05)	0.05 (0.65)	0.05 (0.82)
Remittances received in past 12 months by household women in Rs.	0.00 (0.17)	0.00 (0.94)	0.00 (0.98)
R^2	0.06	0.01	0.01
n =		3718	

Notes: Dependent variables: height-for-age (*haz*), weight-for-height (*whz*), and weight-for-age (*waz*) Z-scores. The numbers in parentheses are t-ratios using Huber–White robust standard errors. The superscripts *, **, and *** indicate significance at the 10%, 5%, and 1% levels, respectively.

between the educational attainments of mother and father is significantly positively related to children's nutrition by the height-for-age and weight-for-age standards. In sum, children's long-term nutritional status as measured by the height-for-age standard significantly increases in the difference between the educational attainments of their mother and father, whereas their shorter-term nutritional status as measured by the weight-for-height

Table 5.4. Determinants of household budgetary share expended upon adult goods: OLS estimates

Variable	Coefficient
Constant	−52.77*** (−12.80)
Household attributes	
Natural log of household per capita annual expenditure	6.43*** (13.65)
Natural log of household size	4.05*** (6.75)
Percentage of household in 0–4 age group	−0.03** (−2.00)
Percentage of household in 5–9 age group	−0.03*** (−2.69)
Percentage of household in 10–14 age group	−0.03** (−2.30)
Household head's years of schooling	−0.38*** (−4.86)
Household head's age in years	−0.22*** (−2.64)
Age in years of wife of household head	0.18* (1.91)
Household net worth in thousands of rupees (Rs.)	−0.001*** (−3.12)
Remittances received in past 12 months by household in Rs.	0.00 (0.50)
Multi-generational household	−0.48 (−1.01)
Rural household	−1.10** (−2.31)
Resident of Punjab Province	5.05*** (5.01)
Resident of Sind Province	1.72 (1.62)
Resident of NWF Province	2.21* (1.88)
Key variables	
Wife of household head worked for cash income in past 12 months	2.16*** (4.63)
Age in years at first marriage of wife of household head	−0.02 (−0.36)
Difference in years of schooling between wife and household head	−0.18** (−2.52)
Per cent age difference between wife and household head	−0.11** (−2.48)
Remittances received in past 12 months by household women in Rs.	−0.00 (−0.36)
R^2	0.15
n =	3745

Notes: Dependent variable: percentage of household budget expended upon adult goods. The numbers in parentheses are t-ratios using Huber–White robust standard errors. The superscripts *, **, and *** indicate significance at the 10%, 5%, and 1% levels, respectively.

standard significantly improves upon their mother working for cash income. Further, children are significantly less likely to be underweight the greater the difference between the educational attainments of their mother and father, and when their mother works for cash income.

Table 5.4 presents estimates of Equation (5.4). The share of a household's budget expended upon the three adult goods of tobacco, adult clothing, and adult footwear appears significantly positively related to the natural logs of household per capita annual expenditure and size. It is clear that the higher the proportion of a household's members in the 0–14 age group, the lower its budget share devoted to adult goods. Given the costs of child rearing, an increase in the proportion of dependent children naturally reduces the share of resources expendable upon adult goods. The share of a household's budget applied to adult goods decreases in the educational attainment of its head. Perhaps this is because a more educated household head is better aware of the critical role of resource allocations to children in human development. It appears wealthier households devote smaller proportions of their budgets to tobacco, adult clothing, and adult footwear as do rural households. Households in the Punjab and in the North West Frontier Province devote larger shares of their budgets to adult goods than do households in Balochistan, the omitted category.

Women's status as measured by the difference between the educational attainments of the wife and household head is significantly negatively related to the share of the household's budget expended upon adult goods, as is women's intra-household status as gauged by the per cent age difference between wife and household head. As argued, this may be considered evidence of a positive relation between women's status and allocations to children. Even the age at first marriage of a household head's wife is negatively related to the share of the household's budget applied to adult goods, though the variable is statistically insignificant. Curiously, the earning of cash income by a household head's wife *raises* the share of the household's budget applied to adult goods. Perhaps working women must increase spending on workplace attire and footwear. There is evidence,[3] however, that more is spent on tobacco as well. Given that mainly men consume tobacco in Pakistan, perhaps working women have less than utter discretion over their earnings. In sum, two of the five measures of women's status may be considered significantly positively correlated with resources allocated to children. Since the bulk of poor households' resources are spent on food, it is likely that more resources allocated to children shall improve their food security.

5.4 Conclusion

This study aims to discover whether improvement in women's intra-household status relative to men raises children's food security in Pakistan, and, therefore, whether bargaining is the mechanism of intra-household resource allocation. Data from the 1991 PIHS yield a measure of evidence of a link between women's status and children's food security. It is found that the more educated a child's mother relative to her father, the better her long-term nutritional status as measured by the height-for-age standard. Further, the earning of cash income by mothers improves children's shorter-term nutritional status as measured by the weight-for-height standard. Additionally, children's weight-for-age anthropometric nutritional Z-scores increase in these two measures of mothers' status. It is also found that women's status as gauged by the difference between the educational attainments of his wife and household head, and the per cent age difference between them, is significantly negatively related to the share of the household's budget expended upon the

[3] Available upon request.

three adult goods of tobacco, adult clothing, and adult footwear. This suggests that resources allocated to children and, by plausible implication, their food security increase in these two measures of women's intra-household status. The chapter's findings of a positive relation between measures of women's intra-household status and children's food security may be taken to imply that households are not monolithic units but that bargaining is the mechanism of intra-household allocation.

References

Becker, G. A. (1965). 'A Theory of the Allocation of Time'. *Economic Journal*, 75 (299): 493–517.

—— (1981). *A Treatise on the Family*. Cambridge, MA: Harvard University Press.

Das Gupta, M. (1987). 'Selective Discrimination against Female Children in Rural Punjab, India'. *Population and Development Review*, 13 (1): 77–100.

Deaton, A. (1989). 'Looking for Boy–Girl Discrimination in Household Expenditure Data'. *World Bank Economic Review*, 3 (1): 1–15.

Foster, A. D. (2002). 'Marriage-Market Selection and Human Capital Allocations in Rural Bangladesh'. Philadelphia: Economics Department, University of Pennsylvania. Mimeo.

Haddad, L., J. Hoddinott, and H. Alderman (eds) (1997). *Intrahousehold Resource Allocation in Developing Countries: Methods, Models, and Policy*. Baltimore, MD: Johns Hopkins University Press for IFPRI.

Handa, S. (1996). 'Expenditure Behaviour and Children's Welfare: An Analysis of Female Headed Households in Jamaica'. *Journal of Development Economics*, 50 (1): 165–87.

Hoddinott, J., and L. Haddad (1995). 'Does Female Income Share Influence Household Expenditures? Evidence from Côte d'Ivoire'. *Oxford Bulletin of Economics and Statistics*, 57 (1): 77–95.

Kishor, S. (2000). 'Empowerment of Women in Egypt and Links to the Survival and Health of Their Infants', in H. Pressler and G. Sen (eds), *Women's Empowerment and Demographic Processes*. Oxford: Oxford University Press.

Levin, C. E., M. T. Ruel, and S. S. Morris (1999). 'Working Women in an Urban Setting: Traders, Vendors and Food Security in Accra'. *World Development*, 27 (11): 1977–91.

Lundberg, S. J., R. A. Pollak, and T. J. Wales (1997). 'Do Husbands and Wives Pool Their Resources?: Evidence from the United Kingdom Child Benefit'. *Journal of Human Resources*, 32 (1): 463–80.

Mahmood, M. A. (2002). 'Determinants of Neonatal and Post-neonatal Mortality in Pakistan'. *Pakistan Development Review*, 41 (4): 723–44.

Mahmood, N. (2002). 'Women's Role in Domestic Decision-Making in Pakistan: Implications for Reproductive Behaviour'. *Pakistan Development Review*, 41 (2): 121–48.

Pelletier, D. L., E. A. Frongillo, Jr., D. G. Schroeder, and J. P. Habicht (1995). 'The Effects of Malnutrition on Child Mortality in Developing Countries'. *Bulletin of the World Health Organization*, 73 (4): 443–8.

Pitt, M. M., and S. Khandker (1998). 'The Impact of Group-Based Credit Programs on Poor Households in Bangladesh: Does the Gender of Participants Matter?'. *Journal of Political Economy*, 106 (5): 958–96.

Quisumbing, A. R., and J. A. Maluccio (2003). 'Resources at Marriage and Intrahousehold Allocation: Evidence from Bangladesh, Ethiopia, Indonesia, and South Africa'. *Oxford Bulletin of Economics and Statistics*, 65 (3): 283–327.

Rubalcava, L., and D. Thomas (2002). 'Family Bargaining and Welfare'. Santa Monica: RAND. Mimeo.

Schultz, T. P. (1990). 'Testing the Neoclassical Model of Family Labour Supply and Fertility'. *The Journal of Human Resources*, 25 (4): 599–634.

Smith, L. C., and L. Haddad (2000). 'Explaining Child Malnutrition in Developing Countries: A Cross-Country Analysis'. Research Report 111. Washington, DC: IFPRI.

—— U. Ramakrishnan, A. Ndiaye, L. Haddad, and R. Martorell (2004). 'The Importance of Women's Status for Child Nutrition in Developing Countries'. Research Report 131. Washington, DC: IFPRI.

Thomas, D. (1990). 'Intra-Household Resource Allocation: An Inferential Approach'. *The Journal of Human Resources*, 25: 635–64.

—— D. Contreras, and E. Frankenberg (2002). 'Distribution of Power Within the Household and Child Health'. Santa Monica: RAND. Mimeo.

Walker, T. S., and J. G. Ryan (1990). *Village and Household Economies in India's Semi-Arid Tropics*. Baltimore, MD: Johns Hopkins University Press.

World Health Organization (WHO) (1983). *Measuring Change in Nutritional Status*. Geneva: WHO.

6

The Changing Pattern of Undernutrition in India: A Comparative Analysis Across Regions

Brinda Viswanathan and J. V. Meenakshi

6.1 Introduction

The proportion of the population that is undernourished has been used as one of the main indicators of poverty. Quoting Osmani (1992: 1):

> Being poor almost always means being deprived of full nutritional capabilities, i.e., the capabilities to avoid premature mortality, to live a life free of avoidable morbidity, and to have the energy for work and leisure. The study of poverty is, therefore, very much a study of the people's state of nutrition.

The study of the 'state of nutrition' is attracting increasing attention precisely because undernourishment is not a problem of low incomes alone, although most undernourished people live in poorer countries. However, not all the variation in undernourishment can be explained by income. Indeed, trends in the prevalence of undernourishment may even move in a direction opposite to that suggested by income poverty; a good case in point is India, as elaborated in this study. This is despite the fact that in India, as in many

We thank the seminar participants at the Development Convention, Chennai; NSS Golden Jubilee Seminar, New Delhi; 38th Indian Econometric Society Conference, Chennai; Workshop on Poverty Measurement, Monitoring, and Evaluation, New Delhi; and UNU-WIDER for useful comments. The paper has benefited greatly from the valuable suggestions of Tony Addison, Basudeb Guha-Khasnobis, Anthony Shorrocks, A. Vaidyanathan and, Guanghua Wan. Part of this work was carried out while the first author was visiting UNU-WIDER and she would like to thank WIDER for providing financial support and a stimulating research environment. We would like to thank Priya Bhalla for her excellent work as research assistant.

other countries, the poverty lines established to quantify income poverty were initially anchored to a caloric norm.

The early contributions to the literature were in the form of estimates of the calorie–income elasticity: for instance, for India, household level data have been used to estimate the calorie–income elasticity by Behrman and Deolalikar (1987); Subramanian and Deaton (1996); Roy (2001); and Viswanathan and Meenakshi (2003). However, most studies do not explicitly focus on the relationship between the prevalence of undernourishment and income. Our own earlier work was among the first to focus on this issue for the rural sector in India (Meenakshi and Viswanathan 2005). The present study extends this work to include related aspects such as income inequality and diet quality: further, it extends the comparison to include urban households.[1]

The present study attempts to describe the pattern of undernourishment in India, disaggregated by state and rural/urban sector, and in the factors associated with these changes. It also attempts to contextualize undernourishment in India in comparison with that in other countries. The underlying objective is to understand the level of and trends in food insecurity in India, at a time when the country has experienced higher economic growth and an improvement in various social indicators.

In measuring undernourishment, we use a household-specific calorie norm, which takes into account the age and gender composition of the household. We believe this to be a superior means of measuring the prevalence of undernourishment, when food intake data are available at the household- (but not individual-) level.

The chapter is organized as follows. Section 6.2 describes the dataset and methodology and section 6.3 compares undernourishment in India with that found across other developing countries. Section 6.4 presents evidence on the prevalence of undernourishment and on how sensitive the magnitudes are to the alternative measures that we propose. Section 6.5 focuses on inequality in energy intakes and how these have changed over time. Section 6.6 considers the relationship between intakes and income, while section 6.7 discusses whether there may be a tradeoff between the intake levels and dietary quality; section 6.8 provides the conclusions.

[1] There is other literature that considers the relationship between incomes and nutritional outcomes, which encompass a broader measure of development. It is the focus of studies such as those by Osmani (1997); Haddad *et al.* (2003); and Svedberg (2004). These studies suggest that some reduction in adverse outcomes can be brought about at lower levels of income growth; and highlight the role of environmental pollution, sanitation, female literacy and presence of a well functioning primary health care system under well-targeted schemes in achieving improvement in nutritional outcomes.

6.2 Data and Methodology

6.2.1 *Data*

The analysis is based on Indian household level (unit record) data from consumer expenditure surveys of the National Sample Survey Organization (NSSO) for the years 1983 (38th round), 1993/94 (50th round) and 1999/2000 (55th round). For two of the years, 1983 and 1999/2000, the unit record data reported energy intakes at the household level. For 1993/94, we computed these following the same procedure as used by the NSSO: that is, by multiplying food intakes with their calorie content using food composition tables as given in GOI (1996).[2] The study focuses on fifteen major states in rural and urban India and compares the variations between the states and sectors over time.

Where comparisons across countries are made, we use the dietary energy supply as reported by the Food and Agricultural Organization (FAO) using food balance sheets (FBS). For the more detailed analysis of Indian data, however, we use the NSSO's consumer expenditure surveys. This is because the FBS data are not disaggregated by rural/urban residence, by state, or by income group. The FBS data reflect energy availability (and, as the name implies, are calculated as disappearance from production), whereas the NSSO data capture consumption at the household level. The household surveys do not, however, canvass intakes of individuals within the household, although details of the demographic composition of the household are available.

6.2.2 *Methodology*

The prevalence of undernourishment (henceforth POU) is simply the head-count percentage of persons whose energy intakes are below a pre-specified norm. That is, given reported caloric intake (C_h) and the recommended intake level, or norm (Z),

$$POU = \frac{1}{N}\sum_{h=1}^{n} I_h w_h \qquad (6.1)$$

where, $I_h = 1$ if $C_h < Z$ and zero otherwise; n is the number of households sampled, and $N = \sum_{h=1}^{n} w_h$ is the estimated population; w_h is the sampling weight associated with the hth household.[3]

In computing these headcount ratios, we follow two approaches. The first is to use the familiar per capita norm with a 2,400 calories per day cutoff

[2] As a consistency check, we replicated results for a subset of states in 1999/2000.

[3] Note that for household-level data, w_h is defined as the household-level multiplier × household size.

recommended by the Indian Council of Medical Research (ICMR) for rural India, and a lower 2,100 norm that is recommended for urban India. Thus, C_h is defined in per capita terms as household caloric intakes divided by the household size, and Z is either the 2,400 or 2,100 norm, depending on whether the household is located in a rural or an urban area. We term this the ICMR POU.

We propose and use a second approach, one that recognizes that there are gender and age specificities to energy requirements, and exploits the demographic information contained in the NSSO household surveys. In this alternative computation, Z is replaced by Z_h in (6.1). That is, we first compute household-specific norm (Z_h) and compare *household* intakes (rather than per capita intakes) with this norm (for more details, see Meenakshi and Viswanathan 2005). Thus $I_h = 1$ if $C_h < Z_h$ and zero otherwise. As in the earlier case, h indexes households. The sampling weight (w_h) (as mentioned before) is used to calculate the percentage of *persons* living in households with insufficient intakes, thereby enabling a direct comparison of the two POUs. This modification, necessitated by the absence of data on consumption by individuals within the households, represents an attempt to capture the impact of demographic composition, and changes in this structure, on the prevalence of undernourishment. We term this the DMG POU.

The age- and gender-norms used in this computation are taken from Gopalan *et al.* (2000) and are as follows for urban (rural) areas:

$$\begin{aligned} Z_h = {} & n_{1h}{}^*713 + n_{2h}{}^*1240 + n_{3h}{}^*1690 + n_{4h}{}^*1950 + b_{1h}{}^*2190 + b_{2h}{}^*2450 \\ & + b_{3h}{}^*2640 + g_{1h}{}^*1970 + g_{2h}{}^*2060 + g_{3h}{}^*2060 + am_h{}^*2425(2875) \\ & + af_h{}^*1875(2225). \end{aligned} \qquad (6.2)$$

Where the variables represent the number of members in different gender and age groups for a given household h:

n_1 = number of children below 1 year;
n_2 = number of children between 1 and 3 years;
n_3 = number of children between 4 and 6 years;
n_4 = number of children between 7 and 9 years;
$b_1(g_1)$ = number of boys (girls) between 10 and 12 years;
$b_2(g_2)$ = number of boys (girls) between 13 and 15 years;
$b_3(g_3)$ = number of boys (girls) between 16 and 18 years, and
$am\ (af)$ = number of men (women) above 18 years.

This formulation uses the assumption of *sedentary* life styles in urban areas; for the rural formulation we use the recommended dietary intake levels for *moderate* activity status (as indicated within parentheses). Note that this affects the coefficients associated with adult males and females only.

This alternative DMG POU approach is related to—but different from—the use of adult-equivalent units to scale consumption. The practice with using adult equivalents is to compute the number of consumer units in each household (e.g. an adult man is assigned a weight of 1, an adult woman: 0.77, and so on), and to divide household energy intake by the number of consumer units. This per consumer unit intake (which is by construction higher than the per capita intake) is then compared with a norm of 2,700 (for India). The approach being followed in this chapter is different: it computes a household-specific norm; that is, the norm itself varies from household to household. We believe this to be a more sensitive measure of the numbers who have inadequate energy intakes.

In computing the household-specific norm, we use the recommended dietary allowance (RDA). This is in contrast to the recent literature that has argued for a change in the way that the prevalence of undernourishment is measured. It is now argued that the use of RDA to measure population prevalence is likely to overstate the number of undernourished, as the RDA is defined to be the level at which there is 97.5 per cent probability that an *individual's* nutrient requirements are met. Instead, the use of estimated energy requirement (EER) is recommended; this is typically 20 per cent lower than the RDA (see Barr *et al.* 2003 and Murphy *et al.* 2002).

While this may be applicable for the ICMR POU approach, for the alternative method that we propose, which compares a household's energy intake with the household's requirement, we continue to use the RDA as this is the more appropriate measure given the level of disaggregation used in the computation. We also continue to use the RDA-based cutoffs for the ICMR POU, in order to maintain comparability across measures. We also note here (but do not discuss) the parallel literature that focuses on the methodological issues related to measurement of insufficiency in energy intakes; see Kakwani (1992); Palmer-Jones and Sen (2001); and Vaidyanathan (2002).

6.3 Comparing India with Other Developing Nations

Before examining in detail the pattern of change in energy intakes in India, it is useful to compare the prevalence of undernourishment in India with that in other developing countries. The FBS of the FAO provide the basis for such a comparison although the FBS provides dietary energy supply rather than actual household consumption in comparison to the NSSO data (as already mentioned in section 6.2). As indicated in Table 6.1 which provides evidence for selected countries, in 1999/2000 average energy availability in India ranked 67th among 173 countries, and were about four-fifths the levels found in China, Argentina or the countries in transition. That is, more than

Table 6.1. Energy availability per capita, and share of cereals in energy availability, in select developing countries 1983/4 to 1999/2000

Country	1983/84		1993/94		1999/2000		Rank in 1999/2000	Country values as proportion of India's intake in 1999/2000
	Total calories	Share (%) of cereal and tubers	Total calories	Share (%) of cereal and tubers	Total calories	Share (%) of cereal and tubers		
Argentina	3048	34.7	3149	33.1	3181	35.0	143	1.28
Bangladesh	2017	85.2	2021	85.1	2140	83.2	26	0.86
Brazil	2623	43.5	2849	37.9	3001	34.2	130	1.20
China	2590	78.5	2792	67.3	2979	60.0	127	1.19
Ghana	1762	65.3	2401	72.7	2597	71.4	79	1.04
India	2206	65.8	2328	63.4	2494	60.6	67	1.00
Indonesia	2367	72.6	2826	69.3	2903	69.5	113	1.16
Korea, DPR	2061	59.4	2230	65.0	2164	67.3	29	0.87
Korea, Rep. of	2949	66.0	2967	52.7	3083	50.0	134	1.24
Malaysia	2705	47.9	2853	43.8	2910	45.7	115	1.17
Mexico	3183	48.9	3141	47.2	3147	47.1	139	1.26
Nepal	2075	81.3	2390	79.6	2434	76.7	61	0.98
Nigeria	1914	58.0	2759	67.2	2779	65.9	103	1.11
Pakistan	2208	57.9	2363	55.4	2459	51.1	64	0.99
Philippines	2130	58.4	2229	56.2	2374	55.4	55	0.95
Rwanda	2260	49.5	2087	48.5	1945	48.2	11	0.78
Sri Lanka	2377	60.6	2218	59.1	2356	56.3	51	0.94
Thailand	2320	65.5	2325	52.9	2456	51.6	63	0.98
Turkey	3314	55.5	3481	53.0	3364	52.9	157	1.35
Viet Nam	2282	82.9	2381	79.2	2486	73.6	65	1.00

Note: Each column is the average for the two years under consideration.

Source: Computed from FBS data of FAOSTAT database, available at www.faostat.fao.org

half the developing countries had prevalence rates of undernourishment that were lower than those of India.

Not only are rates of undernourishment high in India relative to other countries, the Indian NSS data suggest that average caloric intake in India has been declining over time as we elaborate later (although this is not borne out by the FBS data).[4] Note however that this decrease in intakes is not unique

[4] As indicated below, there is a divergence in the mean energy intake figures as reported by the NSSO and the energy supply from FBS: in the 1970s and 1980s the FBS values are lower than the NSS values, but in the 1990s, the NSS estimates are lower.

Energy intake per capita per day in India, FBS and NSSO estimates

	1971/2	1977/8	1983	1993/4	1999/2000
Dietary energy supply (FBS)[a]	2,072	2,085	2,144	2,330	2,494
Caloric intake (NSSO)[b]	2,170	2,370	2,190	2,132	2,283

Sources: [a]FBS (FAO website); [b] cited in Vaidyanathan (2002).

While given the differences in methodology the magnitude of the difference between the two sources may not be considered as very large, the FBS data point to a steady increase in energy

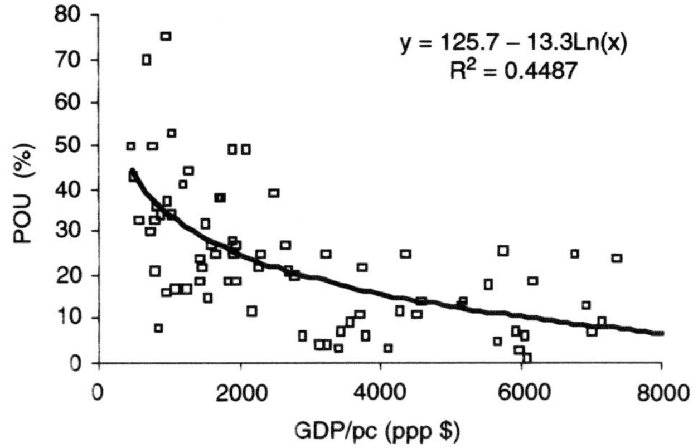

Figure 6.1. Income-POU for 1999/2000 across developing countries

Source: Author's computations based on FBS data from FAOSTAT database, available at www.: foastat.fao.org. GDP data are from World Bank (2003).

to India; the FAO country-profiles data suggest declining intakes for other countries as well, although these surveys are relatively few in number. The limited evidence from the country nutrition profiles of FAO suggests a similar pattern for several countries. For instance, based on consumption expenditure surveys, the average energy intake declined from 2,480 (2,160) kcal in 1984/85 to 2,380 (2,140) in 1987/88 in rural (urban) Pakistan. Similarly based on the national nutritional surveys the per capita average energy intake declined from 2,651 (2,446) in 1982 to 2,294 (2,395) in 1992 in rural (urban) China. Again, these trends are different from the dietary energy supply values as given in the FBS of FAO. That this decline in caloric intakes in India should have happened when average incomes were increasing reinforces the need to study the Indian situation in greater detail. In fact, even in a cross-country comparison, the correlation between per capita gross domestic product (adjusted for PPP in US dollars for countries with values below US$8,000) and POU is not very high (see Figure 6.1). Also, many developing countries have lower POUs but much higher levels of income poverty than India.[5]

supply over time, where as the NSS data indicate an almost secular decline in intakes over time. Svedberg (2000: ch. 7), among others, based on pre-1980s consumption survey data for a few countries, notes that FBS data are usually higher (varying between 10 and 40 per cent) than the consumption surveys and the variation increases with the per capita income of the country. However, this work does not compare trends for a particular country.

[5] We attempted alternative scatter plots relating income and the proportion of underweight children. The correlation is not very high; and is lower still if one considers countries with GDP below PPP US$2,000 per capita. Scatter plots of the prevalence of undernourishment with the proportion of underweight children indicate a higher correlation, but also exhibit a considerable amount of variability across countries. Figures are available from the authors on request.

A decline in intakes need not necessarily be indicative of worsening nutritional wellbeing, provided the fewer calories are compensated by 'better quality' calories. A crude indicator of dietary quality is the share of calories derived from cereals and tubers; the lower the proportion of these starchy staples in the diet, the better its quality. According to FBS data, a decline in this ratio—indicative of an improvement in diet quality—can be seen in over 85 countries worldwide, with the exception of countries in Sub-Saharan Africa. (Note that Table 6.1 presents figures for only a subset of countries, not all countries are reported there.) This decline in the starchy staple ratio between the early 1980s and 1999/2000 is the steepest in some of the newly industrialized economies (NIEs), but is also indicated in all the South Asian countries. The NSSO intake data for India also indicate that the percentage of calories derived from cereals is declining systematically over time, as we note later.

6.4 Trends in the Prevalence of Undernourishment in India

Since the beginning of the 1980s, the per capita GDP in India has grown at an annual rate of 3 per cent. However there were regional differences in terms of both the rate of growth of the state domestic product, as well as the structural composition of growth. Some regions showed larger growth in industry in the 1980s, a pattern which transformed into stagnation in the 1990s, while for other states, the services sector picked up as the manufacturing sector growth showed a decline. Very few states retained agriculture as the largest component of the states' domestic product by 2000 (Shetty 2003), even though per capita food production increased, as did real agricultural wages with inflation rates at fairly low levels. India's human development index (HDI) improved marginally; at the same time, however, inter-state variations in components of HDI seem to have widened (GOI 2001). The states which were growing faster were able to control population growth, improve literacy rates, and reduce infant mortality rates and the proportion of children severely malnourished.

Consider, first, changes in the ICMR POU (Figure 6.2). Note that this measure indicates a high prevalence of undernourishment in the country, much higher indeed than income-based poverty measures would suggest. The ICMR POU is greater than 50 per cent in nearly all states, with undernourishment in urban areas being much lower than in rural areas in most states. Over time, however, the ICMR POU has increased in rural areas, but has declined marginally in the urban areas of most states; this is in contrast to the trends in income poverty, which declined over the same period.[6]

[6] As we show in Meenakshi and Viswanathan (2005, 2003), there is considerable sensitivity of the ICMR POU to the choice of norm used, especially in rural areas, on account of the fact that a considerable mass of the energy intake probability density function is located at around the norm. Indeed, a choice of a cutoff other than the 2,400 (rural) not only affects the magnitude but also the direction of change in the prevalence of *depth of deprivation*.

To what extent might the incorporation of a demographically adjusted norm change these results? The results of this alternative approach, which we term the DMG POU, are also set out in Figure 6.2. The simple demographic adjustment that we propose results in DMG POUs that are much lower than the ICMR POUs, especially in rural areas, where the differences often amount to nearly 10 percentage points. In urban areas, the difference appears to be much smaller, although even here, the difference in some states is as high as 5 percentage points. However, the DMG POU figures continue to be larger than what is indicated by income poverty. Further, both measures yield the same direction of change in the prevalence of undernourishment.

In an alternative formulation, we use the same sedentary activity RDA in computing the household norms for rural areas (results available on request). Not surprisingly, the impact of this change is to reduce prevalence rates in rural areas dramatically, so much so that there is little difference in the prevalence of undernourishment between rural and urban areas. Indeed, if this procedure is adopted, urban undernourishment is higher in many states. Thus the DMG POU is sensitive to the assumption made regarding moderate or sedentary activities in calculating the household norm. Once again, however, there is no change in the trend in the prevalence of undernourishment over time.

To examine whether more generally the ranking of states differs significantly by measure of deprivation used, Table 6.2 presents the rank correlation coefficients between the two measures of POU, income poverty, and related statistics. The rank correlation between the ICMR POU and the DMG POU is above 0.9 in all the three years. Thus while the use of the DMG POU dramatically lowers the headcount per cent of insufficient intakes, the ranking of states is unaltered. Also noteworthy is the lack of correlation between the DMG POU and income poverty, and between the DMG POU and per capita income. As indicated in Table 6.2, while the rank correlation coefficient is positive, it is insignificant except for rural India in 1983. We return to this lack of correlation between income poverty and the POU subsequently.

Interestingly, the DMG-POUs are larger in states where there are fewer children relative to adults. As shown in Table 6.2, the rank correlation between DMG-POU and proportion of children to adults is negative. This is somewhat puzzling since *ceteris paribus* one would expect the per capita energy intakes to be higher in households with a higher proportion of adults. This suggests that the sensitivity of the household energy intakes to changes in demographic structure is much lower than the sensitivity of the household norm; that is, with more adults, household-level intakes increase less than the household's energy requirements.[7]

[7] We are grateful to a referee for pointing this out, s/he further notes that the energy requirements for adult males are quite high relative to that of other members of the household (except boys in the age group of 13–15 and 16–18 years).

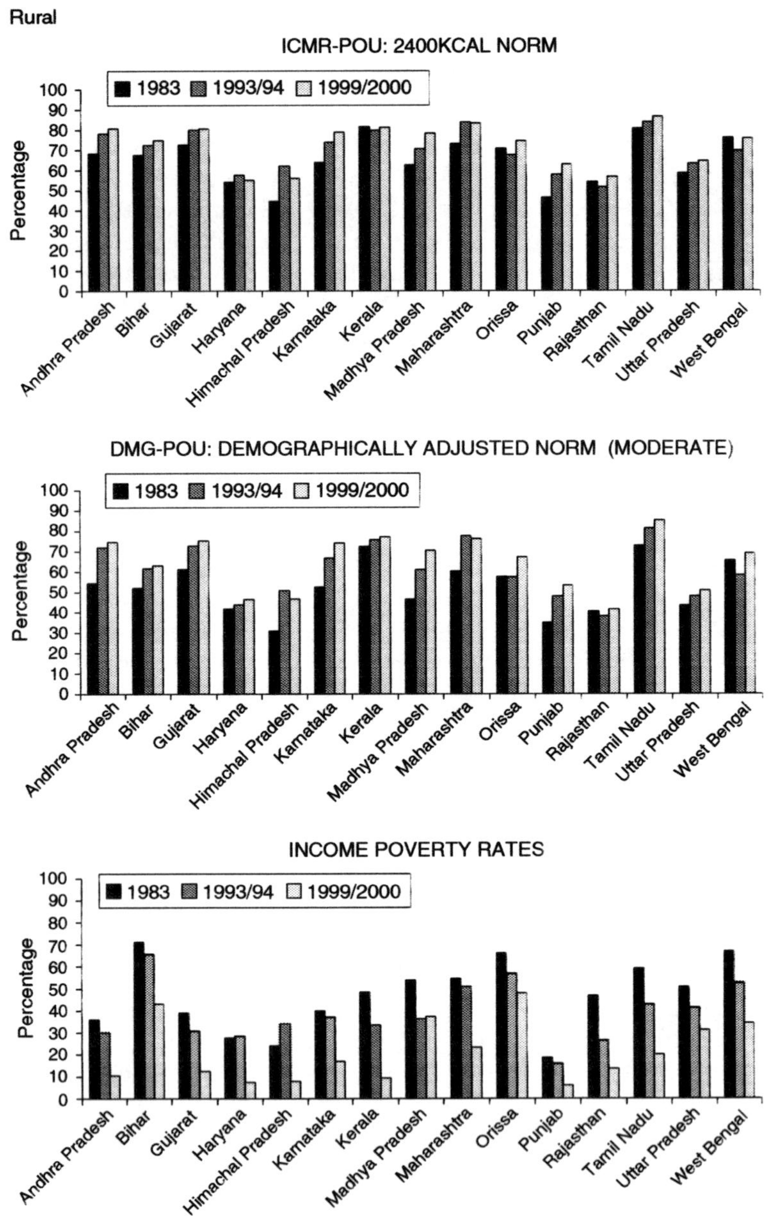

Figure 6.2. Prevalence of undernourishment, alternative norms, and income poverty, 1983, 1993/4, and 1999/2000(%)

Note: (1) ICMR-POU: Prevalance of undernourshment using ICMR recommended norms as discussed in Section 6.2.

(2) DMG-POU: Prevalance of undernourishment using demographically adjusted norms as in Equation (6.2).

(3) The official poverty lines are used for calculating income poverty rates which vary across states and rural and urban areas.

Source: Computed from NSS unit record data for the 38th (1983), 50th (1993/4), and 55th (1999/2000) rounds.

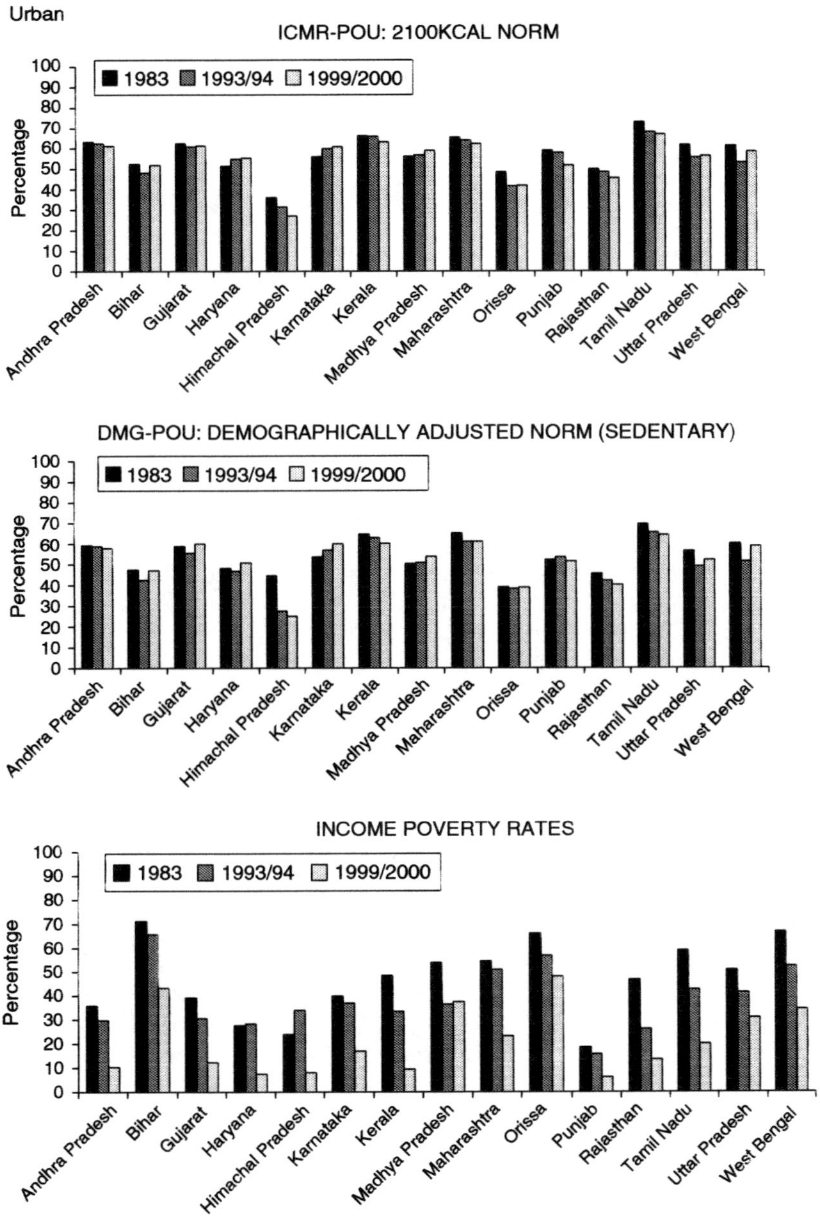

Figure 6.2. (*Continued*)

Table 6.2. Spearman's rank correlation between DMG-POU and select variables

	Child to adult ratio	ICMR-POU	Prop. of income poor	Per capita total expenditure	Cereal share
Rural					
1983	−0.58 (0.02)	0.99 (0.00)	0.56 (0.03)	−0.35 (0.21)	0.34 (0.21)
1993/94	−0.64 (0.009)	0.99 (0.00)	0.36 (0.18)	−0.24 (0.58)	0.08 (0.75)
1999/2000	−0.68 (0.005)	0.97 (0.00)	0.18 (0.52)	−0.08 (0.79)	0.13 (0.71)
Urban					
1983	−0.41 (0.12)	0.96 (0.00)	−0.10 (0.72)	0.19 (0.49)	0.003 (0.98)
1993/94	−0.29 (0.28)	0.97 (0.00)	0.11 (0.70)	0.24 (0.39)	−0.18 (0.52)
1999/2000	−0.40 (0.14)	0.96 (0.00)	0.04 (0.88)	0.39 (0.14)	−0.17 (0.55)

Note: Values in parentheses are *p*-values.

The increase in the POU over time in rural areas is consistent with a decrease in the mean per capita energy intake that is seen in several states, as indicated in Table 6.3. Similarly, the reduction in the POU in urban areas is consistent with increased urban intakes. There are, of course, state-specific trends in that not all the states show the same secular trend as the all India pattern: the terminal period mean intake values are lower than those in initial period for 12 rural states; in urban areas, however, only four states show a similar pattern as all India.

A comparison of the initial and last periods glosses over the interesting changes that appear to have occurred in the intervening years. For example, in some states, while average intakes have declined between 1983 and 1993/94, they appear to have recovered by 1999/2000. This is especially evident in urban areas—among the states which exhibited a decline between 1983 and 1993/94, subsequently, in six states intakes recovered enough to equal or surpass the intake levels of 1983.

Also interesting are the rural–urban comparisons: mean urban intakes were lower in most states in 1983, a result consistent with the largely sedentary urban lifestyles, although the difference was nowhere close to the 300 calorie rural–urban difference in the ICMR norm. Over time, the gap between rural and urban intakes declined; in fact, by 1999/2000 urban intakes were larger than the rural in a majority of the states. This phenomenon itself merits a separate investigation; suffice it to note here that this may be one indication that urban India is headed for the 'double' burden of malnutrition with conditions of overnutrition and undernourishment coexisting. Among the states that continued to have a larger rural intake than urban were the ones with larger share of agriculture in their domestic product compared to the other states.[8]

[8] When the mean intakes are adjusted for demographic changes, the reversal in trend is observed in 1993/4 itself, and in 1999/2000 only two states, Harayana and Punjab, have higher values in rural. These were the only two states which not only have a higher than

Table 6.3. Mean and distribution of per capita calorie intakes across states in rural and urban India, 1983, 1993/4, and 1999/2000

States	Mean (kcal)			Coefficient of variation		
	1983	1993/4	1999/2000	1983	1993/4	1999/2000
Rural						
Andhra Pradesh	2204	2052	2021	0.387	0.321	0.354
Bihar	2190	2115	2121	0.370	0.298	0.629
Gujarat	2110	1994	1986	0.389	0.319	0.297
Haryana	2538	2491	2455	0.462	0.616	0.440
Himachal Pradesh	2613	2325	2454	0.384	0.301	0.533
Karnataka	2260	2073	2028	0.466	0.320	0.460
Kerala	1885	1966	1982	0.450	0.336	0.332
Madhya Pradesh	2324	2165	2062	0.435	0.331	0.463
Maharashtra	2143	1940	2012	0.357	0.482	0.433
Orissa	2103	2199	2119	0.358	0.300	0.281
Punjab	2672	2418	2381	0.464	0.351	0.368
Rajasthan	2434	2470	2425	0.635	0.298	0.364
Tamil Nadu	1861	1884	1826	1.054	0.471	0.396
Uttar Pradesh	2399	2307	2327	0.414	0.343	0.582
West Bengal	2027	2211	2095	0.505	0.284	0.349
All India	2222	2153	2130	0.500	0.359	0.479
Urban						
Andhra Pradesh	2010	1993	2052	0.411	0.298	0.525
Bihar	2133	2188	2169	0.328	0.279	0.369
Gujarat	2000	2028	2058	0.346	0.285	0.533
Haryana	2242	2141	2172	0.458	0.301	0.624
Himachal Pradesh	2430	2416	2655	0.432	0.272	0.652
Karnataka	2124	2026	2046	0.491	0.309	0.328
Kerala	2050	1966	1995	1.041	0.333	0.335
Madhya Pradesh	2139	2083	2132	0.346	0.358	1.383
Maharashtra	2030	1990	2039	1.416	0.286	0.476
Orissa	2220	2262	2302	0.313	0.270	0.452
Punjab	2101	2090	2198	0.482	0.296	0.355
Rajasthan	2255	2185	2337	0.459	0.283	0.881
Tamil Nadu	2140	1923	2032	1.000	0.357	0.663
Uttar Pradesh	2044	2142	2131	0.357	0.302	0.604
West Bengal	2040	2131	2135	0.389	0.272	0.642
All India	2090	2058	2106	1.590	0.479	0.665

Source: Computed from NSS unit record data for the 38th (1983), 50th (1993/4), and 55th (1999/2000) rounds.

6.5 Trends in Inequality

A simple and widely used measure of the inequality in nutrient intakes is the coefficient of variation (CV). Table 6.3 also presents changes in the CV for each of the 16 states and for rural and urban areas separately.[9] The CV values range

average share of agriculture in their domestic product but were also among those few states where the growth rates in agriculture were large during the past decade.

[9] Related measures like the Gini coefficient or the ratio of mean intakes of the richest quintile to the lowest quintile are also discussed elsewhere (Meenakshi and Viswanathan 2003; Viswanathan and Meenakshi 2004).

between 0.3 to 0.5 in rural areas in all the three years. This is also true in urban states, except in 1999/2000 when the CV was substantially higher. Over time, for both rural and urban sectors, the CV declined in 1993/94 as compared to 1983 in a large number of states. In rural India, this decline reflects a decline in standard deviation, given that declining mean intakes should have been reflected in higher CVs.[10] Between 1993/94 and 1999/2000, the CV increased for nine rural states; in six of these mean intakes had declined. In urban areas, however, the CV increased in all states, despite higher intakes.

Also of note is the fact that the CV of intakes in urban areas is higher than that in rural areas in 1999/2000. This is somewhat unexpected since it is widely perceived that a food safety-net, in the form of the public distribution system, caters primarily to the urban areas in India, and contributes to the increased intakes of the poor. Indeed in Kerala and Tamil Nadu, states where the public distribution system is acknowledged to work better than in other states, the CV has declined over time. This is also true in the case of rural Andhra Pradesh, another state where the reach of the food safety net is demonstrably better (see, for example, Dutta and Ramaswami 2001).

6.6 Changes in Income Elasticities of Nutrient Demand

As discussed in section 6.4, the rank correlation of the POU with per capita total expenditure is insignificant. Also, the income poverty rates are much lower than both the ICMR and DMG based measures of the POU.[11] One implication is that a large number of people above the poverty line also have insufficient energy intakes, which is clearly an inappropriate inference, especially if there is a substitution of dietary quality for caloric quantity. Further, the POU across states in rural India has increased, despite increases in real incomes over time. Does this imply that energy intakes are only weakly affected by income? In order to explore this linkage further we look at the relationship between income and calories at the household level using the unit record data.

In particular, Table 6.4 sets out the expenditure elasticity of demand for energy intakes in 1999/2000. We estimate these separately for the poor (first quintile) and the rich (fifth quintile) (Meenakshi and Viswanathan 2005; 2003). The income elasticities of energy demand are significant but magnitudes decline with the level of income. This is evident in several ways: first, states with lower per capita total expenditures exhibit higher elasticities

[10] This is consistent with our earlier results that demonstrated the 'pinching-in' of both tails of the probability density of energy intakes over time (Viswanathan and Meenakshi 2003).

[11] Though the difference between income poverty and POU persists with alternative measures such as the poverty gap ratio and the squared poverty gap, the difference declines with the power of the FGT measure used (results not reported here).

Table 6.4. Calorie income elasticities in rural and urban India, 1999/2000

	Rural			Urban		
	Q1	Q5	All	Q1	Q5	All
Andhra Pradesh	0.771 (0.11)	0.223 (0.06)	0.487 (0.03)	0.429 (0.02)	0.258 (0.02)	0.337 (0.01)
Bihar	0.709 (0.04)	0.390 (0.02)	0.544 (0.01)	0.654 (0.05)	0.167 (0.04)	0.400 (0.02)
Gujarat	0.573 (0.04)	0.294 (0.03)	0.423 (0.02)	0.469 (0.03)	0.125 (0.02)	0.287 (0.01)
Haryana	0.555 (0.05)	0.445 (0.07)	0.496 (0.03)	0.492 (0.04)	0.229 (0.04)	0.345 (0.02)
Himachal Pradesh	0.373 (0.06)	0.347 (0.07)	0.360 (0.03)	0.365 (0.06)	0.180 (0.05)	0.263 (0.03)
Karnataka	0.638 (0.04)	0.345 (0.03)	0.485 (0.02)	0.514 (0.03)	0.145 (0.03)	0.310 (0.02)
Kerala	0.609 (0.03)	0.267 (0.02)	0.430 (0.01)	0.596 (0.03)	0.175 (0.02)	0.363 (0.01)
Madhya Pradesh	0.551 (0.04)	0.394 (0.03)	0.469 (0.02)	0.490 (0.03)	0.212 (0.03)	0.341 (0.01)
Maharashtra	0.556 (0.04)	0.242 (0.04)	0.388 (0.02)	0.383 (0.02)	0.133 (0.01)	0.244 (0.01)
Orissa	0.587 (0.02)	0.301 (0.02)	0.435 (0.01)	0.551	0.229	0.379
Punjab	0.622 (0.04)	0.352 (0.02)	0.480 (0.02)	0.504 (0.05)	0.283 (0.05)	0.388 (0.02)
Rajasthan	0.537 (0.03)	0.505 (0.03)	0.520 (0.01)	0.530 (0.04)	0.206 (0.03)	0.358 (0.02)
Tamil Nadu	0.592 (0.03)	0.270 (0.03)	0.422 (0.02)	0.614 (0.03)	0.234 (0.02)	0.409 (0.02)
Uttar Pradesh	0.595 (0.05)	0.330 (0.03)	0.458 (0.02)	0.540 (0.03)	0.225 (0.03)	0.372 (0.01)
West Bengal	0.643 (0.02)	0.366 (0.02)	0.496 (0.02)	0.337 (0.06)	0.276 (0.07)	0.304 (0.02)

Note: Values in parentheses are standard errors; Q1 = lowest income quintile; Q5 = richest income quintile.

Source: Computed from NSS unit record data for the 55th (1999/2000) round.

than those with larger incomes; second, rural income elasticities are higher than those in urban areas. Finally, in any particular state, the poorer income quintiles have more elastic income elasticities of calorie demand than richer income quintiles. The decline in magnitude of the elasticities across income quintiles is greater in rural areas than in urban. Rural households in Himachal Pradesh are the only exception to this, with an elasticity of 0.3 across all the quintiles. Thus there is a positive association between expenditure levels and the level of energy intakes, especially among the poor, and among poorer regions.

Increases in real incomes are likely to result in declining food shares by Engel's Law and a more diversified diet by Bennett's Law, and each implies higher welfare. The next section tries to understand how the changes in dietary patterns can explain the trends in mean energy intakes observed in rural and urban areas.

6.7 Diet Quality

One 'explanation' for declining mean intakes is that dietary quality is improving, in that there is a tradeoff between the quantity of calories and the quality of its composition. It is suggested that nutritional wellbeing need not be compromised if fewer calories are compensated by 'better' calories. One indicator of dietary quality is the share of calories derived from cereals and tubers; the lower the proportion of starchy staples in the diet, the better its

Table 6.5. Share of cereals in energy intake (per cent)

	Rural		Urban	
	1983	1999/2000	1983	1999/2000
Andhra Pradesh	84.2	72.1	68.6	62.5
Bihar	83.7	74.3	73.3	67.4
Gujarat	67.1	56.7	53.9	47.1
Haryana	66.6	52.6	58.6	48.9
Himachal Pradesh	71.6	59.8	53.9	47.9
Jammu & Kashmir	79.4	63.5	69.0	29.7
Karnataka	80.2	64.9	64.7	57.8
Kerala	71.4	57.4	62.8	54.2
Madhya Pradesh	80.0	71.6	66.0	59.5
Maharashtra	76.1	63.8	58.7	53.0
Orissa	88.0	81.8	74.8	73.1
Punjab	60.0	50.5	52.9	48.0
Rajasthan	77.1	65.3	64.6	56.3
Tamil Nadu	83.0	67.1	67.1	55.8
Uttar Pradesh	75.2	66.7	65.6	57.6
West Bengal	83.1	74.4	67.1	60.3

Source: Computed from NSS unit record data for the 38th (1983), 50th (1993/4), and 55th (1999/2000) rounds.

quality.[12] The NSS intake data for India do indicate that the percentage of calories derived from cereals is declining systematically over time (Table 6.5).

While diets continue to be cereal-based, that is, cereals account for the bulk of energy intakes, but over time, this proportion has declined (Table 6.5). The cereal share in total calories declined in all states between 1983 and 1999/2000 in both rural and urban India. The decline in the urban sector was more modest; urban diets were more diversified than the rural even in 1983. However, with very little variation across states in any given period or sector, the rank correlation of POU with cereal share is not significant as shown in Table 6.2.

The declining cereal share in calories reflects a secular decline in the intake of cereals, especially in rural areas, where the per capita per month cereal intake declined from 14.9 kg to 13.4 kg to 12.7 kg over the two decades, that is, about 1 kg in the first ten-year period and about the same amount in the next five years. The decline in urban areas was rather marginal (perhaps due to the initial level itself being lower). Similar changes have been noticed in China with per capita monthly consumption (for adults in the age 20 to 45) declining from 22.2 (16.5) kg to 17.4 (14.7) kg in rural (urban) areas between 1989 and 1997 (Popkin 2003).

In turn, this decline in cereal intake is associated with a decline in coarse cereals intake. Thus, even within cereals, there has been a switch away from

[12] The percentage of energy from starchy staples may be taken as rough indicator for diet quality as there is no clear empirical evidence which establishes this.

coarse cereals (which often have negative income elasticities of demand) toward the more 'superior' rice and wheat. The average per capita per day intake of cereals other than rice and wheat declined from 130 (40) g in 1983 to 50 (50) g in 1999/2000 for rural (urban) India. In a few states the decline in coarse cereals is compensated to some extent by the increase in refined cereals, thereby reducing the overall decline in cereal intake. In some states, coarse cereals are not preferred and hence there is either no decline in cereal intake or the decline is mainly from the refined ones. This phenomenon is not unique to India and has also been noted in other parts of the world including China. A part of the explanation may also have to do with the decline in the availability of coarse cereals—from 83 g to 61 g per day over this period (GOI 2003).

The declining dependence on cereals is a more widespread phenomenon, and can be found in many other developing countries. While a detailed examination of the constituents of the non-cereal foods and of their implications for the nutrition transition is the subject of a separate paper; suffice it to note that these trends can be discerned even among the poorest two quintiles in both rural and urban areas. These are, all in all, consistent with improvements in dietary quality.

6.8 Summary and Conclusions

There were about 800 million undernourished people in the developing world in 1999/2000 of which the largest number lived in India, accounting for 26.7 per cent followed by China with 17 per cent (FAO 2003). While China made significant progress during the decade of the 1990s, reducing the POU from 17 per cent to 11 per cent, the decline in India in comparison was much more modest. Nevertheless, as many as half the developing countries have POUs that are lower than that in India; only in Sub-Saharan Africa are these prevalences higher.

Given such a scenario, and the concern that many countries, including India, may not be in a position to meet the Millennium Development Goals (MDGs), this chapter examines the pattern of undernourishment across states in India over the two decades ending in 1999/2000, based on large-scale household level data which have information on caloric intakes.

In doing so, we propose and implement an alternative measure of the prevalence of undernourishment, the DMG-POU, that explicitly factors in the demographic composition of the household, even though individual-level intakes are not available. We suggest that this is a superior method for calculating the prevalence of undernourishment; the resulting estimates are much lower than what is suggested by the more traditional methods for calculating the POU.

Our analysis suggests that rural India has seen a decline in energy intakes, while urban India has seen a small increase, although there are substantial state-specific variations. This has led to a reversal in the observed pattern of urban caloric intakes which were lower than the rural in the early 1980s compared to the late 1990s for most states except two agriculturally dominant states.

The results on the proportion of undernourished are not in consonance with changes in income poverty rates. For both rural and urban states the percentage of undernourishment is far higher than the income poverty rates. Further, over time in rural India the POU has increased, while income poverty rates have declined. Interestingly, a decline in inequality in caloric intakes is observed in both rural and urban between 1983 and 1993/4. However, between 1993/4 and 1999/2000, inequalities appear to have increased in urban areas.

Thus, at an aggregate level, the relationship between income and undernourishment is weak, in that the rank-order correlations across states between measures of income/income poverty and prevalence of undernourishment are statistically insignificant. However, results based on household-level data reverse this conclusion. Income elasticity estimates for the poorer households are high, and certainly not close to zero; this indicates that improvements in income would still play a role in improving energy intakes, especially among the poor.

There is some evidence to suggest that despite declining intakes, attributed almost entirely to lower cereal intakes, there is some improvement in dietary quality, as reflected by the decreasing reliance on cereals and tubers as the principal energy source. There is need for further analyses to understand this change, and look at the contribution of other foods like meat, egg, fruits, and vegetables. The extent to which the greater intakes of other components of the food basket, which tend to be important sources of proteins and micronutrients, perhaps compensate for the decline in calories is yet to be studied. The increase in urban energy intakes also needs separate analysis, given the recent concerns related to the problem of overnutrition in developing countries.

References

Barr, S. I., S. Murphy, T. D. Agurs-Collins, and M. I. Poos (2003). 'Planning Diets for Individuals using Dietary Reference Intakes'. *Nutrition Reviews*, 61 (10): 352–60.

Behrman, J. R., and A. B. Deolalikar (1987). 'Will Developing Country Nutrition Improve with Income? A Case Study for Rural South India'. *Journal of Political Economy*, 95 (3): 492–507.

Dutta, B., and B. Ramaswami (2001). 'Targeting and Efficiency in the Public Distribution System: The Case of Andhra Pradesh and Maharashtra'. *Economic and Political Weekly*, 5 May: 1524–32.

FAO (Food and Agriculture Organization) (2003). *State of Food Insecurity in the World 2003: Monitoring Progress Towards the World Food Summit and Millennium Development Goals*. Rome: FAO.

GOI (1996). NSS 50th Round: Nutritional Intake in India 1993–1994. Report No. 405. New Delhi: Ministry of Statistics and Programme Implementation, Government of India.

—— (2001). *National Human Development Report*. New Delhi: Union Planning Commission, Government of India.

—— (2003). *Agricultural Statistics at a Glance: 2003*. New Delhi: Directorate of Economics and Statistics, Government of India. Available at: http://agricoop.nic.in/statistics2003/chap10.htm#chap101

Gopalan, C., B. V. Ramasastri, and S. C. Balasubramanian (2000). *Nutritive Value of Indian Foods* (update by B. S. Narasinga Rao, Y. G. Deosthale, and K. C. Pant) Hyderabad: National Institute of Nutrition.

Haddad, L., H. Alderman, S. Appleton, L. Song, and Y. Yohannes (2003). 'Reducing Child Undernutrition: How Far Does Income Growth Take Us?'. *World Bank Economic Review*, 17 (1): 107–31.

Kakwani, N. (1992). 'Measuring Undernutrition with Variable Caloric Requirement', in S. R. Osmani (ed.), *Nutrition and Poverty*. New York: Oxford University Press for UNU-WIDER.

Meenakshi, J. V., and B. Viswanathan (2003). 'Calorie Deprivation in Rural India: 1983–1999/2000'. *Economic and Political Weekly*, 369–75.

—— (2005). 'Calorie Deprivation in Rural India, 1983–1999/2000: Evidence from Unit Record Data', in A. Deaton and V. Kozel (eds), *The Great Indian Poverty Debate*. New Delhi: Macmillan India.

Murphy, S., S. I. Barr, and M. Poos (2002). 'Using the New Dietary Reference Intakes to Assess Diets: A Map to the Maze'. *Nutrition Reviews*, 60 (9): 267–75.

Osmani, S. R. (1992). 'Introduction', in S. R. Osmani (ed.), *Nutrition and Poverty*. New York: Oxford University Press for UNU-WIDER.

Osmani, S. R. (1997). 'Poverty and Nutrition in South Asia'. Nutrition Policy Paper 16, ACC/SCN. Geneva: WHO.

Palmer-Jones, R., and K. Sen (2001). 'On India's Poverty Puzzles and Statistics of Poverty'. *Economic and Political Weekly*, 36 (3): 211–17

Popkin, B. M. (2003). 'The Nutrition Transition in the Developing World'. *Development Policy Review*, 21 (5–6): 581–97.

Roy, N. (2001). 'A Semiparametric Analysis of Calorie Response to Income Change Across Income Groups and Gender?'. *Journal of International Trade and Economic Development*, 10 (1): 93–109.

Shetty, S. L. (2003). 'Growth of SDP and Structural Changes in State Economies: Interstate Comparisons. *Economic and Political Weekly*, 6 December: 5189–200.

Subramanian, S., and A. Deaton (1996). 'The Demand for Food and Calories'. *Journal of Political Economy*, 104 (1): 133–62.

Svedberg, P. (2000). *Poverty and Undernutrition: Theory, Measurement, and Policy*, Oxford: Oxford University Press for UNU-WIDER.

—— (2004). 'Has the Relationship between Undernutrition and Income Changed?'. Copenhagen Consensus Opponent Note, Copenhagen Consensus.

Vaidyanathan, A. (2002). 'Food Consumption and Nutrition Status: A Re-examination Based on Indian Evidence'. Chennai: Madras Institute of Development Studies. Mimeo.

Viswanathan B., and J. V. Meenakshi (2003). 'Developing Country Nutrition Does Improve with Income: A Look at Calorie and Protein Intakes, 1983 to 1993–94'. *Sarvekshana*.

—— —— (2004). 'Economic Development and Changes in Nutritional Intake in India'. Chennai: Madras School of Economics. Mimeo.

World Bank (2003). *World Development Indicators*, 2003. Washington, DC: World Bank.

7

Food Security in Vietnam During the 1990s: The Empirical Evidence

Vasco Molini

7.1 Introduction

Food security is one of the targets of the Millennium Development Goals and is widely considered a useful measure for evaluating the progress of a country in terms of wellbeing. According to the definition of USAID (1992), we have food security when 'all people all the times have both physical and economic access to sufficient food to meet their dietary needs for a productive and healthy life'.

After a long debate during the 1990s, it is now commonly accepted that wellbeing is multidimensional and that the conventional measures or indexes that are based only on household expenditures miss many aspects. In several recent studies (Palmer-Jones and Sen 2001), the use of purely monetary-based indicators has been combined with non-monetary measures and the results compared in order to assess the phenomena in a more multidimensional way. The results of a non-monetary approach helps to understand the deeper mechanisms that are often overlooked by conventional analysis but which generally are extremely useful in examining poverty dynamics (vulnerability, persistence, etc.).

The use of food security indicators—a broad set of multidimensional measures—moves in this direction by providing useful tools to check the robustness of the findings. To observe relevant improvements in terms of wellbeing, we should see comparable food security improvements. For example, Hoddinott and Yohannes (2002), in analysing the performance of ten

The author is grateful to Brinda Vishwanathan, Madras School of Economics, for useful suggestions regarding the calorie intake approach, Benjamin Davis, FAO-ESA, and Maarten Nube', SOW-VU for useful comments on the first and second revisions, and all the participant of the ICSSR-UNU-WIDER project meetings on Hunger and Food Security. The usual disclaimer applies.

developing countries, find a strong association between two measures of food security (calorie intake and dietary diversity) and the increase in expenditures per capita.

Until now, few scholars have analysed the food security issue in Vietnam (Minot and Goletti 2000). Although there is a conspicuous literature on poverty reduction (including Baulch and Minot 2004; Baulch and Masset 2003; Fritzen 2003), what is missing in particular is a contribution that focuses on the potential food security improvements that occurred in the 1990s.

While in the economic literature no relevant contribution has properly addressed the problem, in nutritional and medical literature some recent contribution shed some light on Vietnam's situation. Thang and Popkin (2004) looking at the per capita calories intake, found that after reaching in the early 1990s the dietary adequacy of 2,100 calories, did not move forward in the late 1990s. By contrast, they found clear improvements in the diet diversification: households tend to consume less starchy staples and more proteins and fats. Thus, authors argue that the situation of food security is controversial. Although there are some signals of improvements in the diet also among more vulnerable groups, the gap in the quantity and quality of calories consumed among different economic groups is widening.

The aim of the present chapter is to analyse the evolution of food security in Vietnam using different measures (e.g. calorie intake, anthropometric measures, elasticities) and conduct a diachronic analysis, as most of the literature on this issue has focused on static/cross countries comparisons, except for a few cases (Skoufias 2003 on Indonesia). Given that the economic performance of Vietnam was astonishing during 1990s (on average over 7 per cent) and that the poverty ratio dropped from 58.1 to 37.4 (World Bank 2004), this study attempts to determine whether a similar pattern existed in terms of food security.

The chapter is organized as follows. Sections 7.2 and 7.3 provide a general overview on data and present the tabulations on the price of food per calorie and the calorie share. Section 7.4 calculates some food security measures and then compares the results among the expenditure deciles and regions while sections 7.5 and 7.6 provide the empirical results.

7.2 Data

The present analysis is based on the Vietnamese Living Standard Surveys (VLSS) of 1993 and 1998 and, in particular, on section 11 regarding food and non-food consumption. The two questionnaires differed only marginally and for 1998 we have information on approximately 4,200 households of 4,800 households interviewed in 1993. Both rounds of surveys ask for data from households on the consumption of 45 different items during a

12-month period preceding the interviews. To take into account specific expenditure patterns unique to Vietnam, information on food items was collected separately for the holiday periods (notably the *Tet* holidays) and the rest of the year. The *Tet* holidays induce a considerable departure from normal spending.

As a major quantity of foodstuff consumed by rural households comes from self-production, respondents were asked to evaluate such consumption as if it were purchased in the market. To obtain annual totals, it is therefore necessary to evaluate both expenditures for food from the *Tet*-period and subsistence production, and correspondingly scale down the normal purchases for the rest of the year. Assuming that the *Tet* and holiday periods cover 2 weeks, the 12-month purchases and subsistence production are multiplied by 11.5/12. We follow a similar procedure for the calorie equivalence. Instead of using values, we transform all quantities into kilograms, converting these into calories according to FAO's conversion table. The procedure has certain shortcomings as the result is not calorie intake but calorie availability (Deaton 1997). In the event of wastage due to inefficient cooking methods, real calorie consumption could be overstated dramatically, but as the data did not provide sufficient information on cooking methods, we assume that the purchased calories are also consumed.

For meals taken outside the home, we preliminarily adopt the Subramanian and Deaton (1996) strategy of using the average price of calories from the remaining data plus an added 50 per cent premium to reflect processing margins. However, for many households eating a considerable number of meals outside the home (households with workers or agricultural labourers working beyond their own land plots) this results in a great underestimation of consumed calories. After several checks and comparing the expenditure data, we decided to use a 'median 1,000 calories price'. This is calculated using the household prices per 1,000 calories of almost every item, except alcoholic beverages and condensed milk, being the most expensive articles and the less likely to be included in a normal meal. We then divide the expenditures for meals outside the home by this price and thus obtain the consumed calories.

Out of 100,000 observations, data on quantities were missing in about 1,000 cases, while values were available. In these instances, the question arose as to what price should be used to evaluate the consumption of these food items: (i) average or median prices calculated from the survey data for other households, (ii) prices from the price (community) questionnaire, or (iii) prices from some other external source? Using the procedure proposed by Deaton and Zaidi (2002) to obtain the quantity consumed, we divide the value of purchase/production by the price of the item prevailing in the cluster/the commune, depending on whichever is the next highest level of aggregation for the price information available. As an indicator of income, we use total household expenditures per capita deflated with a regional price index. The distribution of the two expenditures is fully comparable and the price index based on 1998 prices.

Some observations were dropped: households having an estimated caloric intake below 1,000 kcal per person per day or above 4,000 were eliminated, based on the notion that these figures reflect problems in the consumption data (Minot and Goletti 2000). This reduced the 1993 sample to 4,530 observations (out of 4,800), the 1998 survey to 5,846 (out of 6,000) and the panel to 3,934 for each year (instead of 4,153).

To calculate anthropometric measures we used data collected in section 15 of the VLSS 1993 and 1998 about the height and weight of survey respondents. We reported only the anthropometric measures for adult respondents of working age (18–65). The aim was to use a measure more comparable with calorie intake and more representative of the wellbeing of the entire population.

The comparison with the variation in the BMI might improve, in our opinion, the robustness of our findings. Apart from some methodological flaws typically encountered when estimating per capita food consumption (Nube' 2001) a more fundamental problem is that food expenditure data are only available at the level of households, not at the level of individuals, unless the questionnaire is specifically targeted (Aromolaran 2004). By collecting information on individual household members, an assessment can be made whether an increase in household level food consumption has resulted in an improved nutritional status of all household members, or only of specific members of the households, for example children, adults, males, or females.

As argued by Saith and Harriss-White (1999) anthropometric indicators also have the advantage of ascertaining joint outcomes of nutrition and health functioning. They can thus more easily be used as proxies of morbidity indicators, always difficult to measure and often unreliable. Furthermore, it is important to note that, in strong contrast to data on food consumption, anthropometric measurements are relatively easy to collect by measuring individual's height and weight. In addition, for children accurate information on age is required, but such information is generally available for Vietnamese children.

7.3 Calorie Price, Food Substitution, and Dietary Composition

In Table 7.1, we calculate the median prices for the purchase of 1,000 calories of any specific food category. As expected, rice provides 1,000 calories at the lowest price, followed by pulses and legumes. Rice is the main item consumed by Vietnamese households and its calorie content for 100 g is particularly high (360 kcal for regular and 380 kcal for glutinous). Similar to Deaton's findings in the Maharashtran case (1997), we observe an increase in the cost

Table 7.1. Prices per calorie, 1993 and 1998

	Mean	Bottom 10%	Top 10%	Price relative to cereals		
				Mean	Bottom 10%	Top 10%
1993 survey						
Rice	866	820	931	1	1	1
Other cereals	2358	2043	2901	2.7	2.5	3.1
Roots & tubers	2946	2040	4060	3.4	2.5	4.4
Pulses and legumes	2807	2518	3795	3.2	3.1	4.1
Dairy products and eggs	10701	10151	11149	12.4	12.4	12.0
Meat and offal	8495	7253	11979	9.8	8.8	12.9
Fish and seafood	9154	7697	12627	10.6	9.4	13.6
Oils and fats	1540	1640	1549	1.8	2.0	1.7
Sugar and honey	1916	1729	2331	2.2	2.1	2.5
Fruits	2504	1466	4809	2.9	1.8	5.2
Vegetables	6703	4865	10972	7.7	5.9	11.8
Beverages	36954	25502	49281	42.7	31.1	52.9
Processed food	5397	4262	6664	6.2	5.2	7.2
Other food	3772	3117	5354	4.4	3.8	5.8
Total	7268	5692	9453			
1998 survey						
Rice	1021	983	1147	1	1	1
Other cereals	1929	1542	2423	1.9	1.6	2.1
Roots and tubers	2365	1286	4239	2.3	1.3	3.7
Pulses and legumes	2786	2524	3357	2.7	2.6	2.9
Dairy products and eggs	25112	23745	22732	24.6	24.2	19.8
Meat and offal	10838	9495	14221	10.6	9.7	12.4
Fish and seafood	7745	6084	13523	7.6	6.2	11.8
Oils and fats	1215	1217	1441	1.2	1.2	1.3
Sugar and honey	2369	2073	2982	2.3	2.1	2.6
Fruits	4224	1904	8046	4.1	1.9	7.0
Vegetables	6940	5376	9654	6.8	5.5	8.4
Beverages	39914	26546	55046	39.1	27.0	48.0
Processed food	5750	5098	7113	5.6	5.2	6.2
Other food	4578	3474	6947	4.5	3.5	6.1
Total	8629	6562	11054			

Source: Author's calculations using VLSS 1993 and 1998.

of calories between the poor and richer segments of the population, but also a difference between the prices paid within the same broad food category. Poorer households (bottom 10 per cent in Table 7.1) seem to consume lower-quality items within all food categories; consequently, calorie prices paid by this group are below the mean and far below those paid by richer households (the top 10 per cent).

This is particularly evident in the case of rice in 1998. Compared to 1993, the difference in the price paid by the top 10 per cent increased in comparison to the bottom deciles, suggesting that more rice qualities were available in 1998 than in 1993 and that rich households tended to buy higher-quality items. This is consistent with other contributions (World Bank 2004) analysing the effect of price liberalization on supply diversification.

Table 7.2. Food calorie shares, 1993 and 1998

Products	1993			1998		
	Mean	Bottom 10%	Top 10%	Mean	Bottom 10%	Top 10%
Rice	0.75	0.81	0.53	0.69	0.78	0.47
Cereals	0.03	0.04	0.06	0.04	0.05	0.06
Roots and tubers	0.02	0.05	0.00	0.02	0.05	0.01
Pulses and legumes	0.01	0.01	0.02	0.02	0.01	0.02
Dairy products and eggs	0.00	0.00	0.01	0.00	0.00	0.01
Meat and offal	0.04	0.02	0.08	0.04	0.02	0.06
Fish and seafood	0.02	0.01	0.03	0.04	0.02	0.04
Oils and fats	0.02	0.01	0.03	0.04	0.02	0.04
Sugar and honey	0.02	0.01	0.05	0.02	0.01	0.04
Fruits	0.03	0.02	0.06	0.04	0.02	0.05
Vegetables	0.01	0.01	0.01	0.02	0.01	0.02
Beverages	0.01	0.01	0.02	0.02	0.01	0.03
Processed food	0.06	0.01	0.12	0.08	0.02	0.15
Other food	0.01	0.00	0.02	0.01	0.00	0.02

Source: Author's calculations using VLSS 1993 and 1998.

As suggested by Skoufias (2003), we calculate the relative prices of food items using the mean price of rice as a benchmark. Exploiting the panel nature of the data, we can in fact analyse the relative price variations and determine whether they affect the expenditure elasticity of any commodity demand.

Relative prices changed considerably during the 1990s under price liberalization. Improvements in infrastructure and transportation intensified the exchange, and enabled a greater variety of commodities to reach to all parts of the country. On the demand side, diversification also increased. The combination of both factors, thus, influenced price setting.

The relative price of typical rice substitutes like roots and tubers and other cereals declined, particularly for the bottom ten deciles. Items like cassava, sweet potatoes, rich in calories but less rich in micronutrients and vitamins, are in general in demand only in very poor households. The decline in relative prices and the corresponding drop in calorie shares (Table 7.2) might be interpreted as a good signal: poor households used expenditure improvements not only to increase their daily calorie intake (Table 7.3) but also to improve the nutritional value.

In contrast, the relative prices of micronutrient-rich items, except milk and fish, in general tended to increase (Table 7.1). There is, nevertheless, some variation due to expenditure levels and residential areas. Fish prices increased less from the 1993 and 1998 levels than meat prices. Compared to rice, fish prices and vegetables became more favourable for poor households, thanks to augmented output and the fact that fish was relatively more expensive for rich households. Prices for low-quality rice substitutes depreciated while meat, milk and fruits appreciated. Table 7.2 gives the share of calories provided by each food category.

Table 7.3. Mean calories per day and Simpson index: by deciles by urban and rural areas and by regions, 1993–8

(%) Expenditures deciles	Mean calories per day		Simpson index	
	1993	1998	1993	1998
10	1488	1790	0.29	0.38
20	1716	2024	0.31	0.40
30	1863	2177	0.33	0.42
40	1971	2279	0.35	0.46
50	2060	2331	0.38	0.48
60	2126	2394	0.40	0.51
70	2220	2413	0.44	0.55
80	2274	2484	0.49	0.58
90	2476	2502	0.54	0.63
100	2557	2587	0.66	0.72
Rural	2060	2281	0.39	0.47
Urban	2021	2218	0.54	0.63
Northern uplands	2046	2320	0.43	0.47
Red River Delta	2101	2404	0.39	0.52
Northern coastal	1879	2205	0.39	0.50
Southern coastal	1977	2199	0.43	0.53
Central highlands	2080	2145	0.38	0.43
Ho Chi Minh City	2005	2241	0.49	0.62
Mekong Delta	2173	2209	0.42	0.48
Total	2053	2267	0.42	0.51

Source: Author's calculations using VLSS 1993 and 1998.

Rice has remained the main calorie source for many households but during the interval considered, 1993 and 1998, changes occurred in particular in the top deciles of the expenditure distribution. The share of rice calories declined in five years and rich households tended to diversify their diets. At first glance, these results in conjunction with the average calories per day given in Table 7.3, might suggest low calorie expenditure elasticity.

Poor households spent their expenditure on additional food without modifying the composition of their food balance (Tables 7.2 and 7.3), acquiring most of their calories from carbohydrates (cereals, potatoes, and other starches) and only a marginal amount from proteins (meat, fish, eggs, and legumes) and oils and fats (see also Thang and Popkin 2004).

On the other hand, rich households, instead of increasing their calorie intake, tended to buy more expensive items like fish, beverages, oil, vegetables, and processed food as replacements for rice (Table 7.2). What is surprising, but in line with other findings (Thang and Popkin 2004) is that rich households do not significantly increase the proportion of calories from proteins (only fish increases), while they increase that from lipids and from processed food, typically rich in saturated fats and refined sugar.

This shift towards products that are generally associated with increased risk of obesity, diabetes and heart diseases, and certain types of cancer is of great concern if we consider that it occurred only at the beginning of the economic boom faced by the country. Nevertheless, in the period considered our anthropometric analysis do not detect a particular upsurge in the overweight/obesity rate.[1] Recent studies (Cuong *et al.* 2006; Tesfaye *et al.* 2007) comparing Vietnam with other South East Asian countries confirm the low level of obesity and cardiovascular diseases prevalence. Indeed, in particular urban areas in the south the overweight population is steadily increasing (Cuong *et al.* 2006).

Comparing Tables 7.1 and 7.2 reveals a low sensitivity of calorie shares to relative price variations. Although rice prices were higher in comparison to potential substitutes, their share remained constant. In the bottom 10 per cent, the lower relative price of roots, tubers, pulses, and legumes was apparently ineffective in increasing their share. Also, the big relative price variation determined only a limited variation in the other cereals consumption.

Rich households also do not seem to react in a consistent way to relative price variation. The items-to-rice cross elasticity is not always negative. The elasticity shows the expected sign in the case of fish, oils and fats, processed food, beverages, and fruits, but not for meat. The reduction in the meat consumption, while the relative price declines, is rather difficult to explain.

Changes in relative calorie prices appeared to be only partially linked with how households acquired their calories. Despite the increase in the relative price of rice, poor households seemed to spend the additional expenditure received in 1998 on rice as long as it remained the more convenient calorie source and alternatives were less attractive from a nutritional point of view.

On the other hand, rich households tended to diversify their diet, considering relative price variation not so relevant. The reduction in rice share has not been compensated by strong variation in the consumption of now relatively less expensive items, but by an increase in the share of lipids and in general more expensive items.

7.4 Calorie Consumption Distribution, Dietary Diversity, and Anthropometric Measures

The 1998 situation in comparison to 1993 shows important improvements in calorie consumption and calorie distribution. For a comparison of the two years, we calculate the mean distribution of calories by deciles and by urban and rural areas. Low-expenditure households (Table 7.3) increased their daily calorie consumption and this trend is evident particularly for the poorest households.

The calorie consumption growth rate declined in both survey years, starting from the 3rd decile, thus we suspect that the expenditure calorie relation

[1] We used the 25 cut-off, the same used in (Tesfaye *et al.* 2007). See also Figure 7.2 later.

is monotonically increasing and logarithmic: this pattern contributed to a convergence in calorie availability during the 1990s. This decelerating rate of growth might suggest changes in the composition of commodities evidenced in the previous section. We test this hypothesis using the Simpson Index (see Table 7.4 later), an index of food diversification[2] (see Chapter 2 in this volume).

What clearly emerges is the fact that diversification was associated more with per capita monetary consumption than calorie consumption. Assuming that food diversity is a good indicator of the 'access dimension of food security'[3] (Hoddinot and Yohannes 2002), our data confirm the existence of an improvement in food security from 1993 to 1998 for all expenditure deciles, in all regions as well as for both urban and rural areas (see Table 7.4 later).

To check the robustness of these findings and to better understand the evolution of calorie distribution, we compute and compare the cumulative distribution functions of calorie intake (Meenakashi and Vishwanathan 2003) in the seven Vietnamese administrative regions[4] for 1993 and 1998. To show which distribution is stochastically dominant, or in other words, if associated with a higher welfare, one of the curves should lie to the right of the other function (Figure 7.1).

Based on the results, we can divide the seven regions into two different groups. Five regions exhibit both clear stochastic dominance and evidence of economic improvement. Our data confirm that the increased expenditure per capita was only partially used to increase the per capita calorie intake. The example of north coastal region is straightforward. The strong reduction in the poverty rate (−26 per cent according to available General Statistics Office of Vietnam estimates) introduced a general improvement in calorie distribution, benefiting mostly poor households. The same can be said for the Red River Delta where poverty plummeted about 36 per cent, and an increase in calorie availability is noted. It is interesting to note that economic improvement determined not only an increase in calorie quantity but also in quality. This is evident particularly in the Ho Chi Minh region and the Red River Delta.

[2] The Simpson Index formula is $(1 - \Pi_i)$ where i is the calorie share of food i $(i = 1, 2, \ldots)$. If only one food item was consumed, the index would be zero, so variety increases with the index value, thus establishing a continuum between a 'diverse' and a 'non-diverse' diet (see Chapter 2, this volume).

[3] A measure of the population's ability to acquire available food during a given period.

[4] The stratification of the samples in the two periods is different. The 1993 distribution is stratified by rural and urban areas while 1998 distribution is stratified by rural and urban and by regions. The two distributions are not fully comparable by regions as the 1993 survey is not regionally representative. We decide to include these graphs for the reason that they confirmed the previous analysis, indicating that the results were not inconsistent. Official statistics based on VLSS compare various measures at regional level too, specifying the limits of this type of analysis.

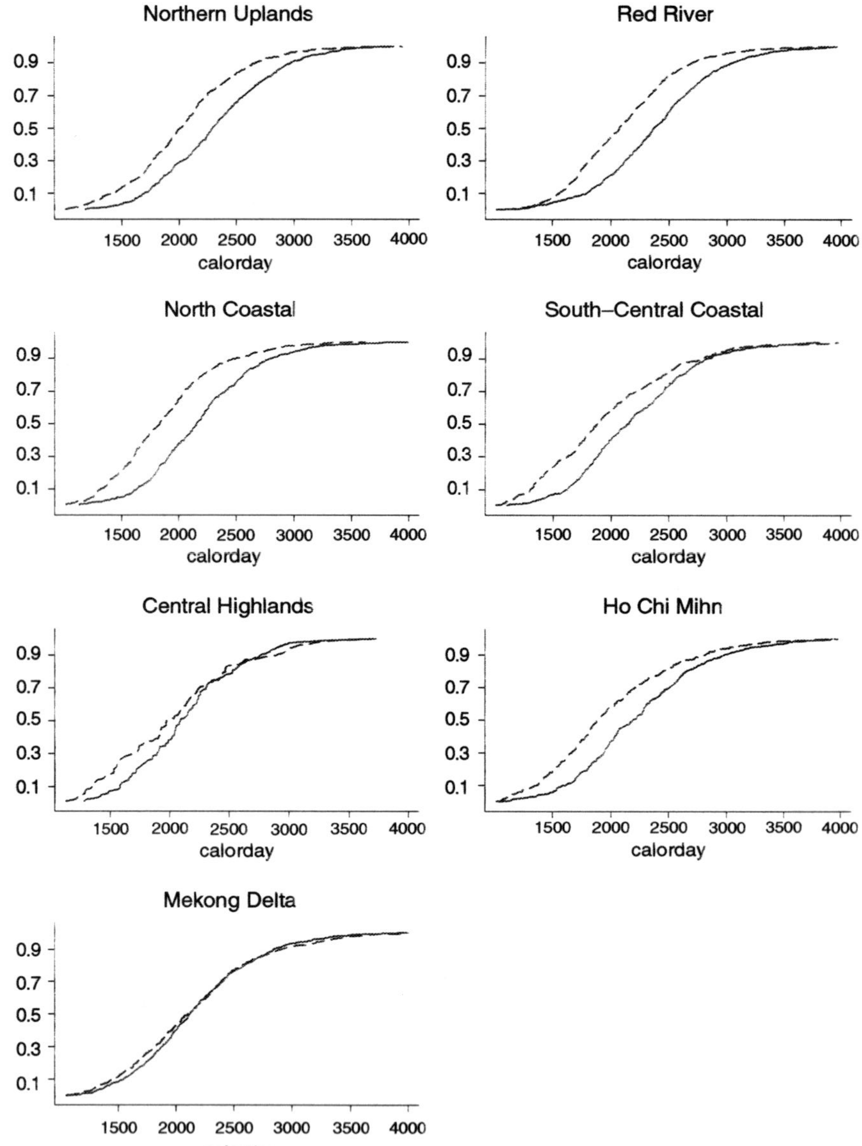

Figure 7.1. Cumulative distribution functions for calories by regions, 1993 and 1998

Note: Continuous line 1998, dashed line 1993.

Source: Author's calculations using VLSS 1993 and 1998.

The curves for the rest of the regions tend to intersect and might not exhibit first-order stochastic dominance. Nevertheless, we observe unambiguous modifications in the distribution. The left tail shifted in both regions. This implies that the proportion of people consuming low calorie quantities has dropped. The intersection occurs close to the limit of 2,100 calories per day, the official Vietnamese calorie norm. In both cases, the number of people consuming less than 2,100 calories per day decreased by almost 50 per cent, but the interpretation of the two variations is different.

The increase in expenditures in the Mekong Delta introduced a greater decline in calories derived from rice and other cereals, but the effect of economic improvement in the central highlands was mostly an addition of consumed calories. Initial conditions, however, were also different. The Mekong Delta is one of the most productive areas of the country and comparatively more urbanized. Therefore, the calorie per day might be a less valid indicator of wellbeing. We analyse this aspect further in the following section but urban households in general have a lower calorie intake as their lives are more sedentary than rural households.

Moreover, richer households tend to have comparatively lower calorie/expenditure elasticity, as they spend more on quality (calorie-poor items like fruit and vegetables) and more in nonfood items. Thus, it is not surprising that beyond a certain threshold, the calorie expenditure elasticity becomes zero or even negative, and in some rich households (Deaton 1997), the daily calorie consumption does not differ substantially form middle-expenditure consumption.

The analysis of the body mass index (BMI) in general confirms the positive trend envisaged by the calorie intake variation. Also looking at the commonly used cut-off point of 18.5, in five out of seven regions there is a clear reduction in the percentage of individuals below that threshold (see Figure 7.2). Nevertheless, there exists some evident dissimilarity between the results of the two indicators.

In two out of three northern regions the big increase in calorie intake is not associated with a similar improvement in BMI. In particular, in the northern uplands the two curves are overlapping and they depict a very fledgling situation in terms of wellbeing. On the other hand, the progress of BMI in the Mekong Delta seems not to be strongly associated with an increase in the calorie availability. While those who were better-off in 1993 in terms of BMI tend to improve their condition in 1998 also, in terms of calorie availability, this trend is not detectable and only those worse-off improve slightly their condition.

More in line with the improvements in BMI is the Simpson Index on dietary diversification (Table 7.3). Once we exclude the north coastal region, all those regions facing a significant increase in their dietary diversification, also

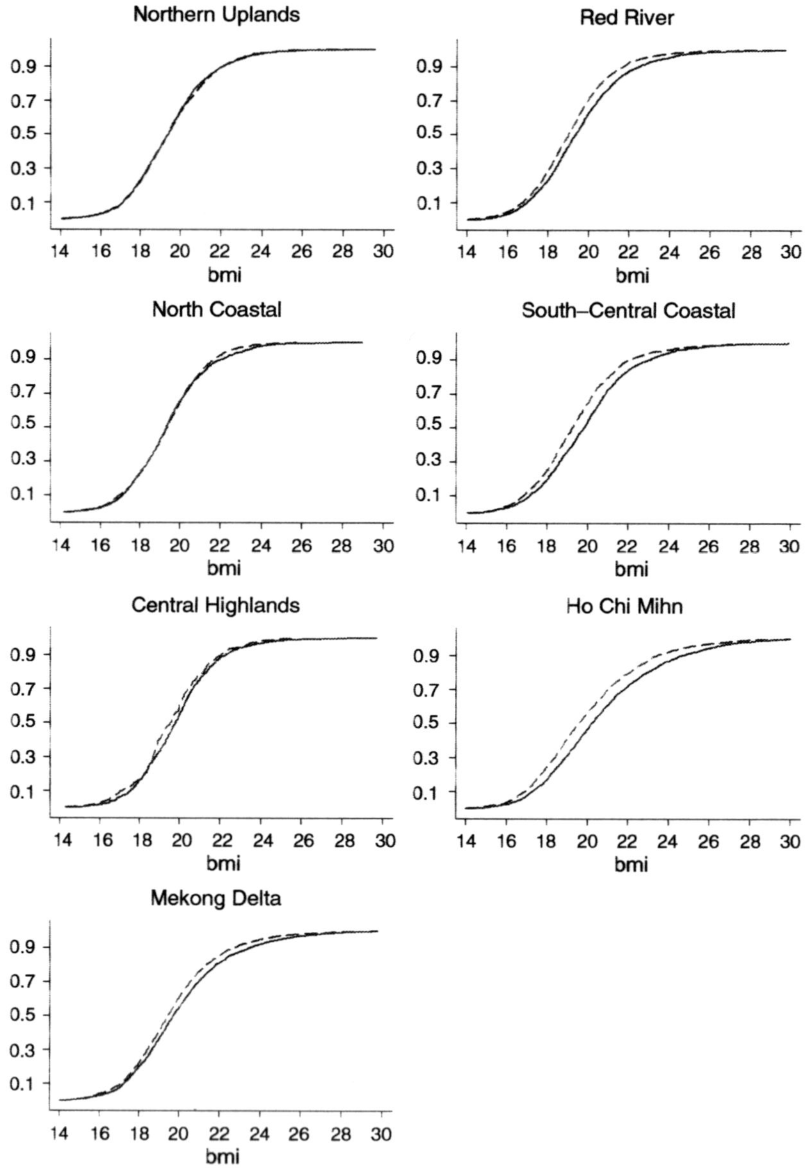

Figure 7.2. Cumulative distribution functions for BMI by regions, 1993 and 1998

Note: Continuous line 1998, dashed line 1993

Source: Author's calculations using VLSS 1993 and 1998

improved in terms of BMI. Similarly, the low level of dietary diversification of the northern uplands matches with the invariance of the BMI.

In conclusion, we might say that the progresses in calorie distribution have been widespread all over the country and the calorie per day intake suggests a clear trend toward convergence, as the richer householders reduce their intake and the poor ones increase theirs. Similar trends are also evidence by the BMI analysis, although the picture is less optimistic since some regions, characterized by extreme poverty, clearly benefit less from the national-scale economic improvements.

Combining the evidence provided by the two measures we can tentatively conclude that food security is improving in four out seven regions, also the most populated ones. In some economically backward areas in the northern region, there is no consistency in the measures. Indeed, assuming that anthropometric measures are in general more reliable than calorie intake ones (Nube' 2001) we can argue that in these regions the wellbeing has hardly improved in the 1990s.

Another important point to stress is that food security, although improved, is not yet fairly distributed and many households are still food insecure or extremely vulnerable. Over the period 1993–8, an increasing number of households augmented their daily calorie consumption, but the calorie source remained almost the same for a great share of population.

We observed important changes in the dietary diversity of even the low-consumption deciles, but poor households continued to acquire most of their calorie needs from rice and other cereals. Only a small portion of the population, located in specific areas of the country, have started to diversify their diets. Ceteris paribus with the same amount of calories per day consumed, households with more diversified diets are better off, as they are nutritionally better protected and more resistant to illness (Vishwanathan and Meenakshi 2001).

7.5 The Calorie Expenditures Relation by Deciles

We have mentioned the potential non-linearity of the calorie expenditures relation—for example, among poor households calorie intakes are likely to respond positively to expenditure variations but as expenditures increase the elasticities tend to decline, sometimes below zero for very high expenditures levels. The empirical evidence for other countries (Subramanian and Deaton 1996; Abdulai and Aubert 2004) suggests that quadratic expenditures terms may not be always sufficient to represent properly these relationships.

After having used additional expenditures to increase their calories per day, households start to be concerned about the monotony of their diet and tend to substitute their calorie sources, devoting extra outlay to more expensive micronutrient-rich items. This desire for variety are derived from the many characteristics such as textures, status value, appearance, taste, aroma that foods possess. As a result, below a subsistence constraint, households focus primarily on acquiring additional calories.

Once the subsistence level is reached, the further increase in income causes households to move off the subsistence constraints, to diversify the diet, and to be less interested in increasing the calories consumed (Hoddinott and Yohannes 2002). The decrease of calorie/expenditures elasticity observed among richer households (Subramanian and Deaton 1996; Abdulai and Aubert 2004) associated with a dietary diversification might be, thus, a good indicator of having met the subsistence constraint and of being more food secure.

We expect, even in the case of Vietnam, that the elasticity of calorie consumption moves downwards from the bottom to the top decile. Furthermore, since we can compare two surveys, we might observe at the same level of income different calorie/income elasticities. This effect is explained by the variation in price elasticities that may have occurred from 1993 to 1998. A ceteris paribus variation in the calorie income elasticity implies, thus, an increased sensitivity of consumers to prices and more propensity to substitute calorie-rich items with items characterized by an higher price per calorie (Tables 7.1 and 7.2).

In order to understand the behaviour of calorie/expenditures elasticity we used non-parametric smoothing techniques running this analysis by expenditures percentiles. Following Subramanian and Deaton (1996) and Deaton (1997), we estimated a regression function of the logarithm of per capita expenditures (x) on the logarithm of per capita calorie availability (y)

$$m(x) = E(y|x) \tag{7.1}$$

using a smooth local regression technique. At any given point of x, we run a locally weighted linear regression choosing weights that diminish with distance from given point x. The weights are also set so that as the sample size increases, the weights given to the immediate neighbourhood of x is increased so that, at the limit, only x is represented.

Instead of estimating a regression for any given point, we subdivided our sample in 50 spaced grids and estimated the regression for any grid. In our case, for the local regression at x observation i get the quartic kernel weight

$$w_i(x) = \frac{15}{16}\left[1 - \left(\frac{x - x_i}{h}\right)^2\right]^2 \tag{7.2}$$

if $-h \leq x - x_i \leq h$ and zero otherwise. The quantity h is a bandwidth that we set at 0.8 value.

A useful feature of this technique is that it allows estimation not only of the regression function, but also of its derivative. In our case as we are regressing logarithms, we can plot the elasticity of calories with respect to expenditures and graphically analyse the non-linearity of which we are concerned. In analysing raw data about urban and rural calorie distribution, we noted a different pattern in relation to income.

This difference is related to the distinguishing features characterizing the two areas. About 80 per cent of the total population lives in rural Vietnam and 90 per cent of poor households. In particular, almost all food-poor live in rural areas. An analysis of wellbeing based on nutritive measures is, therefore, more indicative in rural areas rather than in urban. Moreover, as urban households tend to consume a greater quota of their food balance as outside home expenditures and the calories in this case have been imputed, the risk of measurement error is higher for our urban rather than rural data.

Hence, we decided to regress first urban and rural areas together and then rural areas separately Due to limited space we only reported rural areas results. The functions were constructed using 1993 log per capita expenditures and 1998 log per capita expenditures deflated with regional prices using as base year 1998.

Figure 7.3 (Graph 1) does not indicate any particular non-linearity in the relationship after the logarithmic transformation. In rural areas the logarithm

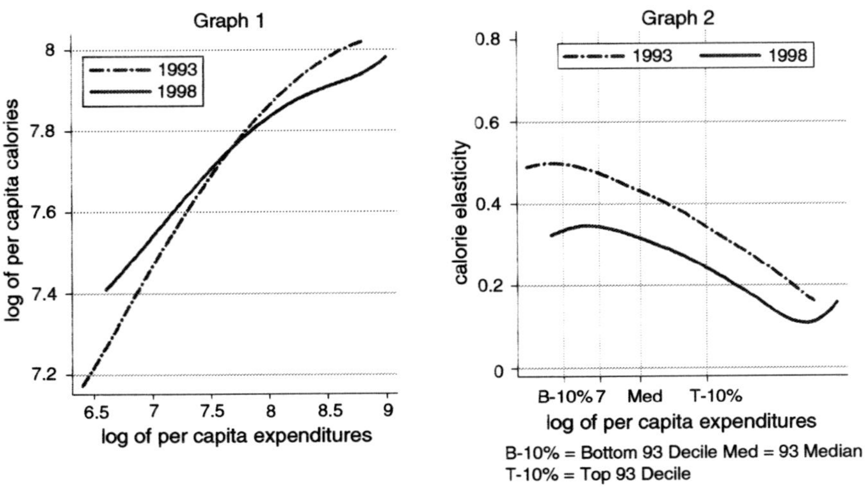

Figure 7.3. 1993 and 1998 regressions functions for log calories and log per capita expenditures (Graph 1) and the calorie expenditures elasticities (Graph 2): rural areas 1993–8

Note: Continuous lines 1998, dashed lines 1993.

Source: Author's calculations using VLSS 1993 and 1998.

transformation seems to be enough to remove skewness in the distribution and the non linearity in the relationship. This result is consistent with Subramanian and Deaton (1996) estimates for India. Comparing the two years, the difference in slopes is particularly evident in 1993 and less accentuated in 1998. In this case, poorer households start with a higher level of per day calories but the slope is more flat than in 1993.

The 1993 elasticity (Figure 7.3, Graph 2) for very poor households is around 0.5 but declines very rapidly below 0.5 in correspondence with the food poverty line (on the x-axis or the log of 1.286 million dong). We cannot compare this trend with similar contributions about Vietnam, but results from Deaton (1997) and Skoufias (2003) about India and Indonesia are similar and present almost the same declining pattern.

The 1998 curve appears to have the same general shape except for the tails of the distribution; 1993 is more leftward shifted since in 1998 it has occurred a massive increase in household income. Poor households in 1993 seem to start from a higher elasticity and the decline is steeper, while for rich households (corresponding to more than 5 million dong per capita) we observe in 1998 an upward movement not observed in 1993.

Other contributions (Abdulai and Aubert 2004) found evidence that after a certain threshold households tend to increase their calorie consumption slightly. In this case, we can think about households that after having increased their nutrition quality and reducing the share of cereals increased their consumption of fats, expensive calorie rich items (milk and candies) and proteins. The great availability of money allows them to substitute items without decreasing the amount of calories consumed. In the case of Vietnam, yet a very poor country, this phenomenon is still limited but we cannot overlook it.

In order to compare the two elasticities curves at same expenditures levels and establish whether they are significantly different we estimated the standard errors associated with each elasticity value. In Figure 7.4, we plot standard error bands separately calculating the formula $m'(x) \pm 2s.e(m'(x))$ (Subramanian and Deaton 1996).

The standard errors are calculated by bootstrapping. To compare the two elasticities, it is enough to check if the standard errors band estimate for 1993 overlap with the 1998 bands (Skoufias 2004). For most of the sample (about 90 per cent of households considered) 1993 bands are clearly above 1998 confirming our hypothesis of declining elasticity in the two years as an effect of increasing price elasticity. Only at the very top the distribution, where confidence intervals bands are wider and elasticity is measured with less precision, the difference seems to be statistically insignificant and bands intersects.

It is interesting to note also that at very low levels of income (close to the lowest decile—10 per cent) the two curves are distanced. Since we have

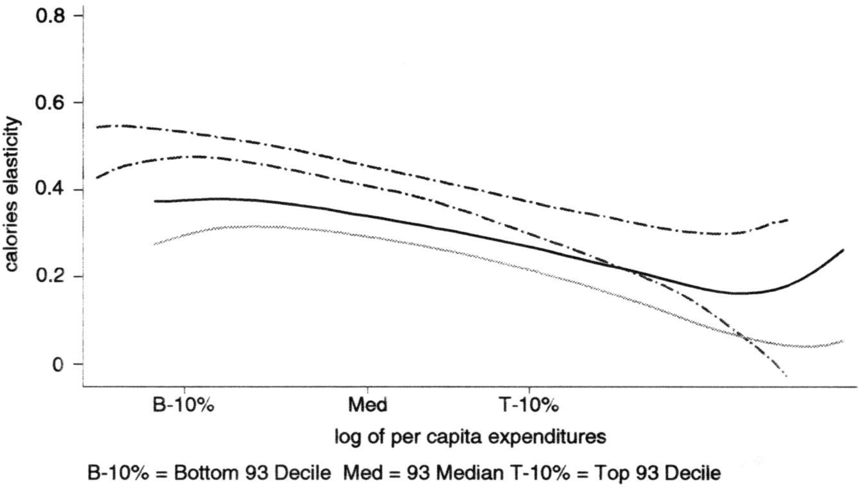

Figure 7.4. 1993 and 1998 standard error bands for elasticities of per capita calories and per capita expenditures in rural areas

Note: Continuous lines 1998, dashed lines 1993.
Source: Author's calculations using VLSS 1993 and 1998.

observed only limited variation between the food groups, the increased price elasticity is explainable by more diversification within the groups, say for example better quality rice and cereals with a lower calorie content, suggesting that also at low level of income distribution the minimum calories requirement is reached by some households.

In conclusion, our preliminary analysis on elasticity adds important elements to our general picture. The calorie/expenditures elasticity is statistically significant and robust to the use of different tools. The comparison of the two periods shows that, following expectations, a decline in calorie expenditures elasticity is associated with an increase in consumption per capita availability and, we guess, to an increase in food security. This is true not only using a static perspective and comparing various deciles of expenditures but dynamically as well. The impressive performance of Vietnamese economy translated in a statistically significant reduction in the calorie expenditures elasticity for almost all deciles.

7.6 The Calorie Expenditures Relation: The Parametric Approach

The bivariate analysis implemented so far does not consider important effects that may influence calorie consumption. It is important checking the robustness of previous section results controlling for household members

Table 7.4. Regression results for rural and urban areas, 1993 and 1998

Dependent variable: calories per capita per day	1993	1998
Log of outlay	0.359**	0.246**
Urban (1:urban; 0:rural)	−0.143**	−0.072*
Age group from 30	0.013	0.021*
Age group from 40	0.071**	0.065**
Age group from 50	0.107**	0.085**
Age group from 60	0.084**	0.078**
Spring dummy	0.015	0.017*
Summer dummy	0.031**	−0.007
Household size	−0.016**	−0.028**
Gender of household head (1:M; 0:F)	0.027**	0.027**
Cereals price (log)	−0.010**	−0.025**
Fish price (log)	−0.009*	−0.009
Rice price (log)	−0.095**	−0.109**
Oils and fats price (log)	0.009*	−0.017**
Constant	4.763**	5.552**
Observations	4530	5846
Robust R-square	0.52	0.43

age, household composition, location, prices, and other observable characteristics. The 1998 regression is a weighted least square one due to sample design while for 1993 we used a simple OLS. In both cases heteroskedasticity problem has been tackled using White correction for robust standard errors.

Exploiting the panel nature of data, we regressed the same equation using a panel fixed effect methodology to control for household heterogeneity. In this way, we further investigated the evolution of calorie consumption over the period reducing potential measurement error (Glewwe and Hall 1998) but we lost various observations due to the big attrition in the data. Regarding the potential endogeneity problem caused by the not clear causality relation between nutrition and income (Stiglitz 1975), we use the same argument proposed by Subramanian and Deaton (1996). In the case of Vietnam in both years it is possible to buy 2,000 calories (rice) for less than 2,000 dong. The average rural worker can easily buy this quantity using 1/20 of the daily wage (GSO 2000) and with this quantity receives enough energy for a full day farming activity. We did not find evidence of any nutrition trap.

Per capita expenditure is significant and has a positive effect on calories (Table 7.4). As expected, the elasticity lowers among 1993 and 1998. In 1993 elasticity was slightly below 0.36 and within a few years it reduced to 0.25. This result is consistent with important economic improvements registered by Vietnam in the period considered and confirms findings of the non-parametric analysis. In the panel analysis the coefficient is positive and between the two OLS values. This again confirms that there was a statistically significant reduction[5] in the elasticity insensitive to changes in the tools.

Most of the other variables have well-determined effects on calorie consumption. Bigger families, presumably those with more children, tend to consume comparatively fewer calories per day while older household consume comparatively more calories than particularly young ones and very old ones (the tails of age cohorts). Rural household require, on average, more calories and, as a consequence, urban dummy is negative and significant.

The prices of most consumed items have in all cases a negative and significant impact. In particular, the rice price elasticity, the main item consumed by almost all households, shows the greatest value in all three regressions. Not surprisingly, the household looks to be extremely sensitive to the 'other cereals' price variations, confirming our analysis on the food balance shares: cereals still provide about 70 per cent of household's calories.

7.7 Conclusions

In this chapter we investigated the changes in wellbeing in Vietnam during the 1990s, analysing, for the first time for this country, the evolution of food security. Our aim was to check the robustness of the impressive economic improvements proposing food security measures and searching a certain degree of association between monetary approach results and ours.

Descriptive statistics were useful to understand the pattern of changes. Between 1993 and 1998 the average caloric intake, the most common measure of food security, has increased in almost all Vietnam even though the intensity has been different. Poor households living generally in rural areas increased their calorie consumption, while rich ones preferred to reduce the quantity of calories consumed opting for an improvement in quality.

The decline in rice cereals and pulses consumption has been massive in particular between the richest strata of the population. Poor households, while increasing the amount of calorie consumed still are too much dependent on energy from carbohydrates and little from proteins and lipids. A preliminary assessment of the food security variation showed that improvements, were, as expected, more concentrated among richer households rather than poor ones since dietary diversity indicators showed little improvement among poorer strata too.

We then compared these findings based with anthropometric data. Anthropometric measures tend to improve less quickly than the calorie intake measures. This tendency is visible in particular in northern regions and among the

[5] We interpret the coefficient of expenditures of the panel regression as a mean value among 1993 and 1998. Being less than 1993, it means that 1998 data contributed to reduce it.

poorest quintile of the population. Furthermore, anthropometric measures show a less optimistic picture in terms of food security. In particular, while calorie intake availability improved in the poorer northern regions (northern upland and north coastal), anthropometric measures hardly envisage any improvements of food security. Indeed, this discrepancy between the two type of measures is circumscribed to few and under-populated regions. In the rest of the country, they both clearly indicate a positive trend in food security.

We then focused on the calorie/expenditures elasticity and compared elasticities between 1993 and 1998. While in the literature, many studies concentrated on the non-linearity of calorie/expenditures elasticity, finding that the more income increases the more elasticity declines, few contributions compared the elasticity function across time and tried to link calorie income elasticity patterns with food security evolution. Our results confirm that this link is strong and show that calorie income elasticity changed in the direction expected among quintiles (static analysis) but over time as well.

We used both parametric and non-parametric tools and the results were convergent, suggesting a steep decline consistent with impressive economic improvements. We concluded that, in general, food security improved in Vietnam during the 1990s though big differences remain among expenditures deciles and, due to the accentuated spatial difference, among regions.

References

Abdulai, A. and D. Aubert (2004). 'Nonparametric and Parametric Analysis of Calorie Consumption in Tanzania'. *Food Policy*, 29: 113–29.

A. B. Aromolaran (2004). 'Household Income, Women's Income Share and Food Calorie Intake in South Western Nigeria'. *Food Policy*, 29: 507–30.

Baulch, B., and N. Masset (2003). 'Do Monetary and Non-Monetary Indicators Tell the Same Story about Chronic Poverty? A Study of Vietnam in 1990s'. *World Development*, 31 (3): 441–53.

Baulch, B., and N. Minot (2004). 'The Spatial Distribution of Poverty in Vietnam and the Potential for Targeting', in D. Dollar, P. Glewwe, and N. Agrawal (eds), *Economic Growth, Poverty and Household Welfare in Vietnam*. Washington, DC: World Bank.

Cuong T. Q., M. J. Dibley, S. Bowe, T. T. M. Hahn, and T. T. H. Loan (2006) 'Obesity in Adults: An Emerging Problem in Urban Areas of Ho Chi Minh City, Vietnam'. *European Journal of Clinical Nutrition*, advance online publication 13 December.

Deaton, A. (1997). *The Analysis of Household Surveys: A Micro-Econometric Approach to Development Policy*. Baltimore, MD: Johns Hopkins University Press.

Deaton, A., and M. Zaidi (2002). 'Guidelines for Constructing Consumption Aggregates for Welfare Analysis'. LSMS Working Paper 135. Washington, DC: World Bank.

Fritzen, S. (2003). 'Growth Inequality and the Future of Poverty Reduction in Vietnam'. *Journal of Asian Economics*, 13 (5): 635–57.

GSO (2000). *Living Standard Survey: Poverty Survey, 1999*. Ha Noi: General Statistics Office of Vietnam.

Hoddinott, J., and Y. Yohannes (2002). 'Dietary Diversity as a Food Security Indicator'. FCND Discussion Paper 136. Washington, DC: Food Consumption and Nutrition Division of the IFPRI.

Meenakshi, J. V., and B. Vishwanathan (2003). 'Developing Country Nutrition Does Improve with Income: A Look at Calorie and Protein Intakes, 1983 to 1993/94'. *Sarvekshana Journal*.

Micklewright, J., and S. Ismail (2001). 'What Can Child Anthropometry Reveal about Living Standards and Public Policy? An Illustration from Central Asia'. *Review of Income and Wealth*, 47 (1): 65–80.

Minot, N., and F. Goletti (2000). 'Rice Market Liberalization and Poverty in Viet Nam'. IFPRI Research Report 114. Washington, DC: IFPRI.

Nube, M., (2001). 'Confronting Dietary Energy Supply with Anthropometry in the Assessment of Undernutrition Prevalence at the Level of Countries'. *World Development*, 29 (7): 1275–89.

Palmer-Jones, R., and K. Sen (2001). 'On India's Poverty Puzzles and Statistics of Poverty'. *Economic and Political Weekly*, 36 (3): 211–17.

Ryan, J. (2002). 'Assessing the Impact of Food Policy Research: Rice Trade Policies in Viet Nam'. *Food Policy*, 27 (1): 1–29.

Saith R. and B. Harriss-White (1999) 'The Gender Sensitivity of Well-Being Indicators'. *Development and Change*, 30: 465–97.

Skoufias, E. (2003). 'Is the Calorie-Expenditures Elasticity Sensitive to Price Changes? Evidence from Indonesia'. *World Development*, 31 (7): 1291–307.

Stiglitz, J. (1975). 'The Efficiency Wages Hypothesis, Surplus Labor and the Distribution of Expenditures in LDCs'. *Oxford Economics Papers*, 28 (2): 185–207.

Subramanian, S., and A. Deaton (1996). 'The Demand for Food and Calories'. *Journal of Political Economy*, 104 (1): 133–62.

Tesfaye F., N. G. Nawi, H. van Minh, P. Byass, Y. Berhane, R. Bonita, and S. Wall (2007). 'Association Between Body Mass Index and Blood Pressure across Three Populations in Africa and Asia'. *Journal of Human Hypertension*, 21: 28–37.

Thang, N. M., and B. M. Popkin (2004). 'Patterns of Food Consumption in Vietnam: Effects on Socioeconomic Groups during an era of Economic Growth'. *European Journal of Clinical Nutrition*, 58: 145–53.

USAID (1992). 'Policy Determination 19, Definition of Food Security'. 13 April. Washington, DC: USAID.

Vishwanatha, B., and J. V. Meenakshi (2003). 'Calorie Deprivation in Rural India 1983–1999/2000'. *Economic and Political Weekly*, 38 (4): 369–75.

World Bank (2004). 'Vietnam Development Report 2004'. Washington, DC: World Bank.

8

Measuring the Efficacy of Targeted Schemes: Public Works Programmes in India

Nilabja Ghosh and Basudeb Guha-Khasnobis

8.1 Introduction

With the advance of agricultural technology, hunger is no longer due to global or national food shortage (Pinstrup-Anderson 2002). The problem lies elsewhere. Conventional macroeconomic and employment generating state policies in developing countries often (Braun 1995) bypass certain sections of the society, leaving them deprived of the purchasing power to meet their minimum and desired intake of food. Even the current processes of structural adjustment and globalization that are expected to bridge areas of shortage and those of abundance and benefit millions can leave many others worse off. The losers would include those disadvantaged due to geography and due to physical, economic, social and gender related reasons. Many believe that mainstream strategies need to be accompanied by direct, well-targeted attempts to eliminate deprivation. The developing country now faces a challenge of balancing mainstream macro-economic policies with micro level safety-netting and development strategies for the excluded sections. Effectively targeted and well-designed welfare programmes backed by positive strategies of development provide the key to this balance. However, the choice of an appropriate strategy to combat poverty and food insecurity has today become an extremely complex task due to policy contradictions and ideological dissension generated by growth-oriented policies and poverty alleviation programmes. The purpose of this chapter is to examine the main targeted hunger elimination schemes in India with a view to measuring their efficacy in reaching the truly needy.

India has a long and diverse history of development and poverty alleviation in which nutrition-based and wage-employment generating programmes were two of the principal instruments. Self-employment generation was a third approach. Both nutrition and employment programmes have gradually taken new shapes in the times of liberalization. While targeting of needy beneficiaries and integration to draw on synergies with other developmental objectives have been the principles for redesigning in both cases, wage employment through public works programmes (PWP) have recently taken a centre stage in India's democracy when the multi-party ruling coalition accepted the giant sized National Rural Employment Guarantee (NREG) programme as a policy instrument and also because the programme has raised scepticism about the expenditure burden it might impose on the national budget.

Of all the rural welfare programmes, PWP has a special appeal in being self-selective that makes targeting its natural property. We, however, question the targeting success of PWP in India. Considering food insecurity as a measure of extreme deprivation we make a comparative assessment of targeting in four different states by examining the convergence of households likely to be food-insecure and households likely to benefit from PWP. Data from national and official sample survey NSSO are used for the purpose.

8.2 India's Approach to Food Security

By the end of the 1980s, the food economy of the country came to a crossroads. First, the green revolution had already offered the coveted self-sufficiency and in fact the stock of foodgrains captured about half of the government's huge food subsidy bill. Second, the excess-producing regions faced problems with saturation. Third, in spite of the abundance, scarcity at the household and sometimes at the regional level still persisted. In fact the lagging rural regions, where more than 70 per cent of the population live, people now grapple with a newly acquired pressure to achieve a higher quality of life in which education of children and health care assume increased importance. Fourth, a severe balance of payment crisis forced India to approach the World Bank and as a result, structural adjustments began to shape the 1990s. This was followed by the emergence of the World Trade Organization (WTO). The paradigm shift was not easy. The policies that the government had to take up since the 1990s generally went contrary to India's own unique economic approach pursued until then. Fiscal and monetary prudence and the tenet of price correction through market facilitation began to take a toll on traditional priority on credit, subsidies and welfare programmes that were meant for the rural poor.

8.2.1 *The Public Distribution System and Other Welfare Schemes in India*

The *public distribution system* (PDS)—a time-tested instrument in India—expressly addresses the issue of household food security.[1] It is an alternative and parallel market that makes foodgrains available at a 'fair price', thus protecting consumers from the high prices generated by the free market mechanism. The PDS became a component in an integrated foodgrain policy of the government: Food Corporation of India (FCI), a public undertaking, conducts the foodgrain operations on behalf of the government. It procures grains at remunerative prices from the farmers, sells at reasonable prices, and maintains buffer and operational stocks. The PDS has time and again been criticized because of its failure to serve the poor, its urban bias, its limited coverage in states with a high concentration of rural poor, and the lack of transparent and accountable delivery arrangements. In other words, the broad-based PDS was perceived as highly untargeted and costly, and there were calls for change, including its dismantling to let the open market adjust prices.

Inevitably, during the reforms of the 1990s, the PDS had to be redesigned. Improved coverage in backwards areas, decentralized procurement of grains by state governments or their agencies in 1997–8, and further modification of the PDS into a two-tiered structure known as the *targeted public distribution system* (TPDS) were some of the new elements introduced. In TPDS the beneficiaries were identified on the basis of a specific poverty line: (i) households existing below the poverty line (BPL households), whose entitlements were subsidized and (ii) above-the-poverty-line households (APL) who were allocated foodgrain at cost price. This was the new beginning of targeting the PDS.[2] To focus the TPDS further, *Antodaya Anna Yojana* (AAY) was launched in 2000 to identify the poorest of the BPL families for the provision of grains at highly subsidized rates. The PDS also supplies to other food-based welfare programmes of the government. In addition, open sales from public stocks are made to stabilize prices and protect consumers against high food prices. Despite the efforts at fine-tuning, at present the PDS is, at best, a partial solution to food insecurity. The subsidy burden is at odds with the economic and fiscal management of the economy while the misery of undernutrition that persists even when stocks exist has been described as 'mass murder' (Drèze 2001). The withdrawals from PDS (off take) fall short of grain allocation because even the BPL price is not always within the reach of the poor. Also, many households mistakenly identified as being 'above the poverty line' cannot afford the APL price. The demarcation of APL and

[1] 'Rationing', as it was originally called, has a long history in India, dating from the Second World War. Introduced by the British government, the PDS was retained after independence as a deliberate social policy.

[2] Initially the BPL entitlement was 10 kg per month per family but was increased as of 2002 to 35 kg for both groups. The entitlement for AAY household was 25 kg per family per month, and is now the same as the APL and BPL entitlements.

BPL itself is rather arbitrary based on a poverty line that is questionable. Further the actual identification of BPL is frequently blamed for local level manipulation.

A number of financial assistance schemes, collectively known as *national social assistance programmes* (NSAPs), were launched in 1995–6. To meet the constitutional commitment towards poor households, NSAPs[3] seek to provide a minimum assurance to those in need or disabled by old age, death of breadwinner, and maternity. *Annapurna*, a scheme started in 2000, provides free food to specific old aged groups. Community grain banks, built with a participatory approach, focus on remote tribal-dominated areas for the prevention of starvation deaths, while the wheat-based nutrition programme is catered to adolescent girls; women's hostels for backward classes serve the traditionally neglected gender. The national nutrition mission, launched in 2001, provides subsidized foodgrains to adolescent girls and expecting and lactating mothers.

One of the most innovative nutrition programmes is the National Programme for Nutritional Support to Primary Education, or the Mid-day Meal scheme (MDM) as it is popularly known, drawing on the successful experience of Tamil Nadu. Initiated in all government and government-aided schools, MDM provides either cooked lunches or raw foodgrains to assure food security without bias. Its goal is to eliminate classroom hunger and promote balanced socialization along with free and compulsory education to all children.

The integrated child development services programme (ICDS), started in 1975, is another community-based outreach programme attending to early childhood care and pregnant and lactating women. The *Anganwadi* centre has become a symbol of the government system providing services to the disadvantaged communities at the village/hamlet level. ICDS also takes an integrated approach contributing to goals of nutrition, health, early childhood development, primary health care and universal elementary education.

8.2.2 *Poverty Programmes and the Evolution of Public Works*

Employment programmes consider the lack of work as the single most important cause of poverty among households. Its rationale is that when the free market fails to provide livelihood opportunities to the poor, particularly the unskilled, the government steps in. In rural India agriculture remains the principal source of employment for the people so that the labour hiring landed class have a monopsony in the labour market. The role of non-farm employment is limited and a matter of concern (Sen and Jha 2005). Lack of

[3] The NSAPs encompass the national old age pension scheme (NOAPS), the national family benefit scheme (NFBS), and the national maternity benefit scheme (NMBS).

Table 8.1. Quality of employment of rural (principal status) workers

Year	Self employed		Regular employed		Casual employed	
	Male	Female	Male	Female	Male	Female
1987–8	57.5	54.9	10.4	4.9	32.1	40.2
1993–4	56.7	51.3	8.7	3.4	34.6	45.3
1999–2000	54.4	50.0	9.0	3.9	36.6	46.1

Note: Figures are percentage share of employment. Self employment includes helping in family enterprise.

Source: NSSO (2001).

earning opportunities manifested as extensive underemployment and a large and increasing share of casual labour in the employment market is a glaring shortcoming. Table 8.1 shows that over time the self employment base has narrowed and regular and salaried employments have a minimal role in the rural economy. As a result, the labourers in farm employment and in particular the women among them, get a poor deal with utter lack of bargaining power. While men often move out to cities for livelihood, the case in appalling for women who have to stay back for household responsibilities as well as inadequacy of living facilities in cities and add to the supply force in rural labour market with little skill or education. Manual, repetitive, arduous, and even injurious jobs are assigned to them along with discriminatingly poor pay (Kaur 1996). Further, with any increase in family affluence the women drop off from this disagreeable labour (which, not surprisingly, also lacks social prestige) market and sometimes fall prey to dependence, vulnerability, and domestic abuse (Boserup 1975). By creating an alternative and well-designed job market, wage-employment programmes can not only create earning opportunities but also improve the bargaining power of workers in conventional market. The benefit could be more to the women who suffer the abysmal employment conditions disproportionately more.

The history of wage employment as public works programmes in India is dotted with programmes more diverse in their names than in content, and these have enjoyed more political importance, while showing a bad implementation record. The *Rural Works Programme*, first initiated in 1970–1, was later re-designated as the *Drought Prone Area Programme* (DPAP). The *Food-for-Work Programme* was started in 1977 with the aim of utilizing the surplus food stocks of the times.

The *National Rural Employment Programme* (NREP) is a pioneering root programme initiated in 1980 for the employment policy to be followed in the years that followed. The *Rural Landless Employment Guarantee Programme* (RLEGP) was another one instituted in 1983 to address the plight of the core rural poor. In 1989 NREP and RLEGP were merged to form the famous *Jawahar Rozhar Yojana* (JRY). In 1993 the JRY was again modified, and two of its components the *Million Wells* and *Indira Awaas Yojana* for rural water and housing respectively were taken out of JRY. Another typical rural works programme, the *Employment Assurance Scheme* (EAS), was also set up in 1993 in districts covered by the modified PDS to provide 100 days of unskilled manual labour to the rural poor who want it. In 2001 the JRY was redesigned again and renamed *Jawahar Gram Samriddhi Yojana* (JGSY). Finally in August 2001 the EAS and the JGSY were merged and a new scheme *Sampoorna Grameen Rozgar Yojana* (SGRY) was created. The objective of the SGRY was to provide additional wage employment with food security in rural areas. Beneficiaries are temporarily employed to build community assets and infrastructure. The cost of the scheme, which includes distribution of foodgrains, is shared by the central and state governments' allotment of funds and foodgrain. For food security the SGRY envisages the distribution of foodgrains at 5 kg per worked-day to the workers as part of wages for which the central government undertakes to supply foodgrains free of cost. Besides this there are area development programmes that also aim to provide employment for the poor. The *Rashtriya Sam Vikas Yojana* that addresses deprivation in the most backward pockets is one such endeavour. It incorporates a special plan for the most backward region of Orissa.

In November 2004 a newly elected coalition government launched the *food-for-work* programme, based on *rozgar badhao* (increase incomes), the slogan of the time. An employment scheme already functional in the state of Maharashtra and acclaimed by both international and national critics inspired the acceptance of the national level employment guarantee scheme and the passing of the National Rural Employment Guarantee Act (NREGA) and its coming into force of February 2006. The major distinction between NREG and the SGRY and the stream of employment programmes that had worked in India is the legal enforceability of right to livelihood conferred by the Act. The Act provides legal guarantee to 100 days of employment in every financial year to every rural household with an adult member willing to do unskilled manual work. A programme officer and the village *panchayat* will implement the programmes without any other middleman such as contractors. The salient features are the inclusion of all willing rural households without arbitrary stipulation of BPL households, reservation of women and a wage rate not falling below the states' statutory agricultural wage rate.

8.2.3 *Advantages of Public Works*

Historically, in the face of natural disasters, 'relief' work has been used as the means of creating income and employment. However, over the past decades, this option has been used in the developing world on a *regular* basis for poverty alleviation. PWP—unlike most anti-poverty measures—is not in the nature of assistance. Rather, it is an alternative job market, in which needy households can participate voluntarily and with dignity, and work to ensure a minimum income to satisfy basic needs. The PWP is also a politically recognized safety-net to the rural poor (Hiraway 1994). Unlike most welfare programmes, it need not entail wasteful subsidies since payment is only made against productive work through which useful assets can be created. If implemented well, PWP can lead to the creation of important rural amenities and the provision of necessary services. Thus, PWP can be productivity enhancing. Housing, approach roads and bridges as well as school buildings add to rural physical and social infrastructure. The construction of wells and restoration of tanks, soil conservation and improvement of the watershed are services that directly impact on agriculture. The poorest population sections benefit from the development and maintenance of common property resources. Thus, the poor and the jobless are, on the one hand, assured of a minimum income through the PWP, while on the other hand, important public goods that the government needs to provide are created. The two-pronged approach has potential for long-term sustainability since productivity is increased in the process.

Public works constitute a tool for conferring purchasing power or direct nutrition to the chosen beneficiary. Most employment programmes have paid wages in cash or in food grains often making use of the stocks in public pool. One important advantage of the PWP is that it can be self-targeting. Identifying the poor presents a challenge in most poverty programmes and results in profligate use of scarce public resources, whereas the PWP, through the type of work and wage rates offered, can be designed to attract the truly needy and to discourage the less deserving. For its target selection, the PWP need not rely on some arbitrary identification of the poor that may not always be accurate or exhaustive. But this can become a disadvantage if the project is not effectively designed and implemented. If the work or conditions become too arduous, unpleasant, gender predisposed or logistically inconvenient, the PWP may in fact discourage the truly needy, given their specific socioeconomic characteristics, and thus become self-defeating. Faulty administration can enable people and political constituencies with more influence to find devious ways of cornering the benefits while the poor stay away. The test of the programme lies in its ability to focus only on the truly needy (Ravallion 1990).

8.2.4 *Institutional Changes for Rural Programmes*

The centralized administration system in India working through a large and complex bureaucracy has traditionally administered the country's rural development programmes. It was all along acknowledged that the system was inadequate for India's vast rural region resulting in inefficiencies and leakages of funds. A more participative system was required. The decade of the 1990s saw important changes in governance for rural development.

The principle of grassroots governance had its roots in the immediate post-independence days (Singh 1999) and was advanced through the Community Development Programmes started in 1952, which enabled administration and planning to be carried out at the sub-state levels. Enactment of the Panchayat Raj Act by some states, following Batwant Rai Mehta's recommendations in 1957 was a further step. Article 40 of the Constitution of India empowered the states to organize the *panchayats* as units of self-government. The cherished principle of grassroots governance embodied in Panchayati Raj institution (PRI) finally received constitutional recognition with an amendment of the constitution only in 1992, which is a landmark episode for the attainment of food security and poverty alleviation at the household level. This allows rural inhabitants, who constitute the vast majority of India's population, to address their own needs, to participate directly in their own development efforts, to select projects according to local needs and to have a voice to air their grievances and problems. Local governments elected by the people, now free of the red tape that characterizes centralized governance, and actual beneficiaries are able to work in close interaction and to monitor progress as well as the utilization of funds. Local governments are encouraged to mobilize local resources locally to complement government resources, to identify beneficiaries and to involve voluntary agencies for programme implementation. Payments can be made transparent through public accountability. The PRI now has the most important role in the conduct of rural development programmes, in identifying the poor and the needy and in implementing the SGRY and the NREG.

8.3 An Empirical Study: Method and Data

Ideally, a targeted PWP should reach the needy—and only the needy households. As food is one of the basic needs of a household, we attempt to examine the linkage between PWP and food security. The study is based on unit-level observations from the 55th round of quinquennial survey (1999–2000) of the National Sample Survey Organization of India (NSSO). The study covers the rural population of four states: Andhra Pradesh, Madhya Pradesh, West Bengal, and Orissa. The choice of the states is based on data availability to us. Further, a model of separate analyses of the four states offered a possibility of a broad based yet comparative view of PWP in India. As food insecurity and public works are relevant for the less skilled and uninformed sections, the study concentrates on households headed by individuals with no education beyond school. This group constitutes the largest section of rural households, excluding less than 2 per cent of households in most cases.

The NSSO provides information at the household *and* member levels on various socioeconomic attributes. Since consumption information is provided at the household level, the household is taken as the unit of study. However, member-level information on age and gender composition of households and education of the head of household are obtained from member files and merged with the household database used for the analysis. The household file provides data on PWP participation though in a limited way. A household is reported as participating in a public works programme if at least one member has been employed for at least 60 days through a PWP over the last 365 days. We had to make use of this information on PWP participation. There are two complexities involved in the kind of analysis undertaken here.

The first one relates to the identification of the deprived households. One way to demarcate the food-insecure households with the available data could be on the basis of conventional poverty line set historically in accordance with a nutritional standard. However, the poverty line effectively allows for substitution among alternative items of requirement within limited means but is blind to the actual allocation and the individualistic requirements of households. Even a nonpoor household could suffer acute undernutrition with this definition. Neither are the poor households a necessary sub-set of the food insecure. In fact the poorest households may have access to cereals, even if of inferior quality such as that obtained by begging or from charity organizations. A less poor household will possibly have constraints on potential sources of income or food, and often other priorities in their expenditure decisions such as when children's education and health take primacy over food. This study therefore uses the household level specific information provided by the NSSO on food consumption in preference to the all encompassing poverty line and considers foodgrains, specifically cereal consumption in physical units, as an indicative measure of food security of the household. To get a cut-off for adequacy of food consumption we used the norm given by India's apex scientific agency ICMR. In Figure 8.1 we find that food is a more extensive problem than income poverty in three of the four states, more so in Andhra. In Orissa however despite high lingering rate of poverty less people are deprived of necessary requirement of food.

Building an analytical food security index is a subject of controversy. We concede that the measure we are using is not above such controversy, although we have very good reasons for using it. The NSSO has been extending its queries beyond physical and calorific intakes to include various questions on meals taken by members, but the results are inconclusive at best. Even the calorie-based indicator is not above question. Human life depends on various nutrients and calorie is but one requirement. Besides, what calorie level can be considered adequate for a healthy life? The answer is far from clear. The government of India, in setting the poverty line, applied a norm based on the ICMR recommendation of 2,400 kcal per consumer unit for

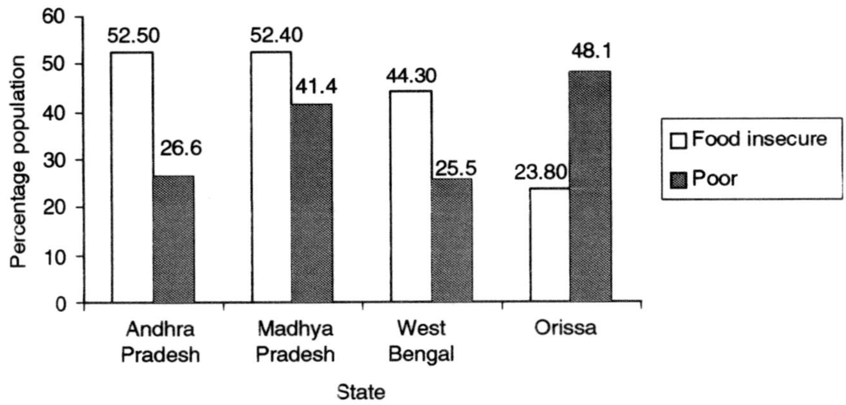

Figure 8.1. Food insecurity and poverty

rural India. FAO, on the other hand, fixed a minimum requirement of 1,890 kcal for a typical citizen in India. Actual calorific requirements depend on factors such as gender, age, body-weight and nature of work, all of which vary among individuals. Fixing a norm, therefore, requires a detailed analysis of the population being studied which is beyond our scope.

We have taken cereal consumption as a measure for two simple reasons:

(1) Cereals are the basic ingredient of the average Indian diet and provide the highest energy share; about 71 per cent of all eaten foods. The Indian government has always recognized the central place of foodgrains in rural basket of consumption and addressed food security of households in PDS and various welfare schemes mainly through provision of cereals and more importantly, by paying wages in PWP partly in terms of foodgrains.

(2) Recognizing the nutritional and human demands and desires for other kinds of foods we have looked at the data on consumption of various other food items given by the NSSO. Computing correlation coefficients across households (Table 8.2) we find that significant statistical correlation exists between consumption of such items and that of cereals in the states concerned. Only in Andhra Pradesh cereal-substitutes seem to replace cereals. Pulses are the chief source of another vital nutrient namely protein for most people in India, particularly the poor, and these show a high correlation, especially in Orissa. Milk and milk products and vegetables, the other two possible dietary diversifications, show a clear positive relation with cereal intake and so do the edible oils. These indications of complementarities also encouraged us to take cereal consumption as a proxy indicator for nutrition and food intake in general.

Table 8.2. Correlation (Spearman's) between household consumption of cereals with other foods

Food	Andhra Pradesh	Madhya Pradesh	West Bengal	Orissa
Cereal substitutes	−0.330**	0.023**	0.115**	0.147**
Pulses and products	0.125**	0.379**	0.413**	0.536**
Milk and products	0.395**	0.324**	0.297**	0.338*
Edible oils	0.541**	0.311**	0.379**	0.517**
Eggs, fish, meat	0.418**	0.282**	0.480**	0.510**
Vegetables	0.388**	0.272**	0.442**	0.653**
Fruit	0.248**	0.231**	0.177**	0.398**

Note: ** Significant at 0.05 level (two tailed).

Source: Computed based on NSSO data.

In Table 8A.1 (in the Appendix) we find that according to *The Food Insecurity Atlas of Rural India*, published by the Swaminathan Research Foundation, the consumption pattern in India is highly cereal based and food consumption in all other items fall short of the ICMR norms. In all the selected states, the average per capita consumption of cereal exceeds the norm and the ratio of cereal consumption to norm is higher than the all-India average, a fact which qualifies these states as dominantly cereal consuming. Cereals still seem to be the main dietary item and chief source of energy. The average cereal consumption in Orissa at 531 g per day is the highest among the states and is well above ICMR norm. Yet, Orissa ranks low in terms of GDP and poverty and NSSO reports the state as deficient in other food security indicators such as meal adequacy indicating that in Orissa a higher standard consumption basket is lacking. West Bengal follows in cereal preference. Madhya Pradesh shows a higher (but below norm) ratio in respect of pulses. Milk and vegetable consumption make up 50 per cent of the norm but is lower in Orissa.

The percentage of food-insecure households by this measure varies from 23 in Orissa to 53 per cent in Andhra and the share is also high in Madhya Pradesh and West Bengal (Figure 8.1). The ranking of the regions within the states (Table 8A.2) also vary. In Orissa the southern region—constituting the districts of Phulbani, Koraput, and Kalahandi—stands out as the most food insecure while the coastal region is the least. In Andhra, too, the coastal region that includes the two Godavari districts is the most food secure and the first places are taken by the inland regions. In Madhya Pradesh, southwest and Malwa have higher share of the food insecure and Chhattisgarh (now new different state) and Vindhya are relatively better off. In West Bengal the hilly Himalayan districts are found relatively better off.

Lately with higher incomes and improved knowledge of nutrition, the consumption patterns in India have shifted from cereals to milk products, fleshy food, and fruit (Radhakrishna and Ravi 1992). In many states, the average cereal consumption has dropped to less than the ICMR norm and is

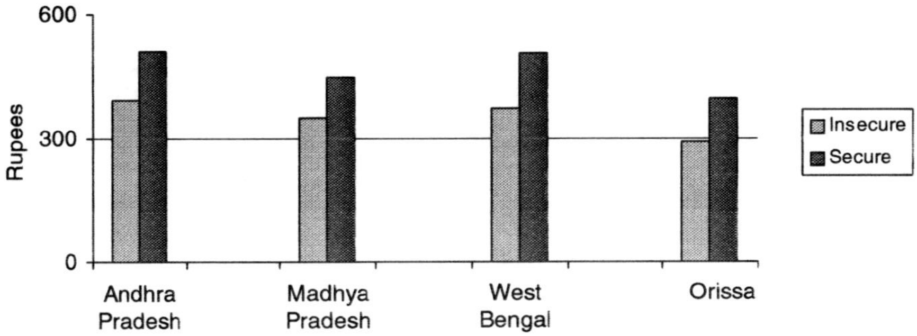

Figure 8.2. Monthly per capita expenditure (total) of food secure and insecure households

generally compensated by other foods. But for the large majority of the rural population having low incomes and limited information, the substitution may not be significant and cereals continue to be the main dietary ingredient. The low consumption of cereals in rural India is of concern in the cases where no improvement in the consumption of other foods is obvious. Perhaps one can conjecture that the high (above 50 per cent) proportion of food-insecure households in Andhra Pradesh and Madhya Pradesh correspond to more affluent groups preferring to substitute higher value foods for cereals. Although this possibility cannot be ruled out, Figure 8.2 finds a positive association between food security and MPCE (monthly per capita expenditure) in all the states. Table 8A.3 consistently shows that the food-secure groups have, on average, a higher MPCE than the corresponding food-insecure group. This holds for all the states analysed and all regions within them. The possibility of dietary diversification associated with higher income is thus not borne out in our demarcation of the food insecure.

The second complexity of analysis is econometric. The relation between participation and food insecurity is fraught with bi-directional causality. A single equation regression to capture the relation would invariably suffer from a simultaneity bias making the results meaningless We have overcome this hurdle by a simple method of using a model of two separate equations, We have considered only exogenous and non-stochastic variables on the right hand side making use of the various social, economic and biological information given by NSSO from the survey. The dependent variables are participation and food insecurity in the two equations which are not likely to have any causal effect on the right hand side variables. The relations draw on the various bias and discriminations inherent in the society that impinge on economic positions and participation decisions of the people. Government policies have also conventionally attacked poverty using this approach of discriminating protection for select sections whose needs are expected to

Table 8.3. Economic access to cereals by households, according to food security status

	Andhra Pradesh	Madhya Pradesh	West Bengal	Orissa
Imputed price (Rs/kg)				
Food insecure	8.67	7.7	10.8	8.7
Food secure	8.88	7.9	10.5	8.9
Economic access (kg)				
Food insecure	45.57	47.7	35.15	33.3
Food secure	57.6	59.4	48.68	44.5

Notes: Economic access is MPCE divided by imputed price;
Coefficients of variations across all households are, respectively, for the four states:
(i) Imputed price: 0.21, 0.23, 0.17, 0.17;
(ii) Economic access: 0.45, 0.55, 0.76, 0.46.
Source: Computed based on NSSO data.

be more and who are known to be historically or otherwise disadvantaged. The overall consumption expenditure on all items, often used as a proxy for income, is also generally associated with these characteristic variables. In any case since the expenditure variable itself is likely to be influenced by participation and possibly food insecurity this variable is also not used as an independent variable to avoid the simultaneity inevitable. The relation between PWP and food insecurity still remains implicit in the two equations although they are now free of the econometric bias.

Food markets are usually hypothesized as fairly perfect markets, and households are often the price-takers subject to locally prevalent prices. In reality, the sources for households accessing food and the quality of consumed food are not always uniform, and the expenditure needed for the same amount of food can differ. In essence, households may pay diverging prices and these can be imputed for cereals from the NSSO data that provide statistics on both expenditures and quantity. The MPCE, taken as a proxy for income, and the paid price convey information on a household's access to food (Table 8.3). Food-insecure households pay marginally less for food than food-secure families except in West Bengal, but the differences are very small. On the whole, imputed prices show modest variation across households. Economic access is substantially higher for the food secure in all states; variations are also larger.

In the states under study, participation is poor, in general less than 5 per cent. The coverage is lowest in Andhra and highest in West Bengal. PWP covers an insignificantly small share of the food-insecure households and notably the households considered as food secure also participate (Table 8.4). Despite the importance of food for sustaining life, a household's perception of its basic wants within today's contemporary world ultimately determines its consumption and earning decisions. Except for Andhra Pradesh, greater share of the food insecure participate compared to the food secure.

Table 8.4. Percentage of households participating in public works programmes, according to food security status

Status	Andhra Pradesh	Madhya Pradesh	West Bengal	Orissa
Insecure	1.2	3.6	3.2	4.7
Secure	1.9	2.7	1.9	3.5
Total	1.5	3.2	2.5	3.8

Source: Computed based on NSSO data.

8.3.1 *Empirical Exercise*

The exercise attempts to study the diverging impacts of important socio-economic factors that are exogenous to the decisionmaking process. Based on discrete choice models of qualitative variables, in a non-coercive system both options[4] can be characterized as binary choice variables (i.e. a household chooses to be or not to be food insecure, or a household chooses to participate or not to participate), given the rational household's individual circumstances. The rationale for the model can be drawn from the random utility class of models, according to which households choose the option if the corresponding net benefit is positive. Correspondingly, a dummy dependent variable Y is defined so that $Y = 1$ if the household chooses the option, $Y = 0$ otherwise.

The probability of the event $P = \text{Prob}(Y = 1)$ is described by a logistic function and the odds are derived as:

$$P/(1 - P) = \exp(\beta' X)$$

where X is a vector of attribute variables describing the household and β is a vector of parameters b_j, showing the direction of relation, the value of β itself being hard to interpret. While the dependent variable taken as the percentage of households in food-insecure states and the percentage of households that participate in PWP takes discrete values indicating the household choice, the exogenous variables are, in most cases, also discrete and the model can help to identify the categories for each possible attribute associated with the option in varying degrees of likelihood. The categories can then be matched for similarity to determine whether the same categories that lead to food insecurity also induce participation. In Table 8.5 the two categories associated with the maximum likelihood of the options are matched and one category with least likelihood is compared. In the case of household features that are continuous variables, direction of the relationship is marked in each case.

[4] Even food insecurity is treated as a state of choice since the household decides on expenditures on various items of requirement depending on their decisions to earn and borrow and allocate in the given market.

Table 8.5. Characteristics of households likely to be food insecure and to participate in public works programmes

	Andhra Pradesh		Madhya Pradesh		Orissa		West Bengal	
	Food insecure	PWP participation	Food insecure	PWP participation	Food insecure	PWP participation	Food insecure	PWP participation
Region								
Most likely	Inland North Southwest	Coastal Inland South	SouthWest Malwa	North Southwest	South North	South Northern	Eastern plains Central plains	Western plains Himalayans
Least likely	Coastal	Southwest	Vindhya	Central	Coastal	Coastal	Himalayans	Central plains
Household type								
Most likely	Others Other labour	Other labour Self-employed agricultural worker	Others Self-employed non-agricultural worker	Other labour Self-employed non-agricultural worker	Others Other labour	Other labour Agricultural labour	Others Other labour	Others Other labour
Least likely	Self-employed agricultural worker	Self-employed non-agricultural worker	Self-employed agricultural worker	Self-employed agricultural worker	Self-employed non-agricultural worker	Self-employed non-agricultural worker	Self-employed agricultural worker	Self-employed agricultural worker
Household composition								
Most likely	More children More working age females	Fewer children Fewer working age females	More children Fewer working age female	More children More working age female	More children Fewer working age female	More children Fewer working age female	More children More working age female members	More children Fewer working age female
Education of head								
Most likely	SEC/HS/ Primary/middle	SEC/HS, illiterate	SEC/HS, illiterate	Non-formal/Pre-primary Primary/middle	Primary/middle, illiterate	Non-formal/Pre-primary, illiterate	Non-formal/Pre-primary, illiterate	Illiterate, SEC/HS
Least likely	Illiterate	Non-formal/Pre-primary	Primary/middle	SEC/HS	SEC/HS	Primary/middle	SEC/HS	Primary/middle
Religion								
Most likely	Hindu, Muslim	Others, Hindu	Muslim, Hindu	Others, Hindu	Muslim, Hindu	Others, Hindu	Others, Muslim	Others, Hindu
Least likely	Others	Muslim	Others	Muslim	Others	Muslim	Hindu	Muslim
Caste								
Most likely	OBC general	SC/ST, OBC	OBC, SC/ST	SC/ST, OBC	SC/ST , OBC	SC/ST OBC	General OBC	OBC General
Least likely	SC/ST	General	General	General	General	General	SC/ST	SC/ST

Source: Based on model results (see tables).

Information on household-level socioeconomic characteristics relevant for the study is collected to the extent possible from the NSSO database. Since geographical advantage plays an important part in the development of a state and the wellbeing of people, the location of the household is important. In this case, the states are divided into different regions according to agro-climatic conditions and other considerations provided by NSSO (see the Appendix). It is known that even when India prospers at the macro-level, people in drought prone, arid and flood-infested regions bear hardship and malnutrition. However, intervention and prioritization by the State endeavour to level out geographical advantages and disadvantages among the states, as balanced regional development is one of the objectives of the state machinery. PWP as a part of state policy, in principle should address this disparity.

Occupation is generally associated with economic conditions, and poverty has been concentrated among certain households, such as agricultural labourers. The NSSO classification of households by 'household type' according to main income source is also applied here to categorize households by occupation. The categories used are self-employed workers in non-agriculture, agricultural labour, other labour, self-employed in agriculture and other occupations. Certain social classes are marginalized for historical reasons, prejudice, or the inevitable majority dominance. Thus, apart from India's main religion Hinduism, other religious groups at times are neglected, although not necessarily. The largest minority group in India are the Muslims. In this model we use three categories Muslim, Hindu and others. The caste system is a well-known complexity of the Indian society and throughout the ages, minority castes, and tribes have been deprived of development approaches. Scheduled castes and tribes (SC/ST) in India are currently protected by the constitution, with a quota in government jobs and special poverty programmes but even now inequality persists. Recently, certain other backward classes (OBCs) have been singled out for special attention, and NSSO reports these households separately as such: SC/ST, OBC, and general.

In the family composition the presence of children creates other demands in addition to food, making a household more vulnerable to food insecurity but less qualified in terms of earning capacity and heavy work. Similarly, female members are at times disadvantaged in the labour market; they are constrained by the nature and condition of the work available, domestic commitments and safety-related issues. Thereby they run the chance of adding to the dependency rate of the household despite their working age. The household composition variables in terms of dependency measured by the proportion of children in family (Children) and gender (Gendratio) by the proportion females in adult members are continuous variables. Education confers information, as well as additional power in the labour market. It also influences consumption decisions and diet awareness. The educational level of the household head is taken to characterize this variable. Admittedly, this variable has its limitation, considering that in some cases, the household head may not be the main source of household finances or awareness. This, however, is not likely for the majority of cases. Based on the assumption that headship implies financial and decisionmaking power, this characterization of the household is retained. Education is taken as a variable with four categories illiterate, non-formal and pre-primary, primary and middle and lastly secondary and higher-secondary, using the NSSO classification of educational attainment. Regression results are reported in Appendix Table 8A.4.

8.3.2 *Results of Regression*

The coefficients with respect to the socio-economic variables in the equation for food security all yield significant parameters. Spatial variation is apparent in the regional effects. Inland North region of Andhra Pradesh, South West of Madhya Pradesh, South of Orissa, and Eastern Plains of West Bengal are the most likely locations of the food insecure.

Households employed in agriculture are less likely to be food insecure, and both the self-employed and the labour in this sector are not represented within the first two likely categories in any of the states. This highlights the importance of agriculture as a minimum support base to the population of India and its role as a food-producing sector. The employment category 'others', which covers a broad range of livelihoods, appears most likely to be food insecure among households in all the states. The other non-agricultural categories other labour and self-employed also appear in the different states. In fact, the self-employed in agriculture group constituting largely the cultivators are the least likely food insecure in three of the states and only in Orissa the self-employed in non-agriculture appear most secure. For a comparison a similar analysis is done for the likelihood of lying below the conventional poverty line and the results are quite different from food insecurity. Agricultural labour leads in income poverty as seen in Appendix Table 8A.5.

The gender composition of the working age members of households goes against females in Andhra and West Bengal implying greater vulnerability of women and households with more shares of women and possibly reflecting on the position of women *vis-à-vis* the employment market. The impact however is negative in Orissa and Madhya Pradesh where women may be participating more in household earning due to reasons like poverty, social norms or employment opportunities. The effect on food insecurity of children's share in household composition is understandably positive and large since they usually add to the mouths to feed but not to the hands that work.

The link between the education of household head and household food insecurity is hardly linear. This is most obvious in Andhra where we have found the presence of relatively higher (school) educated among the food insecure while the illiterate is least likely. Madhya Pradesh presents a more complex case where both the highest and lowest educated in our set appear among the most likely. In Orissa and West Bengal the result is more conservative with the less educated among the like food insecure. This result might be indicative of the employment prospects of educated labour.

Among the religious groups, Muslims are more likely to be food insecure in all the states and the category 'others' least likely except in West Bengal where Hindus are less secure than 'others'. Among the castes the OBC is in the most likely group in all cases and SC/ST, the group drawing maximum policy attention, is present only in Madhya Pradesh and Orissa and incidentally these states have large shares of tribal (ST) population. SC/ST are least likely to be food insecure in Andhra and West Bengal.

There is considerable mismatch in our results between food insecurity and participation. The best match is found in Orissa where regions 'South' and 'North' appear most likely and 'Coastal' as least likely for both food insecurity and participation. Caste also matches perfectly. In Andhra the regional mismatch is striking with the Coastal region, not surprisingly, the least likely food insecure for its agricultural richness. However it gets more of the PWP. Curiously the minority group Muslims are among the food insecure but are least likely participants in all the cases.

8.4 Conclusion

The influence of structural adjustment and globalization is pressuring the government to curb public expenditure, with profound impact on India's historic regime of subsidies and development expenditure. Food insecurity is a form of extreme deprivation that the government of India has always addressed through promotion of food grain production at the macro level and distribution of grains through various nutrition and employment programmes at the household level. In recent times of fiscal restraints, such programmes are being redesigned to be more targeted or integrated with other developmental or social objectives. The targeting is often done with a benchmark poverty line but such a demarcation is not without its weakness.

PWPs known to be broad based, market consistent, and productivity enhancing, are more appealing now for their self-selecting property and this tool has gained more credence both politically and economically resulting in the launch of a national scheme. This chapter examines NSSO survey data on four states, the association between household food insecurity, and participation in public works as it works in India. Based on their importance in rural people's food intake, we have considered household cereal consumption as a proxy for food security and specified a cut-off level using ICMR's norm on cereal consumption and then tried to identify exogenous socioeconomic attributes associated with incidences of food insecurity and participation through logistic models. However cereals are only a part of dietary needs and their physical intake can be used only as a proxy indicator of food security. Besides, the simple method of using two separate equations is adopted only to avoid econometric problems due to the inherent bi-directional causality of the two variables of interest. The regression results at best illustrate how socioeconomic factors have divergent association with food insecurity and with participation and can be considered with caution only.

The regression results on the select four states affirm that food insecurity is a much more complex state than poverty. Diverse and individualistic needs competing for limited incomes, ease of access to physical food, lack of employment opportunities, social stigma about certain ways of earning or acquiring food, and also social compulsions to conceal poverty from public view, are some such factors shaping food insecurity. While income poverty mostly afflicts the labour class, certain regions, the most backward castes and the least educated in expected ways, food insecurity can visit households in various circumstances. Households with less dependency are better off but higher share of women among the adult members can make a household more vulnerable. Agriculture dependent households tend to be more food secure. Participation in PWP is also a complex decision and in the same way, the apparently more privileged in terms of education, caste or occupation can resort to public works. Social stigma, availability of regular employment in the regular market, misallocation of funds across regions, majority domination, and above all quality of design and implementation profoundly impact on participation. Comparing food insecurity and participation in the four states, despite dominant mismatches, success noted in certain cases, most conspicuously in Orissa arouse optimism. The planned nationwide PWP would draw on public resources in a situation of resource shortage and for the best result needs to be targeted towards the neediest. Even the self-selective performance of the PWP is not independent of public action in terms of design and implementation and the nationwide PWP would need constant monitoring.

To the extent the PWP is treated as welfare programme and an essential safety-net in times of globalization targeting is undoubtedly a crucial feature for its feasibility. Human beings have diverse needs with diverse intensities at various times. But food being a primary and biological necessity the state of food insecurity reflects an acute insufficiency of purchasing power. Human beings would avoid this state for oneself and family if possible. Thus a targeted programme should be expected to address food insecurity irrespective of caste, occupation, location, or education. This problem can afflict any household depending on individual circumstances. It is commendable that the NREG has not imposed any poverty-line based eligibility condition for the programme. Our results also show instances of remarkable success of targeting in certain cases, most notably Orissa and affirm the power of the PWP.

However a PWP is also supposed to be developmental by creating valuable rural asset and infrastructure. In the past the JRY and the NREP have shown limited success in this respect and India's rural sector is still starved of any reasonable infrastructure required for economic progress. The NREG's excessive dependence on the capabilities of the PRI, while acceptable on grounds of transparency, may be arguable for its efficiency effect. The method is in stark contrast to how urban infrastructure is built up. Rural infrastructure is extremely important for rural development at this point of time. Also there are other positive programmes promoted by the government to increase incomes in rural India such as by people's enterprise. Emerging services and ancillary prospects in agro-processing and retail industries are some prospects for rural people in the days of liberalization. For the successful transformation of the rural economy there is need for information and marketing infrastructure. The developmental side of NREG can benefit from designing innovation drawing on public and private sector expertise and possibly greater integration with positive income generating programmes. As welfare programmes are a safety net however, targeting remains the key.

Appendix 8.1

Districts in Different Regions

Andhra Pradesh

Region 1—Coastal: Srikakulam, Vizianagaram, Vishakhapatnam, East Godavari, West Godavari Krishna, Guntur, Prakasam, Nellore
Region 2—Inland north: Mahbubnagar, Rangareddi, Hyderabad, Medak, Nizamabad, Adilabad, Karimnagar, Warangal, Khammam, Nalgonda
Region 3—Southwest: Anantapur, Kurnool
Region 4—Inland south: Chittor, Cuddapah

Madhya Pradesh

Region 1—Chattisgarh: Surguja, Bilaspur, Raigarh, Rajnandgaon, Durg Bastar, Raipur
Region 2—Vindhya: Tikamgarh, Chhatarpur, Panna, Satna, Rewa, Shahdol, Sidhi
Region 3—Central: Sagar, Damoh, Vidishah, Bhopal, Sahore, Raisen
Region 4—Malwa: Mandsaur, Ratlam, Ujjain, Shajapur, Dewas, Jhabua, Dhar, Indore

Region 5—South: Jabalpur, Narsimhapur, Mandla, Chhindwara, Seoni, Balaghat
Region 6—Southwest: Khargone, Khandwa, Betul, Kosangabad
Region 7—North: Morena, Bhind, Gwalior, Datia, Shivpuri, Guna

Orissa

Region 1—Coastal: Baleshwar, Cuttak, Ganjam, Puri
Region 2—South: Phulbani, Koraput, Kalahandi
Region 3—North: Sambhalpur, Sundargarh, Keonjhar, Mayurbhanj, Dhenkanal, Bolangir

West Bengal

Region 1—Himalayan: Koch Bihar, Jalpaiguri, Darjeeling
Region 2—Eastern plains: West Dinajpur, Maldah, Murshidabad, Nadia, Birbhum
Region 3—Central plains: North 24-Parganas, Calcutta, Howrah, Hooghly, Burdwan, South 24-Parganas
Region 4—Western plains: Midnapur, Bankura, Purulia

Table 8A.1. Food adequacy in states relative to ICMR norms

	Andhra Pradesh	Madhya Pradesh	Orissa	West Bengal	India	ICMR norm (grams/person per day)
Cereals	1.05	1.13	1.26	1.19	1.04	420
Cereal substitutes	0.00	0.01	0.00	0.00	0.05	75
Pulses	0.58	0.81	0.38	0.35	0.58	40
Vegetables	0.53	0.45	0.47	0.51	0.48	125
Fruit	0.45	0.21	0.27	0.38	0.45	50
Milk and milk products	0.52	0.55	0.15	0.31	0.97	150
Oils	0.56	0.45	0.27	0.52	0.52	22
Meat	0.29	0.08	0.08	0.17	0.15	25
Fish	0.15	0.08	0.39	0.72	0.28	25

Source: Swaminathan Research Foundation (2001).

Table 8A.2. Ranking of regions according to food insecurity

Rank	Andhra Pradesh	Madhya Pradesh	West Bengal	Orissa
1	Inland north	Southwest	Eastern plains	South
2	Southwest:	Malwa	Central plains	North
3	Inland south	Central	Western plains	Coastal
4	Coastal	South	Himalayan	
5		North:		
6		Chattisgarh		
7		Vindhya		

Source: Computed based on NSSO data.

Table 8A.3. Monthly per capita expenditure in Rs (MPCE) according to food-security status of households

Region		Andhra Pradesh		Madhya Pradesh		West Bengal		Orissa	
		Insecure	Secure	Insecure	Secure	Insecure	Secure	Insecure	Secure
1	MPCE	433	529	298	411	369	511	354	444
2	MPCE	378	517	327	417	340	494	194	270
3	MPCE	352	437	371	479	450	537	297	389
4	MPCE	322	446	427	542	317	478		
5	MPCE			299	435				
6	MPCE			343	452				
7	MPCE			389	495				

Source: Computed based on NSSO data.

Table 8A.4. Binary logistic model for food insecurity

	FINSEC			PWP		
	Coefficient (B)	Significance	Exp(B)	Coefficient (B)	Significance	Exp(B)
Part 1: Andhra Pradesh						
Region (base = inland south)						
Coastal	−0.257	0.001	0.774	0.155	0.004	1.167
Inland north	0.272	0.001	1.313	−0.347	0.004	0.707
Southwestern	0.076	0.001	1.079	−1.151	0.008	0.316
Household type (base = self employed workers in agriculture)						
Others	0.395	0.001	1.485	−0.251	0.005	0.778
Self-employed in non-agriculture	0.181	0.001	1.199	−0.800	0.005	0.449
Agricultural labour	0.02	0.001	1.02	−0.204	0.003	0.815
Other labour	0.374	0.001	1.453	0.021	0.005	1.021
Education of head (base = secondary or higher secondary)						
Illiterate	−0.341	0.001	0.711	−1.042	0.004	0.353
Non formal education/ up to primary school	−0.233	0.001	0.792	−1.762	0.005	0.172
Primary/ Middle school	−0.045	0.001	0.956	−1.501	0.005	0.223
Household properties						
Children	1.983	0.001	7.261	−0.759	0.005	0.468
Gender	0.178	0.002	1.195	−0.118	0.007	0.889
Minority religion (base = Hinduism)						
Islam	−0.017	0.001	0.983	−0.286	0.009	0.751
Others	−0.018	0.002	0.982	0.404	0.005	1.497
Caste (base = general)						
SC/ST	−0.087	0.001	0.916	1.108	0.004	3.027
OBCs	0.010	0.001	1.010	0.786	0.004	2.194
Constant	−0.449	0.002	0.638	−3.257	0.007	
% Predicted						
Occurrence		61			72	
Non-occurrence		60			50	
Total		61			51	

(*cont.*)

Table 8A.4. (*Continued*)

	FINSEC			PWP		
	Coefficient (B)	Significance	Exp(B)	Coefficient (B)	Significance	Exp(B)
Part 2: Madhya Pradesh						
Region (base = north)						
Chattisgarh	−0.166	0.001	0.847	−0.959	0.003	0.383
Vindhya	−0.643	0.001	0.526	−0.694	0.003	0.499
Central	0.272	0.001	1.313	−2.919	0.007	0.054
Malwa	0.613	0.001	1.845	−0.689	0.003	0.502
South	0.324	0.001	1.383	−0.899	0.003	0.407
Southwest	0.896	0.001	2.450	−0.577	0.003	0.562
Household type (base = self employed workers in agriculture)						
Others	0.564	0.001	1.758	0.067	0.005	1.070
Self-employed in non-agriculture	0.538	0.001	1.712	0.817	0.003	2.264
Agricultural labour	0.342	0.001	1.407	0.652	0.002	1.919
Other labour	0.456	0.001	1.577	1.296	0.003	3.655
Education of head (base = secondary or higher secondary)						
Illiterate	−0.067	0.001	0.935	0.497	0.004	1.643
Non formal education/ up to primary school	−0.238	0.001	0.788	0.061	0.005	1.955
Primary/ Middle school	−0.269	0.001	0.764	0.502	0.005	1.653
Household properties						
Children	2.236	0.001	9.354	0.304	0.004	1.355
Gender	−0.082	0.002	0.921	0.610	0.005	1.841
Minority religion (base = Hinduism)						
Islam	0.653	0.002	1.921	−0.689	0.006	0.502
Others	−0.021	0.003	0.979	1.132	0.005	3.102
Caste (base = general)						
SC/ST	0.096	0.001	1.100	0.804	0.003	2.236
OBCs	0.140	0.001	1.150	0.302	0.003	1.352
Constant	−1.091	0.002	0.336	−4.528	0.006	0.011
% Predicted						
Occurrence		69			78	
Non-occurrence		59			51	
Total		64			52	
Part 3: Orissa						
Region (base = north)						
Coastal	−0.480	0.001	0.619	−0.352	0.003	0.703
South	0.251	0.001	1.285	0.505	0.003	1.656
Household type (base = self employed workers in agriculture)						
Others	0.481	0.002	1.618	0.344	0.005	1.411
Self-employed in non-agriculture	−0.091	0.002	0.913	−0.305	0.006	0.373
Agricultural labour	−0.025	0.001	0.975	0.783	0.003	2.187
Other labour	0.076	0.002	1.079	2.907	0.004	18.296
Education of head (base = secondary or higher secondary)						
Illiterate	0.164	0.002	1.178	0.011	0.005	1.011
Non formal education/ up to primary school	0.041	0.002	1.042	0.369	0.005	1.466
Primary/ Middle school	0.232	0.002	1.261	−0.223	0.006	0.800

Table 8A.4. (*Continued*)

	FINSEC			PWP		
	Coefficient (B)	Significance	Exp(B)	Coefficient (B)	Significance	Exp(B)
Household properties						
Children	2.469	0.002	11.805	0.176	0.005	1.193
Gender	−0.192	0.003	0.826	0.016	0.007	0.984
Minority religion (base = Hinduism)						
Islam	0.008	0.004	1.008	−3.670	0.096	0.025
Others	−0.284	0.003	0.753	0.683	0.005	1.980
Caste (base = general)						
SC/ST	0.084	0.001	1.087	1.170	0.004	3.222
OBCs	0.052	0.001	1.054	0.614	0.005	1.849
Constant	−2.1	0.003	0.122	−4.971	0.008	0.007
% Predicted						
Occurrence		70			80	
Non-occurrence		56			51	
Total		60			52	
Part 4: West Bengal						
Region (base = western plains)						
Himalayan	−0.503	0.001	0.605	−0.713	0.003	0.490
Eastern plains	0.369	0.001	1.447	−1.192	0.002	0.304
Central plains	0.010	0.001	1.010	−1.492	0.003	0.225
Household type (base = self employed workers in agriculture)						
Others	0.664	0.001	1.943	0.959	0.003	2.610
Self-employed in non-agriculture	0.361	0.001	1.434	0.613	0.003	1.846
Agricultural labour	0.344	0.001	1.410	0.590	0.003	1.805
Other labour	0.452	0.001	1.572	0.861	0.004	2.366
Education of head (base = secondary or higher secondary)						
Illiterate	0.357	0.001	1.429	0.589	0.004	1.802
Non formal education/ up to primary school	0.420	0.001	1.522	−0.217	0.004	0.805
Primary/ Middle school	0.238	0.001	1.268	−0.322	0.004	0.725
Household properties						
Children	1.593	0.002	4.920	0.056	0.004	1.058
Gender	0.345	0.001	1.412	−0.093	0.006	0.912
Minority religion (base = Hinduism)						
Islam	0.376	0.001	1.456	−0.353	0.003	0.703
Others	0.528	0.002	1.696	0.183	0.006	1.201
Caste (base = general)						
SC/ST	−0.052	0.001	0.949	−0.238	0.002	0.788
OBCs	−0.013	0.001	0.987	0.502	0.003	1.652
Constant	−1.859	0.002		−3.413	0.005	0.033
% Predicted						
Occurrence		62			76	
Non-occurrence		60			51	
Total		61			51	

Notes to Tables 8A.4: a. FINSEC-Food insecure. b. PWP-Participation. c. Predictive error is based on a cut-off equivalent to median of probability on account of unbalanced data.

Table 8A.5. Characteristics of households likely to be below the poverty line

	Andhra Pradesh	Madhya Pradesh	Orissa	West Bengal
Most likely	Inland South	South	South	Western plains
	Southwest	Chhattisgarh	North	Himalayan
Least likely	Coastal	Malwa	Coastal	Central plains
Most likely	Agricultural labour	Other labour	Agricultural labour	Agricultural labour
	Others	Agricultural labour	Other labour	Other labour
Least likely	Self-employed agricultural worker	Others	Others	Others
Most likely	More children	More children	More children	More children
	More working age female	More working age female	More working age female	More working age female
Most likely	Illiterate	Illiterate	Illiterate	Illiterate
	Non formal/ Pre-primary	Non formal/ Pre-primary	Non formal/ Pre-primary	Non formal/ Pre-primary
Least likely	SEC/HS	SEC/HS	SEC/HS	SEC/HS
Most likely	Hindu, Muslim	Muslim, Hindu	Hindu, Muslim	Muslim, Others
Least likely	Others	Others	Others	Hindu
Most likely	SC/ST OBC	SC/ST OBC	SC/ST OBC	SC/ST General
Least likely	General	General	General	OBC

Source: Based on model results.

References

Boserup, E. (1975). *Women's Role in Economic Development*, London: Allen & Unwin.

Braun, J. von (1995). 'Employment for Poverty Reduction and Food Security: Concept, Research Issues and Overviews', in J. von Braun (ed.), *Employment for Poverty Reduction and Food Security*. Washington, DC: IFPRI.

Drèze, J. (2001). 'Starving the Poor'. *The Hindu*, 26 February.

Government of Orissa. (1995–6). *Orissa Agricultural Statistics*.

Harriss-White, B. (1999). *'State, Market, Collective and Household Action in India's Social Sector'*, in B. Harriss-White and S. Subramanian (eds), *Illfare in India: Essays on India's Social Sector in Honour of S Guhan*. New Delhi: Sage.

Hirway, I., and P. Terhal (1994). *Towards Employment Guarantee in India: Indian and International Experiences in Rural Public Works Programmes*. New Delhi: Sage.

Kaur S. and S. K. Goyal (1996). 'A Study of Wage Discrimination against Women Agricultural Labourers'. *Agricultural Situation in India*, 53(4).

M. S. Swaminathan Research Foundation (MSSRF) (2001). *Food Insecurity Atlas of Rural India*, 2001. Chennai: MSSRF.

NSSO (2001). *Employment and Unemployment Situation in India, 1999–2000*. New Delhi: National Sample Survey Organization.

Pinstrup-Andersen, P. (2002). 'Food and Agricultural Policy for a Globalizing World: Preparing for the Future'. *American Journal of Agricultural Economics*, 5.

Radhakrishna R. and C. Ravi (1992). 'Effects of Growth, Relative Price and Preferences of Food and Nutrition'. *Indian Economic Review*, 27.

Ravallion, M. (1990). 'Reaching the Poor through Rural Public Employment'. Discussion Paper 94. Washington, DC: World Bank.

Ravallion, M., and Q. Wodon (1998). 'Evaluating a Targeted Social Program when Placement is Decentralized'. Policy Research Working Paper 1945. Washington, DC: World Bank.

Sen, A., and J. Drèze (1999). *The Amaryta Sen and Jean Drèze Omnibus*. New Delhi: Oxford University Press.

Sen, A. and P. Jha (2005). 'Rural Employment: Patterns and Trends from National Sample Survey' in R. Nayyar and A. N. Sharma (eds) *Rural Transformation in India*, Institute of Human Development, Delhi.

Singh, K. (1999). *Rural Development*. New Delhi: Sage Publication.

Swaminathan, M. (2001). 'A Further Attack on the PDS'. *Frontline*, 18 (2).

Part II

Trade Openness, the WTO, and Food Security

9

The Impact of Domestic and International Commodity Price Volatility on Agricultural Income Instability in Ghana, Vietnam, and Peru

George Rapsomanikis and Alexander Sarris

9.1 Introduction

Discussion and analyses of agricultural trade liberalization have focused for the most part on the issue of changes in the level of average prices faced by the producers and consumers of agricultural products under different liberalizing scenarios. However, a rather neglected issue, at least in analytical studies, is the extent to which trade liberalization may affect the instability faced by agricultural producers. More specifically, does increased exposure to international agricultural markets increase the income instability of agricultural producers? The purpose of this chapter is to investigate the issue of income instability of agricultural producers arising from domestic and international causes, and to explore the question of whether increased exposure to international markets will make farmers' incomes more or less unstable.

Agricultural producers are exposed to a variety of income uncertainties, both market related such as price variations as well as non-market related, such as unstable weather patterns. They are also exposed to a variety of idiosyncratic shocks that affect their income, such as illness. Such uncertainties induce substantial income risks that can be particularly detrimental

The research for this study was funded by the FAO Netherlands Partnership Programme and the authors would like to thank Carlo Azzari, Agostina Zanoli, and Panayiotis Karfakis for excellent research assistance, and Nancy Morgan and AliArslan Gurkan of the FAO Trade and Markets Division for useful comments. No senior authorship is assigned.

to small and/or poor producers in developing countries. In particular it has been shown that income instability in the presence of liquidity constraints and inadequate assets that feature rather prominently in many developing countries, can create poverty traps (Zimmerman and Carter 2003).

Farmers in developing countries have developed several ways for dealing with the various risks they face. These involve risk management strategies, namely actions taken ahead of the resolution of any uncertainty to improve the ex ante exposure of the household to various risks, as well as risk-coping strategies, namely rules adopted ex-ante to help the household to deal ex-post with any undesirable consequences. Risk management strategies include, among others, crop diversification, income diversification through off-farm work and sharecropping. Such ex-ante strategies usually sacrifice higher expected income for a more stable income stream. Risk-coping strategies may include the availability of short-term consumption credit, mutual family or village-based reciprocal giving arrangements, and other arrangements.[1]

A significant share of the income variations of rural producers in developing countries seems to be due to idiosyncratic shocks, namely shocks particular to a household (Morduch 1995; Townsend 1995; Carter 1997). Such risks can be insured through formal or informal pooling of a large number of such shocks, such as the village reciprocity relations that are present in many developing countries, or the formal private or public insurance schemes that exist in many developed countries. Covariate shocks, however, namely those that affect all households in a given community or region, such as weather or price shocks, cannot be eliminated by pooling them within a small or even larger region. It is the need to insure farmers against such covariate shocks that has induced the governments of most developed countries to institute various price or income support schemes, under the perception that the private insurance industry would not be able to provide adequate coverage at reasonable cost.

The absence of such arrangements in developing countries is what induces rural households to develop self-insurance, or what has been termed 'consumption smoothing strategies' to deal with covariate shocks. These strategies basically involve building 'precautionary savings', in the form of liquid or near-liquid assets in good years, and depleting them in years of adverse covariate shocks (Deaton 1991). This implies that income shocks translate into smaller contemporaneous consumption variations. There is conflicting evidence, however, on whether such strategies are effective at smoothing consumption (Rosenzweig and Binswanger 1993; Rosenzweig and Wolpin 1993; Fafchamps *et al.* 1998; Dercon 2004; Kazianga and Udry 2006). The

[1] For a recent survey of these practices, see Dercon (2004).

consensus, nevertheless, appears to be that despite the variety of smoothing strategies adopted by poor households in developing countries, there is substantial residual consumption risk (Jalan and Ravallion 1999), and hence vulnerability.

In light of inadequate risk-coping mechanisms and assets, farm households are vulnerable to the vagaries of weather, as well as the market, in the sense that their consumption can easily fall below subsistence levels due to income shocks. Thus, risks may function as a mechanism for economic differentiation within a population, deepening the poverty and food insecurity of some individuals even as aggregate food availability improves (Carter 1997). In the absence of risk management instruments, risk events, such as weather or commodity price shocks, may plunge particularly vulnerable households into poverty (Holzmann and Jorgensen 2000). Although there is no single definition, or measure, of vulnerability to food insecurity in the literature, there is consensus that household vulnerability to poverty is a stochastic phenomenon and that its measurement has to be explicitly forward-looking (Christiansen and Boisvert 2000; Chaudhuri 2002; Ligon and Schechter 2003). While observed poverty provides an ex-post, measure of household's welfare, it may not provide a clear indication of the household's expected welfare in the future. Households tend to remain poor due to low levels of fixed endowments, such as productive assets and human capital, or limited access to markets or credit. However, households that are observed to be nonpoor, in a static manner, may be predisposed to fall into poverty mainly due to variable income that is consequence of large adverse shocks. Vulnerability is often associated with high expected poverty (Christiaensen and Boisvert 2000; Chaudhuri 2002) and identified relative to a poverty line. Other approaches relate vulnerability to low expected utility (Ligon and Schechter 2003). In general, vulnerability to poverty, or hunger, can be expressed as the frequency of poverty, or food scarcity incidence, thus reflecting an ex ante measure that encompasses the uncertainty which households face during a period of time. However, the degree of vulnerability depends on the characteristics of the risk and the household ability to respond to risk through the risk management strategies (Heitzman *et al.* 2002).

Agricultural income instability has long been known to be one of the main contributors to overall income instability for farm households in developing countries. Income instability in turn is one of the main components of overall consumption instability and hence vulnerability. Hence income instability is the building block behind all vulnerability estimates. In this chapter we focus on the impact of covariate shocks on household incomes.

While there has been considerable research devoted to the issue of world commodity market instability and its adverse growth consequences for developing countries,[2] there has been much less research devoted to the domestic market instability faced by many producers in developing countries. Recently Bourguignon *et al.* (2004) showed that international agricultural trade instability implies diverging domestic incomes for different groups of income earners. They do not, however, investigate the impact of increased exposure to international markets. The extent to which domestic markets are exposed to the international market may have important implications for domestic commodity price volatility. Domestic markets can be partly insulated by large marketing margins that arise from high transaction costs. Poor infrastructure, transport, and communication services give rise to large marketing margins due to high costs of delivering the locally produced commodity to the border for export, or the imported commodity to the domestic market for consumption. As a consequence, markets in developing countries may be insulated, resulting in a limited 'buffer' capacity, as the possibility that adverse shocks such as exogenous shifts in supply and demand can be adjusted through trade is limited. Often, in insulated markets, small exogenous shocks may generate relatively large price fluctuations, thus resulting in significant increases in uncertainty. Market integration and trade, in a manner similar to commodity storage, may lead to a reduction in the volatility of domestic prices, given unanticipated shocks in domestic markets, thus reducing the burden of adjustment that is carried by producers and consumers. Partly because of the non, or low tradability of many agricultural products, partly because of the lack of transmission of world prices to domestic markets, domestic agricultural product markets in many developing countries are very unstable, not only from year to year, but also within each crop year. It is not clear how increased exposure to international markets will affect this market instability, and hence it is not clear whether trade liberalization will make the incomes of producers more or less unstable. These are the issues that this paper is set to explore.

The study takes a microeconomic approach, in the sense that it explores potential changes in agricultural income instability caused by increased exposure to international markets. In particular, it analyses the potential changes in various representative groups of agriculture-dependent households in three diverse developing countries, namely Ghana, Peru, and Vietnam. While none of these countries are in the WTO group of least developed countries (LDCs), they are all classified as food insecure according to Diaz-Bonilla *et al.* (2000) and are commodity dependent in the sense that a large share of their exports consists of primary commodities, albeit not all agricultural. Apart from the

[2] For some of the most recent analyses that review earlier studies as well, see Dehn (2000) and Collier and Dehn (2001).

availability of relevant micro-data the countries were chosen because of the diversity of rural household dependency on agriculture and internationally traded commodities, as well as their diverse regions. Per capita GDP (average for 2001–2) is US$280 in Ghana, 420 in Vietnam, and 2,000 in Peru. Employment in agriculture is 61 per cent in Ghana, 69 per cent in Vietnam and 9 per cent in Peru. The share of agriculture in GDP is 34 per cent in Ghana, 23 per cent in Vietnam, and 8 per cent in Peru. Finally the share of agricultural exports in total merchandise exports is 36 per cent in Ghana, 13 per cent in Vietnam, and 10 per cent in Peru.

We estimate household income variances and coefficients of variations under a variety of assumptions, applying a theoretical framework which is an extension of the one developed by Sarris (2002). The framework combines information from both cross-section household data and time-series on prices and yields, and leads to explicit analytical formulae for estimating the household income variance. Our approach relates to household vulnerability to poverty and hunger, as it provides forward-looking measures for the income uncertainty households face in a stochastic manner. The framework is applied to the World Bank's living standards measurement survey (LSMS) data on Ghana, Vietnam, and Peru. Under the assumption that producing households do not change their long-run production and income diversification patterns, household income variance changes are estimated in terms of price and yield uncertainties, in scenarios where households face domestic price uncertainties, and alternatively international price uncertainties.

The plan of the chapter is the following. In section 9.2 we outline the analytical framework of the study. Section 9.3 discusses the data and the income structure of the various income groups in the three countries analysed and presents the results of the analysis of income variability. Section 9.4 summarizes the main conclusions.

9.2 Analytical Framework

Consider a household that produces some agricultural commodities and is also involved in several other income-earning activities. The production-consumption-saving problem of the agricultural household in the context of risk can be formalized mathematically using standard intertemporal stochastic models but it is not our purpose to review these here (for detailed expositions see Fafchamps 2003). Following standard methods outlined in Newberry and Stiglitz (1981), one can write the welfare of the household as a function of the varying income and prices as well as the covariance of income and prices, and a set of demand and risk parameters such as the various income and price elasticities of demand, and the coefficient of relative risk aversion.

In this chapter we do not attempt to estimate the demand and risk characteristics of different groups of households. Rather, we concentrate only on the coefficient of variation (CV) of income, as it is the main component of welfare under risk, especially if prices of the different expenditure categories are not strongly correlated with each other. We develop an explicit expression for the CVs of agricultural income, conditional on information twelve months ahead (in order to capture the inherent uncertainty of agricultural production decisions). Following Sarris (2002) the CV of income of a household can be written as follows:

$$CV^2(Y) = \alpha^2 \sum_i \sum_j s_i s_j E[\Delta p_i \Delta p_j \Delta q_i \Delta q_j + \Delta p_i \Delta p_j + \Delta p_i \Delta q_j + \Delta p_j \Delta q_i + \Delta q_i \Delta q_j] \tag{9.1}$$

where α denotes the share of agriculture[3] in total income, s_i denotes the average shares of each agricultural product i in agricultural income, and q_i is the normalized (by average income) quantity of product i produced.

Consider the relationship between the domestic and international prices of the various commodities. Empirical models of domestic price formation usually adhere to the following generic specification:

$$p_{it}^d = \alpha_i + \zeta_i p_{it}^w + u_{it} \tag{9.2}$$

where p_{it}^d and p_{it}^w denote the domestic and international price of commodity i, respectively, and u_{it} is an error term. Equation (9.2) implies that commodity prices in the domestic market are determined by international market prices, at least in the long run. The parameter ζ_i is interpreted as the elasticity of transmission of world prices to domestic prices, when prices are converted in logarithms, and can be thought of as a measure of the extent to which international price signals pass-through to the domestic market. Nevertheless, the interpretation of ζ_i, and the quantification of the relationship between domestic and international prices depends on the statistical methodology applied for estimation rather than the underlying theoretical concept itself.

Denote by σ_i the CV of production of the ith crop produced by the household, by κ_{ij} the correlation coefficient between the production of the ith crop and the jth other crop produced by the household, by v_i^w the CV of the world price of the ith product, by ρ_{ij} the correlation coefficient of world prices of the ith and jth products (if they are tradable), by v_i the CV of the

[3] This share in the subsequent empirical calculations will comprise only the part of agricultural income for which we have enough information to compute the stochastic variables. Prices are normalized by the average price faced by the household.

random component u_{it} of the domestic price of the ith product, and by ψ_{ij} the correlation coefficient between the random components u_{it} of the domestic prices of the ith and jth products.

Given Equation (9.2), and certain additional normality and independence assumptions, the various terms in Equation (9.1) can be evaluated explicitly as follows:

$$E(\Delta p_i \Delta p_j \Delta q_i \Delta q_j) = (\zeta_i \zeta_j \rho_{ij} v_i^w v_j^w + \psi_{ij} v_i v_j)\kappa_{ij}\sigma_i\sigma_j \tag{9.3}$$

$$E(\Delta p_i \Delta p_j) = \zeta_i \zeta_j \rho_{ij} v_i^w v_j^w + \psi_{ij} v_i v_j \tag{9.4}$$

$$E(\Delta p_i \Delta q_j) = 0 \tag{9.5}$$

$$E(\Delta q_i \Delta q_j) = \kappa_{ij}\sigma_i\sigma_j \tag{9.6}$$

By setting the transmission coefficient ζ_i equal to zero in the above expressions, we obtain the components that are accounted for only by domestic factors such as production, and are not due to international price variability. If, in turn, we set the transmission coefficient ζ_i equal to 1 and, at the same time set the variance of the domestic error term u_{it} equal to zero, then we can simulate the situation where the domestic prices are equal to international prices, with the resulting expressions simulating a scenario in which the household is faced only with international price variability.

In the empirical applications, Equation (9.2) is replaced by a reduced (or standard) Vector Autoregression (VAR) assuming that both domestic and international monthly prices are stochastic in nature, have similar statistical properties and are jointly determined:

$$p_{it}^w = c_1 + \sum_{j=1}^{k} a_{11,j} p_{it-j}^w + \sum_{j=1}^{k} a_{12,j} p_{it-j}^d + \varepsilon_{it}^w \tag{9.7}$$

$$p_{it}^d = c_2 + \sum_{j=1}^{k} a_{21,j} p_{it-j}^d + \sum_{j=1}^{k} a_{22,j} p_{it-j}^w + \varepsilon_{it}^d \tag{9.8}$$

where p_{it}^d and p_{it}^w denote the domestic and international price of commodity i respectively, while the α's are parameters and the ε's are contemporaneously correlated white noise error terms.

Equations (9.7)–(9.8) provide a basis for the estimation of h-step forecast of means and variances of the prices, conditional on the VAR relationships, and, under the implicit assumption that economic agents form expectations according to the VAR relationships, the relative importance of shocks to the domestic and international prices as well as their overall impact on the domestic price can be analysed. The existence and the direction of causal effects between domestic and international prices can be assessed within the VAR environment, by applying Granger's causality tests.[4]

In view of the above discussion, we proceed in the implementation of the conceptual model in two stages. At the first stage, we estimate 12-*month* forecast of conditional variances and covariances for each commodity price on the basis of an estimated vector autoregressive model, or VAR depending on whether or not the commodity is internationally traded. In more detail, we proceed by assessing the statistical properties of the series, specifying and estimating a VAR for the prices that have similar time-series properties, testing for Granger causality and ordering the system, and estimating conditional variances and covariances through variance decomposition. We also estimate the variances of domestic production. In the second step, these estimates are used in conjunction with the income structure of the households in order to estimate household income variances and CVs.

In order to evaluate the impact of the extent to which world market exposure affects household income volatility, we estimate agricultural income CVs under three assumptions:

(i) current conditions of exposure to domestic and international shocks, taking into consideration the estimated price transmission coefficient;
(ii) household exposure to domestic price volatility only, and;
(iii) household exposure to international market prices only, reflecting perfect market integration.

9.3 The Data and Empirical Analysis

We specify the income and expenditure structure of the various farm households in the countries under examination by using the LSMS carried out by the World Bank and the respective national statistical institutions.[5] We restrict our analysis to those households that have some agricultural activities, and classify farm households by first distributing them according to geographical regions in order to capture any agro-climatic conditions that may determine crop production structure. The households are further classified according to

[4] A technical discussion of the estimation of VARs and of the corresponding conditional variances through variance decomposition in the context of a VAR system is beyond the scope of this chapter. Interested readers may refer to Hamilton (1994: ch. 11), and Lütkepohl (1993: ch. 3). Granger (1969, 1988) proposes an empirical definition of causality based only on its forecasting content.

[5] Information on the LSMS data surveys is available at: www.internationalbank.org/html/prdph/lsms/index.htm.

their characterization as poor and nonpoor by utilizing the general poverty thresholds established by studies undertaken by the World Bank and national statistical institutes. The sample is subsequently divided according to the share of income from all agricultural activities (households with shares either larger or smaller than 60 per cent) and their share of agricultural income derived from a main agricultural commodity that depends on the country and the agro-climatic region. These classifications result in 36 classes of households in each country and capture the extent to which households depend on agricultural activities and on the production of specific major commodities. For the households in each classification, we estimate the average income and the shares of income derived from the production of agricultural commodities as well as from wages, self-employment, rents and remittances. We also compute average total expenditure, and the expenditure shares for food, subdivided by food items.

For estimating the vector autoregressions and the conditional measures of price variability for each country, we use monthly data on domestic prices, compiled by the corresponding ministries of agriculture for the period 1992 to 2002. As it was not possible to obtain monthly domestic price data series for all the commodities produced and described in the household classifications, we assume that such agricultural income sources as fruits and vegetables, for which data are not available, present no uncertainties. All prices are in the national currency per ton and have been deflated utilizing the IMF consumer price index. Data on international prices have been collected by the International Financial Statistics (IMF 2005), and have been transformed to domestic prices with the appropriate exchange rates, while conditional measures for yield variability have been estimated utilizing time-series data from FAOSTAT.

9.3.1 *Ghana*

The results of the household classification analysis of the 1998/9 LSMS data on Ghana are given in Table 9.1.[6] The sample represents 2.2 million farm households, out of a total of 4.1 million. The households are divided in three regions: forest, coast and savannah. These are divided according to their income level as poor and nonpoor, utilizing a general poverty threshold of 900,000 cedis per capita per year.[7] The sample is further subdivided according to the contribution of agricultural activities to the total income and according to the portion of cocoa sales contributing to agricultural income

[6] Further information on the Ghana LSMS 1998/9 dataset is available at: www4.internationalbank.org/afr/poverty/pdf/docnav/02684.pdf

[7] The average exchange rate in Ghana for the period of the survey was 2,930 cedis per US$.

Table 9.1. Household classification and characteristics: Ghana

	Share of agriculture in POOR household income						Share of agriculture in NONPOOR household income					
	< 60%			> 60%			< 60%			> 60%		
	Share of cocoa in agricultural income (%)						Share of cocoa in agricultural income (%)					
	< 30	30–60	> 60	< 30	30–60	> 60	< 30	30–60	> 60	< 30	30–60	> 60
Coast												
Estimated no. of households	262,790	7,238	5,190	48,055	1,058	1,151	87,740	982	1 835	19,229	—	—
Share of total households (%)	6.41	0.18	0.13	1.17	0.03	0.03	2.14	0.02	0.04	0.47	—	—
Total income per capita ('000 cedi)	812	1,339	1,669	550	514	804	2,683	1,290	8,399	1,575	—	—
Share of agriculture in total income (%)	16.91	14.66	14.49	71.32	69.94	61.75	17.27	34.96	4.45	75.66	—	—
Forest												
Estimated no. of households	503,790	51,169	31,785	149,464	26,710	8,935	192,334	16,632	11,746	86,874	19,283	6,108
Share of total households (%)	12.29	1.25	0.78	3.65	0.65	0.22	4.69	0.41	0.29	2.12	0.47	0.15
Total income per capita ('000 cedi)	1,017	1,244	1,374	563	647	633	3,103	1,914	3,328	1,577	2,431	4,502
Share of agriculture in total income (%)	22.86	35.21	34.18	70.90	68.66	67.00	21.77	32.49	40.39	74.31	69.87	69.10
Savannah												
Estimated no. of households	488,980	1,393	—	133,115	1,420	1,420	55.436	—	—	37,500	609	—
Share of total households (%)	11.93	0.03	—	3.25	0.03	0.03	1.35	—	—	0.91	0.01	—
Total income per capita ('000 cedi)	759	1,003	—	534	866	7,281	2,700	—	—	1,544	2,431	—
Average share of agriculture in total income (%)	26.92	49.99	—	71.48	64.95	75.94	26.66	—	—	73.82	79.93	—

Source: Authors' computations.

Table 9.2. Decomposed coefficients of variation of domestic prices, Ghana (per cent)*

	CV of domestic prices accounted for by			World price coefficients of variation
	Domestic shocks	International shocks	Total	
Maize	21.24	0.00	21.24	18.4
Cassava	25.80	0.00	25.80	14.9
Plantains	36.06	0.00	36.06	
Cocoyam	17.33	0.00	17.33	
Yam	23.93	0.00	23.93	
Sorghum	24.81	0.00	24.81	16.6
Millet	13.58	0.00	13.58	16.6
Rice	13.30	0.00	13.30	11.5
Cocoa	8.35	0.00	8.35	20.2
Groundnuts	14.46	0.00	14.46	16.0

Note: * Conditional coefficients of variation projected for 12 months ahead.
Source: Authors' calculations.

(i.e. households with shares smaller than 30 per cent, with shares between 30 and 60 per cent or shares larger than 60 per cent). The share of income that derives from the production of cocoa varies considerably between zero cocoa production in the Savannah region and 92 per cent in the Coast region. Poor households are more heavily dependent on the production of cocoa the main internationally traded cash crop, relative to nonpoor households.

Table 9.2 presents the conditional measures of the variability of agricultural prices faced by producers and the conditional CVs of international prices. These have been calculated with estimated single autoregressive models for the domestic price of commodities not traded internationally (cocoyam, yam, cassava, and millet), as well as for the domestic and international prices of goods with dissimilar statistical properties (bananas, maize and sorghum). For the domestic and international prices of rice, which were found to have similar statistical properties on the basis of the unit root tests, the estimated VAR revealed that there was no significant relationship between the two prices, with neither being Granger-caused by the other. Consequently, producers in Ghana are exposed to shocks from domestic markets only and international shocks do not pass through to the domestic market. Table 9.3 presents the estimates of income variability measures. These conditional income CVs may underestimate the actual variability of income as they are estimated on the basis of partial agricultural income for which data on commodity prices are available.[8]

[8] The part of total income accounted by the portion of agricultural income for which we have enough information to compute the income variance is indicated in Appendix Table 9A.1.

Table 9.3. Coefficients of variation (CVs) of agricultural incomes, Ghana (per cent)

	Share of agriculture in POOR household income						Share of agriculture in NONPOOR household income					
	< 60%			> 60%			< 60%			> 60%		
	Share of cocoa in agricultural income (%)						Share of cocoa in agricultural income (%)					
	< 30	30–60	> 60	< 30	30–60	> 60	< 30	30–60	> 60	< 30	30–60	> 60
Coast												
Actual CVs due to:												
Price and production shocks	12.87	13.81	19.00	17.19	16.00	16.68	10.71	13.69	20.90	12.19	—	—
Domestic market price and production shocks only	12.87	13.81	19.00	17.19	16.00	16.68	10.71	13.69	20.90	12.19	—	—
Simulated CVs due to world prices (in US$) and production shocks	8.66	14.68	24.28	8.97	13.07	20.34	7.13	12.69	27.09	6.67	—	—
Forest												
Actual CVs due to:												
Price and production shocks	14.41	14.48	18.23	14.86	14.85	18.30	14.15	15.21	18.09	14.41	15.19	17.64
Domestic market price and production shocks only	14.41	14.48	18.23	14.86	14.85	18.30	14.15	15.21	18.09	14.41	15.19	17.64
Simulated CVs due to world prices (in US$) and production shocks	10.16	15.07	23.05	9.25	14.33	23.06	9.90	15.48	22.68	8.48	14.37	22.18
Savannah												
Actual CVs due to:												
Price and production shocks	10.00	15.22	—	10.62	15.23	20.15	12.78	—	—	14.73	14.94	—
Domestic market price and production shocks only	10.00	15.22	—	10.62	15.23	20.15	12.78	—	—	14.73	14.94	—
Simulated CVs due to world prices (in US$) and production shocks	9.23	16.54	—	9.17	17.60	25.81	10.79	—	—	11.88	17.84	—

Source: Authors' computations.

The estimates suggest that the agricultural income uncertainty faced by farm households is significant. The agricultural income CV for most household groups ranges between 10 and 20 per cent, while several households face CVs that are estimated to be higher than 20 per cent. As the portion of agricultural income in the calculations in Table 9.3 constitutes only a part of the total income variation, the overall income variability of farm households from agricultural shocks is smaller than indicated in the table, but not much less for those households with a large share of agriculture in total income.

Due to high production variability, the households that depend for a larger part of their agricultural income on the main export commodity, cocoa, seem to be exposed to larger agricultural income variability, despite the market intervention policies of Cocobod, the government parastatal, to stabilize producer prices. The per capita incomes of the household groups in Table 9.1 suggest that farm households receiving a larger share of their agricultural income from cocoa have a better income per capita. This indicates that in Ghana, households specializing in cocoa farming are, on average, richer but at the same time more exposed to price and production risks. Income volatility is still significant for the predominantly agricultural households that rely on cocoa to a lesser extent for their agricultural income, mainly because of high variability in domestic prices for maize and cassava. In the coast region, the predominantly poor agricultural households, for whom cocoa sales constitute less than 30 per cent of their agricultural income, experience relatively high uncertainty, with a coefficient of variation raising 12.9 per cent, as cassava and maize production generate up to 68 per cent of their agricultural income. Similarly, poor households in the forest and savannah regions relying on roots and cereals are also subject to significant agricultural income fluctuations. The findings suggest that crop diversification strategies in Ghana, although important as a risk management strategy, may be relatively insufficient in shielding poor producers from large income fluctuations.

The degree of agricultural income fluctuation that producers face if directly exposed to international prices for all globally traded commodities suggests that there would be a considerable increase in income variability of the cocoa-dependent households, irrespective of whether they are poor or nonpoor. On the other hand, agricultural income fluctuations would decrease for those households that are not as dependent on cocoa. This is largely the outcome of the fact that the domestic price of cocoa currently continues to be stabilized by Cocobod. Hence the abolition of this parastatal and full exposure to international prices are bound to have adverse effects on the overall income variability of producers.

9.3.2 *Vietnam*

Table 9.4, utilizing the 1997/8 LSMS dataset, presents the results of the household classification for Vietnam.[9] The sample covers a weighted 13 million households, representing 80 per cent of all households in the country. These are divided in three regions, namely urban and northern Vietnam, Red River and the north coast, and south and central Vietnam. The households are classified as poor and nonpoor on the basis of a total household expenditure threshold of approximately 19.5 million dong per capita per year.[10] They further divided according to the contribution of agricultural activities in the total income (i.e. households with agricultural contributions less than and householders with contributions larger than 60 per cent of total income). The households are also classified according to the portion of internationally tradable commodities in agricultural income (i.e. households with a share less than 30 per cent, a share of 30–60 per cent, and a share larger than 60 per cent). Households in the urban and northern, and Red River and north coast regions are examined according to the share of rice in agricultural income while households in the south and central region are classified according to their activities in coffee production. Production activities are categorized for rice, other cereals (including maize, wheat, barley, malt, millet, and kaoliang), meat (pork, chicken, and beef), fish, cassava, coffee, sugar, fruits, vegetables, and other roots. The classification analysis suggests that rice and meat, especially pork and poultry, contribute significantly to agricultural income in the urban and northern and Red River and north coast regions. Both poor and nonpoor households in these regions are heavily dependent on rice and meat for their incomes, with poor households consuming a relatively larger share of their own production in farm. In the south and central region, both poor and nonpoor households rely on the production of coffee.

Table 9.5 estimates the agricultural price variability of the producers and the share of this variability resulting from domestic and international shocks. The price variations of the producers are largely due to domestic factors, with the exception of rice- and coffee-dependent producers. In addition, except for coffee prices, the US$ denominated international prices are either more unstable than, or equally unstable as, the domestic prices for all commodities. Variability was decomposed to components that are identified with domestic and international shocks with a series of single autoregression models and VARs. For the price pairs with dissimilar statistical properties, namely for sugar and pork, we estimate single autoregressive models. For coffee, the estimated

[9] Further information on the Vietnam LSMS 1997/8 dataset can be found in www.internationalbank.org/lsms/country/vn98/vn98bif.pdf.

[10] The average exchange rate pertinent to the survey period is 13,091 dong per US$. The threshold is 19,590,000 dong per capita per year.

Table 9.4. Household classification and characteristics: Vietnam

	Share of agriculture in POOR household income						Share of agriculture in NONPOOR household income					
	< 60%			> 60%			< 60%			> 60%		
	Share of main commodity in agricultural income (%)						Share of main commodity in agricultural income (%)					
	< 30	30–60	> 60	< 30	30–60	> 60	< 30	30–60	> 60	< 30	30–60	> 60
Urban and northern regions												
Estimated no. of households	164,061	193,203	77,569	316,921	684,132	125,460	1,264,246	179,788	179,154	356,599	223,382	76,235
Share of total households (%)	1.02	1.20	0.48	1.96	4.24	0.78	7.84	1.11	1.11	2.21	1.39	0.47
Total income per capita (dong)	2,662	2,293	1,905	1,546	1,173	745	8,115	5,201	8,121	2,672	1,638	1,886
Share of agriculture in total income (%)	24.97	38.07	30.16	91.98	91.34	94.85	9.90	29.04	13.32	88.14	90.45	93.37
Red River and north coast												
Estimated no. of households	184,308	298,393	234,811	173,966	622,875	369,433	536,795	546,296	282,737	356,527	613,870	169,116
Share of total households (%)	1.14	1.85	1.46	1.08	3.86	2.29	3.33	3.39	1.75	2.21	3.81	1.05
Total income per capita (dong)	2,394	1,894	1,602	1,377	1,116	766	5,175	6,300	4,779	2,574	1,636	1,317
Share of agriculture in total income (%)	22.49	36.17	31.42	91.01	89.59	89.31	19.32	16.51	15.37	81.88	86.15	88.11
Southern and central regions												
Estimated no. of households	412,373	1,168	5,633	1,171,145	26,151	32,370	1,211,060	11,555	24,905	1,559,728	39,217	102,592
Share of total households (%)	2.56	0.01	0.03	7.26	0.16	0.20	7.51	0.07	0.15	9.67	0.24	0.64
Total income per capita (dong)	2,437	4,758	2,896	1,155	1,508	1,676	5,727	5,278	6,448	2,778	2,691	5,445
Share of agriculture in total income (%)	22.00	17.12	35.08	92.47	93.52	95.20	16.96	31.55	24.93	90.80	84.97	92.80

Source: Computed by the authors.

Table 9.5. Decomposed coefficients of variation of domestic prices, Vietnam (per cent)*

	CV of domestic prices accounted for by			World price coefficients of variation
	Domestic shocks	International shocks	Total	
Coffee	51.01	12.68	63.69	45.6
Maize	6.10	0.09	6.20	18.4
Sugarbeet	12.53	0.42	12.95	25.0
Rice	7.74	3.11	10.85	11.5
Beef	2.62	0.01	2.63	9.8
Pork	7.54	0.10	7.64	18.7

Note: * Conditional coefficients of variation projected for 12 months ahead.
Source: Authors' calculations.

VAR parameters are statistically significant, revealing a correlation between domestic and international prices, while the Granger-causality test provides evidence that international prices impact on the Vietnamese domestic price, in the Granger sense. The correlation coefficient between the VAR innovations is estimated to be approximately 0.49, indicating that shocks are passed through from the international to the domestic market to a large extent. The domestic and the international prices account for 80 and 20 per cent of the domestic price forecast variance respectively, while variation in the domestic price can explain 38 per cent of the variation in the international price.

Domestic and international price VARs for maize and beef in conjunction with the corresponding causality tests suggest that domestic prices are not determined, nor Granger-caused by international prices. Consequently, for these commodities, the variance decomposition suggests that the proportion of the domestic price forecast variance attributed to international price fluctuations is nonsignificant. For rice, the VAR estimated parameters suggest a rich dynamic structure. The Granger causality test provides sufficient evidence to suggest that the international price Granger-causes domestic prices. Decomposition of the divergence indicates that 29 per cent of the domestic price variability for rice can be attributed to international rice markets.

Table 9.6 presents the estimates of conditional agricultural income variability for Vietnam. As expected, the results suggest that the uncertainty of the households varies according to production diversification. Households producing a large share of rice and coffee, irrespective of the overall share of these crops in the agricultural income, are exposed to higher income volatility compared to households with less specialized production patterns. Coffee producers in the south and central region are subject to significant income variability. For the producers whose share of coffee in total agricultural income exceeds 60 per cent, irrespective of the share of agriculture in total income, the CV

Table 9.6. Coefficients of variation (CVs) of agricultural incomes, Vietnam (per cent)

	Share of agriculture in POOR household income						Share of agriculture in NONPOOR household income					
	< 60%			> 60%			< 60%			> 60%		
	Share of main commodity in agricultural income (%)						Share of main commodity in agricultural income (%)					
	< 30	30–60	> 60	< 30	30–60	> 60	< 30	30–60	> 60	< 30	30–60	> 60
Urban and northern regions												
Actual CVs due to:												
Price and production shocks	3.56	8.09	10.64	5.58	7.73	10.38	3.71	8.07	12.00	5.05	7.49	11.53
Domestic market price and production shocks only	3.56	8.09	10.64	5.58	7.73	10.38	3.71	8.07	12.00	5.05	7.49	11.53
Simulated CVs due to world prices (in US$) and production shocks	4.91	9.74	12.39	7.23	9.13	12.11	5.40	9.67	14.02	6.88	9.04	13.44
Red River and north coast												
Actual CVs due to:												
Price and production shocks	4.92	8.19	11.09	5.79	7.80	11.04	5.43	8.47	10.78	5.53	8.02	10.68
Domestic market price and production shocks only	4.92	8.19	11.09	5.79	7.80	11.04	5.43	8.47	10.78	5.53	8.02	10.68
Simulated CVs due to world prices (in US$) and production shocks	6.97	9.87	12.93	7.71	9.38	12.88	7.80	10.52	12.56	7.53	9.80	12.47
	Share of coffee in agricultural income (%)						Share of coffee in agricultural income (%)					
South and central regions												
Actual CVs due to:												
Price and production shocks	5.77	19.32	48.92	7.12	27.67	52.45	6.36	26.88	54.28	7.03	27.78	53.19
Domestic market price and production shocks only	5.77	19.21	48.66	7.12	27.54	52.16	6.36	26.74	53.99	7.03	27.64	52.90
Simulated CVs due to world prices (in US$) and production shocks	6.71	18.25	46.26	8.22	26.32	49.55	7.50	25.51	51.31	8.13	26.42	50.28

Source: Computed by the authors.

is around 50 per cent. This is much higher than the CVs of all other household groups. By contrast, even the highly specialized rice producers do not seem to incur a CV larger than 14 per cent.

The results also indicate that almost all of the agricultural income variability faced by the producers is due to domestic factors. Even in highly coffee-dependent households, most of the income variability appears to be due to domestic factors. Such substantial income variation suggests that poor agricultural households may experience serious food security problems *post* adverse coffee price shocks, because of the limited resources used for the production of food crops for own consumption.

The simulation of full exposure to international prices indicates that perfect market integration would increase the CV of agricultural income for almost all households in the urban and northern as well as in the Red River and north coast regions. During the period under examination, Vietnam has implemented a series of policies aimed at maintaining domestic rice prices at a certain level and to reduce its volatility. These included export management through a system of minimum export prices and quotas allocated to authorized export enterprises, both public and private. Minimum export prices were revised frequently in order to follow international prices. In 2001, export quantitative limits were removed, but the new arrangement allows responsibility for exports to be retained by the state trade enterprises (FAO 2001, 2002). Hence it is to be expected that if these policies were replaced with full international market exposure, producers' income variability would increase. This is confirmed by the analysis. In contrast, the results indicate that the highly specialized coffee households in the south and central regions would experience from international exposure a small decline in their overall CV, albeit not large. The remaining income variability would, nevertheless, still be substantial.

9.3.3 *Peru*

The household classifications for Peru are based on the 1994 LSMS dataset (Table 9.7).[11] The sample consists of a weighted 1.9 million producer households, representing 50 per cent of all households in the country, divided in three regions, namely: sierra, coast, and selva. Households are classified as poor and nonpoor according to income-level thresholds that vary across regions.[12]

[11] Further information on the Peru LSMS 1994 dataset is available at: www.internationalbank.org/lsms/country/pe94/docs/i-basica.pdf .

[12] Poverty thresholds in Peru vary across the 12 subregions examined in the LSMS dataset and are calculated according to the cost of a commodity basket. For the purpose of this research, region thresholds are estimated as weighted averages of the constituent subregions. The average exchange rate for the period of the survey was 2.2 nuevo sol per US$.

Table 9.7. Household classification and characteristics: Peru

	Share of agriculture in POOR household income						Share of agriculture in NONPOOR household income					
	< 60%			> 60%			< 60%			> 60%		
	Share of rice in agricultural income (%)						Share of rice in agricultural income (%)					
	< 30	30–60	> 60	< 30	30–60	> 60	< 30	30–60	> 60	< 30	30–60	> 60
Coast												
Estimated no. of households	136,109	3,886	5,505	18,674	1,481	6,085	315,603	9,855	5,344	31,843	2,222	12,170
Share of total households (%)	3.07	0.09	0.12	0.42	0.03	0.14	7.13	0.22	0.12	0.72	0.05	0.27
Total income per capita (nuevo sol)	996	1,095	1,037	482	305	815	4,237	3,300	3,334	4,090	2,181	3,416
Share of agriculture in total income (%)	13.48	11.06	11.67	87.01	90.79	81.97	11.34	16.38	30.82	83.26	76.42	93.33
Sierra												
Estimated no. of households	212,039	2,637	1,195	261,885	1,195	1,195	332,162	8,158	1,195	205,907	2,391	10,759
Share of total households (%)	4.79	0.06	0.03	5.91	0.03	0.03	7.50	0.18	0.03	4.65	0.05	0.24
Total income per capita (nuevo sol)	622	824	116	467	102	676	4,897	2,801	1,207	2,172	1,647	1,947
Share of agriculture in total income (%)	27.65	18.26	36.81	86.47	100.00	93.92	21.16	14.93	43.61	86.77	93.11	89.91
Selva												
Estimated no. of households	69,458	3,364	8,827	61,341	6,835	6,835	120,961	6,128	6,085	51,850	8,228	6,171
Share of total households (%)	1.57	0.08	0.20	1.39	0.15	0.15	2.73	0.14	0.14	1.17	0.19	0.14
Total income per capita (nuevo sol)	681	593	573	618	514	457	3,270	3,411	2,629	2,436	1,407	1,690
Average share of agriculture in total income (%)	24.47	41.69	39.34	86.79	77.91	84.45	20.53	27.18	35.08	86.47	94.19	85.15

Source: Computed by the authors.

Table 9.8. Decomposed coefficients of variation of domestic prices, Peru (per cent)*

	CV of domestic prices accounted for by			World price coefficients of variation
	Domestic shocks	International shocks	Total	
Coffee	10.85	64.65	75.51	45.6
Maize	19.94	0.00	19.94	18.4
Wheat	6.71	11.74	18.44	17.7
Rice	16.20	11.57	27.77	11.5
Beef	16.71	0.00	16.71	9.8
Pork	8.31	0.00	8.31	18.7
Chicken	7.04	34.27	41.31	10.6
Plantains	16.46	0.00	16.46	14.9

Note: * Conditional coefficients of variation projected for 12 months ahead.
Source: Authors' calculations.

The sample is further divided according to the contribution of agricultural activities in total income (i.e. households having contributions less than 60 per cent and those with contributions larger than 60 per cent of total) and according to the contribution of rice production in agricultural income (i.e. households with shares smaller than 30 per cent, with shares between 30 and 60 per cent or shares larger than 60 per cent). The classification suggests that production of rice and cereals are the most important agricultural activities across regions. Both poor and nonpoor households depend heavily on rice and cereals and reveal similar production patterns. Meat is also revealed to constitute an important source of income, especially for the poor households. The proportion of income accruing from coffee production, although small, appears to be relatively more important for poor households, rather than nonpoor households.

Table 9.8 presents the analysis of agricultural price variability of the producers as well as shares of this variability that are accounted for by domestic and international shocks. For commodities like coffee, wheat, and chicken, the major share of the domestic price variability is due to international factors. For other commodities, most of the variability is due to domestic factors and the corresponding CVs of domestic prices do not follow a consistent pattern of instability *vis-à-vis* international prices.

In more detail, the VARs estimated for the domestic and international prices of beef, in conjunction with the Granger causality tests indicated that these prices are related, albeit weakly, with the causality being manifested from the international to the domestic market. In a similar vein, the variance decomposition suggests that most of the variation in domestic prices is attributed to domestic shocks. The estimated VAR parameters and the causality tests provide evidence that on the part of poultry domestic prices are closely related to, and Granger-caused by, international prices. The undertaken variance decomposition indicated that, although domestic prices are highly volatile with a coefficient of variation equal to 0.41, most of this divergence is attributable to international prices. The VAR analysis for domestic and international banana prices reveals that these prices are not determined in parallel. This suggests that international banana prices may not be an appropriate proxy for explaining price fluctuations for plantains in Peru. The VAR for the domestic and international prices for rice revealed that for the period under examination, price shocks in the international market are reflected in the domestic market and *vice versa*, although not to the full extent. The Peruvian government intervenes through tax restitutions on exports and a variable tariff imposed on rice imports. Rice imports originating from non-member countries of the Andean Pact are subject to a 20 per cent tariff plus a supplementary tax of 5 per cent. In mid-2001, the country introduced a price band mechanism based on an external reference price and a basic floor price to be set twice a year. In spite of the existing tariff, the implementation of these policies may have resulted in isolating the domestic market prices from shocks in the international markets, at least during the period covered by the sample.

Table 9.9 gives the results for Peru, which in general suggest that households with relatively less diversified production patterns face higher income uncertainty. In the coast and selva regions, the agricultural income CVs for the predominantly agricultural households with rice production constituting of more than 60 per cent of their agricultural income, is estimated to be around 14–17 per cent. This is considerably higher than the CV of farm households that earn 30–60 per cent of their income from rice. In the sierra, the analysis appears to suggest that lower dependence on rice may not result in a significant income-risk reduction, as households generating less than 30 per cent of their agricultural income from rice cultivation are characterized by higher CVs compared to households with similar characteristics in other regions.

The finding that domestic price and quantity variations are the overwhelming determinants affecting producer incomes is obtained here as well for all income classes. The CVs for the scenario of full exposure to international markets are reported in the last rows of Table 9.9. The results suggest that increasing exposure to international markets would lead to a considerable reduction in all agricultural income CVs (with the exception of one case in the selva region). In general, the reductions in the CVs for most household classifications would be several percentage points. This finding suggests that the domestic price policies aiming to stabilize rice prices may not have resulted in reducing agricultural income volatility. Exposure to international markets would induce an increased income volatility of about 0.4 percentage points for the predominantly agricultural households in the selva region that generate

Table 9.9. Coefficients of variation (CVs) of agricultural incomes, Peru (per cent)

	Share of agriculture in POOR household income						Share of agriculture in NONPOOR household income					
	< 60%			> 60%			< 60%			> 60%		
	share of rice in agricultural income (%)						share of rice in agricultural income (%)					
	< 30	30–60	> 60	< 30	30–60	> 60	< 30	30–60	> 60	< 30	30–60	> 60
Coast												
Actual CVs due to:												
Price and production shocks	4.36	8.65	15.09	8.60	11.64	16.96	3.19	8.00	16.33	8.96	11.58	15.63
Domestic market price and production shocks only	4.35	8.60	14.98	8.60	11.60	16.83	3.16	7.92	16.22	8.95	11.52	15.52
Simulated CVs due to world prices (in US$) and production shocks	2.64	6.95	11.44	6.05	8.48	12.90	2.06	6.36	12.50	6.10	8.96	11.89
Sierra												
Actual CVs due to:												
Price and production shocks	9.92	6.88	15.41	11.71	8.56	12.86	7.16	6.69	17.65	12.24	11.17	14.61
Domestic market price and production shocks only	9.91	6.82	15.32	11.68	8.52	12.77	7.14	6.61	17.52	12.23	11.11	14.50
Simulated CVs due to world prices (in US$) and production shocks	4.40	5.22	11.69	5.43	6.17	9.85	4.02	5.23	13.30	6.13	8.97	11.23
Selva												
Actual CVs due to:												
Price and production shocks	6.13	9.24	14.98	9.25	10.13	14.29	5.04	11.10	13.70	8.85	10.14	14.70
Domestic market price and production shocks only	6.12	9.18	14.87	9.15	10.07	14.19	4.99	11.05	13.60	8.47	10.09	14.60
Simulated CVs due to world prices (in US$) and production shocks	3.55	7.13	11.59	6.44	7.57	11.03	3.52	7.77	10.38	9.17	7.50	11.04

Source: Computed by the authors.

less than 30 per cent of their income from rice, possibly because a higher share of income is accrued from poultry and related meat-production.

9.4 Conclusions

In this study we attempt to answer the question of whether increased exposure to international markets reduces the volatility of domestic market prices and improves the welfare of agricultural commodity households. We develop a theoretical framework that leads to explicit formulae for household income variance on the basis of such covariate shocks as commodity price and yield uncertainties. The empirical work focuses on the estimation of household income uncertainties by linking household microclassifications for a number of different household types in Ghana, Vietnam, and Peru, and time-series analysis. We estimate the household-specific income variability that emanates from market uncertainties, both price and production related, and use this empirical framework in order to conduct simulation experiments on the extent to which full exposure, rather than partial or no exposure, to international market-signals affects commodity prices and thereby agricultural income volatility.

Although the households in the countries under examination are dissimilar in terms of agro-climatic and ecological conditions that may determine crop production structure, as well as in terms of other characteristics, such as consumption patterns, off-household employment, the number of sources of income, transfers and remittances from absent household members, the analysis reveals a uniform pattern, as far as the factors that contribute to household income uncertainty are concerned.

One major result of the study is that, in all countries, almost all of the agricultural income variability of producers seems to result from domestic factors. While domestic prices for tradable commodities exhibit diverse patterns of price transmission from international prices, the impact of international prices on farmer income variability seems to be small, either because of small transmission, or because the relevant commodities constitute only a minimal share of farm income.

We find mixed results of the impact on producer variability from total exposure to international prices. In general, in the countries examined, the results suggest that in the absence of effective price stabilization policies, increased exposure to international markets may result in a reduction in agricultural income volatility, as international markets may act as 'buffers' absorbing large domestic supply or demand shocks in domestic markets. However, with the exception of coffee-producing households in Vietnam, reductions in income variability resulting from increased exposure to international markets are very small. In countries where price stabilization schemes are in place—as in the case of cocoa in Ghana and rice in Vietnam—wider exposure to international markets may result in relatively greater income uncertainty, suggesting that domestic policies in these countries are effective in reducing the uncertainty that emanates from both domestic and international factors.

The extent to which households diversify their income sources and production patterns is noted to affect income uncertainty. As expected, households that rely largely on a single commodity for their earnings face higher income volatility than households adopting a more extensive diversification pattern. For example, the results suggest that the household categories in Vietnam that depend predominantly on rice and coffee experience considerably higher income uncertainty, particularly if opportunities for off-farm earnings do not exist. Similarly, households in Peru depending on rice and cereals face greater uncertainties than those that have a more diversified production pattern. Nevertheless, there are cases where both cash and food crops are subject to high prices and yield volatility, as for example Ghana, implying that crop diversification strategies on their own or as self-insurance may not be sufficient in shielding producers from large income fluctuations. It is, therefore, important that governments intervene in order to establish a mechanism through which commodity insurance can be provided.

The analysis conveys a clear message as far as policy design is concerned. Risks are detrimental to the welfare of poor households and ensuring income security is an essential ingredient of any poverty alleviation strategy (World Bank 2001). However, trade liberalization may not by itself be the panacea for reducing income instability. Thus additional policies are necessary to smooth, or ensure predictability of incomes, as well as to safeguard against sudden income losses. Such policies may include, among others, weather insurance and commodity risk management schemes. The recent initiative of the International Task Force (ITF) on Commodity Risk Management, has proposed using market based derivative instruments to provide price insurance for internationally traded commodities (ITF 1999), while other proposals have suggested using market based weather insurance to cover yield risks (Skees *et al.* 1999). Varangis *et al.* (2002) have suggested using combinations of the above instruments to manage agricultural market risks in developing countries. Such policies aim in providing mechanisms for insuring covariate risks and in creating an environment of more stable income, allowing households to escape poverty traps. Less income uncertainty contributes to poverty alleviation as it allows households to allocate their resources in a more efficient manner by, for example, undertaking investments, or adopting more productive, albeit possibly riskier, technologies and strategies of specialization necessary for agricultural efficiency (Carter 1997), and by avoiding costly risk-coping practices such as consumption smoothing.

Appendix 9.1

Table 9A.1. Shares of included agricultural income in total household income

	Share of agriculture in POOR household income						Share of agriculture in NONPOOR household income					
	< 60%			> 60%			< 60%			> 60%		
	Share of main commodity in agricultural income						Share of main commodity in agricultural income					
	< 30	30–60	> 60	< 30	30–60	> 60	< 30	30–60	> 60	< 30	30–60	> 60
GHANA												
Coast	0.115	0.122	0.137	0.542	0.616	0.574	0.100	0.319	0.044	0.471		
Forest	0.184	0.312	0.324	0.601	0.622	0.643	0.173	0.291	0.390	0.621	0.625	0.666
Savannah	0.182	0.419		0.504	0.569	0.731	0.199			0.539	0.727	
VIETNAM												
Urban & northern regions	0.093	0.282	0.254	0.588	0.655	0.794	0.034	0.209	0.121	0.474	0.625	0.864
Red River & north coast	0.130	0.300	0.290	0.593	0.676	0.797	0.139	0.256	0.221	0.470	0.647	0.770
South & central regions	0.124	0.054	0.339	0.623	0.789	0.888	0.137	0.296	0.268	0.568	0.632	0.875
PERU												
Coast	0.041	0.065	0.083	0.468	0.824	0.794	0.026	0.064	0.322	0.444	0.630	0.821
Sierra	0.135	0.075	0.368	0.590	0.606	0.717	0.068	0.066	0.427	0.595	0.798	0.810
Selva	0.113	0.263	0.355	0.541	0.582	0.754	0.068	0.148	0.222	0.589	0.738	0.785

Source: Computed by authors.

References

Bourguignon, F., S. Lambert, and A. Suwa-Eisenmann (2004). 'Trade Exposure and Income Volatility in Cash-crop Exporting Developing Countries'. *European Review of Agricultural Economics*, 31 (3): 369–87.

Carter, M. R. (1997). 'Environment, Technology, and the Social Articulation of Risk in West African Agriculture'. *Economic Development and Cultural Change*, 45 (3): 557–90.

Chaudhuri, S. (2002). 'Empirical Methods for Assessing Household Vulnerability to Poverty'. Department of Economics, Columbia University. Mimeo.

Christiaensen, L., and R. Boisvert, (2000). 'On Measuring Households Food Vulnerability: Case Evidence from Northern Mali'. Working Paper 2000–5 (March), Department of Agricultural and Managerial Economics.

Collier, P., and J. Dehn (2001). 'Aid, Shocks and Growth'. Policy Research Working Paper 2688. Washington, DC: World Bank.

Deaton, A. (1991). 'Savings and Liquidity Constraints'. *Econometrica*, 59 (5): 1221–48.

Dehn, J. (2000). 'Commodity Price Uncertainty in Developing Countries'. Policy Research Working Paper 2426. Washington, DC: World Bank.

Dercon, S. (2004). 'Risk, Insurance and Poverty', in S. Dercon (ed.), *Insurance against Poverty*. Oxford: Oxford University Press for UNU-WIDER.

Diaz-Bonilla, E. M., M. Thomas, S. Robinson, and A. Cattaneo (2000). 'Food Security and Trade Negotiations in the World Trade Organization: A Cluster Analysis of Country Groups'. TMD Working Paper 59. Washington, DC: IFPRI, Trade and Macroeconomics Division.

Fafchamps, M. (2003). *Rural Poverty, Risk and Development*. Cheltenham: Edward Elgar.

—— C. Udry, and K. Czukas (1998). 'Drought and Saving in West-Africa: are Livestock a Buffer Stock?'. *Journal of Development Economics*, 55 (2): 273–305.

FAO (2001, 2002). *Review of Basic Food Policies*. Rome: Commodities and Trade Division, FAO.

Ghana Statistical Service (2000). *Poverty Trends in Ghana in the 1990s*. Accra: Ghana Statistical Service.

Granger, C. W. J. (1969). 'Investigating Causal Relationships by Econometric Models and Cross Spectral Methods'. *Econometrica*, 37 (3): 424–38.

—— (1988). 'Some Recent Developments in the Concept of Causality', *Journal of Econometrics*, 39: 199–211.

Hamilton, J. D. (1994). *Time Series Analysis*. Princeton: Princeton University Press.

Heitzmann, K., R. S. Canagarajah, and P. B. Siegel (2002). 'Guidelines for Assessing the Sources of Risks and Vulnerability'. Social Protection Discussion Paper 0218. Washington, DC: Social Protection Unit, World Bank.

Holzmann, R., and S. Jorgensen (2000). 'Social Risk Management: A New Conceptual Framework for Social Protection and Beyond'. Social Protection Discussion Paper 006. Washington, DC: Social Protection Unit, World Bank.

IMF (International Monetary Fund) (2005). International Financial Statistics. Washington, DC: IMF.

ITF (International Task Force on Commodity Risk Management in Developing Countries) (1999). 'Dealing with Commodity Price Volatility in Developing Countries: A Proposal for a Market-based Approach'. Discussion paper for

the Roundtable on Commodity Risk Management in Developing Countries, 24 September. Washington, DC.
Jalan, J., and M. Ravallion (1999). 'Are the Poor less Well Insured? Evidence on Vulnerability to Income Risk in Rural China'. *Journal of Development Economics*, 58 (1): 61–81.
Kazianga, H., and C. Udry (2006). 'Consumption Smoothing? Livestock, Insurance and Drought in Rural Burkina Faso'. *Journal of Development Economics*, 79(2): 413–46.
Ligon, E., and L. Schechter, (2003). 'Measuring Vulnerability'. *Economic Journal*, 113 (486): C95–C102.
Lütkepohl, H. (1993). *Introduction to Multiple Time Series Analysis*. Berlin: Springer-Verlag.
Morduch, J. (1995). 'Income Smoothing and Consumption Smoothing'. *Journal of Economic Perspectives*, 9: 103–14.
Newberry, D. M., and J. E. Stiglitz (1981). *The Theory of Commodity Price Stabilization: Study in the Economics of Risk*. New York: Oxford University Press.
Rosenzweig, M., and H. Binswanger (1993). 'Wealth, Weather Risk, and the Composition and Profitability of Agricultural Investments'. *Economic Journal*, 103: 56–78.
—— K. Wolpin (1993). 'Credit Market Constraints, Consumption Smoothing, and the Accumulation of Durable Production Assets in Low-income Countries: Investment in Bullocks in India'. *Journal of Political Economy*, 101 (2): 223–44.
Sarris, A. (2002). 'The Demand for Commodity Insurance by Developing Country Agricultural Producers: Theory and Application to Cocoa in Ghana', Policy Research Working Paper 2887. Washington, DC: World Bank.
Skees, J., P. Hazell, and M. Miranda (1999). 'New Approaches to Crop Yield Insurance in Developing Countries'. EPTD Discussion Paper 55. Washington, DC: IFPRI.
Townsend, R. M. (1995). 'Consumption Insurance: An Evaluation of Risk-bearing Systems in Low-income Economies'. *Journal of Economic Perspectives*, 9: 83–102.
Varangis, P., D. Larson, and J. R. Anderson (2002). 'Agricultural Markets and Risks—Management of the Latter, not the Former', Policy Research Working Paper Series 2793. Washington, DC: World Bank.
World Bank (2001). *World Development Report 2000/2001, Attacking Poverty*. International Bank for Reconstruction and Development. New York: Oxford University Press.
Zimmerman, F. J., and M. R. Carter (2003). 'Asset Smoothing, Consumption Smoothing and the Reproduction of Inequality under Risk and Subsistence Constraints'. *Journal of Development Economics*, 71 (2): 233–60.

10

Agricultural Support Measures of Developed Countries and Food Insecurity in Developing Countries

Michael Herrmann

10.1 Introduction

'There were 815 million people hungry in the developing world in 2002—nine million less than in 1990. Yet in the worst-affected regions—Sub-Saharan Africa [SSA] and Southern Asia—the number of hungry people has increased by tens of millions' (UN 2005: 8; similarly Pingali and Stringer 2003; FAO 2004). Undernourishment and malnutrition continue to cause premature death and to impede the ability of humans to live up to their potentials and make full use of their capabilities (Sen 1999; Nussbaum 1993). The challenge to ensure appropriate nutrition and combat hunger is both a core objective of development and an indispensable prerequisite for it (Benson 2004).

To combat food insecurity and ensure a sufficient food supply is both a moral imperative and an economic necessity. Given the importance of food security, it may be argued that food is a strategic good and that the supply of food should not be left to market forces, but should rather be ensured by the public sector.[1] In countries that do not have the appropriate mix of and/or the appropriate endowments with factors of production, the decision to attain food self-sufficiency would necessitate relatively far-reaching market interventions. While there may be sound political reasons why countries

The author gratefully acknowledges comments of Basudeb Guha-Khasnobis, who directed UNU-WIDER's project on Hunger and Food Security, and comments of participants in WIDER's workshops on the issue. The views expressed in this chapter, however, are those of the author; they do not necessarily reflect views of commentators or views of the UNCTAD Secretariat with which the author is affiliated.

[1] If food is treated as a strategic product, what about water, clothing, medicine, or oil? Could the same argument not be made for all these products?

should attempt to ensure food self-sufficiency, there are compelling economic reasons for why countries should specialize according to their comparative advantage.

One's principal position on this issue will influence one's approach to assess it; the guiding questions, the analysis itself, and the conclusions. Without judging whether the political or the economic reason is more powerful, this chapter assumes an economic rather than a political approach to the challenge of food security. Thus, it treats food like any other product and assumes that food security can potentially be ensured through market mechanisms.

This chapter focuses on the world's poorest countries, namely the least developed countries (LDCs).[2] Almost all of these countries are located in the regions that are most affected by food insecurity—in SSA and South Asia. The LDCs are strongly affected by food insecurity, but the LDCs are also characterized by a generalized level of extreme poverty.[3] According to poverty estimates based on national accounts the LDCs are already the major locus of extreme poverty in the world, but even according to poverty estimates based on household surveys the LDCs are estimated to suffer from an absolute increase of extreme poverty in the coming years. In 2000 every second inhabitant of the LDCs was living in extreme poverty (UNCTAD 2002). Extreme poverty and food insecurity are closely related, as the very poor are least able to take precautions against food insecurity and are therefore the first to be confronted by it. Out of a sample of 227 countries[4] 61 developing countries have experienced food crises during the seven-year period of 1998–2004; according to FAO data (see Table 10.1). The LDCs were, proportionately, affected more often than other developing countries: of the 61 countries facing food crises 29 were LDCs. Of these 29 eleven have suffered from food crises each year over the seven-year period. Of the other 32 countries only four experienced acute food crises each year over this period.

While acknowledging that food crises in LDCs have many potential causes, this chapter argues that food dilemma in the LDCs is closely related to distortions of the global agricultural markets, which can be attributed to agricultural support policies of advanced countries. Agricultural support measures as defined here include both subsidies and border measures; advanced countries include OECD countries but also advanced non-OECD countries. It is important to extend the analysis beyond OECD countries, as several

[2] The LDCs are a group of developing countries that the UN has identified as least developed, owing to low income per capita, weak human resources, and fragile economies. At present the group of LDCs includes a total of 50 developing economies.

[3] In accordance with international standards, extreme poverty is measured by a poverty line of US$1 per person per day in 1985 PPP.

[4] The term 'countries' as used here includes other territories. The use of this term is not intended to question the legal status of any country, territory, city, or area, or its authorities, or its frontiers or boundaries.

advanced non-OECD countries also provide considerable support to domestic agriculture.

The chapter has four sections. The section 10.2 examines the patterns of agricultural specialization and food insecurity, and 10.3 assesses effects of agricultural support measures on food insecurity. In this context, the chapter distinguishes between a trade-centric approach and a development-oriented approach to evaluate agricultural support measures. Section 10.4 concludes the analysis with a series of policy implications.

10.2 Agricultural Specialization and Food Crises

10.2.1 *Pattern of Agricultural Specialization*

Table 10.1 shows the LDCs' specialization in the agricultural sector and their exposure to food crises, giving, where possible, individual values for the LDCs and for different developing-country groups. The developing countries are divided into three subgroups: namely low-income countries (World Bank definition), low-income, food-deficit countries (FAO definition), and the LDCs (UN definition). These three subgroups have overlapping memberships.

Data on agriculture value added as share of GDP were collected for 171 countries. Out of these 171 countries there are 95 countries where the share of agriculture value added in GDP is higher than the developing countries' average; out of these 95 countries there are 45 countries where the share of agriculture population in total population is higher than the developing countries' average; and out of these 45 countries there are 24 countries where the share of agricultural land area in total land area is higher than the developing countries' average.[5]

Based on these indicators, these 24 countries, including no less than 19 LDCs, have a relatively strong specialization in agriculture and appear to have a comparative advantage in agricultural production. It would not be an exaggeration to expect these countries to be, at best, net food exporters to the world, or to assume that they are able, at the least, to satisfy the food needs of their own population. Yet 23 out of 24 countries (i.e. 96 per cent) that appear to have a comparative advantage in agricultural production have received food aid during the reference period 1998–2004. By contrast, only

[5] Based on the same measures all three sub-groups of the developing-country group also have a strong agricultural specialization. The only notable deviation from this picture is that the group of LDCs has, on average, less agricultural land than the group of developing countries. But the average for the LDC group somewhat distorts the values for individual LDCs. A breakdown shows that while there are LDCs where agricultural land is scarce, there are numerous LDCs where it is not. It is important to emphasize however that the indicator of agricultural land does not provide any meaningful indication of land quality. The indicator can therefore only be used as a rough proxy for the ability to expand agricultural production.

Table 10.1. Agriculture and food security indicators for LDCs and selected developing-country groups, 1998–2002

	Agriculture			Food			Food aid		Frequency of acute food crises*	Reasons for acute food crises
	Value added as % of GDP	Population as % of total	Land as % of total	Trade balance (US$ million)	Trade balance per capita (US$)	Supply per capita (kcal/day)	Per capita, cereals (kg)	Per capita non-cereals (kg)		
Developing countries	11.3	52.0	40.7	−1958.6	−0.4	2651.3	1.6	0.2		
LDCs	29.0	70.0	36.2	−3631.8	−5.4	2111.5	5.3	0.5		
LICs	20.3	55.2	41.4	1542.0	0.6	2390.0	2.6	0.3		
LICs, food-deficit	19.0	57.4	44.3	3229.6	0.8	2595.5	1.9	0.2		
Afghanistan	54.1	67.0	58.4	−97.6	−4.5	—	10.7	1.3	7.0	Civil strife, drought, war
Angola	8.2	71.9	46.0	−287.4	−23.0	2008.5	14.8	2.6	7.0	Civil strife, IDPs, returnees
Bangladesh	24.8	55.7	62.7	−812.6	−5.9	2168.1	5.3	0.0	3.0	Floods
Benin	36.8	54.0	28.4	−98.9	−16.0	2507.5	—	—		
Bhutan	35.9	93.7	12.1	−3.7	−1.8	—	—	—		
Burkina Faso	33.8	92.3	36.9	−98.0	−8.3	2393.8	2.3	0.5		
Burundi	51.3	90.4	80.9	23.2	3.8	1638.2	4.1	1.0	7.0	Civil strife, insecurity, IDPs, returnees
Cambodia	41.0	70.1	29.3	−77.8	−5.9	1998.0	2.1	0.3	2.0	Floods
Cape Verde	11.6	23.0	17.4	−58.6	−134.6	3193.8	107.7	2.7	2.0	Drought
Central African Republic	54.9	72.7	8.3	−9.9	−2.7	1967.3	1.1	0.2	3.0	Civil strife, IDPs
Chad	38.6	75.2	37.8	15.5	2.0	2121.9	2.0	0.1	1.0	Refugees
Comoros	39.8	73.6	64.8	−12.3	−17.6	1750.4	7.2	0.0		
Congo, DR	53.4	63.2	9.7	−157.3	−3.2	1658.4	0.7	0.2	7.0	Civil strife, IDPs
Djibouti	3.8	78.5	56.1	−62.9	−94.5	2128.2	17.6	2.0		
Equatorial Guinea	11.8	70.5	11.9	−2.0	−4.2	—	1.4	0.6		
Eritrea	18.7	77.6	63.5	−45.2	−12.2	1538.4	46.2	4.6	7.0	Drought, IDPs, returnees
Ethiopia	44.5	82.4	27.9	116.3	1.8	1792.5	12.8	0.4	7.0	Drought, IDPs
Gambia	31.2	79.0	61.5	−50.5	−38.7	2266.9	4.0	1.1		
Guinea	23.8	83.8	49.7	−95.6	−11.8	2342.8	3.0	0.7	4.0	IDPs and refugees
Guinea-Bissau	60.1	82.8	44.7	31.9	23.0	2075.8	7.0	2.6	3.0	
Haiti	26.9	62.3	57.3	−268.2	−33.5	2064.5	16.1	2.1	7.0	Civil strife, drought, floods
Kiribati	17.2	27.4	53.4	—	—	2854.9	—	—		
Lao PDR	42.1	76.5	7.7	−17.1	−3.2	2261.1	2.9	0.2	2.0	
Lesotho	17.3	39.2	76.8	−105.2	−59.2	2595.0	6.2	1.2	3.0	Adverse weather, drought

(cont.)

Table 10.1. (*Continued*)

	Agriculture			Food			Food aid		Frequency of acute food crises*	Reasons for acute food crises
	Value added as % of GDP	Population as % of total	Land as % of total	Trade balance (US$ million)	Trade balance per capita (US$)	Supply per capita (kcal/day)	Per capita, cereals (kg)	Per capita non-cereals (kg)		
Liberia	—	67.6	23.3	−58.2	−20.0	2030.0	18.2	4.6	7.0	Civil strife, IDPs, shortage of inputs
Madagascar	30.1	74.2	46.9	61.5	3.7	2043.4	1.6	0.8	4.0	Drought, cyclones
Malawi	35.7	77.6	34.8	34.7	3.1	2144.9	5.6	0.3	2.0	Adverse weather, drought
Maldives	—	27.1	34.7	−65.0	−223.5	2514.1	11.0	—		
Mali	41.3	81.0	28.0	−30.8	−2.6	2213.3	0.4	0.1		
Mauritania	22.6	52.9	38.8	−139.0	−52.7	2757.7	12.4	1.5	3.0	Drought
Mozambique	28.0	76.9	60.2	−148.3	−8.3	1998.9	7.8	0.6	2.0	Drought
Myanmar	58.7	70.2	15.9	208.9	4.4	2855.7	—	0.0		
Nepal	40.5	93.0	33.3	−80.6	−3.5	2406.0	0.4	0.0		
Niger	40.3	87.7	13.0	−37.4	−3.5	2135.6	2.1	0.1		
Rwanda	42.1	90.8	64.9	−12.2	−1.7	1941.2	13.5	5.7	4.0	Drought
Samoa	13.1	34.5	45.1	−18.4	−106.1	2821.5	—	—		
São Tomé and Principe	20.5	64.2	53.5	−2.8	−18.4	2328.8	26.0	1.5		
Senegal	18.1	73.8	41.0	−361.4	−38.5	2270.4	2.1	0.5		
Sierra Leone	47.6	62.2	38.5	−110.8	−24.9	1940.4	9.5	2.8	7.0	Civil strife, IDPs, returnees
Solomon Islands	—	73.2	4.0	−13.5	−30.6	2238.0	—	—		
Somalia	—	71.2	69.1	12.8	1.4	—	3.1	0.4	7.0	Drought, civil strife
Sudan	40.0	61.1	53.4	−164.3	−5.1	2284.6	4.7	0.8	7.0	Civil strife, drought
Tanzania, UR	44.8	78.2	42.3	70.7	2.0	3750.6	—	—	6.0	Drought, refugees
Timor-Leste	33.9	81.7	19.3	−31.7	−43.9	2702.4	10.3	1.9	1.0	Drought
Togo	39.5	59.7	63.6	−13.2	−2.8	2307.0	0.8	0.0		
Tuvalu	—	36.0	—	—	—	—	—	—		
Uganda	37.2	79.0	50.9	135.1	5.9	2333.2	2.5	0.5	7.0	Civil strife, IDPs, drought in parts
Vanuatu	15.8	36.7	13.3	−9.1	−46.2	2559.0	0.1	0.0		
Yemen	16.3	50.4	33.6	−600.1	−33.3	2047.4	8.0	0.5		
Zambia	22.4	69.3	46.9	−39.7	−3.9	1893.1	2.8	0.7	4.0	Rain, floods, drought

Source: Agriculture value added and GDP calculations based on World Bank (2003a); all other variables from FAO, FAOSTAT on-line data.
Note: *Number of years in which country was affected by food crises, in the period 1998–2004.

eleven out of 36 countries (i.e. 37 per cent) that appear to be comparatively disadvantaged with regard to agricultural production have received food aid over the same period.[6] This chapter focuses on countries which have a potential comparative advantage in agriculture and therefore may face competition from other agricultural producers, including those in the advanced countries.

In the group of countries characterized by a relatively strong dependency on food aid only 14 out of 23 countries were net food importers. By contrast, in the group of countries characterized by a relatively low dependence on food aid 29 out of 34 countries (for which food trade data were available) were net food importers. This suggests that the food insecurity situation of a country cannot systematically be linked to its food trade balance. This has important implications as the discussion of food insecurity within the multilateral trading system centers around net food-importing developing countries rather than food insecure countries as such.

It is somewhat paradoxical that the countries which appear to have a comparative advantage in agricultural production are the very same countries with the greatest exposure to food crises. The situation is particularly pronounced in the least developed countries. On average they have a stronger specialization in agriculture than other developing countries and yet they receive more food aid than other developing countries. In order to understand this situation, it is necessary to examine the causes of food crises.

10.2.2 *Causes of Food Crises*

Table 10.1 lists reasons for food crises, wherever provided by FAO. These 'causes' of food crises can be broadly grouped into three categories of causes, namely political instability, natural disasters and factors that contribute to high dependency ratios. These causes for food crises are more pronounced in the least developed countries than in other developing countries.

POLITICAL INSTABILITY

Political instability, which may or may not result in armed conflict, is one of the most cited causes for food crises. Political instability and armed conflict can cause displacement of persons, depletion of human capital, destruction of land, decrease of economic activities and/or an unequal distribution of economic output. Many of the least developed countries are affected by conflict. Between 1992 and 2001 the number of LDCs that experienced conflict increased, while the number of other developing countries that experienced conflict decreased. In the 1970s and 1980s about 40 per cent of the LDCs were

[6] The countries with an apparent disadvantage in the production of agricultural goods have a relatively low share of agriculture value added in GDP, a relatively small share of the agriculture population in total population and a relatively small share of agriculture land in total land.

affected by conflict, but this figure has increased to 50 per cent in 1990–5 and to 58 per cent in 1996–2001 (UNCTAD 2004).

NATURAL DISASTERS

The second most cited causes for food insecurity are natural disasters, including droughts, floods, and storms. Today the LDCs are not only the world's major centre of humanitarian crises; they are also a major locus of natural disasters. While many natural disasters can neither exclusively nor directly be attributed to policies of LDCs, natural disasters can be exaggerate by practices in LDCs, including a rapid rate of deforestation, which is reflected in low levels of genuine domestic savings. Over the past two decades the LDCs have seen rapid rate of deforestation. By the late 1990s they had a rate of net forest depletion which was equivalent to two per cent of their GDP; about three times as high as in other developing countries (UNCTAD 2002: 91). There are important differences between the LDCs however. Those that have been characterized by a decrease of poverty have typically seen a lower rate of deforestation and an increase of genuine domestic savings, while those that have been characterized by an increase of poverty have seen a higher rate of deforestation and a decrease of genuine domestic savings.

HIGH DEPENDENCY RATIOS

Other causes of food insecurity have to do with factors that contribute to high and increasing dependency ratios. An increasing number of dependants per income earner results from at least four developments, namely higher birth rates, which increase the number of children per household; longer life expectancies, which increase the number of elders per household; the spread of disease, which worsens the ratio of capable income earners to ill persons per household; and political conflict, which has similar effects. A net increase of immigration may also contribute to an increase of the dependency ratio, especially if immigrants are not allowed to work or are not able to find work. Consequently dependency ratios in LDCs are higher than in other developing countries; in 2002 they where 0.862 in the LDCs and 0.582 in other developing countries.

The previous section has highlighted two facts: food crises are particularly frequent in the LDCs, and the reasons for food crises are particularly pronounced in the LDCs. There thus appears to be a straightforward explanation for food insecurity, which suggests similarly straightforward, although not necessarily simple, solutions to food insecurity: countries need to identify the exact cause of food crises and they need to take measures to tackle this cause. But frequently it is even more complicated than that. Factors which appear to be under the control of food-insecure countries frequently are beyond the control of these countries; what may appear to be a cause of a food crisis may sometimes be a consequence of a food crisis; and what may appear to be the sole cause of food crises may be compounded by other, less obvious causes of food crises.[7]

While it is apparent how the outlined factors may contribute to the outbreak of a food crisis, they cannot provide a full understanding of the problem. Why, for example, do countries continue to specialize in certain agricultural goods even though adverse environmental conditions regularly destroy their harvest? Why do these countries not diversify into other types of products in order to reduce their exposure to environmental shocks? Or why do they not at least change the method of production in order to reduce their exposure to such shocks? To answer such questions, the chapter proposes a methodological distinction between the causes for food crises, which goes beyond the distinction that has been made so far.

The study proposes a distinction between relatively obvious trigger causes of food crises, on the one side, and less obvious systemic causes of food crises, on the other. Trigger causes create the short-term changes necessary actually to bring about an outbreak of a food crisis. Systemic causes, by contrast, create the long-term conditions that are conducive to the outbreak of a food crisis. Unlike the trigger causes, which are often of a non-economic nature, systemic causes tend to be of an economic nature. The systemic causes have to do with the economic environment that makes it relatively easy for countries to slip into food crises, while making it relatively difficult for countries to get out of food crises. The chapter argues that agricultural support measures of advanced countries can act as a systemic cause of food insecurity in the developing countries.

In order to understand how agricultural support measures of advanced countries can negatively affect food security in developing countries, it is important to distinguish between a trade-centric perspective and a development-oriented perspective. Contrary to the development-oriented perspective, the trade-centric perspective suggest that agricultural support measures of advanced countries may actually counteract rather than cause food insecurity in developing countries. Both perspectives will be discussed in the subsequent section.

[7] Poverty and hunger may not only be consequences of conflict, high dependency ratios and natural resource depletion; poverty and hunger may also be factors that contribute to conflicts, higher dependency ratios and excessive natural resource use. UNCTAD (2002) has highlighted a complex, over-determined relationship between poverty, environmental degradation and population growth. Furthermore, UNCTAD (2004) has argued that there is no simple, linear relationship between conflict and poverty. Most low-income countries have experienced an economic crisis, which deepens poverty, before they have experienced the outbreak of conflict, which further exacerbates poverty (see also David 2004). In economic terms: poor populations tend to have relatively low opportunity costs and they may therefore be more prone to get involved in conflict.

10.3 Agricultural Support Measures and Food Insecurity

10.3.1 *Nature of Agricultural Support*

Agricultural support takes two principal forms: it can be provided in the form of payments, including producer and consumer subsidies, or in form of border measures, including tariff and non-tariff barriers. Tariff barriers are associated with relatively high average tariff rates, relatively high tariff peaks, and tariff escalations. By contrast, non-tariff barriers include import quotas, but also overly complex rules of origin and overly stringent sanitary and phytosanitary (SPS) and technical product standards. As many non-tariff barriers are difficult to quantify they are not captured in measures of total aggregate support.

Figure 10.1 provides an overview of the development of agricultural support in the OECD countries. In 2001 OECD countries provided support to their own agricultural sector of about US$311 billion. At the same time,

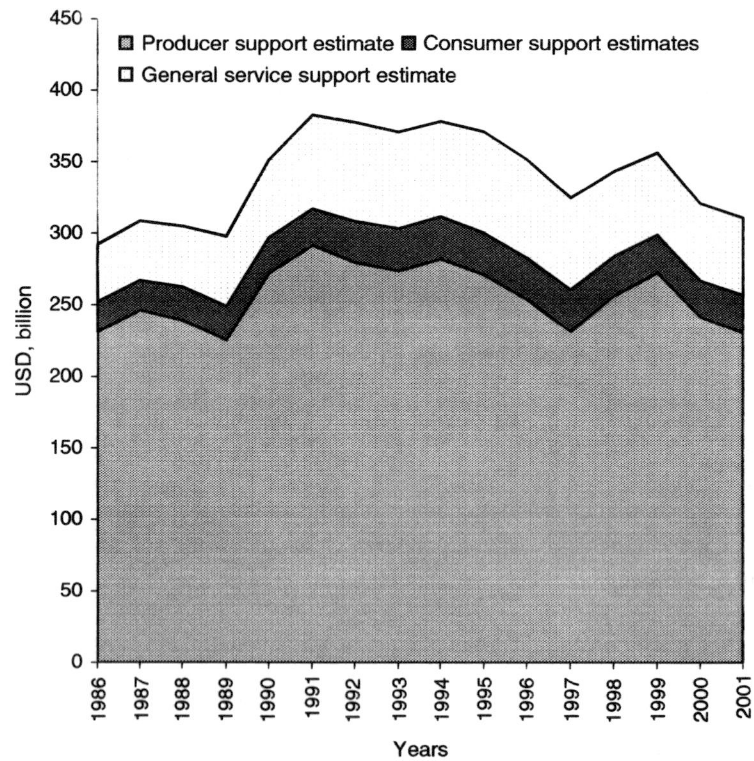

Figure 10.1. OECD agricultural support and its components, 1986–2001

Note: Consumer support refers to transfers from taxpayers to consumers; all figures are estimates.
Source: Calculations based on OECD PSE/CSE on-line data.

OECD countries provided development assistance to all LDCs of only US$12 billion—an amount equivalent to about two-weeks' worth of domestic agricultural support.[8] The most important form of support is producer support which can be broken down into two types, namely market price support, which includes import restrictions, and direct payments, which include actual subsidies paid to producers.

Both types of support are associated with major distortions of market mechanisms. Market price support delinks product prices, on the one side, and supply and demand, on the other; direct payments to producers decouple produce prices, on the one side, and the income of producers, on the other. First-round effects of such distortions can be an excessive production of agricultural goods, adding-up problems in agricultural markets and a decline of agricultural prices. Reactions to these distortions can bring about second-round effects, including further downward pressure on product prices, as is highlighted below.

Whether agricultural support measures of advanced countries actually affect agricultural production in developing countries is theoretically dependent on two conditions, namely the economic size of advanced countries, and the economic openness of the developing countries. In accordance with real-world conditions it can safely be assumed that the advanced countries constitute large economies, which have the potential to affect world prices, and that especially the least developing countries are relatively open economies, which can be affected by world prices (Ray *et al.* 2003). The Trade Restrictiveness Index of the IMF shows that the LDCs have particularly open trade regimes (UNCTAD 2004, 2006).

The Doha Round has given impetus to numerous studies in international trade on agricultural support measures. These studies have helped to highlight the ways in which and the extent to which agricultural support measures of advanced countries affect developing countries. The following section will discuss aspects of these trade-centric evaluations of agricultural support measures, while the section after that will describe aspects of a more development-oriented evaluation of agricultural support measures.

10.3.2 *Effects of Agricultural Support: Trade-Centric Perspective*

Hypothetically there are three effects that agricultural support measures of advanced countries may have on agricultural production in developing countries:

[8] In 2001 the group of LDCs included 49 countries. Calculations are based on OECD producer support estimates and consumer support estimates, and OECD aid data. Development assistance is net disbursement of official development assistance, which includes imputed multilateral flows.

No effects. This is because advanced countries produce and support temperate agricultural products, whereas most developing countries specialize in tropical agricultural products.

Negative net effects. This is because the elimination of agricultural support in advanced countries will lead to an increase of the food import bill of developing countries. The negative effect associated with an increased food import bill of developing countries is expected to exceed the positive effect associated with increased agricultural production in developing countries.

Positive effect. This is because the elimination of agricultural support in advanced countries will lead to an increase of agricultural production in developing countries. The positive effect associated with an increased production of agricultural goods in developing countries is expected to exceed the negative effect associated with an increased food import bill of developing countries.

While the first hypothetical effects assumes that there are no links between agricultural support in advanced countries and agricultural production in developing countries, the second and third hypothetical effect suggest links between these two factors, although with inverse signs.

Table 10.2 shows that the first hypothetical effect is inconsistent with empirical data. The table provides an overview of the products which receive support in OECD countries and the five most important producers of these products and their substitutes in the LDCs. From this it becomes apparent that LDCs produce virtually all the goods supported by OECD countries. Furthermore, the LDCs produce many goods that are substitutes for the goods supported by OECD countries.[9]

It can therefore be concluded that agricultural support measures of advanced countries affect agricultural production in developing countries. The case of cotton provides a particularly dramatic illustration of these effects (Badiane *et al.* 2002; Oxfam 2003). But is it possible to generalize the case of cotton, and what exactly are the net effects of agricultural support measures?

When analysing the effects of agricultural support measures of advanced countries on developing countries, it is important to focus not only on effects on producers and consumers, but to focus also on the effects in the short run and the long run. While producers of agricultural goods may suffer from import of subsidized food, the consumers of agricultural goods may benefit from the import of such food. Furthermore, while producers may suffer from such imports in the short run, they may be able to cope with negative effects in the long run. In other words, negative effects do not only depend on the

[9] While this distinction between temperate and tropical goods has always been difficult, it becomes increasingly blurred, as progress in technology, including biotechnology, allows for an increasing number of goods to be produced in diverse climatic zones.

Table 10.2. Products supported by OECD countries, and the top-five LCD producers of these products,[a] based on average annual production in metric tonnes 1991–2000

	Animal products						Primary crops																											
	Meats				Non-meats		Cereals						Oil crops			Fruits					Vegetables									Others		Textiles		
	Beef and veal	Pork	Poultry	Mutton	Eggs	Milk (cow)	Barley	Maize	Oats	Rice	Sorghum	Wheat	Rapeseed	Soybeans	Sunflower	Apples	Grapes	Mandarins	Pears	Strawberries	Beans	Cabbage	Cucumbers	Garlic	Onions	Pepper, red	Potatoes	Spinach	Tomatoes	Coffeebeans[c]	Sugar	Cotton	Wool	Tobacco
LDC producers of equivalents[b]																																		
Afghanistan				1		2	2					1			4	1	1		1														2	
Angola																5																		
Bangladesh	4		2		1	3				1		2	1									1	1	2	3		1	1	5		1			3
Benin																										1			4			2		
Bhutan																3										3								
Burkina Faso											2															4						3		
Burundi																					4													
Cambodia		1								4				3																				
Chad																																5		
Congo, Dem. Rep.		5						5														4	5							3				
Eritrea							5																											
Ethiopia	3		3	3	3	4	1	2	1		3	4	2	5			5	4			3	2								2			3	
Haiti																		3										2						
Laos People's Dem. Rep.																		1																5
Lesotho									2																									
Madagascar	5	3								5						2	4		2			5	3				5			4	4			
Malawi								3														3					3				5			1
Mali											4																					1		
Mozambique															5																			
Myanmar		2	1		2					2				2	1						1			1	1						3			2
Nepal							4	4		3		3															2							

(*cont.*)

Table 10.2. (*Continued*)

	Animal products						Primary crops																											
	Meats				Non-meats		Cereals						Oil crops			Fruits					Vegetables									Others		Textiles		
	Beef and veal	Pork	Poultry	Mutton	Eggs	Milk (cow)	Barley	Maize	Oats	Rice	Sorghum	Wheat	Rapeseed	Soybeans	Sunflower	Apples	Grapes	Mandarins	Pears	Strawberries	Beans	Cabbage	Cucumbers	Garlic	Onions	Pepper, red	Potatoes	Spinach	Tomatoes	Coffeebeans[c]	Sugar	Cotton	Wool	Tobacco
Niger																									2									
Senegal			4																				4					3						
Somalia				4																														
Sudan	1			2	5	1					1	5			3			5						3		5			1		2	4	1	
Tanzania	2				4	5		1			5				2		3				5			5					3	5			5	4
Uganda		4												1							2				4		4			1				
Yemen			5	5			3									4	2	2	3				2	4	5	2			2				4	
Zambia														4					4															
LDC producers of substitutes[b]																																		
Afghanistan						5																												
Angola																															2			
Bangladesh	5	5	5	5		3																										1	1	
Burkina Faso							3	3	3	3	3	3																						
Burundi																5	5	5	5	5														
Central African Republic																															4			
Congo, Dem. Rep.	3	3	3	3									4	4	4	2	2	2	2	2	1	1	1	1	1	1	1	1	1					
Ethiopia	2	2	2	2			2	2	2	2	2	2									5	5	5	5	5	5	5	5	5		3	5	5	
Madagascar																															5	4	4	
Mali							4	4	4	4	4	4																						
Mozambique													5	5	5						4	4	4	4	4	4	4	4	4					
Myanmar													2	2	2																	3	3	
Nepal	4	4	4	4		4																												

Niger						1	1	1	1	1	1																				
Rwanda															3	3	3	3	3												
Senegal												3	3	3																	
Somalia					1																										
Sudan	1	1	1	1	2							1	1	1																	
Tanzania															4	4	4	4	4	2	2	2	2	2	2	2	2	2	1	2	2
Uganda						5	5	5	5	5	5				1	1	1	1	1	3	3	3	3	3	3	3	3	3			

Source: Agricultural subsidies calculations based on OECD PSE/ CSE on-line data, and agricultural production on FAO, FAOSTAT on-line data.

Notes: [a] The table includes all goods that receive support from OECD countries, regardless of the type and the level. The largest LDC producer for each product is identified by the number '1', . . . the fifth largest LDC producer for each product is identified by the number '5'. In the case of strawberries no significant LDC producer has been identified; in the case of oats and rapeseeds there are only two LDC producers; in the case of spinach there are only three LDC producers; and in the case of pears there are only four LDC producers. For all other products there are at least five LDC producers. No substitutes have been identified for eggs, coffee, and tobacco.

[b] 'Equivalents' are products included in the FAO database on agricultural production that can be directly compared with the products that are subsidized by OECD countries, whereas 'substitutes' are products included in FAO database on agricultural production that have similar properties to those products that are supported by OECD countries. While the category of 'equivalents' includes only goods in their unprocessed form, the category of 'substitutes' includes goods in both their unprocessed and processed forms. For a detailed description of the methodology, see Herrmann (2003a).

[c] Amongst the OECD countries only Mexico provides support for coffee; support is provided in form of consumer support.

current specialization of producers, but they also depend on the future potential specialization of producers. In the short run, when economies display relatively little flexibility, producers of food will find it difficult to compete against imports of foods that receive subsidies abroad. But in the long run, when economies display greater flexibility, producers of food may decide to increase production of goods that do not receive subsidies abroad; they may decide to switch to the production of other agricultural goods or they may even decide to switch to the production of non-agricultural goods. Thus while resources may be unemployed in the short run, they are likely to be re-employed in the long run, although in other types of economic activities.

Assuming that producers can potentially produce any product, and that economies tend to full employment, it would be rational if countries stopped the production of goods that they may import and consume at subsidized prices, and if they specialized instead in the production of goods that they can sell at normal prices. Under these circumstances, but only under these circumstances, imports of subsidized goods essentially amounts to a transfer of income from the country that subsidizes the product to the country that imports the subsidized product. While the transfer of income is a relatively static effect, imports of subsidized food may also have more dynamic effects. Imports of subsidized food, which ensure low levels of consumer prices, can also help to discourage an increase of wage rates and thus support the international competitiveness of an economy. Furthermore, imports of subsidized food, which lead to a contraction of the agricultural sector, may allow for scarce resources to be employed in non-agricultural sectors and thus support a more rapid structural transformation of an economy. Arguably subsidized food imports by developing countries can therefore be a good thing for developing countries.

In short, to evaluate the effects of agricultural support measures of advanced countries on agricultural development in developing countries is a formidable challenge. A comprehensive evaluation of the effects would add up the benefits and costs that developing countries incurred over the past years because of the provision of agricultural support. By contrast, current evaluations of these effects focus on the benefits and cost that developing countries are expected to incur in the coming years in case of an elimination of agricultural support measures. It is important to emphasize that past benefits and costs are very different from future potential benefits and costs. It would therefore be misguided to use the latter as a proxy for the former. In other words, even if the benefits of eliminating agricultural support today may appear very small, it would be a hasty to conclude that the costs of maintaining agricultural support over the past years were very small as well.

Most current valuations of the effects of agricultural policy reform are based on simulations with general equilibrium models. Many simulation exercises derive at similar results. The similarities between estimated effects are attributable to the fact that virtually all simulations use the same general equilibrium model, albeit different versions (UNCTAD 2003b); differences between estimated effects are attributable to the fact that the simulations make varying assumptions about elasticities (Anderson *et al.* 2000; Diao *et al.* 2001; World Bank 2003b). Different studies assume different supply responses to multilateral trade liberalization and different poverty reduction responses to economic growth.

The results of the simulations are also attributable to the current pattern of protection. On average agricultural markets are more protected than industrial markets, and within agricultural markets tariffs remain more important than subsidies (Hoekman *et al.* 2002; Tokarick 2003). This pattern of protection suggests that the liberalization of agricultural markets tends to bring about higher benefits than the liberalization of industrial markets, and that the elimination of tariffs tends to bring about higher benefits than the elimination of subsidies. Yet, several advanced countries have increased subsidies to agricultural producers as they have reduced tariff barriers on agricultural goods. It would therefore be misguided to focus agricultural policy reform on border measures and to disregard the negative effects of direct payments.

The simulation exercises show that gains from trade liberalization are not evenly distributed among countries. Countries that currently do not have an advantage in the production of agricultural goods and are currently dependent on the import of food will suffer, whereas countries that have an advantage in the production of agricultural goods and are currently exporters of agricultural goods will benefit. There is broad consensus that the largest and most advanced agricultural producers among the developing countries, namely the Cairns Group, would benefit from the elimination of agricultural support, but there is no agreement whether the smaller and less-developed agricultural producers, namely the LDCs, would benefit from the elimination of agricultural support.[10]

The International Food Policy Research Institute (IFPRI 2003) estimates that annual agricultural and agro-industry income of developing countries is US$24 billion lower because of agricultural support in industrialized countries. If industrialized countries were to eliminate agricultural support, all developing countries would have income gains. Typically the income gain of advanced developing countries would be higher in value terms, but the income gain of the lesser developed countries would be higher as a share of their total income. According to the IFPRI study the annual income of SSA would be almost US$2 billion higher. Yet, the study maintains that these

[10] Please note that the results of the different studies are not easily comparable, since they are based on distinct assumptions about the nature of agricultural liberalization. Peters (2006) suggests that the LDCs may have welfare losses focuses on an elimination of export subsidies, while Hoekman *et al.* (2002), suggest that the LDCs will have welfare gains focus on the reduction of all protective measures.

benefits are likely to be underestimated. The subsequent section explains why these benefits may be underestimated.

10.3.3 *Effects of Agricultural Support: Development-Oriented Perspective*

General equilibrium models can provide important insights into the ways in which trade liberalization affects economies and people, but they cannot provide accurate estimates of the effects of trade liberalization on economies or people. There are several reasons why poverty reduction in response to exports growth is likely to be overestimated. Furthermore, there are several reasons why export growth in response agricultural reform may be overestimated or underestimated. Agricultural exports may be weaker than expected because countries face considerable non-tariff barriers to trade, which simulation exercises do not take into consideration. But agricultural exports may be stronger than expected because countries may have a latent comparative advantage in agricultural sector, which simulations also fail to consider.[11]

On balance, simulations appear to underestimate the benefits that developing countries may derive from an elimination of agricultural support measures in advanced countries, since the simulations disregard substantial costs that developing countries are forced to bear because of the continuation of agricultural support in advanced countries:

The costs of agricultural support are underestimated because simulations focus only on products that receive agricultural support, and disregard effects in substitute markets. This is because such support measures not only discourage the production of goods that receive support abroad, but also discourage the production of their substitutes (Herrmann 2003a).

The costs of agricultural support are underestimated because simulations focus only on the current pattern of agricultural production and trade (which is itself the result of distorting agricultural policies) rather than past or potential patterns (which would be a better reflection of the country's underlying comparative advantage). While past performance is not a reliable indicator of future potential, it is nonetheless important to recall that the group of LDC was a net food exporter until 1988.[12]

[11] While agricultural trade liberalization decreases tariffs on agricultural goods, it does not reduce non-tariff barriers affecting agricultural goods. Yet, non-tariff barriers to trade—overly complex rules of origin or overly stringent SPS and technical product standards—can result in actual supply responses well below projected supply responses. Indeed non-tariff barriers to trade are a particularly great impediment to trade for many of the poorest countries. In 1999–2001 environment-related trade barriers affected 42 per cent of the LDC exports. For comparison, in the same period tariff barriers affected only 24 per cent of LDC exports. Other developing countries have the inverse problem. In the same period about 38 per cent of their exports were negatively affected by tariff barriers but only 20 per cent of their exports were negatively affected by environment-related barriers to trade (Fontagné *et al.* 2001; Herrmann 2003b).

[12] Calculations based on UN Comtrade data.

According to Cline (2004) many LDCs still have a latent comparative advantage in production of food even though many of them are currently net importers of food.

The costs of agricultural support are underestimated because simulations disregard the importance of agricultural development for poverty reduction. In developing countries, but especially least developed countries, the development of the agricultural sector is an important mean to reduce poverty, as the majority of the poor live in rural areas and as their livelihoods directly or indirectly depend on agricultural production. In the LDCs in 2000–3 the agricultural sector accounted still for 33 per cent of GDP (compared with 11 per cent in other developing countries and only two per cent in developed countries), and the agricultural sector provided livelihoods for 70 per cent of the labour force (compared with 52 per cent in other developing countries and only three per cent in developed countries). The agricultural sector in least developed countries thus continues to be very important for the economy and the people; considerable more important than in other developing countries or the developed countries which provide the lion's share of agricultural support. Premature de-agrarianization in the least developed countries could therefore dramatically increase poverty and food insecurity.

The costs of agricultural support are underestimated because simulations disregard the importance of agricultural development for the development of non-agricultural sectors. Dual economy theories highlight many vital linkages between the development of the agricultural sector, on the one side, and the development of non-agricultural sectors on the other (Lewis 1954, 1968; Ranis and Fei 1961; Jorgenson 1961). Higher agricultural output, for example, will allow countries to save foreign exchange by reducing food imports but it may even enable countries to increase foreign exchange by rising food exports. Foreign exchange is essential for the poorest countries as it enables them to import capital goods which they could not otherwise afford and make investments which they could not otherwise conceive as possible.

The costs of agricultural support are underestimated because simulations disregard perverse incentives for producers and negative effects for economic upgrading. Agricultural support measures put downward pressure on important wage goods (namely food), and subsequently place downward pressure on wage rates (and payroll fringe costs). While low wags in developing countries can help to increase the competitiveness of these countries in labour-intensive and low-tech sectors, it can discourage a specialization of these countries in more capital-intensive and high-tech sectors. The specialization in labour-intensive rather than capital-intensive, in low-tech rather than high-tech products has far-reaching implications. It influences current production structures, but it also influences future development prospects. This is because this pattern of specialization constrains the propensity of economies to increase productivity levels and ultimately constrains their ability to enlarge production possibilities. The effects of agricultural support measures in advanced countries are thus similar to the effects of an unlimited supply of unskilled labour in developing countries. While the development literature has paid some attention to the ways in which an unlimited supply of unskilled labour in developing countries can discourage favourable structural change (Lewis 1954; Sachs 2000), recent studies have not paid attention to the ways in which agricultural support measures of advanced countries can discourage economic upgrading in developing countries.

TRANSMISSION MECHANISMS AND EFFECTS

Figure 10.2 presents a stylized picture of the ways in which agricultural support by advanced countries affects agricultural production in developing countries. In correspondence with actual patterns of agricultural production the figure assumes that developing countries produce tropical agricultural goods, which are not produced by advanced countries, and that they produce temperate agricultural goods, which are also produced by advanced countries. The temperate agricultural goods may therefore be referred to as shared agricultural good. For simplicity, and because it would not change the basic message, the flow diagram does not include additional products. The flow diagram examines possible responses of advanced developing countries, on the one side, and the least developed countries, on the other, to agricultural support measures of advanced countries.

Agricultural support measures of advanced countries lead to lower prices of agricultural goods at both the international level and farm gates. The lower prices of the shared agricultural good leave developing countries with two principal alternatives: they may decide to continue the production of the shared agricultural good, in which case they need to decrease the price of their produce, or they can decide to stop the production of the shared agricultural good, in which case they need to diversify into other goods.

If the developing countries continue with the production of the shared agricultural good, they need to lower the relative prices of these goods. This can be achieved through an increased level of productivity and/or a decreased level of production costs.[13] While any country can hardly increase productivity levels in the short run, more advanced countries may be able

[13] Assuming a Ricardian-type formula, where the comparative advantage of countries, expressed by the prices of its products (P), is determined by the relationship between wages (w) and labour productivity (Y) (i.e. $P = w/Y$). In a model with multiple factors of production wage costs would be replaced by aggregate production costs.

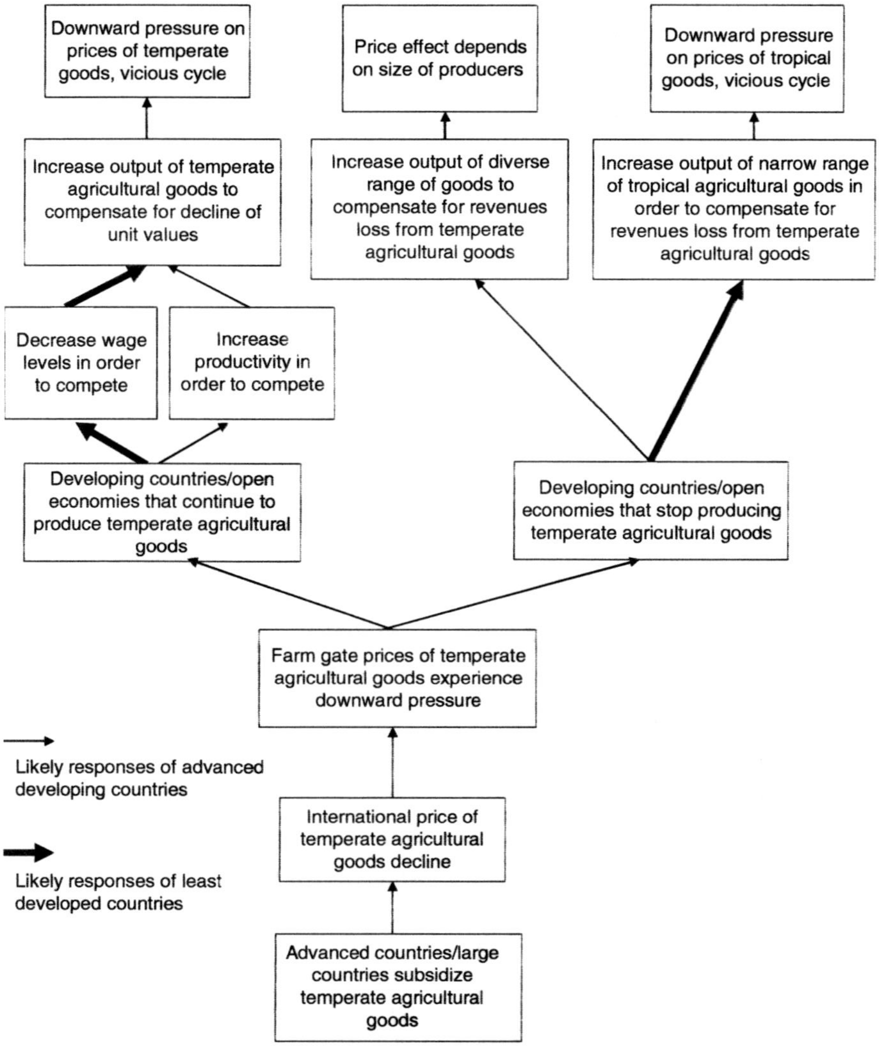

Figure 10.2. Links between agricultural support measures of advanced countries and production decisions in developing countries

Source: Author.

to increase productivity levels in the medium to long run. This is also true for the more advanced countries *among* the developing countries. Thus while advanced developing countries may have the possibility to increase productivity levels and pursue the 'high road' to competitiveness, least developed countries are most likely forced to cut costs and take the 'low road' to competitiveness. Given that labour is the most intensively used factor of production in the majority of lesser developed countries, this means downward pressure on wage rates and/or payroll fringe costs. The question is how realistic this would be in countries where the wages are already at subsistence levels.

Whether developing countries achieve their competitiveness from higher productivity or lower wage levels, the unit value of agricultural products will fall and, all else equal, the return to agricultural producers will fall as well. In order to make up for a lower unit value of goods, producers are likely to increase the sales volume of the goods. While this is a perfectly rational reaction at the level of the individual, it can have undesired effects at the level of the community. This is because a simultaneous increase of agricultural production is likely to lead to adding-up problems in agricultural markets (fallacy of composition) which puts further downward pressure on agricultural prices (second-round effects on prices).

But will the developing countries fare better if they decide to stop rather than continue the production of temperate agricultural goods? The answer to this question depends on a country's productive capacities which determine its production possibilities. Relatively advanced developing countries which have relatively strong productive capacities and extended production possibilities may be able to diversify in a broad range of other products. Indeed countries that have this option should probably make use of it. This way they can enjoy the benefit of importing goods at prices below normal price levels, and they can increase their aggregate output by focusing on products for which they can get normal returns.

The situation is different for the LDCs as they typically have very weak productive capacities. The weak productive capacities prevent them from diversifying into new types of agricultural and non-agricultural products. As a consequence they are encouraged to specialize in a narrow range of products in which they are almost exclusive producers. Goods which are produced almost exclusively by the poorest countries, and are therefore rarely supported by advanced countries, are tropical goods. A notable exception is cotton. But while an increasing specialization in tropical goods may seem to make economic sense, it is associated with considerable economic difficulties. Many of the tropical produce are characterized by unstable prices, and many economies that have a strong specialization in these produce are therefore prone to suffer from unstable export revenues and economic shocks. These problems are exaggerated by the fact that an increased production of tropical goods, like an increased production of any common good, is likely to lead to a further deterioration of prices. Confronted by falling revenues producers of tropical agricultural goods may decide to further increase the production of tropical agricultural goods and subsequently contribute to a second-round of price deteriorations.

The highlighted transmission mechanisms and transmission effects are supported by evidence from case studies. Case study evidence shows that subsidized food exports of advanced countries have led to surges of food imports by many poor countries (FAO 2003). Furthermore, case study evidence shows that subsidized food exports of advanced countries caused the demise of food industries in poor countries (UNCTAD 2002: 108). While this is not the only reasons why LDCs have become net food importers, it is certainly a factor that can help explain why LDCs have become less successful food exporters.

In sum, agricultural support measures of advanced countries can alter the specialization of developing countries and subsequently agricultural support measures of advanced countries may have considerable effects on the trade structure of developing countries. Effects on export specialization and export revenues as well as effects on import structures are highlighted in the following sub-sections.

EFFECTS ON EXPORT REVENUES

Agricultural support measures are neither the only reason for declining prices of agricultural goods in world markets, nor are they the only reasons for a narrow specialization of developing countries in a few primary commodities. But agricultural support measures of advanced countries can contribute to both of these developments. Several studies during recent years have focused on how support to agricultural producers has affected world market prices of agricultural goods (e.g. Ray *et al.* 2003; Institute for Agriculture and Trade Policy 2003).

The combination of declining prices of commodities, on the one hand, and a narrow specialization in commodities, on the other, implies significant costs. Table 10.3 shows that changes of commodity prices over the period 1980–2001 had serious effects on export revenues of LDCs. The decline of many commodity prices has led to large forgone export revenues of developing countries.[14] In 2001, forgone export revenues of LDCs due to falling prices of food amounted to about US$2.0 billion, and forgone export revenues of LDCs due to falling prices of agricultural raw materials amounted to about US$0.5 billion. The lion's share of the latter is attributable to falling prices of cotton. If the USA had not provided cotton subsidies, the cotton price in 2001 could have been considerably higher. Some studies (Badiane *et al.* 2002) suggest that the cotton price on world markets could have been 12 cents higher,

[14] It is important to emphasize that this is an analysis of long-term commodity price trends, which does not take into account recent commodity price changes. The rapid expansion of manufacturing production in China (and a few other emerging markets) has lead to a rapid increase of demand for and prices of raw materials (especially oil, ores, metals, and minerals). The rising prices of these raw materials benefit a number of resource-rich countries; including some of the poorest countries (see also UNCTAD 2003a, 2005; Mayer and Fajarnes 2005).

Table 10.3. Estimated effect of international commodity price changes since 1980 on the export revenues of the LDCs, 2001

	International commodity prices, 1980–2001				LDCs export values, 2001		
	Product code	Index, 1980 = 100		Change (%)	US$ million		
	(SITC 3 Rev. 2)	1991	2001	1980–2001	Actual	Potential	Loss/gain
All foods	0,1,22,4	59	51	−49	4166	6191	−2025
Beverages							
Cocoa & products	072–073	47	45	−55	28	43	−15
Coffee & substitutes	071	44	30	−70	444	755	−312
Tea & maté	074	92	120	20	142	114	28
Foods							
Bananas & other fruits	057	151	156	56	186	82	104
Beef & other meats	011–012,014	96	77	−23	37	46	−9
Fish	034–037	95	96	−4	1562	1617	−55
Maize	044	86	79	−21	32	39	−7
Pepper & other vegetables	054	69	119	19	239	192	47
Rice	042	72	40	−60	37	59	−22
Sugar & products	061–062	31	30	−70	229	388	−160
Wheat	041,046	59	64	−36	23	32	−8
Vegetable oil seeds & oils							
Oilseeds, incl. soybeans	222–223	77	66	−34	236	315	−80
Oils, incl. linseed oil	423–424	68	57	−43	96	138	−42
Agricultural raw materials	21,23–26,29	97	76	−24	2177	2702	−525
Textiles							
Cotton, raw	263	85	54	−46	831	1217	−386
Cotton, manufactured	652	85	54	−46	97	142	−45
Jute	264	110	105	5	59	56	3
Sisal & other textiles	651,659	88	99	−1	301	305	−4
Wool	268	118	75	−25	3	3	−1
Wood							
Wood, rough	245–248	123	128	28	863	620	243
Plywood & other manufactured woods	634–635	136	150	50	75	38	37
Others							
Cattle hides & other hides, manufactured	211	111	127	27	378	276	102
Cattle hides & other hides, raw	611–612	111	127	27	126	92	34
Rubber, raw	232–233	75	42	−58	36	57	−21
Rubber, manufactured	621,625,628	75	42	−58	10	16	−6
Tobacco	121–122	154	131	31	377	259	118
Memo:							
Minerals, ores & metals	27–28,68	95	78	−22	2085	2546	−461

Source: Calculations based on UN Comtrade data (exports), and UNCTAD Commodity Price Bulletin (prices).

which would have increased export revenues of Central and Western African countries by US$250 million; other studies (Oxfam 2003) estimate that the cotton price on world markets could have been 11 cents higher, which would have increased the export revenues of all African producers by US$302 million.

EFFECTS ON IMPORT STRUCTURES

Agricultural support measures of advanced countries can also negatively affect structural change in developing countries. Developing countries witness a premature contraction of domestic agricultural production and subsequently they grow dependent on agricultural imports. This means that they are encouraged to spend scarce foreign exchange on the import of basic consumer goods, which they should be able to produce at home; and that they are increasingly unable to spend foreign exchange on the import of capital good, which they are not able to produce domestically. The poorest developing countries, which have few economic activities outside the agricultural sector, are particularly affected by these developments.

Figure 10.3 shows that in comparison with other, more advanced developing countries, the LDCs spend now a large proportion of their foreign exchange on the import of basic consumption goods (i.e. goods which ensure human survival) rather than the import of capital goods (i.e. goods which enable investment).

For 'scientifically lagging countries' such as the LDCs, the import of capital goods is the principal means of technology acquisition. The low imports of capital goods is therefore a major impediment to technological upgrading.

In conclusion, the trade-centric perspective, on the one side, and the development-oriented perspective, on the other, are characterized by important differences. These differences are attributable to the fact that the trade-centric perspective tends to emphasize short-run effects on consumers, whereas the development-oriented perspective emphasizes long-run effects on production. The differences between the perspectives are particularly apparent in the case of the least developed countries. The trade-centric perspective suggests that the poor in LDCs are likely to suffer from the elimination of agricultural support measures. This is because it will lead to higher prices of imported foods, which effectively decrease the real income of the poor. By contrast, the development-oriented perspective suggests that the poor in LDCs are likely to benefit from the elimination of agricultural support. This is because it will encourage an increased production of agricultural goods, which provides employment and income to the poor. Overall it seems that the net effects on the poor are likely to be negative. This is because the majority of the poor directly or indirectly derive their livelihood from agricultural production. A contraction of agricultural production is therefore likely to affect their income negatively (cash or in kind). At the same time the majority of the poor have a very low consumption of imported goods. An expansion of subsidized food imports is therefore unlikely to raise their real income significantly (see also Paarlberg 1999).

In sum, development-oriented perspective is not ignorant of short-term adjustment costs that are associated with the elimination of agricultural

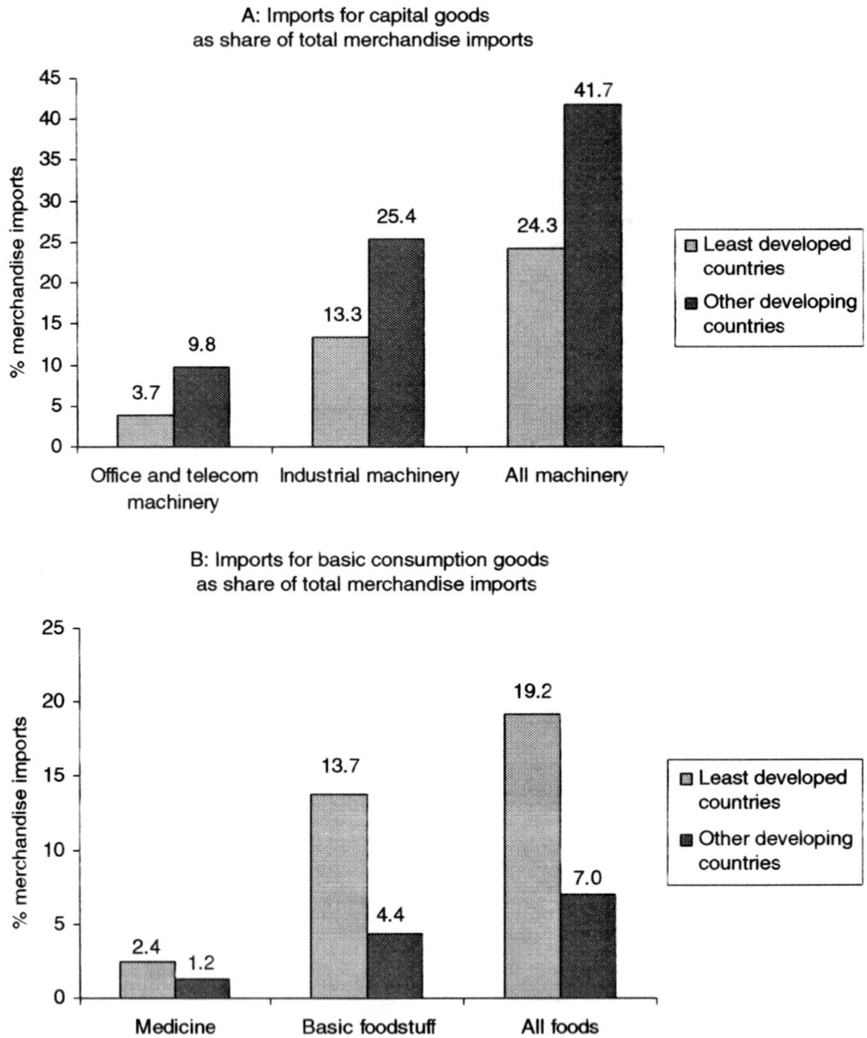

Figure 10.3. The structure of merchandise imports of the LDCs and other developing countries, 1999–2001

Note: [a] Product groups are defined in accordance with SITC Rev. 2: Office and telecommunications machinery: code 75 and 76; industrial machinery: code 71 + 72 + 73 + 74 + 77 − 775; all machinery: 7 − 775 − 781 + 87 + 881 + 884 (includes all previous). Medicine: code 541; basic foodstuffs: code: 00 + 01 + 02 + 04 + 054 + 056 + 09 + 22 + 4; all foods: 0 + 1 + 22 + 4 (includes all previous).
[b] Basic foodstuffs are defined in accordance with FAO.

Source: Calculations based on UN Comtrade database.

support, but the development-oriented perspective emphasizes the grave long-term costs that result from the continuation of agricultural support. The development-oriented perspective also emphasizes that for the developing countries long-term costs weigh heavier than short-term adjustments costs. By contrast, the trade-centric perspective typically disregards the long-term costs discussed in this section.

10.4 Policy Implications

At its core food insecurity has to do with economic underdevelopment of countries. In other words, countries are food insecure either because they do not have the capacity to produce sufficient food at home or because they do not have the foreign exchange to import necessary food from abroad.

While this chapter acknowledges that trigger causes can lead to food insecurity, the study focuses on systemic causes of food insecurity, which are often neglected in the discussion of food insecurity but are no less important for a comprehensive understanding of food crises. While there are many potential systemic causes for food insecurity the chapter focuses on only one systemic cause of food insecurity, namely agricultural support measures of advanced countries. Agricultural support measures of advanced countries are a systemic cause for food insecurity in developing countries. They negatively effect the development of the agricultural sector and subsequently they also negatively impact on the development of non-agricultural sectors. Agricultural support measures of advanced countries therefore contribute to economic underdevelopment of developing countries, which is at the core of food insecurity.

One key conclusion is that food security in developing countries is best achieved through the economic development of developing countries; another key conclusion is that economic development of developing countries is best supported through agricultural policy reform in advanced countries. These conclusions have various policy implications:

ECONOMIC GROWTH IN DEVELOPING COUNTRIES

'Solving hunger isn't about providing food, except for acute cases. It's about solving poverty' (Kripke quoted in Reuters 2005). While relatively advanced developing countries may combat poverty through a redistribution of existing resources, least developed countries can combat poverty only through high and sustained rates of economic growth. While economic development is about more than economic growth, economic development must be accompanied by economic growth. In poor developing countries high and sustained rates of economic growth are a precondition for the creation of productive employment opportunities, an increase of household incomes and ultimately poverty reduction and food security.

For poor countries to promote economic growth, they have to have strong productive capacities. Given the importance of productive capacities the development of productive capacities should be a core objective of poor developing countries and a core objective of their development partners. As such the development of productive capacities should assume a central position in national development, poverty reduction, and food security strategies.

AGRICULTURAL LIBERALIZATION IN ADVANCED COUNTRIES

The WTO Agreement on Agriculture has the ambitious aim of applying the same rules to agricultural trade as for non-agricultural trade, and the Doha Agenda used to have the ambitious aim to encourage significant liberalization of the agricultural sector. These objectives are well taken, but actual reforms fall far short of required reforms. In principle advanced countries should change their agricultural policies in order to eliminate dangerous market distortions. But in practice advanced countries have very little incentives to undertake such adjustments. This is because advanced countries do get benefits from providing agricultural support and they do not bear the full costs of these policies. The costs that they bear are mainly associated with higher food prices for consumers in the advanced countries; the costs that they effectively externalize are associated with a lower production in the developing countries. If advanced countries were to internalize the full cost of their policies, they may be more likely to consider a change of these policies. A way to encourage such an internalization of costs by advanced countries may be the introduction of targeted trade barriers in other countries, which effectively limit trade in subsidized goods. Safeguard measures of developing countries appear justifiable and in line with multilateral trade rules, given that agricultural support measures of advanced countries threaten agricultural industries in developing countries.

But safeguards against subsidized agricultural imports should only be a mean of last resort. A credible phasing-out of agricultural support should receive priority in multilateral trade negotiations. Such an approach would be based on an economic rather than a political rational. In accordance all support measures that alter the relative price of the factors of production, or directly alter the prices of final products, should be considered trade-distorting support measures. This is because they change the comparative advantage of a country and subsequently they redirect trade flows between countries.

This chapter has discussed simulation exercises which suggest the benefits of LDCs from agricultural policy reform are small, but it has also highlighted reasons why these exercises may underestimate the benefits of LDCs from such reforms. While there are important reasons why LDCs may not be able to significantly increase agricultural production and exports in the short-run there is no reason to believe that many LDCs cannot significantly increase their agricultural production and exports in the long run. Many LDCs have favourable resource endowments and many of the LDCs may be able to strengthen their productive and supply capacities. Overall it appears that even least developed countries can derive considerable gains from multilateral trade liberalization if focuses on the elimination of agricultural support, and if the elimination of agricultural support is accompanied by the following measures:

Elimination of all unnecessary non-tariff barriers to trade (overly complex rules of origin, overly SPS and technical product standards, etc.);

Aid to help LDCs effectively comply with the remaining trade barriers (reasonable product standards, various trade rules, etc.); and

Aid to help LDCs effectively strengthen productive capacities (infrastructure, finance, technology, skills, etc.).

'Aid for trade' can potentially help to develop productive capacities, but currently aid for trade falls short of this objective. At present there is only little aid for trade on offer, and the little aid for trade that is on offer focuses on compliance of developing countries with multilateral trade rules, and the compliance of their producers and exporters with product standards and customs procedures. While this is important, it is not enough. Countries will only be able to increase the supply of their exports, if they are able to produce internationally competitive goods.

DEVELOPMENT AID AND EMERGENCY FOOD AID

The focus on the development of productive capacities, and the complementary focus on the development of trade capacities, requires a substantial increase of aid to the productive sectors as well as an increase of aid for trade. While the level of aid to least developed countries has significantly increased during recent years, the share of aid for productive sectors development has significantly declined during the past decades. Donors must reverse this trend.

But it is not sufficient to increase the level of aid for productive sectors development, it is also necessary to increase the coherence between aid and trade policies. At present good aid policies are often undermined by bad trade policies. Efforts, for example, to develop the agricultural sector in developing countries are undermined by agricultural support measures of the developed countries.

It is important that countries do not refrain from phasing out agricultural support because of possible adjustment costs. It is better to address adjustment costs, such as an increase of the food import bill, than to maintain market-distorting policies. Aid to help countries cope with adjustment costs should be provided to countries that are most in need (i.e. the low-income countries) and it should be provided in a non-debt creating form (i.e. grants). Developing countries have made only little use of existing instruments to finance food imports during balance-of-payments crisis. This is not necessarily an indication that developing countries are not willing to use such funds, it is rather an indication that the funds are not provided at attractive conditions (i.e. loans rather than grants and in conjunction with conditionalities).

It is important that aid, including emergency food aid, is provided in ways that prevent the accumulation of unsustainable external debt and subsequently increase the likelihood of future debt crises. While aid which is used to finance commercial activities that are expected to generate a future stream of income may be provided in form of loans, aid that is used for activities that cannot be expected to generate a future stream of income should always be provided in form of grants. Aid which is used to finance consumption goods (e.g. food imports) or aid that is used to finance public goods (e.g. health, education, research, certain types of infrastructure) should therefore be provided in form of grants.

Short-term measures to deal with food crises in developing economies should not impinge on long-term strategies for developing productive sectors in these countries. This means, for example, that food aid should be provided in a manner that minimizes distortions of agricultural markets.

Similar to agricultural support measures of advanced countries, food aid of advanced countries, may negatively affect the long-term development of developing countries. On the one side, recipient countries, which have an actual or potential comparative advantage in agricultural production, may be discouraged from developing their agricultural production as long as subsidized food imports or food aid offer access to inexpensive foods. On the other side, donor countries, which provide support to their agricultural production, may wish to continue this support as long as increased food exports and food aid provide them with the opportunity to dispose of surplus food (von Braun 2003). Marianne Fischer Boel, EU Farm Commissioner, said that 'genuine food aid is both desirable and legal [...] [but] we have focused on the problem of using food aid as a way to get rid of surplus production' (quoted in Reuters 2005).

In order to improve the delivery of food aid in a way that it does not discourage the development of agricultural sectors, it is important that donors have a better understanding of why developing countries require food aid and why they fail to produce sufficient food domestically. So far much emphasis has been given to the food trade balance of countries but the food trade balance provides no information about the probability of food crises or about the potential of food production. It therefore appears desirable to evaluate not only whether countries are net importers of food, but to also determine whether countries can import or produce food on a sustainable basis.

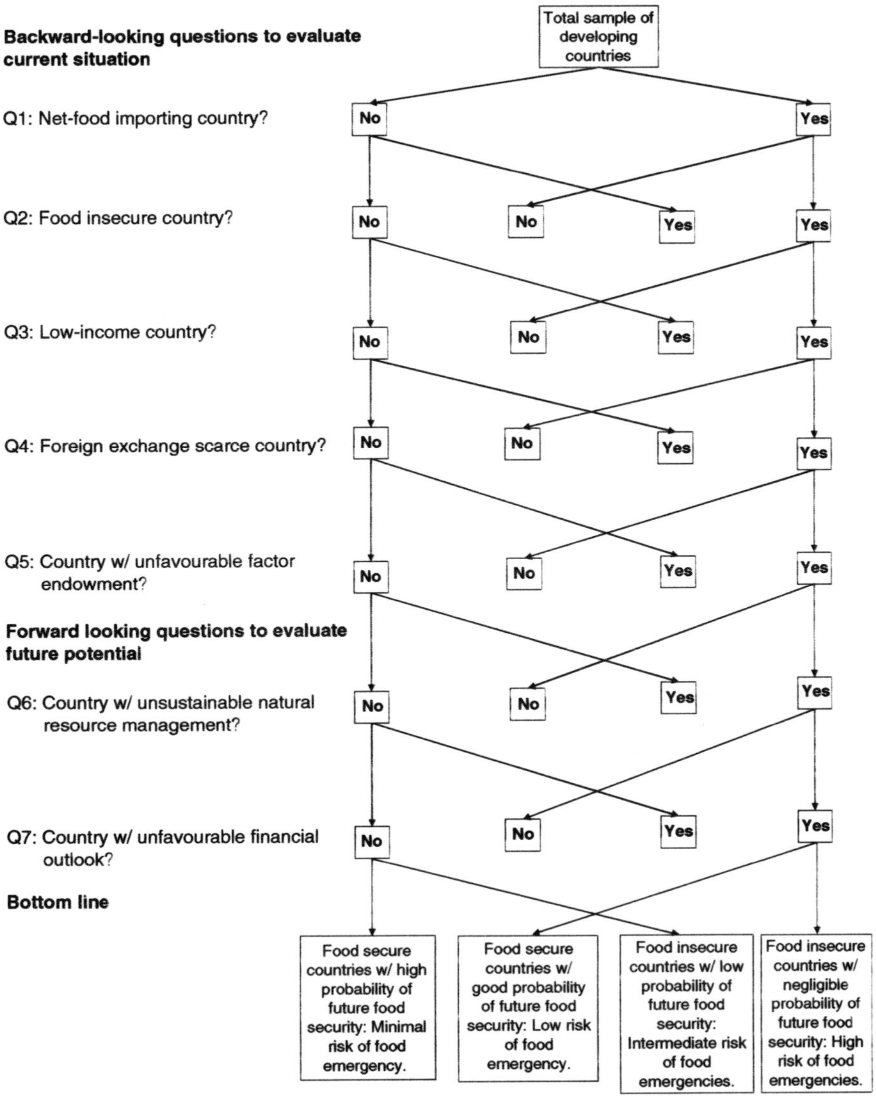

Figure 10.4. Scheme for identification of countries that face risk of food insecurity and countries that require particular assistance with agricultural development

Note: A final country classification depends on specific thresholds. Low incomes may be defined in accordance with the World Bank's definition of low-income countries; food insecurity may be defined in accordance with FAO's definition of food insecurity. Countries may be said to have a foreign exchange scarcity if their reserves cover less than 6 months worth of imports and debt service obligations, and they may be said to have an unfavorable factor endowment if they have limited fertile land, which constrains an expansion of agricultural production, or limited agricultural machinery, fertilizer, irrigation, and skilled workers, which constrains an intensification of production. In this context, see also FAO (2002).

Source: Author.

A series of backward and forward looking questions may help to better evaluate current and future prospects of food security. Based on such questions, Figure 10.4 offers a possible classification scheme.

It is important to emphasize that these questions are merely indicative and that the list is not exhaustive. On the basis of such questions it may be possible to gain a more refined understanding of which countries are prone to suffer from food crises and which are less likely to be affected. In addition, these questions indicate whether countries have a capacity to produce food domestically or whether they do not. Such information is useful for the design of food aid policies, but it can also provide clues about the potential of agricultural development.

References

Anderson, K., J. François, T. Hertel, B. Hoekman, and W. Martin (2000). 'Potential Gains from Trade Reform in the New Millennium'. Paper presented at the Third Annual Conference on Global Economic Analysis, 20–2 June. Monash University.

Badiane, O., D. Ghura, L. Goreux, and P. R. Masson (2002). 'Cotton Sector Strategy in West and Central Africa'. IMF Working Paper 02/173. Washington, DC: IMF.

Benson, T. (2004). 'Africa's Food and Nutrition Security Situation: Where Are We and How Did We Get Here?'. IFPRI 20/20 Discussion Paper 37. Washington, DC: IFPRI.

Cline, W. (2004). 'Trade Policy and Global Poverty'. Washington, DC: Center for Global Development and the Institute for International Economics.

David, M. (2004). 'Civil Conflict in LDCs: Background Paper for the Least Developed Countries Report, 2004'. Geneva: UNCTAD.

Diao, X., T. Roe, and A. Somwaru (2001). '"A Global Analysis of Agricultural Trade Reform in WTO Member Countries", in Agricultural Policy Reform: The Road Ahead'. *American Economic Review*, 802: 25–42.

FAO (2002). 'The LIFDC Classification: an Exploration'. Report of the 28th Session of Committee on World Food Security, 6–8 June. Rome: FAO.

—— (2003). 'Some Trade Policy Issues Relating to Trends in Agricultural Imports in the Context of Food Security'. Report of the 64th Session of the Committee on Commodity Problems, 18–21 March. Rome: FAO.

—— (2004). *The State of Food Insecurity in the World 2004: Monitoring Progress towards the World Food Summit and Millennium Development Goals*. Rome. FAO.

Fontagné, L., F. von Kirchbach, and M. Mimouni (2001). 'A First Assessment of Environment-Related Trade Barriers'. CEPII Document de Travail 01–10. Paris: Centre d'Etudes Prospectives et d'Informations Internationales.

Herrmann, M. (2003a). 'Agricultural Support Measures of Advanced Countries and Agricultural Production in LDCs: Conceptualization of Transmission Effects'. Background Paper for the Least Developed Countries Report, 2004. Geneva: UNCTAD.

—— (2003b). 'Trading under Adversity: The Marginalization of LDCs in World Trade'. Background Paper for the Least Developed Countries Report, 2004. Geneva: UNCTAD.

Hoekman, B., F. Ng, and M. Olareaga (2002). 'Reducing Agricultural Tariffs versus Domestic Support: What's More Important for Developing Countries?'. Policy Research Working Paper 2918. Washington, DC: World Bank.

Institute for Agriculture and Trade Policy (2003). *United States Dumping on World Agricultural Markets*. Minneapolis: Institute for Agriculture and Trade Policy.

IFPRI (2003). *How Much Does It Hurt? The Impact of Agricultural Trade Policies on Developing Countries*. Washington, DC: IFPRI.

Jorgenson, D. (1961). 'The Development of a Dual Economy'. *Economic Journal*, 71: 309–34.

Lewis, W. A. (1954). 'Economic Development with Unlimited Supplies of Labour'. *Manchester School*, 22 (2): 139–91.

____ (1968). 'Reflection on Unlimited Labour'. Princeton Special Paper. Princeton.

Mayer, J., and P. Fajarnes, P. (2005). 'Tripling Africa's Primary Exports: What, How, Where?'. Discussion Paper 180. Geneva: UNCTAD.

Messer, E., and M. J. Cohen (2004). 'Breaking the Links between Conflict and Hunger in Africa'. 2020 Africa Conference Brief 10. Washington, DC: IFPRI.

Nussbaum, M. (1993). 'Non-relative Virtues: An Aristotelian Approach', in M. Nussbaum and A. Sen (eds), *The Quality of Life*. Oxford: Clarendon Press for UNU-WIDER.

Oxfam (2003). 'Cultivating Poverty: The Impact of US Cotton Subsidies on Africa'. Briefing Paper 30. Oxford: Oxfam.

Paarlberg, R. (1999). 'The Weak Link between World Food Markets and World Food Security: Policy Reform, Market Stability and Food Security'. Proceedings of a Conference of the International Agricultural Trade Research Consortium. Minneapolis: University of Minnesota.

Peters, R. (2006). 'Roadblock to Reform: The Persistence of Agricultural Export Subsidies'. Policy Issues in International Trade and Commodities, Study Series 32. Geneva: UNCTAD.

Pingali, P., and R. Stringer (2003). 'Food Security and Agriculture in the Low Income Food Deficit Countries: 10 Years after the Uruguay Round'. FAO/ESA Working Paper 03–18. Rome: FAO.

Ranis, G., and J. C. Fei (1961). 'A Theory of Economic Development'. *American Economic Review*, 51 (4): 533–58.

Ray, D. E., D. de la Torre Ugarte, and K. Tiller (2003). 'Rethinking US Agricultural Policy: Changing Course to Secure Farmer Livelihoods Worldwide'. Knoxville: Agricultural Policy Analysis Center, University of Tennessee.

Reuters (2005). 'Rich Nations Square up for WTO Food Aid Fight'. 23 September.

Sachs, J. D. (2000). 'Tropical Underdevelopment'. Plenary lecture at the Economic History Association meeting, September. Los Angeles.

Sen, A. (1999). *Development as Freedom*. New York: Kopf, and Oxford: Oxford University Press.

Tokarick, S. (2003). 'Measuring the Impact of Distortions in Agricultural Trade in Partial and General Equilibrium'. IMF Working Paper. Washington, DC: IMF.

UN (2005). *The Millennium Development Goals Report 2005*. New York.

UNCTAD (2000). *Least Developed Countries Report, 2000*. New York and Geneva: United Nations.

UNCTAD (2002). *Least Developed Countries Report, 2002*. New York and Geneva: United Nations.

—— (2003a). *Trade and Development Report, 2003*. New York and Geneva: United Nations.

—— (2003b). *Back to Basics: Market Access Issues in the Doha Agenda*. New York and Geneva: United Nations.

—— (2004). *Least Developed Countries Report, 2004*. New York and Geneva: United Nations.

—— (2005). *Trade and Development Report 2005*. New York and Geneva: United Nations.

—— (2006). *Least Developed Countries Report, 2006*. New York and Geneva: United Nations.

von Braun, J. (2003). 'Berlin Statement on Food Aid for Sustainable Food Security'. Tabled at the International Workshop on Policies against Hunger II: Food Aid—Contributions and Risks to Sustainable Food Security, 3–4 September. Berlin.

World Bank (2003a). *World Development Indicators*. CD-Rom. Washington, DC: World Bank.

—— (2003b). *Global Economic Prospects 2004*. Washington, DC: World Bank.

11

An Analysis of the Potential Impact of the Current WTO Agricultural Negotiations on Government Strategies in the SADC Region

James Hodge and Andrew Charman

11.1 Introduction

The Agreement on Agriculture (AoA) emerging from the Uruguay Round (UR) brought agriculture under the World Trade Organization (WTO) disciplines applied to goods and tropical agricultural products. It focused on the tariffication of agricultural protection measures, the limitations of domestic support programmes, and of export subsidies. Its main achievement was not greater levels of liberalization, but rather the establishment of a framework for future agricultural liberalization.

There has been much concern over the possible negative impact of the AoA on agriculture and rural livelihoods in developing countries. The consequence on food security within Sub-Saharan African (SSA) has been of particular concern to African countries due to the seriously underdeveloped state of agriculture on the continent. The African Group joint proposal on the WTO negotiations on agriculture (WTO 2001b: 1, para. 2) notes that the current state of agriculture in SSA 'reinforces and perpetuates the low growth syndrome and pervasive poverty' evident throughout the continent.

Scholars have expressed three concerns with the AoA: Has the Agreement resulted in changes in domestic agriculture policies in developing countries? How much flexibility do developing countries have under the current agreement? And what is the current and potential impact of the agreements on national food security?

There is, at the present juncture, no evidence to show that the AoA has had had a significant impact in either constraining government policy options or curtailing agricultural development programmes for the poor (see Matthews 2000). One reason is that the agreed market access and subsidy targets of the Agreement have limited impact since the special and differential (S&D) exemptions and *de minimis* provisions are adequate. However, it has been argued that the AoA provides a framework for the global agreement of trade rules which could constrain country actions with respect to domestic subsidies, tariffs and export subsidies—the three main issues on the current agenda of negotiations.

This study aims to help identify how the AoA, in terms of the proposed tariff and subsidy reduction modalities, could potentially constrain government action to achieve food security in the Southern African Development Community (SADC). The research examines the current phase of agriculture negotiations. The main focus is on the direct effects of the agreement on food security policy in SADC—hence, the domestic subsidy and market access concerns. It is believed that these effects may pose constraints on the policy options of governments; this question we seek to address in the SADC context.

The chapter does not substantially consider trade-related aspects of intellectual property rights (TRIPS) agreements and the agreement on sanitary and phytosanitary (SPS) measures. Nor does it consider the indirect effect on developing countries resulting from the reduction of export subsidies and preference erosion in developed countries. This topic has been extensively analysed. The study does, however, reflect on the feasibility of the Marrakech Decision in addressing least developed country (LDC) and net food importing developing country (NFIDC) food security concerns.

11.2 The SADC Food Security Context

SADC is a regional trade grouping founded in 1992 and comprises 14 southern African countries, namely Angola, Botswana, DR Congo, Lesotho, Mauritius, Malawi, Mozambique, Namibia, South Africa, Swaziland, Seychelles, Tanzania, Zambia, and Zimbabwe. Seven of these countries (Angola, DR Congo, Lesotho, Malawi, Mozambique, Tanzania, and Zambia) have been afforded LDC status, while Botswana, Mauritius, and Namibia are characterized as NFIDCs.[1]

Agricultural development is important to national economic development and poverty reduction strategies in all SADC countries. The contribution of agriculture to GDP ranges from 5 per cent to 50 per cent; it holds a

[1] See www.fao.org/trade/negoc_aoa_marrakech_enasp#7.

particular significance in the case of Botswana, Mauritius, Malawi, Mozambique, Swaziland, Tanzania, Zambia, and Zimbabwe as an engine for economic development and source of foreign revenue. Across the southern African region, the agricultural sector is the largest employer of seasonal and low skilled labour (Official SADC Trade, Industry, and Investment Review, annual review, 2003–5).

At the time that the SADC group came into being (in the early 1990s), national agricultural policies sought to achieve the twin objectives of ensuring national food self-sufficiency and promoting the production and export of industrial crops.

The national food self-sufficiency objective was, in the case of all members (apart from Mauritius and South Africa), directed towards ensuring the production of sufficient maize to meet national requirements. The main recipients of this policy were smallholder farmers, operating within subsistence-oriented farming systems. These farmers accounted for the bulk of food crop production in all SADC members, bar South Africa where food production was undertaken by commercial farmers. In policy terms, the fulfilment of national maize requirements was seen as synonymous with food security and maize deficiency equated to crisis. Small grains (including rice, millet, and sorghum) and root and tuber crops (such as cassava and sweet potato), though an important part of household nutrition, attracted comparatively little state support in terms of subsidies and measures to secure market access (for a more extensive analysis of national food baskets, see Charman and Hodge 2005).

The objective of supporting export oriented industrial crops, such as tobacco (Malawi and Zimbabwe), cotton (Mozambique, Tanzania, and Zambia), sugar (Malawi, Mauritius, Mozambique, and Zimbabwe), and tea/coffee (Malawi and Tanzania), was aggressively pursued through subsidies, labour market controls, and para-statal marketing bodies. The production was undertaken by commercial growers and smallholders, with both the state and agribusiness providing services and securing market access. Livestock production is an important component of the agricultural economies of all SADC members and a valuable export in the case of Botswana, Zimbabwe (prior to 2002), and South Africa.

The LDC bloc within SADC, along with Zimbabwe (post-2002), is highly vulnerable to food crisis. Widespread famine occurred throughout the region in 1992–4 and 2001–3, while isolated food insecurity crises have been recorded annually in most of the LDC member countries as a result of drought or floods. The high vulnerability of agriculture (and maize production especially) in these countries is attributable to the low level of skills within the smallholder sector, the inadequacy of the technology and financial resources available to farmers, weakly develop infrastructure and linkages to markets, the absence of private sector actors in providing agricultural services to food crop production, political and social insecurity (civil strife and land reform) and the HIV/AIDS pandemic. While maize is the major food staple for rural peoples throughout SADC, South Africa (through its commercial farming sector) currently accounts for 49 per cent of the total production, Mozambique and Tanzania account for 30 per cent, and the DR Congo, Malawi, Zambia, and Zimbabwe combined for 20 per cent (Vink *et al.* 2006).

Over the past decade, SADC governments have reformed their agricultural development strategies. A noticeable policy shift has been the recognition that the goal of national food self-sufficiently, while ideologically desirable given the rural nature of these countries, is simply not attainable (Charman and Hodge 2005). This has resulted in trade reforms and generally added weight to liberalization measures, though in cases such as Zimbabwe, her increasing reliance on grain trade has caused the government to more strictly regulate the sector. The NFIDCs and the LDCs depend significantly on food imports to meet their food requirements, although demand varies on a seasonal basis, due largely to the bearing of climatic factors on maize production. For Botswana, Lesotho, Namibia, and Mauritius, cereal imports (maize, rice, and wheat) account for more than 50 per cent of their total national average requirements. Most SADC members are deficit in wheat and rice and depend on trade to supply these crops, whose demand is rapidly expanding among urban populations. Whereas wheat and rice are imported into the region, much to the regional maize trade involves intra-regional arbitrage, both through formal channels and informally through uncontrolled borders.

SADC members are less trade reliant in non-cereal foods. Most members are self-reliant in starchy roots, fruit, and vegetable crops. The central African members are, however, dependent on imported vegetable oil crops and dairy products. Only Mauritius relies heavily on trade to fulfil its domestic food requirements for animal products; other countries export animal products. National food consumption, in per capita terms, shows a trend of gradual improvement since 1990, mainly due to the improved availability of cereals and increased root and tuber production, though the net gains have been periodically off-set by episodes of drought. The human development status of the region's population is well reflected in the consumption levels of non-cereal and non-starchy foods. An analysis of national Food Balance Sheets from 1991 to 2001, using FAOSTAT data, has identified the under-nourishment of a large proportion of the population in terms of protein and vitamin requirements. The data show a dramatic distinction between the annual per capita intake in the food categories of sugar, meat, animal fats, and milk in the SADC LDC countries by comparison to the corresponding figures for the developing countries (Mauritius, South Africa, and Zimbabwe) (see Charman and Hodge 2005).

11.3 Agricultural Trade Liberalization

Agricultural trade liberalization in SADC predates the WTO. Significant reforms were undertaken in the central African member countries under the respective conditions of structural adjustment programmes. In the cases of Malawi and Zambia, trade liberalization began in the late 1980s when their respective governments first lowered and amalgamated duty rates. The Malawi government, for instance, reduced the maximum MFN (most favoured-nation) tariff from 70 per cent to 45 per cent in 1988; this was further lowered in 1996–7 to 35 per cent, while no tariffs were applied on raw materials in manufacturing to encourage sector growth (FAO 2003c). In the early 1990s, the economic reform process emanating from SAPs in Malawi, Zambia, Tanzania, and Mozambique resulted in the elimination of import restrictions, currency devaluations, and market deregulation, thus ending the role of state monopolies and liberalizing grain trade. Zimbabwe in 1991 introduced a range of market reforms, aimed at deregulating markets, removing price controls, and fostering a growth in export oriented production (FAO 2003b).

The South African Custom Union members (Botswana, Lesotho, Namibia, South Africa, and Swaziland) all embraced economic reforms after the achievement of political stability post 1990s and following specific interventions to deregulation of the South African agricultural sector. The latter included the de-regulation of agricultural marketing, tariff reductions, and the elimination of export subsidy measures (Kirsten 2006).

In 1996 the SADC trade protocol was adopted. This set out an architecture for liberalizing regional trade through the planned (phased) removal of tariffs and non-tariff barriers (NTB). The trade protocol commenced implementation in 2000. The aim is to eliminate tariff and NTB to intra-SADC trade within an eight-year timeframe on a staggered basis. South Africa, as the region's dominant trading nation, has agreed to lower its border barriers to SADC imports immediately, whereas other SADC members will progressively liberalize. Special concessionary rules are contained in the agreement to protect sensitive sectors, such as sugar.

The relevance of the SADC trade protocol on food security needs to be seen in the context of the regional trade patterns. Studies of inter-regional agricultural trade show that South African dominates trade in exports and imports with very little inter-regional trade conducted among other members in all crops bar cereals (see Vink *et al.* 2006). In value terms, however, South Africa currently trades as much with its Southern African Customs Union (SACU) partners ($459.6 million in 2001) as it does with the rest of the SADC region ($496.6 million in 2001) (Charman and Hodge 2005). SADC agricultural trade with SACU is characterized by high value agricultural products, notably meat (Botswana), fruit and vegetables (Mauritius), sugar

(Malawi and Zimbabwe), tobacco (Malawi and Zimbabwe), and fish (Mozambique and Namibia), which are then processed or re-exported from South Africa. The data suggest a robust growth in intra-regional agricultural trade since the mid-1990s. Scholars (see Vink *et al.* 2006) have expressed the concern that the eventual elimination of trade barriers under the protocol will enable South African producers to consolidate their position within the region through their price competitiveness and through their linkages to complex value chains.

SADC members are aligned to regional groupings (COMESA and EAC) which, independently, provide a custom union framework. These agreements shall provide across-the-board duty-free trade on all products which fulfil rules of origin criteria. SADC members are furthermore party to a host of trade agreements (including the Contonou Agreement, EBA, AGOA, and the SA–EU Trade, Development and Cooperation Agreement) that provide preferential access to European and North American markets. Members have also (long standing) bi-lateral trade agreements, such as the Malawi–Zimbabwe and the Malawi–Mozambique agreements, under which many food imports enter at preferential rates below the MFN applied tariffs.

Preferential market access has emerged as the most critical issue in SADC member trade engagements. This is true for both producers of sensitive crops, Malawi, Mauritius, Zambia, and Zimbabwe in the case of sugar, and also in the context of non-compensated losses from tariff revenues that have affected the smaller SACU members. The major challenges to further economic integration among the SADC members relate to the persistence of NTB, high transaction costs due to poor infrastructure, and disharmony in the application of trade rules, notably in terms of S&P agreements.

11.4 The AoA: Impact Assessment

11.4.1 *The Initial Agriculture Agreement*

The purpose of the AoA in the UR was first and foremost to bring agriculture under the disciplines of the WTO. The UR saw considerable pressure to liberalize the agriculture sector. This is apparent from the commitments that countries made under agriculture, especially developing countries:

SUBSIDIES

The initial agreement provided enormous scope for developing countries to provide domestic support for their agricultural sectors, despite registering low levels of actual aggregate measures of support (AMS). Not only was the *de minimis* level set at a high 10 per cent of the value of production, but Article 6.2 provided special and differential (S&D) provisions for investment and input subsidies for resource-poor farmers (a key element of food security at the household level). Developing countries could also take advantage of the Green Box provisions for nontrade-distorting agricultural support. At the time, all SADC countries with the exception of Mozambique were providing trade-distorting domestic support for producers beyond the support for resource-poor farmers only. Of particular importance were credit and input subsidization (e.g. general fertilizer price subsidies and low interest loans), and price support. However, only South Africa was forced by the agreement to reduce support as it had an AMS that fell outside the *de minimis* at the time (its AMS was 5.9 per cent of production).[2] For the other SADC countries, Malawi offered the greatest level of support at 2.9 per cent of production. As a result, many have failed to even notify support that fell within the Green Box as total support (Green Box, S&D, and Blue/Amber Box) fell below the *de minimis*.

MARKET ACCESS

In terms of tariffs, developing countries were allowed a once-off opportunity to bind all tariffs at a high ceiling rate that far exceeded their applied tariffs. SADC members not part of SACU took full advantage of this provision and bound all tariff lines covered by the agreement at very high ceiling rates (with the exception of a few selected tariff lines). Zimbabwe bound at 150 per cent, Malawi and Zambia at 125 per cent, Mauritius at 122 per cent, Mozambique at 100 per cent and Angola and the DR Congo at 55 per cent. These bound rates far exceeded actual tariffs that have a mean between 18 per cent and 28 per cent for non-SACU members of SADC. This implies substantial 'water' in the tariffs, giving countries considerable scope for further reductions in future negotiations before actual tariff rates become affected. It also currently provides countries with scope to increase actual tariffs in response to a perceived threat to their agricultural sector without breaking their WTO commitment.

Furthermore, as LDCs were not required to make any reductions in the UR, the necessity for strategic reductions was not necessary. SACU countries operate with a common external tariff and therefore their applied tariffs are identical. The SACU agreement permits individual countries some limited deviation for the purpose of industry development. SACU therefore bound around the lowest common denominator—South Africa—at far lower rates (a mean bound rate of 34 per cent). Lesotho, however, used its discretion to bind at 200 per cent without any exceptions, even though they still implement the lower applied rates of SACU. Despite the lower binding in the SACU members of SADC, there is still considerable 'water' in their bound rates as

[2] Note that South Africa is classified as a developed economy within the WTO and so faced the lower AMS level of 5 per cent.

their mean tariff in 2003 was only 8.6 per cent (and a median of 0 per cent). Some of these bindings must have impacted on applied tariffs, as 27.4 per cent of SACU tariffs were bound at the applied rate in 2003 (though only 5.6 per cent were bound at non-zero rates).

11.4.2 *The Current Round*

There is no evidence that the initial agreement has affected food security policy in SADC. The current Doha Round, nevertheless, has the potential to do so, given that it envisages far deeper agricultural liberalization. The Doha Round may fail to deliver on these promises given the widespread opposition to significant agricultural reform. This is apparent by the fact that there is still no agreed modality for agricultural liberalization in the Doha Round despite four years of negotiation. The Draft General Council Decision of 31 July 2004 (WTO 2004) is only a framework for establishing modalities, and lacks any clear details of formulae for both domestic support and market access liberalization. The only clarity it provides is that LDCs will not be required to make any reduction commitments; this is important to SADC as seven of the 14 members are LDCs and hence the agriculture negotiations present no direct threat to their strategies for agricultural development. It is important for them still to have an interest in negotiations because they will be bound by the negotiated provisions should they be reclassified as developing countries at a later point.

The clearest modalities are contained in the texts circulated around the time of the Cancun Ministerial in July 2003, specifically the joint US–EU text, the Group of 20 Developing Countries (G20) text and the Debraz text that sought to compromise between the two. While none of these texts were agreed, they provide an insight into what key players are thinking and the shape of modalities that may emerge in the end. Given the lack of a clear modality, we now seek to identify which modalities might potentially threaten current SADC food security policies.

11.5 Subsidies: Domestic Support and Export Subsidies

11.5.1 *Negotiating Texts*

The Draft General Council Decision of 31 July 2004 reaffirmed its support for special and differential treatment as laid out in Article 6.2 of the AoA. Furthermore, Paragraph 45 of the Annex on Agriculture states that LDCs will be exempt from all subsidy related reductions. The draft calls for a tiered reduction in all measures of support to achieve some harmonization. In terms of specific categories of support:

- Aggregate measures of support (AMS): tiered approach to achieve greater cuts for those with higher AMSs;
- *De minimis*: developing countries that allocate most of their *de minimis* to subsistence and poor farmers will be exempt;[3]
- Blue Box: should not exceed 5 per cent of a member's total value of agricultural production;
- Green Box: criteria to be reviewed to ensure no trade-distorting effects; and
- Export subsidies: to be phased out with a longer time period for developing countries.

This text is a clear compromise between the joint US–EU text and the G20 text, and is not dissimilar to the Debraz text. It calls for a tiered approach (G20), offers scope for greater support by developing countries (G20), specifically no commitments from LDCs (G20), while setting overall limits (US–EU and G20) and a 5 per cent maximum on the Blue Box (US–EU). What needs to be negotiated is the specific tier formula for reductions in total support and AMSs.

11.5.2 *Potential Constraints to SADC Countries*

While the original commitments under the AoA were not constraining, there has since been a dramatic shift away from general producer subsidies of one form or another in SADC. Additionally, there has been a growing focus on targeted support for smallholder farmers (the S&D provision) and more general support measures that would fall within the Green Box provisions. The primary reason for these shifts in agricultural strategy has been structural adjustment policies aimed at reducing state debt and improving the sustainability of the fiscus. This is particularly evident amongst the LDCs (especially Lesotho, Malawi, Mozambique, Tanzania, and Zambia) that have effectively eliminated all support for commercial farmers.

The currently applied and notified support measures offered by SADC countries, including the value of that support where data are available, are shown in Table 11.1. It is ordered into the LDCs (no reduction obligations), developing countries, and developed economies (South Africa only). Table 11.1 provides some insights into how SADC food security policies might be threatened by any proposed reductions in agricultural subsidies.

It is only the wealthier SADC members (notably South Africa) that are able to sustain these support measures fiscally, but even South Africa has significantly cut back on such support. The reduction also does not appear to be WTO driven, because the reductions have been dramatic and the current

[3] Essentially this is in lieu of a development box that has been a constant call from developing countries.

Table 11.1. SADC domestic support, current (WTO notified and applied)

Domestic Support Commitment	Least developed countries					Developing countries					Developed
	Lesotho	Malawi	Mozambique	Tanzania	Zambia	Botswana	Namibia	Mauritius	Swaziland	Zimbabwe	South Africa
S&D 'Box'											
Production (inputs and technology) for resource poor farmers	A	N		A	N	A	N		A	A	
Technology and animal subsidies					A	A	N			A	
Welfare transfers (assets and land)	A	A					N			A	
Investment subsidies			A			A	N				
Value (% of production)		0.73			0.88		0.48				(1.5)*
Green Box (Annex 2)											
General public agricultural services											
Administration	A	A	A	A	N	A	A	A	A	A	N
Research		A		A	N	N	N	A	A	N	N
Pest and disease control	A	A	A	A	N	N	N		A	N	N
Training	A	A	A	A	N	A	A	A	A	N	N
Extension service	A	A	A	A	N	N	N	A	A	N	N
Inspection services	A	A	A	A	N	A	A	A	A	N	N
Marketing		A			N		A	A			
Resource conservation	A	A	A	A	A	A	A	A	A	A	N
Infrastructure				A	N	N	A		A	N	N
Food stockholding		A			A					A	
Domestic food aid	A	A	A		A		A		A	A	

Blue Box							
Direct payments to producers							
Domestic support commitment							
Decoupled income support							
Income insurance						N	
Disaster relief		N	N				
Structural adjustment (producer and resource retirement)							
Environment/conservation							
Regional development							N
Value (% of production)	5.50		1.84			0.62	5.56 (4.06)**
Other (product and non-product AMS)							
Credit subsidization			A		A		N
Inputs subsidization			A		A	A	
Infrastructure (on farm-) development		A					
Resource allocation							N
Price support				A	A		N
Value (% of production)							1.72

Source: Authors' informed assessments, drawing on WTO notifications by SADC members.

Notes: N = WTO notified; A = applied support (author's assessment);

* Although notified under the Green Box, South Africa offers substantial development aid (R 323) to producers in disadvantaged areas to encourage agriculture and rural development (predominantly former homelands). This might be considered S&D.

** The figure in parentheses excludes the value ascribed to S&D.

level of support is well below the permissible bound levels. For instance, South Africa has a US$310 million limit on total AMS on top of the R750 million *de minimis* allocation but has reduced total support to US$70 million (or only 1.72 per cent of production). It has also eliminated export subsidies even though it is permitted an expenditure of US$100 million. Most SADC countries reduced their Green Box expenditure over the course of the past decade, mainly in response to SAP, a measure not required under the AoA. For instance, Zambia reduced Green Box support from 12 per cent to 5.5 per cent of the value of production, and Namibia from 4.7 per cent to 1.8 per cent.

We therefore conclude that in light of the substantial changes in food security and general agricultural policy within the region, shifting from a focus on national production to an increasing dependence on trade, reductions in the *de minimis* are still highly unlikely to dig into current domestic support. Furthermore, much of the support outside of the Green Box is targeted at resource-poor farmers and so would fall within the S&D provision (i.e. exempt from *de minimis*). However, even this is small in comparison to likely *de minimis* reductions. For example, in Malawi, policies under the S&D provision are valued at only 0.73 per cent of the value of production, while in Zambia the figure is 0.88 per cent of production. Namibia, the only other country where data are available through notifications, had a total S&D provision value of 0.48 per cent of production. South Africa, which has listed development aid under the Green Box, reaches 1.5 per cent of production. In contrast, Green Box support is 1.84 per cent of production for Namibia, 5.5 per cent for Zambia, and 4.06 per cent for South Africa (excluding the development aid of 1.5 per cent).

Although current subsidy proposals pose no real constraint on SADC countries, it may still be strategically important for SADC countries to try retaining a high *de minimis* level in order to provide policy space for the future. It is apparent that while most countries offer typical Green Box support for their agricultural sector (of varying sizes), more extensive support is mostly offered by those that can afford to (i.e. the developing countries and South Africa). This is evident from the range and value of support under S&D provisions, Blue Box and trade-distorting support measures. As income in these countries grows, they may be more able to provide domestic support and may wish to do so in order to accelerate agricultural growth. We have argued elsewhere (Charman and Hodge 2005) that if the poorer countries in the region are to attain food security, then the levels of support to agriculture need to be increased substantially. This includes policies that may not fall into the S&D provision or Green Box; for instance support for emerging farmers and long-term welfare transfers (especially in light of the devastation caused by the HIV/AIDS pandemic in rural areas).

A further reason for caution is that there is no clarity on whether extra-budgetary foreign aid (government and nongovernmental organization aid) may be included in the estimation of domestic support for countries in the region. This support is substantial and could raise measures of support considerably. SADC countries should recognize the advantage of keeping *de minimis* support bindings at levels that far exceed current and possibly future support. Policy space will allow developing countries to offer trade concessions without harming current strategies.

11.6 Market Access

11.6.1 *Negotiating Texts*

The Draft General Council Decision of 31 July 2004 provides few details on what modalities will be used to address tariff reductions in the Doha Round. It merely notes agreement to use a tiered formula that will be applied to bound, not applied, rates and that each member may designate a number of tariff lines as sensitive products that will receive more flexible treatment. It also reaffirms that developing countries will receive special and differential treatment on all aspects of the modality and a special safeguard mechanism will be established for their use. Finally, LDCs will be exempt from any reductions.

The US–EU and G20 texts provide at least some insights into the thinking of key members of what tiered formulae might be used. The EU–US Joint Text provides for a blended formula for tariff reduction that would include lower requirements for developing countries. The blended formula is comprised of the following components:

(i) [.] per cent of tariff lines subject to a [.] per cent average tariff cut and a minimum of [.] per cent;
(ii) [.] per cent of tariff lines subject to a Swiss formula coefficient [.];
(iii) [.] per cent of tariff lines shall be duty-free; and
(iv) A maximum tariff of [.] per cent.

In contrast, the G20 proposed framework is harder on developed economies but softer on developing. For developed economies, the average cut for [.] per cent of lines is replaced by a linear cut for [.] per cent of lines. It also looks to address tariff escalation in these countries. For developing countries, the G20 proposal calls for only an average cut of [.] per cent with a minimum cut of [.] per cent for all lines, except where tariff bindings are already low (no reduction) or for special products (SP) (minimum linear cut). No maximum tariffs, no Swiss formula, and no duty-free tariffs.

The proposed modality included as an annex to the Cancun Ministerial (Debraz text), largely follows the EU–US text for developed countries (but includes tariff escalation). For developing countries, it also follows the EU–US text but with some concessions. These include [.] per cent of tariffs bound between 0 and 5 per cent instead of being bound duty-free, and the two exceptions to the average cut proposed by the G20 (the SP designation and no reduction on low tariffs).

11.6.2 *Constraints for SADC Countries*

SADC countries, going into negotiations, need to assess what sort of tariff structure would best suit their development objectives in agriculture. It is thought that many SADC countries would identify modest tariffs as necessary to provide incentives for production of both raw and processed food products. This is currently the case with several members. Regional food production needs to be encouraged because it is cheaper than food imports for many food staples in the region, and would limit the extent to which countries struggle to import their basic requirements. Production incentives are also negatively affected by occasional low and variable prices that result from high levels of subsidization in the developed countries[4] and surplus dumping in time of a global glut.[5] An important consideration is the high transport cost both in reaching the region and within the region. Transport costs offer some degree of protection (mainly to landlocked countries in the region), and this should be reflected in lower tariff levels. The exception is if the threat is from regional producers such as South Africa or Zimbabwe. NTBs similarly afford protection to the domestic producers. However, NTBs are second-best tools because they work against the rapid and effective importation of food in times of crisis. In contrast, tariffs can be adjusted downwards in crisis years to facilitate imports and thus reduce the price of food to the consumer.

This chapter does not attempt to determine an optimal tariff regime for each SADC country. It is however apparent—from an examination of agricultural tariffs at a detailed level for many SADC countries—that there has been little strategic thinking in this regard. The setting of tariffs has been motivated, for some SADC members, by the fiscus dependence on tariff revenue. Often blanket rates are applied to an entire range of products without regard to whether or not it is necessary to fulfil a policy objective. For instance, most of Malawi's MFN tariffs are either 10 or 40 per cent, for Mozambique they are 2.5, 7.5, or 35 per cent, for Zambia 5, 15, or 25 per cent. While there are definite benefits to the simplicity of the tariff regime, these tariff decisions are also evidence of the weak trade negotiation pressure on government policy. SADC countries have not carefully considered which tariffs are

[4] For instance, SACU's tariff on wheat is purely to counteract the European subsidies.

[5] Surplus dumping in times of global glut does not justify a high applied tariff but rather a high bound tariff that gives scope to raise a low applied tariff in these periods. A safeguard mechanism, alternatively, can achieve the same goal.

important and which are not and thus can be given up strategically in trade negotiations.

The chapter now considers whether the negotiating modalities will make reduction of some tariffs unavoidable or not.

11.6.3 *Tariff Reductions*

The exclusion of LDCs from making any reduction commitments in this round clearly implies that the negotiations, at this point, offer no threat to most of the SADC countries. For the non-LDCs the threat to existing policy differs according to the type of formula that may be used in negotiations. Tables 11.2 and 11.3 examine the implications on all current agricultural tariff (Table 11.2) and food security tariff lines separately (Table 11.3) from different formulae (based on existing proposals) and different coefficients applied to these formulae. Our analysis considers a range of products as 'food security products', not simply cereals, but other components necessary for a diversified nutritional diet (meats, dairy, starchy roots, vegetables, fruit/nuts). The analysis further includes the main regional cash crops, as these are inextricably linked to regional food security and are part of the smallholder cropping strategy.

While the LDCs are included for completeness, the main focus is on the developing countries (Botswana, Mauritius, Namibia, Swaziland, and Zimbabwe) and the one developed country (South Africa). It must be noted that SACU has a common external tariff and so will experience the same reductions. There is some scope within SACU to have special safeguards for development, and so the BLNS countries (Botswana, Lesotho, Namibia, and Swaziland) may be able to bind at a higher level. Our analysis examines SACU tariffs as a single entity.

SADC countries used the opportunity in the UR to bind at very high tariff levels, typically over 100 per cent. The main exception was SACU (mean bound rate of 34 per cent) as there was greater pressure on South Africa to bind lower. Across the region, applied tariffs on the food security lines we examine are much lower than bound rates, with mean applied rates in the range of 15–20 per cent, with Zimbabwe the highest with 27 per cent and SACU the lowest with 8.6 per cent. This means that there is considerable 'air' in the tariffs, which can protect these countries from possible large average cuts in future negotiations. For example, were SADC countries to undergo average cuts of 60 per cent, the effect on applied tariffs would be negligible or none. SACU is the exception where 5.6 per cent of tariff lines are bound at their applied rate and so a cut of any magnitude will enforce a reduction. But because the median tariff in SACU is 0 per cent, cuts of greater and greater magnitude do not have vastly different effects on the number of lines affected.

Table 11.2. Impact on SADC agricultural tariff lines from different formula and coefficients

	Least developed countries						Developing		Developed
	Angola	DR Congo	Malawi	Mozambique	Tanzania	Zambia	Mauritius	Zimbabwe	SACU
Mean tariffs, %									
Mean bound tariff	53.0	54.0	124.0	100.0	120.0	125.0	120.0	150.0	34.0
Mean applied tariff	9.7	13.5	15.5	16.2	18.0	18.6	20.5	27.4	8.6
Median applied tariff	5.0	10.0	10.0	25.0	25.0	25.0	15.0	25.0	0.0
Maximum applied tariff	35.0	20.0	25.0	25.0	25.0	25.0	80.0	100.0	55.0
Average cut									
% of lines affected by average cut of									
20	0.0	0.0	0.0	0.0	0.0	0.0	0.0	0.1	10.2
30	0.0	0.0	0.0	0.0	0.0	0.0	0.0	0.1	11.4
40	4.9	0.3	0.0	0.0	0.0	0.0	7.1	4.7	15.3
50	9.3	0.3	0.0	0.0	0.0	0.0	7.1	6.2	24.0
60	10.5	1.3	1.1	0.0	0.0	0.7	14.8	7.0	29.0
70	18.2	43.5	1.2	0.0	0.0	0.7	29.9	7.4	31.5
Maximum tariff, %									
% of lines with a tariff greater than									
20	13.7	42.2	46.4	57.7	66.6	58.6	34.9	55.8	13.0
30	9.3	0.0	0.0	0.0	0.0	0.0	33.1	45.6	3.8
40	0.0	0.0	0.0	0.0	0.0	0.0	29.8	43.8	0.7
50	0.0	0.0	0.0	0.0	0.0	0.0	13.9	6.4	0.1
Low tariffs									
% of lines									
tariff = 0	0.0	0.0	11.6	0.8	22.3	2.1	39.7	6.4	51.3
tariff ≤ 5	54.5	15.6	17.2	27.2	22.3	21.1	40.3	26.2	57.1
Swiss coefficients									
% of lines affected by a Swiss coefficient of									
10	45.3	84.1	82.8	57.7	77.7	78.9	59.7	73.7	42.0
15	13.7	43.7	46.4	57.7	72.1	78.9	52.6	71.9	34.4
20	13.7	42.6	46.4	57.7	66.6	59.1	35.1	56.4	33.3
25	13.7	42.5	46.4	57.7	66.6	58.6	33.2	55.2	31.9

Source: Authors' calculations. Tariff rates obtained from WTO, UNCTAD Trains, and SA Customs and Excise databases.

Table 11.3. Impact on SADC food security-relevant tariff lines from different formula and coefficients

	Least developed countries						Developing		Developed
	Angola	DR Congo	Malawi	Mozambique	Tanzania	Zambia	Mauritius	Zimbabwe	SACU
Mean tariffs, %									
Mean bound tariff	55.0	52.0	125.0	100.0	120.0	125.0	115.0	149.0	43.1
Mean applied tariff	2.0	13.6	15.7	19.8	22.7	22.1	27.0	40.7	11.6
Median applied tariff	2.0	10.0	10.0	25.0	25.0	25.0	15.0	40.0	4.0
Maximum applied tariff	2.0	20.0	25.0	25.0	25.0	25.0	80.0	100.0	45.0
Average cut									
% of lines affected by average cut of									
20	0.0	0.0	0.0	0.0	0.0	0.0	0.0	0.0	15.6
30	0.0	0.0	0.0	0.0	0.0	0.0	0.0	0.0	17.0
40	0.0	1.0	0.0	0.0	0.0	0.0	14.7	9.1	20.6
50	0.0	1.0	0.0	0.0	0.0	0.0	14.7	13.2	26.2
60	0.0	8.1	0.0	0.0	0.0	0.0	24.9	13.2	39.7
70	0.0	49.2	0.0	0.0	0.0	0.0	44.7	13.2	42.6
Maximum tariff, %									
% of lines with a tariff greater than									
20	0.0	41.1	43.1	75.6	88.8	77.2	44.2	85.3	21.3
30	0.0	0.0	0.0	0.0	0.0	0.0	44.2	73.6	17.0
40	0.0	0.0	0.0	0.0	0.0	0.0	44.2	73.6	3.5
50	0.0	0.0	0.0	0.0	0.0	0.0	21.8	12.7	0.0
Low tariffs									
% of lines									
tariff = 0	0.0	0.0	7.1	1.0	7.1	1.5	38.6	0.0	44.7
tariff $\leq$ 5	100.0	9.6	7.6	18.8	7.1	5.6	40.6	5.6	54.6
Swiss coefficients									
% of lines affected by a Swiss coefficient of									
10	0.0	90.4	92.4	75.6	92.9	94.4	59.4	94.4	70.9
15	0.0	49.2	43.1	75.6	90.9	94.4	59.4	90.4	65.2
20	0.0	42.1	43.1	75.6	88.8	77.2	44.7	85.8	63.8
25	0.0	42.1	43.1	75.6	88.8	77.2	44.7	84.8	61.0

Source: Authors' calculations. Tariff rates obtained from WTO, UNCTAD Trains, SA Customs and Excise databases.

The EU–US joint text proposed a maximum tariff as a means to harmonize and bring some extreme bindings in developing countries to a level that is closer to applied rates. Yet it is the developing, rather than the developed, countries with SADC that make use of high maximum tariffs. This may in part be due to the imposition of structural adjustment programmes where tariff reduction and simplification are often components. Given that the developing countries are the ones that will face reduction commitments, the use of a maximum tariff in the formula is likely to affect Mauritius and Zimbabwe significantly, as well as even at levels of 40 per cent (this would affect 30 per cent of Mauritius tariff lines and 44 per cent of Zimbabwe's). SACU has few very high tariffs and would therefore be marginally affected by the use of a maximum in the formula, even at levels of 20 per cent (this would have an affect on 13 per cent of SACU tariff lines).

A further component of the EU–US proposal is to have a set percentage of tariff lines duty free. This would pose a greater threat to the LDCs in the group rather than the developing countries which generally (with the exception of Zimbabwe) have a significant percentage of duty free lines. Yet as we have argued, there is considerable scope for countries like Zimbabwe to be more strategic in their tariff setting. Zimbabwe has only 6.4 per cent of tariff lines duty-free, but almost 29 per cent of tariff lines see no trade activity. This may be due, in part, to prohibitive tariffs, though a significant part is due to a lack of domestic demand for some very narrowly defined product groups. Additionally Zimbabwe has almost 30 per cent of its tariff lines at a rate of 5 per cent or less, a portion of which could be moved to zero with minimal effect on tariff revenues or production internally.

The EU–US proposal also includes a Swiss formula that would be applied to a certain proportion of tariffs. The Swiss formula would be the most threatening component of any formula. Among the developing countries that need to make reduction commitments, a modest Swiss formula coefficient of 25 would impact on a third of all tariff lines in the case of SACU and Mauritius, and up to 55 per cent of all tariff lines in the case of Zimbabwe.

11.6.4 *Food Security Tariff Lines*

When we examine the tariff lines associated with key food security products, then a similar picture emerges. Tariff rates on these lines are generally higher than those on other agricultural products, except in Angola where they are lower. In SACU, for example, the mean bound rate in food security products is 9 per cent higher than that of all agricultural products. Food security tariff lines may be the first to be affected by reduction commitments. The threat can be seen by comparing the effect of an average cut on food security products in comparison to all agricultural products for the countries that face reductions in this round. While for Mauritius and Zimbabwe any low average cut will still not have an impact, the impact would double for food security products (in percentage terms) once cuts reach reasonable levels (40 per cent or above).

Similarly, the use of a maximum tariff in the formula would have a far greater effect on food security product lines, most notably for Zimbabwe which has a very high mean tariff of 40 per cent for food security products. The use of a percentage of products duty free would have no impact on food security lines if countries choose to allocate reductions to other agricultural products. Both Mauritius and SACU both have a large portion of food security products already subject to duty free access, reflecting a policy of cheaper essentials where no home production takes place (most obvious in the case of Mauritius) or it is internationally competitive (more obvious in the case of South Africa). Swiss coefficients would have an even more dramatic effect. However, the EU–US proposal stresses that the Swiss formula would be applied only to a proportion of tariffs, and not all. Given the broad impact of even modest coefficients of 25, it is likely that some food security tariff lines will be threatened if applied to 50 per cent of all tariff lines.

11.7 Marrakech Decision

In the course of the WTO negotiations, different views on how to take into account nontrade concerns have been raised. The most contentious issues concern food security, livelihoods and poverty alleviation, rural development, environmental issues, food safety and animal welfare. LDCs and NFIDCs see a clear link between the case for concessionary modalities towards these development issues and the overarching objective of levelling global disparities through liberalization of agricultural trade.

LDCs have acquired a degree of support for their concerns over the food security issue from a broad spectrum of stakeholders. There is general consensus that a mechanism is required to ensure that food aid does not disrupt domestic production in recipient countries. But what actually constitutes 'disruption' is not agreed, and there is disagreement on how the impact can or should be evaluated. In food crisis situations, such as the recent southern African famine, stakeholders accept that WTO agreements should not hinder 'food aid' delivery. Furthermore, there were significant differences on the following important issues:

- The criteria for types of food aid;
- The provision of grants, thus facilitating regional procurement, verses direct food aid;

- The issue of genetically modified organisms (GMOs) and environmental concerns; and
- The need for a commitment not to reduce food aid volumes when prices increase.

Within the debate there is acceptance that developed countries have a role in providing continued technical and financial cooperation to LDCs for enhancing agricultural productivity, diversifying crop production, marketing information dissemination, export development, and SPS measures. It is not clear how far this developmental role should go or where its boundaries should end. Furthermore, the implications of financial and technical support in terms of the negotiations on trade have not been fully considered.

The Marrakech Decision focused on the possible negative effects of the reform programme on LDCs and NFIDCs and identified potential actions by countries to alleviate these threats. In particular, the Marrakech Decision expressed the concern that liberalization might lead to negative effects in getting adequate supplies of basic foodstuffs externally on reasonable conditions. It further identified the difficulties countries may experience in financing food imports. The Decision provides recommendations on food aid, export credits, and financing facilities. In terms of food aid, the ministers agreed to review levels of food aid, adopt guidelines to ensure food aid is fully in grant form, and give full consideration to requests for technical and financial assistance to improve agricultural productivity and infrastructure. In terms of export credits, the ministers agreed to ensure that the AoA covering export credits made appropriate provision for LDCs and NFIDCs. Finally, the ministers recognized that these countries may be eligible to draw on the resources of existing international financial institutions or such facilities as may be established.

Developing countries claim that this decision has never been implemented, but the careful wording of this decision imposes no obligations on the members (it is a 'best endeavour' agreement). LDCs are, nevertheless, anxious to have the Marrakech Decision implemented. The Draft General Council Decision of 31 July 2004 included for negotiation aspects of the Marrakech Decision.

The concern in the decision that food aid levels would decrease was unfounded given the response to the recent SADC food security crisis (Charman and Hodge 2005). In this experience, a central issue became the delivery of food aid in the form of GM maize and not grants. The Draft General Council Decision of 31 July 2004 does not agree to provide food aid in fully grant form but leaves it open to further negotiation. It states, however, that the provision of food aid should not cause commercial displacement, which underlines the necessity of maintaining effective incentives for local farmers. The Marrakech Decision argued for the establishment of a financing facility to assist countries during crisis. The southern African food crises highlighted not only the need for such a facility, but most importantly for access to grant financing. The main weakness with the Marrakech Decision is that it imposes no binding commitments on members and therefore is unlikely to be implemented in full. Furthermore, it is questionable whether the WTO will make the Marrakech commitments mandatory, as they fall outside the mandate of the WTO itself, especially in respect to the financing facility issue.

11.8 Conclusion

Several studies have argued that the initial AoA does not constrain food security objectives in LDCs and NFIDCs. Our study endorses this view; we conclude that the proposed modalities in the current round are also unlikely to restrict SADC policies to enhance and assure food availability, improve household access to food and secure stability in the supply of food. The high level of 'water' in the tariffs on food security crops ensures that agreed reductions, where applicable (excluding LDCs) would still leave member countries with sufficient policy space to pursue agriculture development through affording producers protection from increased trade. The current proposed tariff reductions will not affect applied tariffs in these crops. The most worrying scenario in terms of the current negotiations on tariff reductions would be the setting of a low maximum tariff. This could potentially minimize the use of tariffs to protect national markets from international dumping. While this is a matter of concern for some agricultural produce lines (where demand is relatively stable, such as vegetable oils, poultry and dairy products), it would have limited impact on local cereal markets where demand fluctuates both seasonally and inter-seasonally and supply is met largely through home production. Furthermore, the transaction costs of engaging in cereal markets are high, due to the poor state of the region's infrastructure and the absence of accurate market information as much trade crosses national boundaries illegally and thus goes unrecorded. Our study notes that while many non-essential agricultural tariff lines may come under pressure for reduction through Swiss formula and duty free components of the modality, SADC members have scope for reducing irrelevant tariffs on lines for which imports are minimal or zero.

This study concludes that the AoA's primary threat for domestic support for SADC countries would come from a reduction in the *de minimis* allocation to a level that would start to cut into current or future planned subsidization. In additional, the removal of Article 6.2 privileges that would result in these domestic support measures counting under the *de minimis* allocation would also present a significant threat. Current support levels are comparatively low (even in the case of South Africa and the region's developing countries) and decreasing in real and absolute terms due to budgetary constraints, as is the case with the LDCs (notably Malawi and Zambia). Yet is has been acknowledged that if household food security is to be achieved, then levels of support need to be increased substantially in the future. The New Partnership for Africa's Development (NEPAD) Comprehensive Africa Agriculture Development Programme (CAADP), for example, calls upon member countries to align their budget expenditure to the CAADP framework, which requires that at least 10 per cent of budget expenditure is directed to agriculture (see *SADC Today*, volume 8, number 1, April 2005). The required level of support to bring about the NEPAD vision will include the provision of subsidies that do not fall into the S&D provision or Green Box; these include, direct input subsidies for emerging farmers and long-term welfare transfers to the rural poor and specifically those smallholders unable to achieve household food self-sufficiency.

We argue that in order for SADC countries to pursue policies in line with the NEPAD' CAADP, it is important that they retain sufficient policy space to allow them room for manoeuvre. In this context it is important for SADC countries to recognize the advantage of keeping *de minimis* support bindings at levels that far exceed current and possibly future support. Policy space will allow them to offer trade concessions without harming future strategies. We further caution that it is important for SADC countries to begin notifying their Green Box policies. The bulk of farmer support current given by SADC members falls within the Green Box, and notification will ensure that fiscal resources allocated to these support measures are not lumped in with general AMS or the S&D provision. This would provide countries with even greater differences between actual support, and support permitted within the *de minimis* allocation. Such a strategy allows developing countries more scope to accept a reduction in their own *de minimis* in return for greater reductions from the developed countries in future negotiations. It also assists in the negotiation process as it demonstrates that current requirements are appropriate.

Finally, we concur with the argument that the failure to implement the Marrakech Decision may hinder the expedient resolution of future food crises, especially among the SADC LDCs.

References

Charman, A. J. E., and J. Hodge (2005). 'SADC Food Security: An Analysis of the Potential Impact of the Current WTO Agricultural Negotiations on Government Strategy'. Paper presented at the UNU-WIDER–ICSSR project (in collaboration with FAO) on Hunger and Food Security: New Challenges and New Opportunities. 12–14 October. Helsinki: UNU-WIDER.

FAO (2003a). 'Some Trade Policy Issues Relating to Trends in Agricultural Imports in the Context of Food Security'. Sixty-fourth section of the FAO Committee on Commodity Problems, 18–21 March. Rome: FAO.

—— (2003b). 'Zimbabwe', in *WTO Agreement on Agriculture: The Implementation Experience—Developing Country Case Studies*. Rome: FAO.

—— (2003c). 'Malawi', in *WTO Agreement on Agriculture: The Implementation Experience—Developing Country Case Studies*. Rome: FAO.

Kirsten, J. (2006). 'Socio-Economic Dynamics of the South African Agricultural Sector'. *Trade Policy Briefing*, 10. South African Institute of International Affairs.

Matthews, A. (2000). 'Synthesis of the Findings of 23 Country Case Studies', in *WTO Agreement on Agriculture: The Implementation Experience—Developing Country Case Studies*. Rome: FAO.

Vink, N., R. Sandrey, C. L. McCarthy, and H. E. Zunckel (2006). 'Promoting Agricultural Trade and Investment Synergies between South Africa and other SADC Member Countries'. *TRALAC Working Paper*, 20. Stellenbosch: US Printers.

WTO (1995a). *Agreement on Agriculture*. Geneva: WTO.

—— (1995b). *SADC Agricultural Schedules*. Geneva: WTO.

—— (1995–2003). *SADC Notifications to the Committee of Agriculture*. Geneva: WTO

—— (2000). 'Committee on Agriculture, Special Session: Decision on Measures concerning the Possible Negative Effects of the Reform Programme on Least Developed and Net Food Importing Developing Countries (NFIDC Decision)'. UN document G/AG/NG/S/4, 27 April. Geneva: WTO.

—— (2001a). *Mauritius Trade Policy Review*. Geneva: WTO.

—— (2001b). 'Committee on Agriculture, Special Session: WTO Africa Group: Joint Proposal on the Negotiations on Agriculture'. UN document G/AG/NG/W/142, 23 March. Geneva: WTO.

—— (2001c). 'WTO Agriculture Negotiations. The Issues, and Where We Are Now. Media Briefing'. UN document TN/AG/6, 21 October. Geneva: Committee on Agriculture, WTO.

—— (2002a). *Malawi: Trade Policy Review*. Geneva: WTO.

—— (2002b). *Zambia: Trade Policy Review*. Geneva: WTO.

—— (2002c). 'Committee on Agriculture, Special Session: Negotiations on Agriculture. Overview (18 December)'. Geneva: WTO.

—— (2003a). 'Draft Cancun Ministerial Text'. UN document JOB(03)/150/Rev.1. Geneva: WTO.

—— (2003b). 'EU–US Joint Text on Agriculture', 13 August. Geneva: WTO: Geneva.

—— (2003c). 'G20 Framework for Establishing Modalities in Agriculture'. Geneva WTO.

—— (2003d). *SACU Trade Policy Review*. Geneva: WTO.

—— (2003e). 'Committee on Agriculture. Negotiations on Agriculture. First draft of modalities for further commitments'. UN document TN/AG/W/1/Rev. 1, 18 March. Geneva: WTO.

—— (2004). 'Draft General Council Decision of 31 July 2004'. UN document WTO/GC/W/535. Geneva: WTO.

12

International Trade, Food Security, and the Response to the WTO in South Asian Countries

Ramesh Chand

12.1 Introduction

Agriculture is the mainstay of the South Asian economies. About 20 to 41 per cent of national output and 44 to 73 per cent employment are contributed by this sector in various countries in the region. Heavy dependence on agriculture, low productivity, low growth rate of economy and slow growth in employment opportunities in nonagriculture sector are the salient features of South Asian countries (SACs) and are largely responsible for widespread poverty and undernutrition in the region. As seen from Table 12.1, more than 30 per cent of the rural population in India, 36 per cent in Pakistan, 44 per cent in Nepal, and more than 50 per cent in Bangladesh live under poverty. Similarly, the incidence of undernutrition varies from 17 per cent in Nepal to 32 per cent in Bangladesh. Any adverse impact on agriculture sector in these countries, from forces like trade liberalization, has widespread ramifications in terms of employment, nutrition, livelihood, and food security.

Historically, SACs have followed inward-looking trade policies. Sri Lanka was the first country in the region to undertake trade reforms. It initiated liberalization in the late 1970s. Other countries initiated serious trade liberalization policies during early 1990s primarily in nonagriculture sector. Reforms in agriculture trade were missing, or were quite slow until the Uruguay Round of GATT, which was implemented in 1995 with the establishment of the World Trade Organization (WTO). The Uruguay Round (UR) requires adjustments in domestic policies involving greater importance to trade rather than supporting self-sufficiency to achieve or maintain food security. This is a serious concern to SACs as food security has remained the chief concern

Table 12.1. Agro-economic profile of the SACs

Particular	Ref. year(s)	Bangladesh	India	Nepal	Pakistan	Sri Lanka
Per capita gross national income US$	2002	380	495	230	420	850
Income rank in the world	2002	171	161	191	168	142
Arable land: ha per capita	1999–2001	0.06	0.16	0.13	0.15	0.05
Share of agriculture in GDP %	2002	23	23	41	23	20
Workforce in agriculture	around 2000					
Male		53	58.4	NA	44	49
Female		77	(Total)	NA	73	38
Agriculture value added/worker 1995 US$	2000–2	318	401	203	716	725
Population under poverty %	late 1990s					
Rural		53.0	30.2	44.0	35.9	27.0
Urban		36.8	24.7	23.0	24.2	15.0
Undernourished population %	1999–2001	32	21	17	19	25

Source: World Bank (2004).

of development policy of these countries and they have striven hard to attain this goal by improving or acquiring self sufficiency in foodgrain. Though these countries sometimes faced situations of availability of cheap foodgrain in the international markets, it was considered highly desirable to develop domestic capability, as trade was not considered a reliable source to meet the needs of principal food items of domestic population.

This chapter analyses the changes in agricultural trade, changes in the dependence on food imports, trade orientation of agriculture, agricultural growth in SACs before and after WTO, and food security issues related to trade liberalization. Based on the experience with implementation of UR, the chapter discusses issues of concern to the SACs for negotiations in the next round of WTO agreement. This analysis is based on the data covering the period from 1991 to 2004. The whole period was studied by taking four yearly averages of trade data, terming 1991–4 as before WTO, 1995–8 as the launching or initial years of WTO and 1999–2002 as post-WTO. The analysis was then further extended up to the year 2004 to include more recent data.

12.2 Agriculture Trade Before and After WTO

A general idea about the impact of UR on the agriculture trade of the SACs can be obtained by looking at agricultural trade before and after 1995 when the WTO Agreement came into effect. Basic information on SAC trade before and after WTO is provided in Table 12.2.

Agricultural exports of Bangladesh increased from US$128 million in the four years before WTO to US$139 million in the initial years of

Table 12.2. Agriculture trade of SACs before and after WTO, US$ million

	1991–4: Before WTO	1995–8: Start of WTO	1999–2002: After WTO	2003–4
Bangladesh				
Exports	128	139	105	108
Imports	663	1248	1623	1905
Net trade	−535	−1109	−1518	−1797
India				
Exports	3085	5557	5087	6781
Imports	1336	2711	3699	5006
Net trade	1749	2846	1388	1776
Nepal				
Exports	49	48	58	125
Imports	141	217	194	278
Net trade	−92	−169	−136	−153
Pakistan				
Exports	956	1101	1067	1244
Imports	1405	2135	1814	1993
Net trade	−448	−1034	−747	−749
Sri Lanka				
Exports	528	923	969	1077
Imports	500	779	766	878
Net trade	29	144	202	199

Source: Calculated by author from the FAOSTAT Database.

implementation of Agreement on Agriculture (AoA). The post-WTO period (1999–2002) saw a sharp fall in exports. On the other hand, agricultural imports increased from US$1.248 billion to US$1.623 billion since the implementation of WTO. The net result has been that trade deficit of Bangladesh rose by more than 38 per cent with the implementation of AoA.

In the case of India, agricultural exports as well as imports followed a substantial increase in the initial years of WTO. India's trade surplus, which increased from US$1.7 billion in the early 1990s to US$2.8 billion by 1998, dropped to US$1.388 billion in the post-WTO period.

The agricultural trade of Nepal shows a substantial increase in imports and a trade deficit in the initial years of WTO. Although there was some decline in imports and the trade deficit in the later years, these remained higher than in the pre-WTO years.

Agricultural exports of Pakistan, as in India and Bangladesh, turned out to be lower in the post-WTO period. However, its imports behaved differently as they declined from US$2.135 billion in the beginning of the WTO to US$1.814 billion after the WTO. This helped Pakistan to reduce its worsening trade deficit that had reached more than US$1 billion with the implementation of WTO agreement.

Agricultural exports of Sri Lanka were only slightly higher than its imports during 1991–4. The situation turned favourable for exports after 1995 and resulted in a large trade surplus. There was further improvement in the trade

Table 12.3. Summary indicators of impact of WTO on agricultural trade of SACs

Country	Impact on imports	Impact on exports	Net impact
Bangladesh	Highly adverse	Highly Adverse	Highly adverse
India	Highly adverse	Favourable	Adverse
Pakistan	Adverse	Slightly favourable	Adverse
Sri Lanka	Adverse	Favourable	Favourable
Nepal	Adverse	Favourable	Adverse

Source: Calculated by the author based on Table 12.2.

surplus of agriculture during post-WTO period. Based on this analysis, the summary impact of WTO AoA trade of SACs is generalized in Table 12.3.

12.2.1 *Composition of Trade*

Major items of exports and imports and changes in their trading volume during 1991 to 2002 in the five SACs are presented in Table 12.4.

BANGLADESH

Wheat, vegetable oil, oilseeds, cotton, and rice are the major items of farm imports for Bangladesh. There was a substantial increase in the import of these items at the beginning of WTO and the increase continued at a moderate rate in the post-WTO period. The biggest increase took place in the case of rice whose imports increased from US$5.6 million before WTO to US$186.7 million in the initial years of WTO. Wheat emerged as the largest import item, followed by soybean oil. Bangladesh's import of vegetable oil moved close to 100 thousand tonnes and constituted 30 per cent of its total agricultural imports in value term. In addition, more than US$100 million is spent on oilseeds and oilcake. Oilcake has emerged as a new import item in recent years.

Bangladesh has a very small volume of agricultural exports, which is less than one-tenth of its imports. Exports of fruit and vegetables showed promising growth with the start of WTO but then stagnated to around US$12 million. The export of tea halved in the post-WTO period and jute exports dropped by about 16 per cent.

INDIA

Vegetable oil, cotton, and pulses are the major items of India's agricultural imports. In the last ten years, import of vegetable oils and cotton has seen an amazing increase more than tenfold. Import bill for vegetable oil was US$130 million in early 1990s,that is, before WTO, but increased to US$1632 million in the late 1990s (Table 12.4: Panel B). India's imports volume has exceeded

Table 12.4. Changes in major agricultural exports and imports for selected SACs, 1991–2004, US$ million per year

Trade	1991–4	1995–8	1999–2002	2003–4
Panel A: BANGLADESH				
Imports:				
Cotton lint	89.8	167.6	197.9	170.5
Rice	5.6	186.7	193.4	211.2
Sugar (raw equivalent)	18.2	40.2	66.1	135.2
Wheat and flour, wheat equiv.	164.2	185.5	259.5	317.9
Dairy products and eggs	69.0	58.0	84.5	76.0
Fixed vegetable oils	137.7	293.8	391.7	384.0
Palm oil	37.4	70.3	109.6	215.0
Soybean oil	94.6	217.1	273.8	153.0
Oilseed cake meal	0.1	1.7	19.1	73.7
Oilseeds	47.8	91.1	83.9	75.3
Exports:				
Fruit and vegetables	5.9	11.3	12.1	15.2
Jute	75.2	82.4	69.2	61.3
Tea	39.7	35.0	16.6	10.2
Panel B: INDIA				
Imports:				
Cotton lint	63.2	70.5	314.8	286.3
Fixed vegetable oils	129.9	1047.2	1632.2	2462.6
Palm oil	85.8	732.1	1045.9	1746.6
Soybeans oil	28.3	105.0	382.9	596.4
Pulses	159.4	254.8	386.9	491.8
Exports:				
Rice	369.5	1180.5	825.2	1186.7
Sugar (raw equivalent)	63.5	106.9	211.5	146.2
Cotton lint	108.9	174.4	10.2	116.3
Fruit and vegetables	536.2	704.7	929.2	1064.0
Tea	372.9	414.3	382.9	355.6
Coffee	194	430	256	226.5
Oilseed cake meal	571.1	775.4	411.6	700.8
Oilseeds	65.6	181.9	198.2	324.7
Spices	166	336	352	368.0
Tobacco	136	204	200	254.8
Cashew nuts	308	374	452	440.5
Panel C: PAKISTAN				
Imports:				
Fruit and vegetables	94.0	139.7	198.6	163.2
Pulses	55.6	71.9	109.3	95.9
Sugar (raw equivalent.)	60.2	31.8	138.7	7.8
Wheat and flour, wheat equiv.	297.2	432.1	160.1	26.5
Cotton lint	24.4	154.1	182.1	379.4
Fixed vegetable oils	474.3	864.6	528.4	644.6
Palm oil	354.0	702.4	410.9	576.0
Soybean oil	114.4	145.2	87.7	46.4
Tea	182.8	185.6	201.8	182.5
Oilseed cake meal	0.1	11.7	20.8	14.4
Oilseeds	19.7	36.0	124.2	226.5
Exports:				
Cotton lint	322.0	167.3	59.8	48.4
Fruit and vegetables	58.0	80.1	119.9	160.8

Table 12.4. *(Continued)*

Trade	1991–4	1995–8	1999–2002	2003–4
Rice	329.8	506.1	526.4	594.5
Sugar (raw equivalent)	9.9	85.9	65.8	20.2
Oilseeds	14.9	14.8	15.5	11.0
Panel D: NEPAL				
Imports:				
Fruit and vegetables	11.4	61.8	27.2	45.9
Fixed vegetable oils	24.4	41.5	33.1	60.6
Palm oil	7.7	8.0	20.7	44.1
Soybean oil	14.5	8.9	7.7	10.7
Rice	6.0	8.1	15.0	8.1
Sugar, total (raw equiv.)	5.2	5.8	7.9	1.8
Oilseeds	2.6	2.6	18.2	19.6
Exports:				
Butter	0.5	0.6	3.1	0.6
Fruit and vegetables	21.4	13.9	15.2	18.0
Pulses	15.8	13.8	14.1	12.5
Oilseed cake meal	2.1	1.8	2.8	7.2
Oilseeds	6.1	9.0	0.9	0.5
Panel E: SRI LANKA				
Imports:				
Milk equivalent	55.7	95.2	111.8	121.1
Rice	38.9	46.5	19.7	37.5
Fixed vegetable oils	18.2	37.8	42.1	67.8
Pulses	30.0	47.4	53.0	48.4
Sugar (raw equiv.)	102.5	141.9	127.1	122.1
Wheat and flour, wheat equiv.	115.5	146.3	123.1	164.5
Oilseed cake meal	7.4	12.7	16.2	26.0
Oilseeds	1.8	1.5	4.2	1.9
Exports:				
Fruit and vegetables	56.0	86.7	83.5	84.5
Rubber natural dry	51.1	72.7	27.2	44.7
Tea	308.4	594.6	654.9	702.5
Oilseeds	3.9	6.2	8.3	12.0

Source: Calculated by author from the FAOSTAT Database.

one million tonnes of soybean oil and three million tonnes of palm oil. The imports of cotton and pulses have reached US$315 million and US$387 million, respectively.

During 1991 to 2004, the export of rice, fruit, and vegetables has seen substantial growth. In the case of rice, a major boost to exports came from the domestic front in the removal of restrictions on the export of non-basmati rice. Rice exports crossed US$1 billion mark with the beginning of WTO. The later years of WTO membership turned out to be unfavourable for rice exports. In contrast, the exports of fruit and vegetables and cashew nuts have seen a smooth and steady growth, indicating the favourable impact of WTO.

Exports of oilcake, which was the most important item of agricultural exports during the early 1990s, has received a serious setback in the post WTO period, though there was some recovery during 2003 and 2004. Coffee exports more than doubled in the beginning years of the WTO compared to the quadrennium before 1995, but then faced very sharp decline. Tobacco and spices were big beneficiaries of liberalization but in the later years their export either stagnated or showed sluggish growth. India also exports some oilseeds and their export has risen steadily and crossed US$324 million in the recent years as against US$66 million before WTO. Exports of cotton had almost dried up during 1999–2002 when India had to import large quantity of cotton lint to meet its demand. Export of sugar has moved on a rising trend till 2002.

PAKISTAN

Pakistan witnessed a substantial increase in imports of fruit and vegetables, pulses, cotton and oilseeds and sharp fluctuations in imports of wheat, sugar, and vegetable oils (Table 12.4: Panel C). Cotton crop was badly affected even before WTO as its exports declined from more than US$322 million in early the 1990s to US$167 million by the quadrennium ending 1998, and imports increased from US$24 million to more than US$154 million. In the post-WTO period, imports increased further and exports declined sharply.

In recent years, Pakistan has succeeded in reducing its dependence on import of wheat and edible oil. A closer look at vegetable oil imports shows that this decrease is purely due to a decline in price, and the quantity of imports has remained almost the same. As is the case with India, the export of horticultural crops moved on a steadily rising trend. Rice exports remained above US$500 million after the early 1990s. Sugar exports show large swings.

NEPAL

Nepal's imports of major agricultural products, mainly fruit/vegetables and vegetable oil show substantial increases in the beginning of the WTO-years, after which there was a large decline. Rice imports have almost doubled in the post-WTO period while oilseeds imports increased sevenfold. The import of palm oil more than doubled whereas soybean oil shows a small decline. Sugar imports show a steady increase during the entire period after 1991 (Table 12.4: Panel D). Fruit and vegetable remained the largest export items, followed by pulses. In both cases, exports show a decline with the beginning of WTO but some recovery thereafter.

SRI LANKA

Sri Lanka spent more than US$100 million on the import of sugar and wheat in the early 1990s (Table 12.4: Panel E). Their imports went up with the beginning of WTO, then decreasing slightly. A similar trend is observed in the case of pulses and rice. The imports of milk and related products, pulses

Table 12.5. Share (per cent) of trade in GDP agriculture of SACs

Country	Trade	1991–4	1995–8	1999–2002	2003 and 2004
Bangladesh	Imports	7.8	13.2	12.9	18.0
	Exports	1.5	1.5	0.8	1.0
	Total trade	9.3	14.6	13.7	19.0
India	Imports	1.7	2.8	3.7	4.4
	Exports	3.9	5.7	5.2	5.9
	Total trade	5.6	8.4	8.9	10.3
Nepal	Imports	9.1	12.7	8.8	12.9
	Exports	3.2	2.8	2.9	5.8
	Total trade	12.3	15.5	11.7	18.7
Pakistan	Imports	13.7	15.9	10.8	11.6
	Exports	9.3	8.2	7.1	7.2
	Total trade	23.1	24.0	17.9	18.9
Sri Lanka	Imports	25.1	29.5	26.8	28.8
	Exports	26.5	34.9	30.3	35.4
	Total trade	51.6	64.4	57.1	64.2

Source: Calculated by author from the FAOSTAT Database, and ADB (various issues).

and oilseed cake saw significant increases in the initial years of WTO, followed by a slow increase in the post-WTO period.

Tea alone accounts for more than two-thirds of Sri Lankan agricultural exports, which almost doubled with the beginning of WTO. Exports continued to increase in later years, but at a slower rate. Rubber exports received a serious setback in the post-WTO period while on fruit and vegetable there was a small adverse impact.

12.2.2 *Trade Orientation of Agriculture*

The ratio of import, export, and total trade to GDP agriculture increased considerably in the beginning years of WTO in all the countries (see Table 12.5). In the post WTO period the share of trade showed an increase in India, Bangladesh, Nepal, and Sri Lanka and decline in the case of Pakistan.

During 2003 and 2004 trade constituted around 10 per cent of GDP agriculture in India, 19 per cent in the case of Nepal, Bangladesh, and Pakistan. Trade orientation of agriculture was very high in the case of Sri Lanka where trade constituted more than 60 per cent of GDP agriculture.

12.3 Trade Liberalization and Food Security

The relationship between food security and trade is quite complex and hardly uniform across countries. This relationship is determined by the choice of domestic policies and their effectiveness, production opportunities, infrastructure for commodity trade and exchange, comparative advantages and purchasing power of the people. It is because of this complexity of the relationship between trade and food security that there is no consensus in the literature on the impact of trade liberalization on food security. According to one school of thought, food self-sufficiency is essential for the food security of low-income countries as volatility in international prices can render them out of the reach of common people with small wages. This may not necessarily be the case for high-income people who have deep pockets. According to this view, temporary phase of low international prices should not be taken as a permanent opportunity and domestic capabilities of food production should be safeguarded in such times (Chand 2002).

It is also pointed out that a significant proportion of the population in SACs are not only dependent on agriculture for their livelihood, but also for survival in circumstances just around the poverty line. Therefore, it has been proposed that non-trade concerns such as maintenance of the livelihood of agrarian peasantry and the production of sufficient food to meet domestic needs are taken into consideration.

According to an alternative view, national self-sufficiency should not be confused with food security. It is believed that national self-sufficiency is neither necessary nor sufficient to guarantee food security at the individual level. In this context, the example of India is quite apt. Even though the country had 30 per cent of its grain production (more than 60 million tonnes) in public stock by the year 2000, every fourth Indian was reported to be undernourished and food insecure. This implies that entitlement and prices are very critical to food security.

According to this alternative stand, what a country needs is sufficient capacity to generate foreign exchange by specializing in goods based on the country's comparative advantage and importing what cannot be covered by domestic production (Panagariya 2002).

According to the first school of thought, an increase in imports to meet domestic demand adversely affects food self-sufficiency and, in turn, food security. According to the alternative view, imports should not be seen as having adverse impact on food security if they do not cause adverse effect on self reliance. The following section examines the impact of trade liberalization both on food self-sufficiency and self-reliance and then draws some inferences about impact of trade liberalization on food security.

12.3.1 *Impact on Self Sufficiency*

The impact on food self-sufficiency in the various SACs can be seen from the share of imports in domestic consumption. These estimates for major food commodities are given in Table 12.6 and for whole of food sector in Table 12.7.

Table 12.6. The dependence of selected SACs on imports for food (per cent)

Country	Cereal	Wheat	Rice	Sugar & sweeteners	Pulses	Vegetable oils	Vegetables	Fruit	Meat	Milk	Marine products, fish
India											
1991–4	0.37	0.81	0.17	2.33	4.45	5.73	0.01	0.35	0.01	0.06	0.04
1995–8	0.67	1.73	0.05	1.64	6.08	24.39	0.01	0.61	0.00	0.04	2.40
1999–2002	0.30	0.59	0.05	1.38	10.66	47.89	0.08	0.74	0.00	0.08	1.38
Pakistan											
1991–4	11.02	13.04	0.17	6.03	22.65	98.04	0.84	1.34	0.00	0.71	0.00
1995–8	11.99	14.34	0.05	6.25	20.86	95.40	2.00	2.08	0.01	0.52	0.00
1999–2002	5.39	6.44	0.33	12.86	36.37	88.40	2.55	3.19	0.01	0.36	0.00
Sri Lanka											
1991–4	40.51	100.78	9.00	76.03	60.23	101.39	10.52	1.60	1.04	49.24	0.01
1995–8	47.18	104.67	11.44	89.13	79.41	166.15	17.32	3.47	1.89	57.88	0.00
1999–2002	41.65	102.98	5.13	98.88	94.32	199.13	21.20	6.87	2.17	64.29	0.01
Nepal											
1991–4	1.15	1.25	1.90	26.68	11.79	58.13	0.19	0.96	0.00	1.65	100.00
1995–8	1.19	0.66	1.97	23.71	4.29	62.16	2.57	1.07	0.00	0.17	100.00
1999–2002	2.21	1.27	3.27	29.37	11.17	89.49	0.42	1.88	0.05	1.41	100.00
Bangladesh											
1991–4	6.26	54.57	0.17	7.30	12.10	70.50	5.90	2.38	0.19	16.35	0.18
1995–8	9.96	48.60	4.43	15.25	8.10	95.59	2.87	6.75	0.21	11.65	0.54
1999–2002	12.55	62.36	4.04	32.98	25.00	120.49	3.77	8.61	0.06	18.31	19.97

Source: Calculated by author based on data from the FAOSTAT Database.

Table 12.7. The dependence on import for food: aggregate

Country	1991–4	1995–8	1999–2002
India	0.89	2.02	3.76
Pakistan	8.46	8.12	7.45
Bangladesh	9.20	13.57	17.87
Sri Lanka	34.47	41.08	43.24
Nepal	2.89	2.93	4.87

Notes: Aggregation based on weighted average of selected commodities using prices as weight; Imports exceeding domestic consumption, observed in the case of vegetable oil, are considered to constitute maximum domestic consumption.

Source: Calculated by author from the FAOSTAT Database.

India's reliance on imports to meet domestic demand for cereals, fruit, vegetables, and milk remained quite low, less than 1 per cent of demand during the twelve-year period between 1991 and 2002. With the beginning of WTO-tenure, fruit imports started to increase and gained momentum over time but have remained below one per cent of total fruit intake. Dependence on sugar imports to meet domestic demand declined to less than 1.5 per cent with the implementation of WTO AoA.

The dependence on imports increased sharply for pulses, doubling in the last twelve years, and very heavily for vegetable oil. More than 10 per cent of pulses consumed in India are now imported. Imports met less than 6 per cent of vegetable oil used for food before WTO. This increased to 24 per cent in the initial years of WTO and is now approaching half of the total vegetable oil demand in India, forcing the country to import more than four million tonnes to meet domestic demand. With liberalization there has been small increase in fish imports but still remaining below 2.5 per cent.

Pakistan witnessed a decline in import dependence for cereals from more than 10 per cent prior to 1998 to 5.4 per cent in the post-WTO period. Reliance on imported vegetable oil also declined but is still very high, above 88 per cent. Between the quadrennium 1991 to 1994 and 1998 to 2002, the share of imported food items in domestic consumption increased from 6 per cent to 12 per cent for sugar, 23 per cent to 36 per cent for pulses, 1.3 per cent to 3.9 per cent for fruit and for vegetables from less than 1 per cent to more than 2.5 per cent.

Sri Lanka's import dependence indicates a tremendous increase for all food products except cereals, for which import reliance initially increased with the beginning of WTO but then dropped back to the level of the early 1990s. Imported cereals constitute more than 40 per cent of cereal consumption. The country's almost entire demand for sugar, 64 per cent of the milk demand, and 20 per cent of the vegetable demand are met from imports. The import of vegetable oils is double the level of consumption, perhaps a reflection of the fact some vegetable oil is used for industrial purposes and some is diverted to

India via Sri Lanka, as Sri Lanka has much lower tariff than India and the free trade pact between the two countries is favourable for such trade deflection.

Nepal was not a member of WTO during the period under review, but has been affected by changes in agriculture brought about by WTO and globalization, particularly in its neighbouring country, India, which accounts for an overwhelming share of Nepal's trade. Highest share of imported items in food intake is for vegetable oil which has increased from 58 per cent in the early 1990s to 89 per cent in the post-WTO period. Sugar is another food item whose import dependence is quite high (29.4 per cent). Reliance on imported cereals and fruit indicates a rising trend, though around two per cent, it is low. For other products, imports witnessed a decline with the implementation of WTO but increased during the post-WTO period.

Table 12.6 shows a considerable increase for Bangladesh in imports for most food products after the early 1990s. Share of imported food items in domestic consumption increased from 6.2 per cent before WTO to 10 per cent in the initial years of WTO. This dependency increased further to 12.55 per cent in the post-WTO years. The share of imports in sugar consumption has more than doubled every four years. Similarly, the dependence on imported pulses has doubled from 12.1 per cent before WTO to more than 25 per cent in the post-WTO period. Imports of vegetable oil were as high as 70 per cent of domestic demand during 1991 to 1994, increasing after mid-1995 to 95.6 per cent. Currently vegetable oil imports are 20 per cent higher than consumption. The country has also seen an increased import content in the domestic demand for fruit, milk, and marine products.

There were concerns that trade liberalization would result in increased dependence on food import. Actual experience shows that in all SACs the reliance on imports has increased very sharply for vegetable oil, and almost half of all requirements are met through imports. Even high tariff rates could not deter the import increase. The reason is that price of palm oil is very low compared to vegetable oils produced in SACs. Though other vegetable oils are considered to be of better quality, the general populations have attached greater weight to price than quality. Dependence on imports has also increased for pulses in all SACs except Nepal. The results vary across countries for other commodities. India has guarded effectively against the import of cereals, fruit and dairy products in the post-WTO period by with high tariffs, or in some instances, non-tariff measures. Pakistan and Sri Lanka could manage the same only in the case of cereals, and thus experienced increased import dependency on the part of all other foods. Bangladesh and Nepal have seen moderate to sharp increases in their import dependence of most food items.

Calculations on India's import dependence for total food show that the country met less than one per cent of its domestic food demand from abroad before WTO. During initial years of WTO this dependence increased to about

2 per cent (Table 12.7). In the post-WTO period pertaining to the years 1999 to 2002, there was a sharp decline in food self-sufficiency.

In the case of Nepal, the dependency on imports for food increased from 2.9 per cent in the pre-WTO period to 4.87 per cent in the post-WTO period. Food self-sufficiency in Bangladesh has suffered a sharp decline since 1995, and has met close to 18 per cent of its food requirement from imports in the recent years compared to 9.2 per cent in the pre-WTO period.

Sri Lanka was affected by low food self-sufficiency already in the pre-WTO period, as more than one-third of its food demands were met from imports. With the WTO-led trade liberalization, its dependence on imports accelerated further and is around 43 per cent. Pakistan, on the other hand, is the only nation among all SACs where food self-sufficiency has seen slight improvement since the beginning of WTO.

These results imply that if self-sufficiency is used as an indicator of food security, then with the progress of trade liberalization, food security has suffered a significant decrease in all SACs except Pakistan.

12.3.2 *Impact on Self-Reliance*

It is often asserted that trade liberalization promotes the allocation of resources based on comparative advantage. According to this logic, a country benefits, or improves its self-reliance, by specializing in the production of goods in which it has comparative advantage and imports items in which it does not have comparative advantage. This implies that trade liberalization provides opportunities to increase exports which can be used to finance imports. Based on this reasoning, two simple indicators of self-reliance are estimated. The first indicator is net trade, that is, excess of exports over imports. This indicator is further refined by taking the ratio of net trade to GDP agriculture. The second indicator is taken as ratio of imports to exports to determine percentage of exports needed to finance imports.

The pattern of the two indicators of self-sufficiency discussed above can be seen from Table 12.8. Out of the five SACs, only India and Sri Lanka have positive net trade in agriculture whereas the other three countries have negative agricultural trade balance. Net earnings from agriculture increased in the case of India from 2.2 per cent of GDP agriculture in pre-WTO period to 2.90 per cent in the initial phase of WTO. In the post-WTO period, the ratio of net trade in GDP declined to 1.28 per cent. Similarly, India spent only 43 per cent of its export earnings to finance imports during 1991–4. During 1999 to 2004, more than 72 per cent of export earnings were used for meeting agricultural imports. Thus, both the indicators of self-reliance reveal sharp decline in the post-WTO period.

In the case of Bangladesh, agriculture imports exceeded exports and trade deficit was 6.46 per cent of GDP agriculture in the pre-WTO period. With the

Table 12.8. Self-reliance in agriculture, measured as the ratio of net trade to GDP and the ratio of imports to exports

Country	Aspect %	1991–4	1995–8	1999–2002
India	Net trade/GDP	2.22	2.90	1.28
	Imports/exports	43.31	48.78	72.72
Bangladesh	Net trade/GDP	–6.26	–11.70	–12.47
	Imports/exports	517.99	900.64	1547.56
Nepal	Net trade/GDP	–5.96	–9.87	–7.06
	Imports/exports	288.16	452.76	332.65
Pakistan	Net trade/GDP	–4.38	–7.68	–5.00
	Imports/exports	146.89	193.91	170.07
Sri Lanka	Net trade/GDP	1.44	5.44	6.98
	Imports/exports	94.57	84.42	79.10

Source: Calculated by author from the FAOSTAT Database and ADB (various issues).

implementation of the WTO Agreement, this deficit increased to 11.7 per cent of GDP agriculture and has in recent years increased further. For comparison, the agricultural imports for Bangladesh were only five times its export during 1991–4. The value of imports has increased to more than fifteen times the value of imports since the implementation of trade liberalization.

Nepal's and Pakistan's trade deficits have increased faster than GDP agriculture between the pre-WTO and the initial years of WTO. After 1998, the ratio of trade deficit to GDP declined somewhat but has remained higher than what it was in the pre-WTO period. Sri Lanka is the only country in South Asia that was able to improve its self-reliance in agriculture after WTO-related trade liberalization.

12.3.3 *Trade Liberalization and Agriculture Growth*

Growth in GDP agriculture is an important and all encompassing indicator of the performance of the farming sector. Annual agricultural GDP growth rates for the different SACs during 1992 to 2003 are given in Figure 12.1. In order to give a better picture, the growth rates were computed from three yearly moving average series of GDP agriculture, as annual series showed considerable fluctuation. Growth rates are given as the per cent change over the previous year.

As can be seen from Figure 12.1, the agriculture GDP growth rate shows a sharp deceleration in Bangladesh, India, and Sri Lanka. In the case of Pakistan there was a deceleration with the beginning of WTO but growth rates have recovered in the post-WTO period. Agriculture growth rate in Nepal remained unaffected by trade liberalization and WTO.

In contrast to agriculture, growth rates of total and non-agricultural GDP during the post liberalization period show significant rise. This is widening disparities in income of workers in non-agriculture and agriculture sectors and

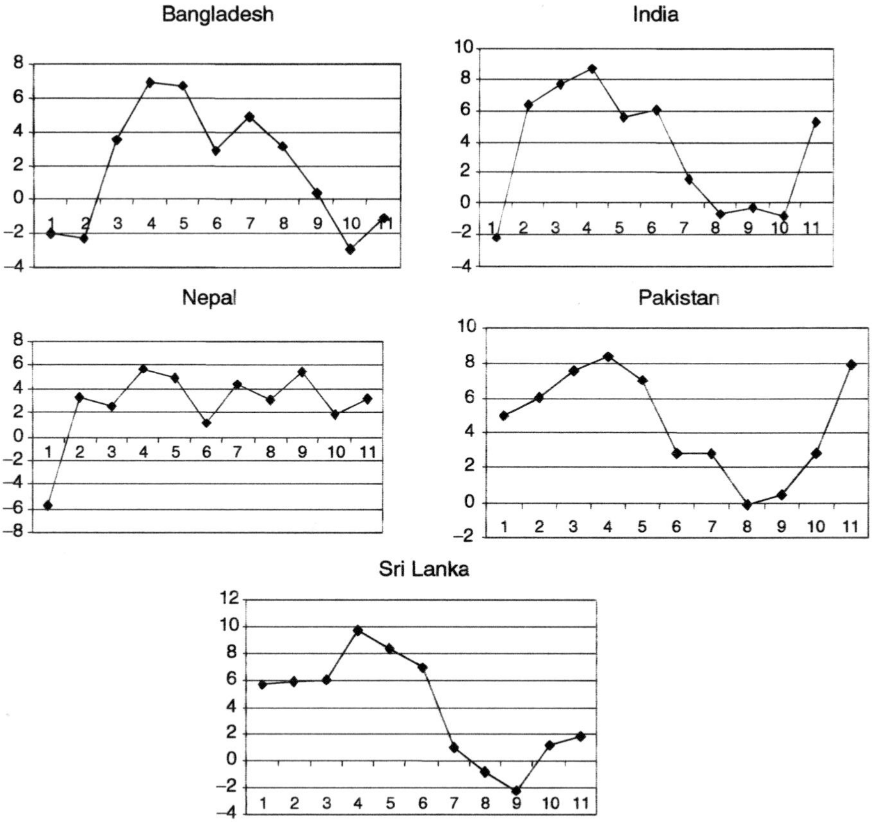

Figure 12.1. Agricultural GDP growth rates for selected SACs, 1992–2003
Source: Computed by author from the FAOSTAT Database.

also adversely affecting the welfare of the majority of the population of South Asia that is dependent on agriculture. For instance, in India, the ratio of per worker income in non-agriculture and agriculture sectors increased from 3.52 around 1991 to 5.2 around 2001. It has also been brought out by some studies that incidence of undernutrition has increased during 1993–4 and 1999–2000. The sluggish growth of agriculture is also resulting into agrarian distress in most parts of South Asia.

12.4 Volatility in Domestic and International Prices

International agricultural prices generally exhibit a cyclical pattern and are characterized by high volatility. A comparison of volatility in international

Table 12.9. Instability in domestic and international prices of selected food commodities

Commodity	Bangladesh	India	Nepal	Pakistan	Sri Lanka	International
Rice	0.124	0.126	0.129		0.099	0.145
Maize	0.122		0.148			0.177
Wheat		0.064		0.093		0.163
Groundnut		0.102				0.198
Rapeseed		0.086		0.181		
Coconut		0.195			0.227	0.266

Note: Instability in series, say (Y), was measured as std dev. of [$Ln(Y_{t+1}/Y_t)$]
Source: Calculated by author from the FAOSTAT Database.

prices and domestic prices in SACs for selected food products during 1991 to 2002 is shown in Table 12.9. Instability in international prices is higher than domestic prices in all SACs for all the selected commodities.

If international price shocks are transmitted to the domestic market, it would destabilize crop patterns and supply, and would cause uncertainty in crop incomes. Based on a comprehensive analysis of international and Indian prices in the last fifty years, Chand and Jha (2001) observe that government intervention has been quite effective in insulating domestic prices from the effect of instability in international prices in developing countries like India. This implies that unregulated and free trade would impart instability to domestic prices and there is strong case to regulate trade to maintain price stability. While domestic production must compete with the trend level of international prices, it must be protected against instability. One way to do so is to impose variable tariffs that restore level of current import prices to a long-term trend.

12.5 Implementation of the Uruguay Round AoA and Issues for Negotiations

Implementation of the UR AoA has been a mixed blessing for SACs. It helped to create a favourable environment for trade reforms and for initiating trade liberalization, which were considered highly desirable for these countries. However, what was projected as the benefits from AoA for the SACs and expectations based on that did not come true.

12.5.1 *Domestic Support*

Domestic policies in the SACs have been such that domestic prices of major agricultural produce were kept lower than global prices. This resulted in negative product-specific support or net taxation on agriculture. These countries provide some non-product specific support through subsidizing inputs like fertilizer, irrigation, power and credit supplied to agriculture. The magnitude of non-product specific support remained smaller compared to the negative product-specific support, which rendered the aggregate measure of support (AMS) negative for these countries. So far AMS in SACs remained within permissible, de minimus, level of support as per the UR AoA.

Agriculture in South Asia is in a transitional stage. Large segments are still underdeveloped and thus, in the initial stages, require considerable government assistance in order to harness its potential and for development. Huge investments are required in infrastructure and institutional development, as farmers are generally resource poor and do not have the capital to invest in agriculture. Markets are not well developed, and government intervention is needed to ensure a remunerative price environment that would lead to the adoption of improved technology. Therefore, SACs need provisions for product-specific as well as nonproduct-specific support for agriculture. Agriculture also has special needs that require assistance in the form of infrastructure development, research, extension, insurance, and market development. SACs need the Green Box subsidies for providing such assistance.

In a liberalized trade regime, competitiveness is affected by policies both on the domestic scene and the international scene. In this context it is important to see the various provisions of domestic support used by other countries. OECD countries particularly, EU members, USA, Canada, and Japan provide huge subsidies to their farmers in various forms that give their production an advantageous position *vis-à-vis* farmers in developing countries. Moreover, Green and Blue Box subsidies have been used to compensate for any reduction in the Amber Box subsidy. This support enables developed-country farmers to reduce production costs and offer produce at lower prices, resulting in the developing countries being disadvantaged in exports and in competing with imports.

There is no justification for the developed countries to provide such support because their agricultural sector is highly commercialized and at an advanced stage of development. Infrastructure and markets are well developed and farmers are resourceful and capable of operating without government assistance. Therefore, in the new AoA, the developed countries should disallowed from providing Amber or Blue Box support. Some well-defined measures could be considered under the Green Box option but their level should be capped to avoid misuse, as has been done in the past.

12.5.2 *Market Access*

In the area of market access SACs have supported their commitments by (i) replacing nontariff border measures with tariffs, (ii) removing quantitative restrictions (QRs) and (iii) liberalizing their trade by lowering applied

Table 12.10. Changes in tariff barriers on primary products in SACs with WTO

Country	Year	Simple mean %	Weighted mean %
Bangladesh	1989	79.9	53.5
	1999	21.1	21.0
	2004	16.2	12.7
India	1990	69.6	26.0
	1997	25.7	22.6
	2004	29.0	36.9
Nepal	1993	15.7	14.2
	1998	16.2	12.0
	2004	13.9	9.3
Pakistan	1995	46.3	24.0
	1998	42.7	26.2
	2004	14.7	9.4
Sri Lanka	1993	24.2	23.0
	1997	24.0	20.7
	2004	14.4	8.0

Source: World Bank (various years).

tariffs, even though these were below the bound rates, as can be seen from Table 12.10. Bangladesh bound its tariff on agricultural imports at 200 per cent with the exception of a few commodities with 150 per cent and 50 per cent tariff. Against this, the average applied tariff has been brought down to 16.2 per cent and 12.7 per cent by the year 2004, as compared to 79.9 per cent and 53.5 per cent, respectively in 1989. India has mainly three bands of bound tariffs; 100–104 per cent for raw products such as cereals, most fruit and vegetables, as well as oilseeds and pulses; 150 per cent for semiprocessed items (tea, chicken, wheat flour) and 300 per cent for processed products like vegetable oils, fats. There is some deviation from these broad norms for certain individual products. The simple mean and weighted average of applied tariffs on agricultural imports was 69.5 per cent and 26.0 per cent respectively during 1990; these rates were reduced to 25.7 per cent and 22.6 per cent by 1997. Pakistan bound its agricultural import tariffs at 100 per cent for most products, but the bound tariff for wheat, sugar and tea was 150 per cent. Its applied tariffs during 1995, given as a simple mean and weighted mean were 46.3 and 24.0 per cent; currently tariff rates are 14.7 and 9.4 per cent. Sri Lanka was first among the SACs to initiate trade liberalization and progressively brought down its tariff rates even before WTO. Accordingly, it bound all its tariff rates at 50 per cent. Applied tariff rates were around 24 per cent during 1993, which have been reduced to 14.4 per cent on simple mean basis and 8.3 per cent on weighted mean basis.

Bound tariff in all SACs except Sri Lanka are very high on certain items. There is no justification to have bound tariffs above 100 per cent, as this would provide adequate protection even when international prices drop.

The liberalization of trade and the removal of QRs in the initial years of implementation of WTO agreement did not cause much difficulty because international prices of bulk products were quite high during the first three years. Subsequently, as international prices declined to a very low level and developed countries responded by granting huge subsidies to their producers, South Asian agriculture faced severe difficulties. Domestic production of staples also experienced the threat of disruption, and some countries resorted to desperate measures to deter cheap imports. This experience highlights the important lesson that due to the high volatility in international prices, the SACs are unable to safeguard domestic production against imports with the standard tariff measures if and when global prices drop to very low levels. In order to deal with similar situations, the SACs either need to bind their tariffs at very high levels so that applied tariffs can be raised appropriately, or, to initiate special safeguards to regulate imports of sensitive products.

Setbacks to exports occur because of poor or reduced access in other countries' markets. Developed countries have very high bound tariffs for selected products and they also have special safeguards to prevent the imports of certain products (WTO 2002). Some countries have variable tariffs, which rise in response to a fall in prices. All these measures reduce access to developed-country markets. If these measures fail, then at times sanitary and phytosanitary measures (SPS) are invoked without justification to check imports. Based on this experience, the strategy of the SACs should focus on seeking reasonable protection for their markets and greater access to developed-country markets.

12.5.3 *Export Competition and Subsidies*

The EU and USA, representatives of the major trading group, along with 23 other countries can subsidize exports. EU export subsidies in particularly have caused concern to the developing countries. Among SACs, Pakistan occasionally resorts to freight subsidies on fruit and vegetables, or undertakes state trading for cotton and rice. At times, concession is provided on export credit (Khan 2003). Sri Lanka provides limited subsidies for some agricultural exports and duty concessions for exporters on the import of capital goods. The Sri Lanka Export Credit Insurance Corporation provides export insurance and guarantee service for the development of exports (Kelegama 2003). India provides income tax exemptions on profits from agricultural exports, as well as domestic and international freight subsidies for some exported commodities. Bangladesh also extends assistance to agricultural exports in the form of concessional interest rates and export credit guarantee. SACs provide only indirect support on some agricultural exports on some agricultural exports permitted within the UR AoA. These do not parallel the direct export subsidies provided by the industrialized countries (Gulati 2003).

Among the SACs, there is no deviating from the issue of export subsidies. These countries should make a strong plea for immediate and complete elimination of export subsidies as these are highly trade distorting. Due to underdeveloped infrastructure, markets and trade institutions in the SACs, government intervention at times in terms of measures to provide freight subsidy, incur certain marketing costs or promote export incentives during initial stages become essential in order to develop export potential. SACs need to seek exemption in these as a part of their special and differential (S&D) treatment.

12.5.4 *State Trading Enterprises*

State trading enterprises (STEs) have played an important role in all SACs in creating a remunerative price environment for producers that has resulted in output growth, commercialized promotion of agricultural trade and an improvement in food security. The main functions of a STE include price administration, procurement and the sale of a significant part of domestic production, the maintenance of commodity stock, and monopoly in imports and exports. Some STE functions are considered trade-distorting, while most are of regulatory and promotional nature.

There has been considerable change in the role of STEs and their importance in the recent past. Bangladesh has considerably diminished the role of the Bangladesh Food and Allied Corporation, Trading Corporation of Bangladesh and other parastatals during the 1990s, but the country maintains a national foodstock under the public foodgrain distribution system. In Pakistan, an increasing number of the functions of PASCO are being commercialized and STEs like Rice Export Corporation, Cotton Export Corporation and Trading Corporation of Pakistan are operating on a commercial principle. Sri Lanka has couple of STEs in the food sector. The Cooperative Wholesale Establishment (CWE) is the major STE entrusted with the task of price stabilization and food security. CWE undertakes the bulk purchase of agriculture commodities and imports wheat with exclusive trading right. Market intervention role of CWE and other STE has diminished over time (Kelegama 2003). The Food Corporation of India (FCI) plays a predominant role in price administration of wheat and paddy/rice through bulk purchases of marketed surplus at pre-determined prices, the maintenance of large stocks and the release of stock for public distribution, for the open market and, of late, for exports. FCI has the cereal-import monopoly; this was partly lifted in 1999 and shortly re-instated after cheap imports glutted India's coastal areas despite adequate stocks in government warehouses. India has virtually eliminated the function of several other STEs in the imports and exports of vegetable oil, cotton, sugar, etc.

In the long run, it is in the interests of SACs to reduce the role of STEs and to promote private enterprise in agricultural marketing and trade. However, the global market is unreliable for meeting the food-security concerns of the low-income populations of South Asia because of price volatility, the strong hold of commodity cartels over global trade, and the international market's limited capacity to absorb major supply-and-demand shocks. Therefore the SACs need the state trading enterprises address food-security concerns, particularly of weaker sections of society. But these STEs should play a minimalist role, and should operate without either domestic or international trade monopolies along with private trade.

12.6 Summing up

The policy of trade liberalization as followed by the SACs, particularly since implementation of the WTO Agreement in 1995, has considerably increased their dependence on imports for meeting food requirements. All SACs, with the exception of Sri Lanka, indicate a deterioration in agricultural self-reliance in the post-WTO period. The deterioration is a reflection of the much higher growth in food imports than in the growth in agricultural exports because domestic production of the SACs, even after high tariffs, cannot compete with cheap imports. Furthermore, their exports faced stiff competition in global markets. The underlying reason for both developments was an unexpectedly low level of international prices.

The subsidies in OECD countries have a major impact on the level of international prices and market distortions. Thus, the SACs need to adopt an agenda that leads to a reduction in production subsidies, and in support and export subsidies, as all of these cause distortions and low prices on the global markets. This would eliminate the possibility of import threats for several products, and prospects for exports could improve.

One of the reasons for deceleration in agriculture growth in SACs is the deterioration in agricultural terms of trade resulting from low international prices. SACs need to safeguard their farmers against price shocks that can have an adverse impact on production. This can be done with special safeguards to check large-scale imports of cheap goods.

Trade has an important role in food security, as it offers the possibility of stabilizing domestic prices, to balance food deficiency, and to harness comparative advantage. In fact, satisfying a small fraction of demand through trade can have a positive impact on improving the efficiency of domestic production and thus should not be seen as a threat to domestic producers. However, domestic capacity for food production should not be stifled by the dependence on trade. The SACs need to strike a balance between food self-sufficiency and trade, by carefully evaluating the diverging crop production across countries.

Per capita income in SACs is quite low and more than half of household expenditure is spent on food. A vast majority of the population is not able to absorb volatility and shocks in the international markets. Therefore, these countries need to pursue food self-sufficiency, particularly for main staples, to maintain food security until such a time that the per capita incomes increase. This necessitates that domestic capacity in food production be strengthened and developed further in an efficient manner so that the domestic produce is competitive with normal international prices.

References

ADB (various issues). *Key Indicators of Developing Asian and Pacific Countries*. Manila: Asian Development Bank.

Chand, R. (2002). *WTO, Trade Liberalization and Indian Agriculture*. New Delhi: Mittal Publications.

____ D. Jha (2001). 'Trade Liberalization, Agricultural Prices and Social Welfare', in S. S Acharya and D. P. Chaudhri (eds.), *Indian Agricultural Policy at the Crossroads*. Jaipur: Rawat Publications.

Dowlah, C. A. F. (2003). 'Bangladesh', in M. D. Ingco (ed.), *Agriculture, Trade and WTO in South Asia*. Washington, DC: World Bank.

Gulati, A. (2003). 'India', in M. D. Ingco (ed.), *Agriculture, Trade and WTO in South Asia*. Washington, DC: World Bank.

Kelegama, S. (2003). 'Sri Lanka', in M. D. Ingco (ed.), *Agriculture, Trade and WTO in South Asia*. Washington, DC: World Bank.

Khan, S. (2003). 'Pakistan', in M. D. Ingco (ed.), *Agriculture, Trade and WTO in South Asia*. Washington, DC: World Bank.

Panagariya, A. (2003). 'Trade Liberalization and Food Security: Conceptual Links', in *Trade Reforms and Food Security*. Rome: FAO, 25–42.

World Bank (various years). *World Development Indicators*. Washington, DC: World Bank.

WTO (2002). 'Special Agriculture Safeguard'. Background Paper by the Secretariat. G/AG/NG/S/9/Rev.1. Rome: WTO.

13

Does the WTO Agreement on Agriculture Endanger Food Security in Sub-Saharan Africa?

Samuel K. Gayi

13.1 Introduction

The use and application of the concept *food security* changed significantly with the seminal work of Sen (1981) on the causes of famine. The concept of *entitlement* (the means or the ability to access food) rather than aggregate food supplies has since been critical to the food security debate. The Food and Agriculture Organization (FAO) and the World Bank introduced a dynamic perspective to this concept when they defined it as the access by all people at all times to nutritious food for an active and healthy life (FAO 1996c; World Bank 1986; see also Sen 1981; Drèze and Sen 1989; Maxwell 1989; Schulthes 1994). And guided by this long-term framework, the World Bank (1986: 1) identifies two types of food insecurity: chronic and transitory.

In most developing countries, an important determinant of food security is food production. This is because most of the food-insecure people live in rural areas, earn a substantial share of their income from agriculture, and meet a significant share of their food requirements directly from their own food production (Salih 1994: 7; Maxwell 1996: 157; FAO 1996d: 3). Experiences of the famine that ravaged Africa in the mid-1980s have, however, exposed the dynamic and long-term notion entailed in the concept. The overriding concern of these famine victims was not only short-term access to food, but also the preservation of their assets, future livelihoods, and resilience to future shocks (Maxwell 1996: 1578) primarily defined within the *food production* framework thereby emphasizing food self-sufficiency. On the other hand, the notion of food security for the non-rural (urban) households, who do not meet most of their food needs from own agricultural production, would generally entail not only the ability to command access to food, but also the availability of food supply in the long term. Central to this second interpretation is the notion of *food availability* in which food imports could play a significant role, as the major concern in this scenario is food self-reliance.

In a recent work, the FAO acknowledges that food security is a multifaceted concept, which incorporates the availability of adequate food supplies at the global and national levels as well as the principle of all people at all times having economic access to adequate and nutritious food (FAO 2003b: 25–9), thereby emphasizing the stability of both access to, and availability of, food.

The WTO Agreement on Agriculture (AoA), thus, clearly has implications for food security in poor countries of Africa, as it is aimed at attaining enhanced liberalization in international agricultural trade in three main policy areas: domestic support, export subsidies and border measures.[1] Full implementation by developed countries of the three reduction commitments embodied in the AoA was expected to lead to increased variability in world food prices and world food price increases (Greenfield *et al.* 1996; UNCTAD 1995b), although with significant regional differences (Africa, for example, was expected to increase its dependence on food imports: Greenfield *et al.* 1996).

The objective of this chapter is to examine the state of food security in Sub-Saharan Africa (SSA) during the period 1990–2002 within the context of the AoA, and suggest a policy framework for improving food security in the region. It attempts to find answers to the following questions:

(i) Are there identifiable changes in the food security situation (and in domestic food production) in SSA countries in the post-Uruguay Round (UR) period?

(ii) If so, could these be explained by the WTO AoA?

(iii) What domestic policy options under the Agreement are available for these countries to improve their food security situation?

(iv) What improvements in the Agreement (within the framework of the on-going negotiations in agriculture) are likely to safeguard food security in net food importing/deficit countries in SSA?

The chapter attempts to identify trends in the food security situation of SSA based on selected indicators: for example, food import dependence; food import capacity; and daily energy supplies (or, calories per capita per day). These are supplemented by an analysis of selected indicators of nutritional wellbeing such as nutritional levels, under-five mortality rate and life

[1] This has spawned a wide range of literature on the potential impact of the Agreement on the prices of food imports; and on the agricultural production. See, for example, Greenfield *et al.* (1996); Hamilton and Whalley (1995); Konandreas and Greenfield (1996); Lindland (1997); UNCTAD (1995a, 1995b), and FAO (1996a, 1996b, 1996c, 1996d, 1999, 2003a, 2003b).

expectancy. It also analyses the trend in food aid levels since 1990. Issues of intra-household food security and the differential impact of the AoA on urban and rural households are not examined, as a serious analysis of these would require more disaggregated data.

It argues that considering the large rural farming population in those SSA countries with both static and dynamic comparative advantage in agriculture, it may be advisable for them to pursue policies towards food self-sufficiency as a means of attaining food security—at least until such a time when international trade in agriculture is fully integrated into the WTO disciplines—for four main reasons. First, the agricultural sector has large multiplier effects in these economies; second, it is a major source of livelihoods and income for the majority of the populations living in rural areas; third, agricultural development is the best means of preserving the livelihoods (entitlements) of the rural poor as well as developing the rural areas; and fourth, arguably, current agricultural production structures in SSA have evolved in response to agricultural protectionism in the north (i.e. distorted price signals) and might require a transitional period to (re)adjust liberalized trade in agriculture. Those SSA countries that lack comparative advantage in agriculture may want to aim for a food self-reliance strategy (i.e. meeting most of their food requirements through imports) to attain food security.

The study is structured as follows. Section 13.2 briefly discusses the concept of food security and the main elements of the AoA, while the relationship between trade liberalization and food security is examined in section 13.3. The food security situation in SSA in the post-UR era is discussed in section 13.4. This is followed by an investigation into the permissible policy options contained in the AoA that could be utilized by SSA to attain its food security (or agricultural) objectives; and an exploration of improvements in the AoA (within the context of the Doha Round on the ongoing negotiations in agriculture) likely to safeguard food security in SSA is given in section 13.5. The last section presents some concluding remarks.

13.2 Main Elements of the WTO Agreement on Agriculture[2]

Agricultural trade is one of five new areas[3] included in the agenda of the UR of trade negotiations. The concluded WTO AoA was expected to initiate a process of greater liberalization in international agricultural trade, as it

[2] Negotiations within the framework of the Doha Round are not directly addressed here as most of the issues are still under negotiation. For progress on these issues, see WTO (2004) (for July 2004 Package), UNCTAD (2004), and Laird *et al.* (2004) (for an analysis of the issues involved for developing countries).

[3] The other new areas are: services, intellectual property rights, investment measures, and trade in textiles and clothing, which had hitherto been conducted within the framework of the multi-fibre arrangement (MFA).

brought the sector under the disciplines of the General Agreement on Tariffs and Trade (GATT). It aims at attaining enhanced transparency in three main areas: market access, domestic support and subsidies. Specifically, developed and developing countries are to reduce tariffs by at least 15 per cent and 10 per cent, respectively, on particular products (*market access*); all indirect subsidies to agriculture are to be restrained (domestic support); while *export subsidies* are to be rationalized and reduced (see Table 13.1, and Table 13.8 later).

The least developed countries (LDCs), two-thirds of which are in SSA, are required—like other countries—to 'tariffy' non-tariff barriers (NTBs) and bind their tariffs, although within a longer timeframe. Unlike other countries, however, they are exempted from all reduction commitments. Additional special and differential treatment (S&D) measures with respect to the implementation of the AoA are provided for the LDCs and a group of net food-importing countries, which includes almost all countries in SSA,[4] in two ministerial decisions and declarations annexed to the main agreements.[5] Some of these measures are taken up in section 13.5 on policies.

13.3 Trade Liberalization and Food Security in SSA

The link between trade policy (or liberalization) and food security is complex, and can be better assessed in country-specific or regional contexts. For food-importing countries, changes in trade policy orientation could have a significant impact on their foreign exchange earnings, and therefore have critical implications for their food security situation. In SSA, for example, the relative ease of collecting taxes on international trade as well as the lack of alternative 'tax handles' have increased governments' dependence on taxes levied on imports and exports. This makes total revenues highly vulnerable to changes in the value of export earnings (UNCTAD 2003) (stemming from changes to trade policy orientations) which could jeopardize food security. Trade policy changes in these countries may also have positive or negative implications for rural incomes, depending in particular on how these changes impact on the country's main agricultural exports, and on domestic food prices. In countries where these changes encourage economic activities in the tradeable sector, they could in time be expected to lead to increased income for primary crop producers in rural areas, particularly if other government

[4] As of July 1999, five SSA countries (Botswana, Côte d'Ivoire, Kenya, Senegal, and Mauritius) were on this list in addition to the 33 African LDCs. Note that Senegal has since then been classified as an LDC.

[5] These are the 'Decision on Measures in Favour of Least Developed Countries' and the 'Decision on Measures Concerning the Possible Negative Effects of the Reform programme on Least Developed and Net Food-Importing Developing Countries'.

Table 13.1. Summary of selected provisions in the WTO Agreement on Agriculture

	Rules	Liberalization	Safeguards	Special treatment
Market access	(i) 'Tariffy' of all NTBs (ii) Bind all tariffs (iii) No new NTBs	(i) Cut overall tariffs by 36% over 6 years (1995–2000); developing countries by 24% over 10 years (1995–2004) (ii) Minimum tariff cut by 15%; developing countries by 10%	(i) Guaranteed current or minimum access (ii) Protection against import surges	(i) No reduction by LDCs (ii) Longer implementation period of tariffication (10 years)
Domestic support	Specify 'amber' type and 'green box' policies	Reduce total outlays (calculated as aggregate measure of support during base period of 1986–8) on 'amber' policies by 20% over 6 years. Developing countries to reduce by 13.3% over 10 years	'Green box' policies can continue	(i) *De minimis* rule (i.e. product and non-product specific domestic subsidy excluded if less than 10% of value of agricultural production) (ii) Decoupled support payment excluded (iii) Extra exemptions for developing countries and LDCs (S&D measures)
Export subsidy	(i) Commodity-specific categorization of assistance (ii) No new subsidies on other commodities	(i) Reduce expenditure by 36% (base period, 1986 = 100) in equal instalments over 6 years; developing countries over 10 years (ii) Reduce volume of subsidized imports by 21% (base year, 1986 = 90) over 6 years; developing countries to reduce by 14% over 10 years	(i) Adhere to food aid rules (ii) Export credit provisions and guarantees	Internal transport and marketing costs exempted for developing countries and LDCs

Notes: S&D—Special and differential treatment; LDCs—Least developed countries.

Sources: GATT (1994) and WTO (1995).

policies do not interfere with the transmission mechanism of border prices and if there is a positive supply response.

The aggregate impact of changes in trade policy on the food security of a particular country would depend on the relevant strategy pursued: food self-reliance or food self-sufficiency. Self-reliance in food is when a country pursues an externally oriented trade regime with a view to earning enough from its exports of goods and services to finance its food requirements. On the other hand, the food self-sufficiency approach entails the country meeting its food requirements—or a substantial part of it—from domestic production.

In situations where countries are prone to terms-of-trade (ToT) losses that reduce their purchasing power (foreign exchange earnings), greater external orientation could increase variability in food supplies, thus creating conditions that threaten food security.[6] This risk is particularly great for SSA, which has been plagued by secular declines in ToT, exacerbated by price fluctuations in its major exports[7] (FAO 2003a; UNCTAD 2003). According to UNCTAD research (2003), for example, all commodities lost more than half their purchasing power in terms of manufactured goods between 1997 and 2001.

Another risk associated with the food self-reliance strategy of SSA relates to the emergence of competitive advantage as distinct from comparative advantage (FAO 2003a). This stems primarily from the strategic position of certain economic actors (in particular, multinational firms) in the value chain, the power that goes with this position and the ability of these actors to exploit rents from comparative advantage (UNCTAD 2003; FAO 2003a; see also Kaplinsky 2000, 2002; Fitter and Kaplinsky 2001). The asymmetrical nature of power in these value chains has led to unequal distributions of total income. Small producers in developing countries incur large income losses (relative to the retail prices they received in the past) while traders and firms have reaped significant benefits (Fitter and Kaplinsky 2001). The impact of the constantly diminishing share of total income accruing to these small producers has been devastating in terms of social dislocation, reduced entitlements and poverty as well as food insecurity (UNCTAD 2003).

The fact that the benefits of trade liberalization have failed to match its positive predictions in SSA also means that the strategy of self-reliant food security entails some risks in the countries of the region. In particular, the fallacy of composition, a perennial problem faced by commodity producers, suggests that the value of exports may not increase as fast as increases in volume (Mayer 2002; UNCTAD 2003; FAO 2003a). Thus, despite its potential

[6] The collapse of the international price of coffee, for example, has been cited as the major factor undermining food security in Central America, where four countries faced food emergencies in 2000–3 (FAO 2004).

[7] For more discussions on secular declines in terms of trade for Africa, see UNCTAD (2003: 33); and for the risks these pose for food security, FAO (2003a: 43–4).

beneficial effects, trade liberalization may not guarantee food security for SSA countries, as decreasing commodity prices and escalating tariffs in OECD countries remain major hurdles to increasing income and food security in SSA (Pingali and Stringer 2003: 6).

13.3.1 *WTO AoA and Food Security*

The trade-liberalizing impact of the AoA, at least in the short run, was expected to lead to higher food prices with diverging effects on net food-importing and exporting countries, as the practical outcome of the OECD countries' protectionist regimes has been to lower world market prices. It would also entail significant redistributive impact in both developed and developing countries with gains and losses to producers and consumers, respectively, in the developing countries (Laird *et al.* 2004). While higher export prices are good for producers (and exporters), they hurt those countries that depend on subsidized imports (and hurt the urban poor) as they face higher food bills (and prices for basic foods). This could undermine food security.

The WTO AoA is expected to have a positive impact on net food-exporting countries because higher world food prices increase export revenues, even if export volumes were to remain fairly stable, or do not fall more than the proportionate increase in price. Thus, depending on the transmission effect of world prices, producer income, and their food security could be boosted.

For the group of net food-importing countries, the level and variability of prices induced by the AoA raise two interrelated issues: first, how would these influence household food security; and second, how to track this impact with regard to the different sections of the community, in particular the urban and rural poor, and producers versus consumers. This in turn raises one conceptual and practical issue—what are the main income (entitlement) sources of the poor, and how will liberalization impact on these? Considering that labour is the income source for most of the poor, how will liberalization affect real wages? And for those poor who earn a part of their income from the production and sale of agricultural products (as in SSA, for example), what will liberalization do to their profits (Panagariya 2002)?

The increase in world food prices attributable to the AoA has been modelled to be much lower than predicted at the beginning of the UR. This in particular concerns grains *vis-à-vis* certain types of meat, sugar, and diary products, while World Bank and OECD estimates suggest the reverse (UNCTAD 1996: 62; Tyers and Anderson 1992: table 2). Trade liberalization as encompassed in the AoA is also expected to lead to net increases in income in primary agriculture and agro-industrial production as well as in agricultural trade (Diao *et al.* 2003). If all developing and OECD countries attain full liberalization of their goods market by 2005, global welfare gains have been estimated at US$260 billion (Anderson *et al.* 1999). Developing countries are estimated to gain more that US$45 billion per annum from liberalization in international trade in agriculture (Anderson 2004), but increases in net agricultural trade in SSA are relatively small (Diao *et al.* 2003).

Concerns had been expressed about the possible impact of the AoA on poverty and food security in LDCs and net food-importing countries before the conclusion of the UR (Husain 1993), and after the Agreement became effective (FAO 1999; Michalopoulus 1999, 2000). Indeed, much of the pre- and immediate post-UR literature suggests that the AoA would impact negatively on food security in much of Africa through higher and more volatile food prices and declining levels of food aid (see, for example, UNCTAD 1995b). However, it has been noted that the predicted price increases and volatility would depend on the pace of agricultural liberalization in the OECD countries and the specific response to the Agreement of the (developing) countries with comparative advantage in agriculture (Gayi 1998). Furthermore, changes in world food prices reflect the ongoing liberalization of agriculture in developed countries rather than the AoA per se (Page and Davenport 1994). Differences in regional response to the Agreement have also been highlighted, with Africa increasing its food import dependence (Greenfield *et al.* 1996), although some analyses also suggest that the case for food price increases and volatility might have been exaggerated (Greenfield *et al.* 1996; Sharma *et al.* 1996).

These notwithstanding, the AoA could potentially have great repercussions on food security in SSA. This impact would depend on the response of developed countries' food exports and SSA agricultural exports to the actual level of liberalization attained in international agricultural trade (which, to date, is limited), and the elasticity of SSA's import capacity to changes in international food prices as well as the amount of food requirements the region covers from its imports and food aid.

13.4 Post-Uruguay Round Food Security Situation in SSA

SSA is highly dependent on the agricultural sector for the livelihood of its population, growth of real output, and export earnings. About 64 per cent of the region's population derive their livelihood from the sector[8] (the highest for any region in the world). The sector contributes about one-fifth of total gross domestic product, and about 12 per cent of the total export earnings

[8] The proportion of total population engaged in agriculture for some individual SSA countries is very high: for example, about 90 per cent in Burkina Faso and Burundi. However, it is important to note that in the Sahel and the Horn of Africa, there are millions of pastoralists living in arid and semi-arid, and for whom animal husbandry constitutes a more critical component of income than crop agriculture.

for the region. The sector is particularly important for the poor, most of whom reside in the rural areas and undertake subsistence agriculture. About 95 per cent of the rural population is engaged in the agricultural sector. Thus, raising agricultural productivity, output and exports is critical not only for the region's economic growth, but also for its food security.

However, low productivity and output, stemming from a lack of investment in the sector, (e.g. irrigation facilities, high-yielding seed varieties and improving soil quality) mean that the region has been relying on food imports and food aid to close the gap between demand and supply. In this regard, the region's export performance is critical in determining the food security in these countries. This extends to the ability to attract additional foreign exchange from other sources such as remittances (a measure of its ability to finance food imports), international (and donor countries') policies regarding food aid (which affect the overall level of available food aid), and trade policies agreed within the framework of the multilateral trading system (which impact on food production and supplies, and therefore food prices).

It would appear that the concerns over higher and more volatile world food prices and food security risks for the developing countries, in particular the net food-importing nations (which includes much of SSA) in the post-UR, have been exaggerated, as the long-term trends depict falling real food prices (FAO 2003a; Valdés and McCalla 1999). High prices have not materialized because of increased productivity and yields driven by substantial subsidies in the major producing countries (World Bank 2001: 3), suggesting AoA's weak effect in reducing such subsidies (domestic support). At the global level, other food security indicators also indicate positive trends: consumption and average kcal/person/day have increased, and there is a growing diversification of diets away from starchy (roots and tubers) to non-starchy foods (eggs, meat, and milk). The same trend is witnessed in the developing world where the incidence of undernourishment has declined from about 20 per cent of total population (1990–2) to less than 17 per cent (1999–2001) (FAO 2003a).

About 60 per cent of the total number of the undernourished people are in Asia and the Pacific, but SSA, with 33 per cent of its population undernourished, registers the highest incidence of undernourishment. Over the past two decades, developing countries have, on the whole, reduced the incidence of undernourishment from about 28 per cent to 17 per cent of their total population in 1999–2001, but in absolute numbers the decline has been much slower, particularly in SSA and Latin America, where the decline in the proportion of the undernourished population is more than offset by population growth (FAO 2004).

The rest of this section assesses the state of food security in SSA based on the trends in selected indicators such as world food prices, daily energy supplies (or calories per capita per day), food import dependence, and food import capacity. This is supplemented by an analysis of selected indicators of

Table 13.2. Effects of the implementation of the WTO AoA on world food prices by the year 2000 (percentage change)

Commodity[a]	FAO[b]	UNCTAD[c]		OECD/WB[f]
		(1)[d]	(2)[e]	
Wheat	7.0	8.6	3.2	6.6
Rice	7.0	9.6	0.7	1.3
Maize	4.0	—	—	—
Millet/sorghum	4.0	—	—	—
Other grains	7.0	—	—	—
Coarse grains	—	9.0	2.9	3.3
Oil—seeds	—	7.7	3.8	—
Vegetable oils	—	5.9	2.5	4.6
Fats and oils	4.0	—	—	—
Beef	8.0	10.1	5.3	2.3
Pork	10.0	6.3	2.7	0.6[g]
Lamb	10.0	10.2	5.5	2.3
Poultry	8.0	9.3	4.9	0.6[g]
Dairy products	—	7.9	4.5	2.5
Milk	7.0	—	—	—
Sugar	—	11.3	4.5	3.0
Weighted average	6.6	8.6	3.8	3.3

Notes: [a] The three institutions adopted slightly different definitions for commodities; e.g., FAO's category 'other grains' includes 'coarse grains'; [b] FAO data taken from FAO (1995); [c] Revised figures from UNCTAD (1995c), which are different from those in the original source, UNCTAD (1995b); [d] This assumes no price response in non-OECD countries to changes in world market prices; [e] Assumes a price response in non-OECD countries; [f] Scenario allows for unemployment; [g] Other meats.

Source: UNCTAD (1996: 62).

nutritional wellbeing such as nutritional levels, under-five mortality rate, and life expectancy. It also analyses the trend in food aid levels since 1990.

The free-market food price index between 1994 and 2003 depicts a more or less steady decline in real food prices, in particular during 1997–2002, after the post-UR peak of 1996 (see Table 13.2). Prices fell, particularly for rice and sugar, with real prices in 2002 at about two-thirds and half of their 1990 levels, respectively. A slightly different picture, however, emerges from the analysis of the prices of vegetable oilseeds and oils. These increased steadily between 1994–8, experienced a slight decline thereafter, with the 2002 prices 10 per cent higher than the 1990 prices but still below the 1994 level. Thus, the predictions of price hikes in food after the implementation of the AoA appear not to have been borne out. The line of best-fit clearly shows a declining trend for world food prices during 1994 and 2003 (Figure 13.1).

Price instability or trends in stocks and flows of global cereal markets are, however, less robust indicators of food security compared to a country's ability to finance its import requirements from export earnings (FAO 2003a: 14). Considering that about 40 per cent of SSA relies on food imports to meet its

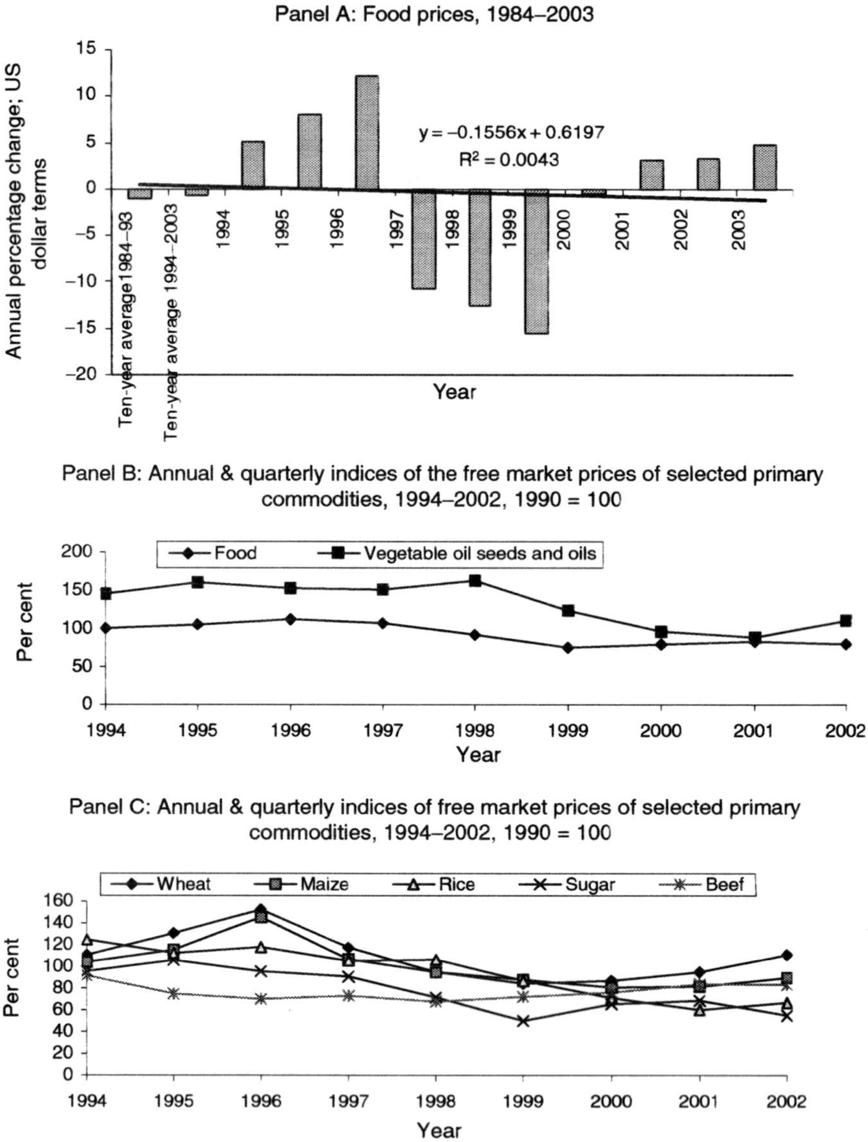

Figure 13.1. Food price trends in Sub-Saharan Africa, 1984–2003
Source: Computations based on FAO online data.

total requirement, and the fact that the region's import dependence[9] increased from by about 10 per cent to 13.6 per cent between 1973 and 1993 (FAO 2003a: 4), food import capacity (FIC) is probably a more reliable indicator of its food security level. Following Valdés and McCalla (1999), food import capacity is defined as the ratio of food import value (expenditure) to the total export value/revenue (excluding services). Essentially, the FIC captures changes in food import requirements for a particular country and its ability to finance these from its own resources.

Over the period 1990–2 and 2000–2, FIC decreased (that is, increased ratio of FIC) for about two-thirds (29 nations) of the 42 SSA countries for which there are data. Overall, the situation is serious for the eighteen countries for which food import dependence increased, even though their capacity to import food has diminished (Table 13.3). The situation appears to be most serious for the Gambia, which suffered a marginal increase in food import dependence but a collapse in food import capacity (an increase in FIC ratio from 157 per cent to 606 per cent).[10] Although Sierra Leone suffered the largest collapse in FIC, the country reduced its food import dependence by about 20 per cent over the period. Generally, a high FIC (more than 0.25) suggests some level of vulnerability to food insecurity that may stem from domestic harvest shortfalls or higher world prices (shortfalls in export earnings) which would require measures to improve food security: food or financial aid, and diversification of the economic base, including improvements in agricultural productivity (Valdés and McCalla 1999). Thus, the increase in FIC for the majority of SSA countries over the period suggests added vulnerability to food insecurity in the region, particularly in view of the fact that just over half of all these countries have increased their dependence on food imports (Table 13.3).

In terms of a food availability indicator, dietary energy supply (DES), average kcal/person/day at the global level has grown by about one-third, and the proportion of non-starchy food in total food consumption has increased by about 8 percentage points since the mid-1960s (FAO 2003a). Data on DES between 1990 and 2002 confirm the long-term positive trend in food security identified by the FAO at the global level as well as in all regions of the world. Indeed, the 4 per cent increase in the annual average value of DES of SSA

[9] Import dependence is defined (calculated) as the share of food import costs to total import costs.

[10] These results have to be interpreted with caution because FIC is overestimated for countries with large workers' remittances and service (or tourism) exports (such as Cape Verde, Seychelles, Mauritius, and to some extent, the Gambia) as these are not taken into account in tallying the export receipts used in calculating it. The FIC is generally high (that is, a ratio of more than 0.25) for small island developing countries (such as Sao Tome and Principe among the 18 countries), while the converse is true for large countries. That is they have rates lower than 0.25 (Valdés and McCalla 1999).

Table 13.3. Import dependence and import capacity of food in Sub-Saharan Africa

Country	Import dependence of food ratio (%)		Food import capacity ratio (%)	
	1990–92	2000–02	1990–92	2000–02
Angola	27.5	23	5.8	14.3
Benin	31.6	22.2	57.7	61.7
Burkina Faso	17.2	18.1	24.1	63.6
Burundi	9.9	16	29.1	60.1
Cameroon	18.5	17.2	12.9	16.6
Cape Verde	33.3	32.9	431.6	345.1
Central African Republic	18.6	26.1	25.1	24.6
Chad	19.8	8.9	27.3	30.5
Comoros	31.9	21.9	87.6	139
Congo, Republic of	17.2	20.9	8.8	8.8
Congo, DR	13.5	26.5	12.1	23
Côte d'Ivoire	21.5	19	16.3	11.7
Djibouti	28.3	27	315.7	329.9
Equatorial Guinea	26.5	11.2	30.9	4.7
Ethiopia	12	11.4	38.6	40.9
Gabon	17.6	18.5	6.6	6.7
Gambia	33.6	34.5	156.9	605.5
Ghana	11.2	12.8	13.8	19.5
Guinea	22.3	23.6	23.3	27.3
Guinea-Bissau	13.8	27.2	93	36.1
Kenya	11.9	12.8	18.8	23.8
Liberia	20	9.3	15.6	20.2
Madagascar	11.8	17.1	18.9	30
Malawi	8.4	15.8	12.7	23.9
Mali	25.5	15.1	43.2	20.3
Mauritania	27.4	26.4	16	28.1
Mauritius	12.6	16.3	17.4	21.4
Mozambique	26.8	14	165.1	29.3
Niger	24.3	38.8	51.9	64.5
Nigeria	8	19.9	4.2	7.1
Rwanda	11.9	19.3	35.7	92.7
Saint Helena	15	16.8	56	140.8
São Tomé and Principe	21	36.5	112.7	313.9
Senegal	29.2	23.7	53.7	66.2
Seychelles	20.3	18.8	72.9	56.3
Sierra Leone	35.5	27.9	40.8	227.9
Somalia	41.4	58.2	43.4	93.6
South Africa	6.2	4.8	5.3	4.8
Tanzania, UR	5.2	14.5	17.9	31.4
Togo	24.1	21.2	43.1	34.7
Uganda	7.9	13.5	23.3	30.8
Zambia	6.9	9.8	7.7	13.5
Zimbabwe	8.3	8.3	12.6	9.2

Note: Import dependence of food-ratio of food imports to total imports.

Source: Computations based on FAO online data.

Table 13.4. Annual average value of DES (kcal/person/day), Africa and other regions, 1992–2002

Region	Annual average		% change
	1990–2	2000–2	
Africa	2,315	2,389	3
Sub-Saharan Africa	2,116	2,200	4
Asia	2,548	2,687	5
Latin America & the Caribbean	2,705	2,848	5
Memo items			
World	2,704	2,795	3
Developed countries	3,259	3,300	1
Developing countries	2,531	2,657	5

Source: Computations based on FAO online data.

between 1990 and 1992, and 2000 and 2002[11] is slightly higher than the 3 per cent average for both the world and Africa as a whole, although marginally below that of other developing-country regions. However, the DES was the lowest in SSA in the two periods with per capita calorific intake still below that of all developing countries (by 21 per cent) and Latin American and Caribbean countries (by almost 30 per cent), which registered the highest DES among developing countries (Table 13.4). Based on daily per capita calorific intake, food security has improved in SSA over the period 1990–2 and 2000–2. Out of the total of 48 SSA countries for which DES data are available, the number of countries recording less than 2,000 calories per day (the minimum non-adjusted calorie limit per day needed to sustain moderate activity) dropped from fifteen to ten. Four additional countries also exceeded the higher limit of 2,310 calories per day[12] (that is, an increase from 14 countries to 18 over the period) (Table 13.5).

All five SSA countries (Burundi, Comoros, DR Congo, Guinea Bissau, and Liberia), which suffered a 5 per cent decline or more in DES over the period under consideration (Table 13.5), experienced political instability in one form or the other. Unsurprisingly DES declined in the DR Congo by as much as a quarter. For the other countries, the decline can be explained by civil war in Sierra Leone, a worsening and erratic economic performance in Zambia and Tanzania, respectively, and probably the high incidence of HIV/AIDS in Botswana and Swaziland.[13]

[11] Barring inconsistency in data, this would seem to suggest that the fall in FIC identified earlier did not translate into lower food supplies per capita.

[12] The FAO estimates that the daily energy supply or per capita food supply, measured as calories per day required to sustain moderate activity is between 2,000–2,310 calories, although this has been adjusted to 2,600–2,950 calories per day, considering moderate inequality in food consumption (FAO 1996b: 4–5).

[13] The explanatory factor(s) in the decline of kcal/person/day in this category of countries, however, need(s) to be properly analysed based on prevailing specific domestic social and economic conditions during the period under consideration.

Table 13.5. Annual average value of DES (cal/person/day), African countries, 1992–2002, grand total

	Annual average value		% change
	1990–2	2000–2	
Ghana	2073.3	2619.3	26.3
Djibouti	1802.2	2201.8	22.2
Chad	1782.5	2145.5	20.4
Mozambique	1735.2	2033.4	17.2
Malawi	1880.8	2154.9	14.6
Angola	1782.8	2040.8	14.5
Guinea	2105.3	2381.8	13.1
Congo, Republic of	1861.0	2085.5	12.1
Ethiopia PDR*	1637.8	1826.1	11.5
Namibia	2061.0	2268.9	10.1
Kenya	1921.0	2107.0	9.7
Mauritania	2555.6	2770.6	8.4
Benin	2337.8	2515.4	7.6
Cameroon	2114.4	2266.7	7.2
Lesotho	2445.3	2617.1	7.0
Togo	2151.4	2296.2	6.7
Cape Verde	3010.8	3209.0	6.6
Nigeria	2537.6	2704.6	6.6
Gabon	2454.3	2613.6	6.5
Seychelles	2311.2	2452.4	6.1
Côte d'Ivoire	2471.7	2620.3	6.0
Central African Republic	1874.4	1976.9	5.5
Niger	2020.4	2130.0	5.4
Rwanda	1947.1	2048.7	5.2
São Tomé and Principe	2272.2	2389.9	5.2
Sudan	2159.4	2260.0	4.7
Uganda	2274.6	2362.7	3.9
Tunisia	3151.7	3271.3	3.8
South Africa	2826.8	2917.2	3.2
Zimbabwe	1975.2	2024.0	2.5
Southern Africa	2293.6	2349.0	2.4
Mauritius	2886.5	2955.3	2.4
Burkina Faso	2353.1	2407.7	2.3
Senegal	2276.0	2279.7	0.2
Mali	2215.7	2199.7	−0.7
Madagascar	2084.0	2061.4	−1.1
Zambia	1929.2	1904.1	−1.3
Sierra Leone	1990.7	1925.7	−3.3
Swaziland	2454.7	2360.3	−3.8
Gambia	2366.7	2269.3	−4.1
Tanzania, UR	2049.5	1958.7	−4.4
Botswana	2263.4	2155.4	−4.8
Guinea-Bissau	2299.9	2101.4	−8.6
Comoros	1914.7	1747.7	−8.7
Liberia	2211.0	1996.6	−9.7
Burundi	1896.2	1635.4	−13.8
Congo, DR	2172.5	1627.1	−25.1
Unweighted average	2195.6	2281.8	4.2

Note: *Including Eritrea.

Source: UNCTAD calculations based on FAO online data.

The FAO reports that as of August 2003, 60 per cent of the countries worldwide[14] experiencing serious food shortages that required international intervention were in Africa. These food shortages are exacerbated by the HIV/AIDS pandemic affecting various aspects of food production, including marketing, transport, and utilization. More than half of the reported food emergencies in Africa are, among other reasons, due to civil strife and refugees while conflict and economic problems were cited as the main cause in more than a third of the cases[15] between 1992 and 2003 (FAO 2004). Most conflicts in SSA have led to large internal displacement of populations, which makes communities less food secure. These communities—even those previously food self-sufficient—are forced to rely on food aid. Often this situation persists long after the cessation of conflicts while victims await mine clearance for their agricultural lands, and/or because non-agricultural businesses have been destroyed.[16]

For a more complete picture of the food security situation in SSA, trends in protein supply per capita per day, under-five mortality rates and life expectancy at birth are examined as proxies for the overall wellbeing of the population. The daily protein supply per capita remained generally stable in the early 1990s at about 51 before increasing marginally to 53.4 during 2000–2, which is slightly better than the developed and developing country averages for the period, (but much below the average for the LDCs—see Figure 13.2). In 2002, SSA registered the worst under-five mortality rate in the developing world—174 deaths per 1,000, three times the rate (54 per 1,000) for the Middle East and North Africa, the second worst region. Also, life expectancy in SSA deteriorated from 51 to 49 years over the 1990–2002 period in contrast to other developing regions, which experienced increases (World Bank various issues).

Based on the incidence of undernourishment in the total population, however, the food security situation in the majority of countries in SSA has remained more or less the same. Over the periods, 1990–2 and 1999–2001, about 25 per cent of the populations of thirty countries were undernourished, and 35 per cent of the population of sixteen nations were undernourished (FAO 2000: table 1; FAO 2003a: table 2). While the proportion of the undernourished population dropped between 1990–2 and 1999–2001, the number of undernourished people increased by 20 per cent to almost 200 million over the same period (FAO 2003a: 31–3). The incidence of undernourishment is greater in all regions of SSA (with the exception of West Africa) than in all

[14] This means 23 out of the total of 38 countries needing international intervention were in Africa.

[15] IFPRI also reports a strong association between food insecurity and conflict (Messer and Cohen 2004).

[16] For the costs associated with internal conflicts, including food insecurity, in the LDCs, see, for example, UNCTAD (1997: 125–47).

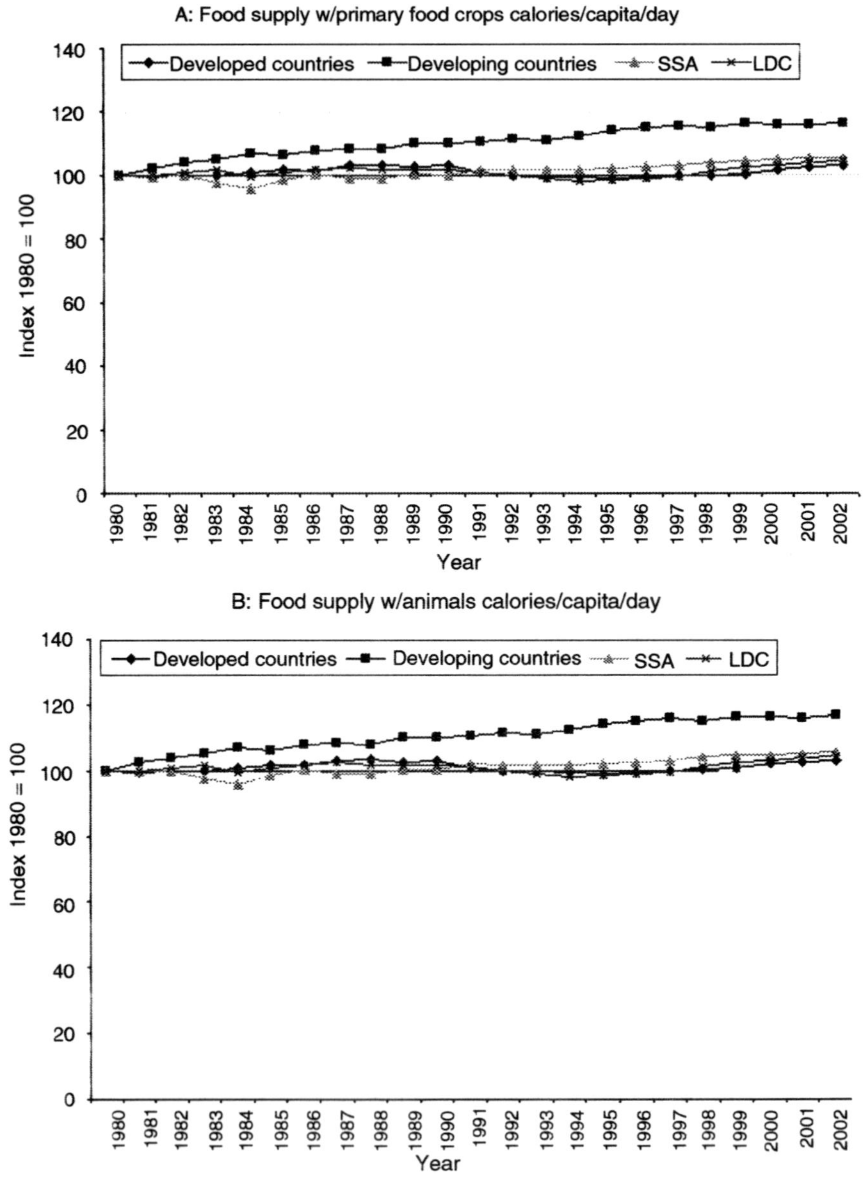

Figure 13.2. Food supply in selected country groups, 1980–2002
Source: Computations based on FAO online data.

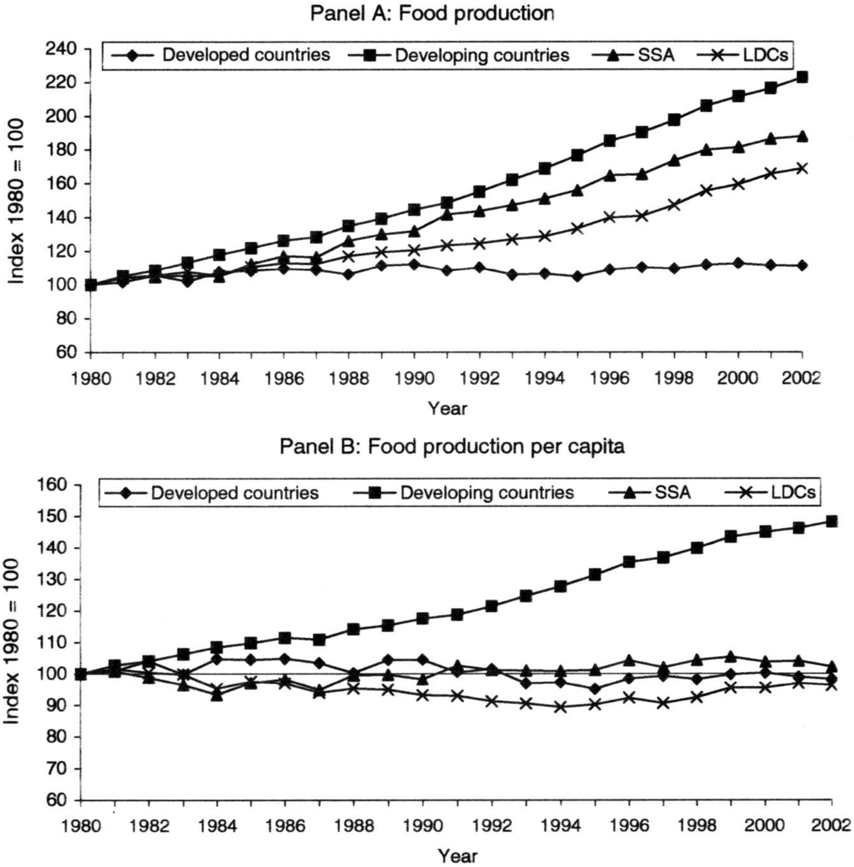

Figure 13.3. Food production in selected country groups, 1980–2002
Source: Computations based on FAO online data.

the developing-country regions. The main reasons here appear to be the civil wars, deterioration in some economies since the late 1990s and possibly in some instances the HIV/AIDS pandemic.

What is the domestic situation in terms of food production, imports and exports? In absolute terms, food production grew by about a third between 1990 and 2002, although it stagnated in per capita terms (Figure 13.3). Food exports increased by about 20 per cent, while food imports increased by 30 per cent over the same period (Figure 13.4). Food aid levels fluctuated. By 2002 cereal and non-cereal food aid shipments to SSA were almost 25 per cent and 10 per cent below their 1990–2 levels, respectively (Figure 13.5), suggesting that SSA food requirements were being met increasingly from food

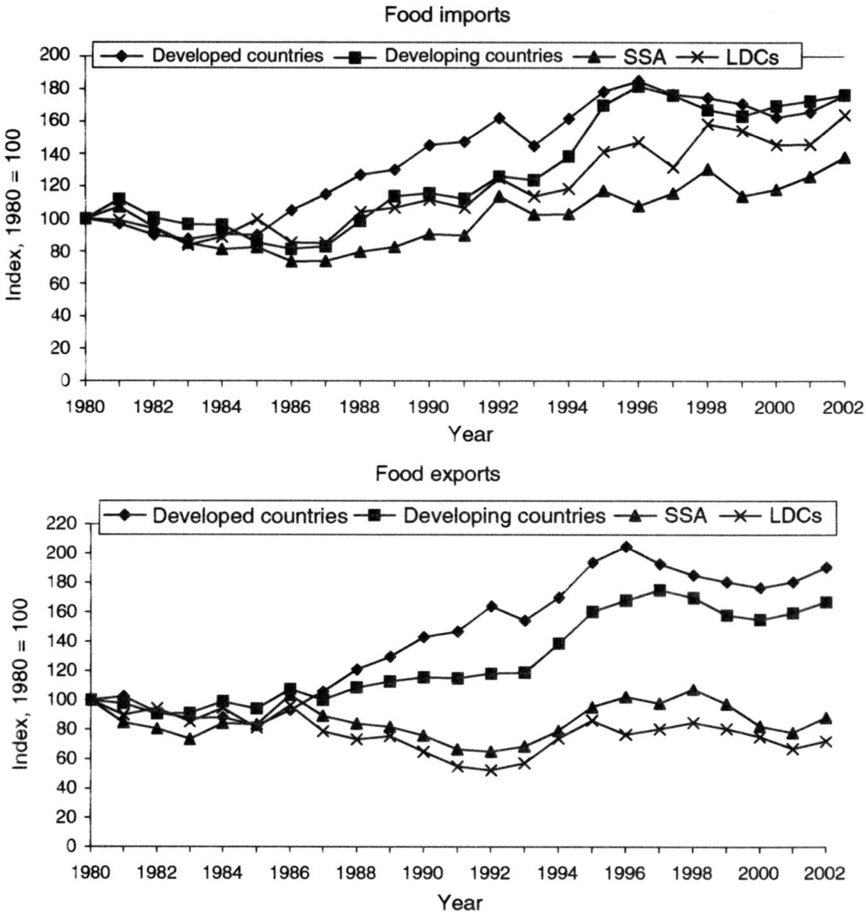

Figure 13.4. Food imports and exports in selected country groups, 1980–2002
Source: Computations based on FAO online data.

imports rather than food aid. This tends to confirm the observation by Pingali and Stringer (2003) that only a small part of concessional food aid goes to SSA.

In their analysis of the state of food availability in West Africa based on a simple exponential growth model, Nouve and Staaz (2003) concluded that there was no structural change in the four components[17] of the region's aggregate food availability in the pre- and post-WTO AoA periods (1989–95 and

[17] The test was performed on aggregate food availability and its major components, grain and root/tuber production, imports and food aid.

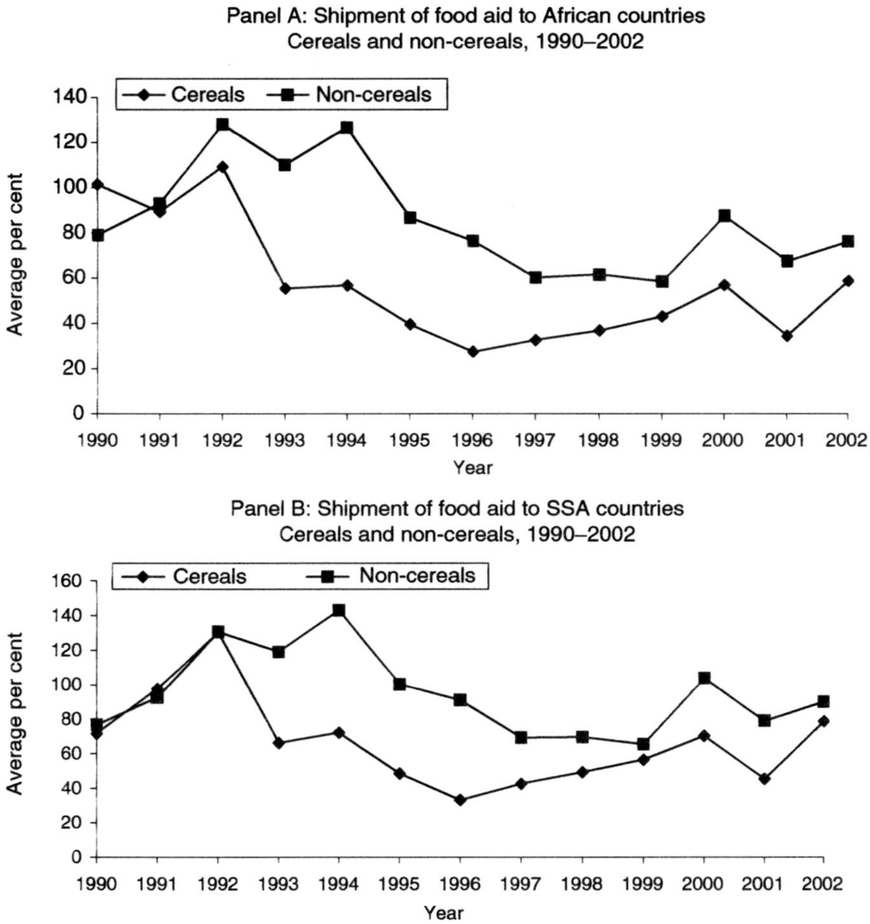

Figure 13.5. Shipment of food aid to African countries, 1990–2002
Source: Computations based on FAO online data.

1996–9 respectively).[18] On the region's capacity to finance its food imports before and after WTO-AoA, their study suggests that this did not change significantly change between the two periods: the regional trade-weighted average of the share of food imports as a percentage of total merchandise exports were 21 per cent and 21.2 per cent respectively.[19] Their regression

[18] A slight slow down in the growth in total per capita food availability in the post-WTO AoA did not reverse the growth in per capita food availability during this period. They attributed the changes in total availability to other components of total food availability not included in the four indicators used to determine aggregate food availability.

[19] This was attributed this to limited liberalization in the OECD and the fact that food prices did not rise as expected.

Table 13.6. State of food security in SSA, 1990–2002: summary of indicators

Indicators	Direction	Impact on food security	
		Positive	Negative
World food prices	Reduced	X	
Food import capacity	Reduced		X
Daily energy supply	Increased	X	
Prot/Cap/day	Increased	X	
Under-5 mortality	Increased		X
Life expectancy	Reduced		X
Undernourishment	Reduced	X	

Source: Compiled by the author.

results also confirm that that there was no statistical difference in the food import shares between the two periods.

While Nouve and Staaz (2003) concluded that both food availability in West Africa and the food import financing capacity of the countries in the region have not deteriorated in post-AoA period, other analysts have argued to the contrary. Oyejide (cited in endnote 10 of Nouve and Staaz 2003) for example contends that the AoA has had a negative impact in Africa as most countries which are low-income net food importers have experienced higher import bills within a context of preference erosion and export earnings which are not rising as fast as import bills.

The overall conclusions of Nouve and Staaz (2003) are consonant with the general analysis of the post AoA food security situation in SSA despite the different cut-off points in the definition of pre- and post-AoA periods. Nevertheless, the latter view (of Oyejide) would seem to confirm our earlier analysis of FIC in SSA based on Table 13.3. Indeed, a study on Kenya supports this latter position as the country's capacity to import declined in the post AoA period because of the poor performance of exports, and there were indications that the county was spending a large proportion of its export earnings on food imports thereby incurring high import bills. (Nyangito *et al.* 2004: 76).

Overall, the analysis of selected indicators of food security suggest that, on balance, the food security situation in SSA has at best improved, or at worst remained stable (Table 13.6). This situation appears to have little to do with the AoA, as the predicted food price increases never materialized. Thus, one would have to examine other factors which could be influencing the state of food security in SSA. Our analysis seems to suggest that weak agricultural performance, political instability, and the poor economic performance of these countries are the main culprits.

More than other factors, political instability and macroeconomic performance appear to be the main explanatory factors for the food insecurity situation. For example, Botswana, Mauritius, and Seychelles (except perhaps

Table 13.7. Land use: SSA and developing regions, 2001

Region	Agriculture area per capita (ha/person)	Arable land (% of agric. area)	Irrigated area (% of arable & permanent crops area)	Fertilizer consumption kg/ha/arable land)
World	0.82	27.9	17.8	98.3
Developed countries	1.36	34.3	10.7	84.0
Developing countries	0.67	24.5	22.7	109.0
Asia & the Pacific	0.32	39.8	33.2	163.2
Latin America & the Caribbean	1.49	19.0	11.0	84.8
Middle East & North Africa	1.12	18.9	28.5	70.9
Sub-Saharan Africa	1.51	15.8	3.7	12.6

Source: FAO (2004: 175–81).

Comoros)—the SSA countries that stopped receiving food aid in the last four decades—have become much richer. And Burundi, Guinea Bissau, DR Congo, Liberia, and Sierra Leone—the countries in which food insecurity appears to have increased—have all experienced serious internal conflicts in one form or the other over the past decade. This has resulted in the contraction of their economies; or economies have not performed well, as in Zambia.

Can the weak agricultural performance of SSA be explained by the policy restrictions stemming out of the AoA? It is indeed very doubtful if this were the cause. First, per capita food production in SSA has more or less stagnated since the 1980s, although the absolute level of food production has increased, suggesting that high population growth rates are at the heart of per capita declines in food production. Furthermore, the failure of food production to keep pace with population growth could be explained by the low productivity of African agriculture as depicted in the use of agricultural inputs, for example, fertilizer and irrigation. In the developing world, Africa has the highest agricultural area per capita but the lowest irrigated area (3.7 per cent) and fertilizer consumption (12.6 kg/ha/arable land) compared with the developing-country average of 22.7 per cent and 109.0 kg/ha/arable land respectively (Table 13.7).

Indeed, if the AoA has not had a negative impact on the SSA food security situation to date, it could be explained by various factors. Liberalization attained under the AoA is limited because of the choice of baseyears with high rates of protection, uneven product coverage, and 'dirty tariffication'[20] in developed countries (Gayi 1998; World Bank 2001: 9). Also, restrictions on domestic agricultural policies in very poor countries of the region are not as constraining as they might first have appeared. While price support policies operating through producer (or administered) prices to farmers have

[20] This refers to the overestimation of NTBs in the tarrification process resulting in post-UR tariff levels that are higher than the pre-UR tariff levels, even after the mandatory reductions for temperate products like cereals and meat.

Table 13.8. Permissible domestic policy measures ('green box' policies)

Type of policy	Description of measures
General services	• Research, extension, training, pest and disease control, inspection, marketing and promotion, and infrastructural services.
Direct payments	• Decoupled income support, income insurance, safety net programmes, disaster relief, retirement schemes, structural adjustment policies, environmental and regional assistance programmes.
Food stocks	• Purchase at market prices; part of national food security programme.
Domestic food aid	• Nutritional programmes and programmes for poverty relief.

Source: Extracted from the WTO Agreement on Agriculture.

to be reigned in, there are no constraints on policies that target the poor and vulnerable directly; for example, policies to promote agricultural investments, (rural) infrastructure, nutritional and other poverty-reducing programmes. Domestic policies which are likely to have a more direct impact on food production, food stock, prices, and food security in SSA are permitted under the 'Green Box' or S&D measures specifically granted for poor developing and least developed countries (Gayi 1998). For instance, governments could provide input subsidies or diversification support to poor farmers (see also Table 13.8). The critical issue for SSA countries is the lack of technical and administrative capacity to establish clearly defined criteria for selecting groups that are vulnerable to food security, and to design and implement programmes targeted at these groups. Fiscal constraints and restrictions (or conditionalities) under various IMF/World Bank supported programmes may also limit ability of these countries, and constrict their policy space, in undertaking such programmes.

Within the context of the discussion above, what then are the policy options for SSA if it is to improve the state of its food security?

13.5 Policy Issues

The predicted price increases stemming from the WTO AoA, and associated possible negative impact on food security in SSA have yet to materialize (or, at least, not on the scale predicted). The corollary of this is that SSA's expected supply response has also been weak, and may remain so in the short to medium term. One may thus be tempted to conclude that in this context, SSA would be better off pursuing a strategy of food self-reliance. This may be particularly true when one considers that the standard neoclassical economic argument against erecting trade barriers to promote food self-sufficiency is that barriers will hurt food security as they increase the price of imported food.

Nonetheless, on a deeper analysis, this recommendation may in the context of SSA be somewhat flawed, not least because a number of these countries have static or dynamic comparative advantage in agriculture. For a variety of additional reasons, discussed below, this group of SSA countries might want to take advantage of the AoA to increase agricultural sector investment as a means of diversifying into more high-value products, and increasing productivity and output (food production) to attain food security (i.e. a strategy of food self-sufficiency)—at least, until such a time that the agricultural sector is fully integrated into WTO disciplines. As acknowledged by the World Bank (2001: 2), food security objectives are best pursued through increased agricultural productivity.

Indeed, in many parts of Africa, agricultural development (crop farming or animal husbandry) is intertwined with 'entitlements'—as a source of jobs (incomes) and for providing food. And in addition to other factors, the failure of particular agricultural (and food) policies has been identified as a major cause of the food and humanitarian crisis that afflicted Southern Africa[21] during 2001–2 (Wiggins 2003, 2005). Even in situations where developing countries may have benefited from the AoA via international trade, it has been cautioned, 'food security remains a domestic issue, involving questions of land structure, infrastructure, domestic policies in general, domestic institutions and processes' (Nouve and Staaz 2003).

Trade is a critical part of any food security strategy. However, trade *per se* does not address the issue of *extreme* poverty in SSA countries, which in turn gives rise to food insecurity. There is therefore the need to address food security in a holistic manner, not only through improving access to food (i.e. enhancing 'entitlements'), but also through food availability (Nouve and Staaz 2003). Even in countries such as Kenya, where food purchases make up about 70 per cent of rural households' food consumption, Nyangito *et al.* (2004: 78–9) have been argued that as the decline in rural household incomes moves in the same direction as the decline in farm incomes, there is positive correlation between food security and the performance of the agricultural sector. That is, rural households become more food insecure as the performance of the agricultural sector declines, although a redistribution of income or food through remittances has 'buffered' household consumption patterns during times of food stress. Thus, while imports may increase food supplies, households are unable to buy these simply because of limited incomes, particularly from agriculture and related activities (Nyangito *et al.* 2004: 78–87).

[21] The six most affected countries are: Lesotho, Malawi, Mozambique, Swaziland, Zambia, and Zimbabwe

It is important to note that these are not arguments against liberalization *per se*, but are intended just to signal the potential problems for vulnerable regions like SSA as well as highlight the need for appropriate action, particularly at the national level, but also at the multinational level, to forestall these problems.

First, the experiences of African famine situations in the mid-1980s suggest that the poor are primarily concerned about their resilience to future shocks to food supplies, and therefore the preservation of their assets and future livelihoods (entitlements). Increasing investment in agriculture offers a solution. In the medium to long run, agricultural development may also enable these countries to trade their way out of poverty, as is often suggested by various writers (for example, Winters 2000; Diao *et al.* 2003).

Second, the neoclassical argument in favour of a self-reliant strategy for food may not necessarily hold for countries with large rural farming populations, which is the case of those SSA nations with a comparative advantage (static or dynamic) for agriculture or food production. While food import restrictions may have some adverse effects on food security in these countries in the short run, higher world food prices could serve as an incentive for farmers to produce marketable surpluses, particularly if these are accompanied by complementary policies that promote agriculture, increase productivity, and facilitate access to export markets (see discussion below). Within an appropriate incentive policy framework for agriculture, food security in the medium to long run could be enhanced, particularly as agriculture could have multiplier effects, creating non-farm jobs in distribution and marketing and even in processing. Estimates suggest that for every US$1 generated through agricultural production in developing countries, economic linkages can add another US$3 to the rural economy (Diao *et al.* 2003; Watkins and von Braun 2003).

Third, recent attempts to reform the Common Agricultural Policy (CAP) of the EU remain modest, with the EU subsidies set to continue to rise until 2013 (Diao *et al.* 2003). Proposed reforms are focused on domestic support measures (which do not directly affect consumer prices and are therefore less trade-distorting), not on trade, and contain no new provisions on tariffs or improving market access for African agricultural exports (UNCTAD 2003: 26). And border measures, one of the pernicious means of agricultural protection in these countries, remain more or less intact (Hoekman *et al.* 2002). However, without a significant reform of CAP or agricultural trade barriers in the industrialized countries, import liberalization in the developing countries will simply perpetuate unfair competition, and undermine the gains the latter could derive from trade liberalization.[22] Indeed, simulation exercises have

[22] About 70 per cent of the increase in the value of exports from SSA, for example, is estimated to come from liberalization in the EU alone. And when Haiti liberalized its rice

shown that developing-country benefits from eliminating agricultural support measures are relatively small compared to total elimination of trade barriers (Hoekman *et al.* 2002).

It should also be mentioned that developing-country gains from the liberalization of international trade in agriculture can only be assured with an objective application of various measures on sanitary and phytosanitary (SPS), technical barriers to trade (TBT), and environmental standards, which are increasingly being deployed as non-tariff barriers, even as tariffs are being eliminated. Recent evidence suggests that the overly stringent application of these standards has led to significant losses for developing countries in terms of export revenues (Wilson and Otsuki 2001; CUTS 2002).

Fourth, we recall that the agricultural sector makes an immense contribution to the economies of these SSA countries in terms of GDP, export earnings, and employment (rural livelihoods/entitlement). Considering that the agricultural sector's role is particularly critical in rural economies, it deserves special treatment. Several studies have suggested that agricultural-led growth strategy may, for the world's poorest countries, produce greater multiplier effects to the rest of the economy than other alternative growth strategies. Prominent among these are the dual economy models of Lewis (1954) and Ranis and Fei (1961), which underscore the importance of promoting the agricultural sector as a necessary condition for industrial and overall development of underdeveloped economies. Recent studies also suggest that even modest investments in agriculture could yield high returns (Word Bank 2001: 4). Increased profits from agriculture could stimulate expanded economic activity, with knock-on effects in four areas: (i) employment (creation of farm and farm-related activities with spin-offs in non-farm and non-rural sectors); (ii) land (increased agricultural profits reinvested in the sector); (iii) capital (additional attraction of investments which in turn augment growth), and; (iv) technology (better investment climate leads to technological improvements which in turn increase productivity) (Diao *et al.* 2003).

From cross-national observations, the most important strategy for national food security relates to economic growth and widespread income improvement. Thus, an evaluation of any food security strategy must be within the context of its impact on economic growth, and, in particular, the opportunities it creates for improving the income of the poor. Thus, it is sensible for food security policy in poor countries to focus on the income of food producers (Summer 2000). In Southern African countries such as Lesotho, Malawi, Mozambique, Swaziland, Zambia, and Zimbabwe, the dependence of poor households on agriculture as a source of jobs, incomes, and foreign exchange (entitlements) increased at the turn of the century. This was triggered by

market in 1995, prices collapsed by about 25 per cent, with grave consequences for local farmers who became displaced (Diao *et al.* 2003).

the collapse of mining and industrial sectors in the region, and subsequent steep fall in remittances to these households (Wiggins 2005). In much of SSA, low-per capita productivity of small-scale farm households contributes significantly to their food insecurity. And finally, as argued by Herrmann (2003), full liberalization of the agricultural sector may create opportunities for the production and exports of not only those products that receive direct production support in OECD countries but also for other items that are potential substitutes. For example, locally grown millet and sorghum (flour) are close substitutes for imported wheat (flour) and rice, and locally produced palm oil for imported vegetable oil.

Fifth, examples abound of countries where trade has not attained sustained growth due to the lack of supply capacity or its weakness (Laird *et al.* 2004). This is particularly the case in poor developing countries, and highlights the fact that free trade may not—and should not—be regarded as an end in itself. Benefits accrue only if countries implement complementary policies at the domestic level to increase agricultural productivity and meet the burgeoning national and international safety requirements (e.g. SPS measures) in order to increase competitiveness in global markets. In SSA these policies would typically encompass institutional issues such as land reforms and improved access to agricultural inputs (credit, fertilizer, pesticides, etc.) as well as infrastructural developments (irrigation facilities) and improvements in marketing channels (rural roads).

Sixth, as discussed earlier, SSA is highly vulnerable to international price fluctuations as reflected in secular declines in the terms-of-trade over the past few decades. Therefore if trade liberalization leads to added dependence on food imports to attain food security (food self-reliance), this could increase the vulnerability of these countries to food insecurity in the event of a severe terms-of-trade deterioration. As observed by Summer (2000), in some cases, import barriers and other policies to enhance food self-sufficiency may reduce variability in food prices, or at least reduce the likelihood of a high spike or other access interruptions.[23]

In the light of the foregoing discussions, it might be rational for SSA countries, which have some comparative advantage in agriculture, to aim for food self-sufficiency strategy, at least in the short to medium term. This would limit their exposure to fluctuations in both world food and commodity prices—that is, until such a time when international trade in agriculture becomes fully liberalized. At present, agricultural production structures in these countries have evolved more or less in response to agricultural protectionism of the

[23] He cautions though that while this is a theoretical possibility, its practical application depends on internal and global commodity price distributions (Summer 2000). Our argument in this chapter is that the facts in the case of SSA suggest this would be case, hence the recommendation of a food self-sufficiency strategy as interim strategy pending the full integration of agriculture into WTO disciplines.

north (and to some extent benign policy neglect in individual countries),[24] and arguably these do not reflect the true comparative (and competitive) advantage of the region's agricultural sector. As contended by Diaz-Bonilla and Gulati (2003), depressed world prices of many food products caused by the north's agricultural protectionism 'may have contributed to some developing countries becoming net food importers, pushing them into a more extreme specialization in tropical products'.

With national governments implementing the necessary agriculture policy reforms within a context of ongoing agricultural trade liberalization in the north, allocation of resources in SSA countries should in time reflect optimal outcomes. A clear and an unambiguous international commodity policy[25] should also contribute to improving food security (Summer 2000), in particular if it guarantees remunerative prices for producers and therefore reduces the possibility of a sharp ToT deterioration for these countries. Under these conditions, countries could then move gradually from a strategy of food self-sufficiency to self-reliance, as full agricultural liberalization combined with an international commodities policy would help ensure some protection of the entitlements of individual rural producers (income) as well as national governments (export revenues).

Fortunately, macroeconomic stability has been attained in all but a handful of SSA countries, where inflation is still in double digits, and anti-agricultural bias in domestic policies in these countries has been addressed. The conditions are therefore propitious for the implementation of specific policies to increase agricultural investment for the development of the rural and entire economy. The question then is what type of agricultural investments could these governments make to improve agricultural productivity, enhance food security and reduce the vulnerability of the poor to food insecurity? What policies are these countries able to implement to develop their agricultural sectors without falling foul of the AoA? The next section attempts to respond to these questions.

13.5.1 *Agricultural Development Policies Consonant with the WTO AoA*

As argued in the previous section, an important element in safeguarding food security in SSA is the performance of the agricultural sector, particularly in countries with a comparative advantage in the sector. Government policies aimed at increasing investment in the agricultural sector, improving productivity on smallholder farms, improving the supply of inputs and facilitating

[24] This could also be attributed to the wrong signals that food dumping sends to SSA governments, which are more interested in cheap food for their urban populations than in developing agricultural sector for the benefit of small-scale farmers (Watkins and von Braun 2003).

[25] See UNCTAD (2003: 45–60) for examples of these policies.

the marketing of output through the provision of rural infrastructure, and generally supporting rural development are becoming important. Most crucially, the gamut of policies that can be deployed to support poor farmers in remote rural areas and the agricultural sectors of SSA falls within the 'Green Box'. That is to say, they are not proscribed by the AoA. Neither is there a ban on other measures such as increasing expenditure for agricultural research, extension, training with regard to specific food crops (including measures to facilitate the transfer of information and research results to producers), pest and disease control and even marketing. SSA governments could also provide infrastructure in support of agricultural development without falling foul of the provisions of the AoA. These include physical infrastructure to promote agricultural activities, including roads, electricity, water, dams, and drainage schemes,[26] environmental programmes and assistance for the deprived regions.

It is also important to note that the calculation and application of the aggregate measures of support (AMS) is not product-specific and as such, guarantees some flexibility in domestic support policies as long as global commitments reflected in individual country schedules are not exceeded.[27] LDCs and other poor developing countries, including SSA, are accorded special and differential treatment. This enables governments to use a special category of production support policies that are exempt from the calculation of the country's current total AMS. These policies encompass agricultural input subsidies to low-income or resource-poor producers, investment subsidies, and government assistance to encourage agricultural and rural development. These exemptions allow considerable leeway for SSA governments to support their agricultural sectors.

If governments are able to design effective programmes and implement them successfully, agricultural productivity should increase and farmer incomes be boosted. A dynamic agricultural sector should provide inputs for agro-processing industrialization, thus expanding employment opportunities in both rural and urban areas, and thereby contributing significantly to enhanced entitlements. Such programmes could be different, even in the same country, and need to take into account the diversity in topography and rainfall patterns. In those areas where most rural dwellers have restricted options for diversification, as in the Sahel, crop production may have to be supplemented with other activities such as (agro-)forestry, and livestock production (Sanders 2002).

General rural development programmes should also create opportunities for off-farm income—generating activities in rural areas—thus boosting incomes

[26] This, however, excludes subsidies to inputs or operating costs, or preferential user charges.

[27] The problems relating to this for most of the developing countries are discussed later.

from these sources. All of this should have a positive impact on food security. Also possible are the knock-on effects such as qualitative improvements in rural life, and expansion of domestic demand for consumer goods, which in turn will stimulate increased domestic demand for food or production of consumer goods, and or/or higher imports of these goods (UNCTAD 1997: 45).

One important and worrying observation, however, is the clearly limited ability of SSA governments to finance all these programmes in view of the resource constraints, including the paucity of administrative and technical expertise that these countries face. Second, while these programmes are permissible within the framework of the AoA and the WTO in general, some could be prohibited under various IMF/World Bank programmes (standby arrangements) explicitly as part of the conditionalities governing these programmes; or implicitly because of requirements, limiting the level of fiscal deficits each country can incur within a budget cycle. These highlight the need for donor assistance (technical and financial resources) in supporting the programmes, and the importance of policy coherence, whereby international financial (or development) institutions ensure that their respective policy advice and prescriptions to these countries are in consonance and not in conflict with each other, if not at the national level, then at the sectoral level.

13.5.2 *The Doha Round of Trade Negotiations: What Difference Does It Make?*[28]

The continued availability of these policies and exemptions for the use of poor developing countries depends on the outcome of the ongoing agricultural negotiations within the context of the Doha Round (which incorporates the revision of the AoA as part of the built-in agricultural sector agenda). As of yet, there does not appear to be a threat to this country group of a roll-back of these special and differential treatment measures. Nevertheless, it is important as a starting point to continue to defend these and then seek clarification and improvement by arguing specifically that food security enhancement measures be incorporated into the AoA.

It is worth noting therefore that since the late 1990s, special and differential treatment measures (e.g. preferential market access and certain exemptions from domestic disciplines) have been proposed as the solution to the food security problems that might arise from the AoA (e.g. Whalley 1999; Fukasaku 2000; Michalopoulus 2000). These measures continue to be

[28] Discussions in this chapter on reform of the AoA during the ongoing Doha negotiations are limited to those likely to have a direct impact on food security in poor countries. For further details on other proposals discussed for the reform of the AoA, see for example, WTO (2004) and UNCTAD (2004: 16–23).

Table 13.9. The Doha Agricultural Negotiations Summary of issues raised by developing countries

General

- The final balance, equity and sequencing between and within the three pillars of the agricultural negotiations, as well as within the single undertaking. Credible and expeditious commencement and completion of the implementation of the negotiated commitments.

Domestic support

- The choice of a reduction formula for the AMS that reduces the currently applied support on a product-specific basis so that substantial reduction is achieved for all products of export interest to developing countries;
- Setting stringent criteria for the blue and green boxes to prevent box shifting;
- The implication of *de minimis* cuts by developing countries, and identifying the type of *de minimis* support that qualifies as being given to subsistence and resource-poor farmers.

Export competition

- Set credible date for the elimination of all forms of export subsidies, in particular direct export subsidies;
- Role of export credits and STE used by developing countries in their development strategies, and their appropriate reflection in S&D provisions;
- Due priority given to putting in place mechanisms (trade, aid and financing mechanisms) to alleviate possible negative impacts on LDCs and net food importing developing countries (NFIDCs).

Market access

- Choice a tariff reduction formula that effectively eliminates tariff peaks and tariff escalation in developed countries for products of export interest to developing countries;
- Restraining the flexibility given to sensitive products of developed countries (product selection, tariff cuts and tariff rate quota, TRQ, expansion) so as not to undermine market access opportunities for developing countries. The elimination of special safeguard measures for developed countries;
- Ways to link market access improvement to market entry enhancement;
- Appropriate degree of 'proportionality' in tariff cuts for developing countries, taking into account the fact that tariffs are the only protection given to their agricultural producers to counter subsidized production and exports of developed countries;
- Design of SP and SSM that would allow developing countries sufficient policy flexibility with respect to food security and rural development.

Source: UNCTAD (2004: 11).

discussed within the context of the Doha negotiations; and it has been argued that they should form an integral part of the negotiations, taking into account the special development needs of developing countries, including food security and rural development (UNCTAD 2004). Much of this discussion is taking place with reference to instituting a new 'development box' to address food security, rural development, and other needs of developing countries (Laird *et al.* 2004). See Table 13.9 for the specific concerns and issues on agriculture raised by developing countries in the Doha negotiations.

One specific measure under discussion is allowing developing countries to make lower reductions for trade-distorting domestic support over longer implementation periods, with those that allocate almost all *de minimis* support for subsistence and resource-poor farmers to be exempted from *de minimis* reductions. Indeed, it may be in the interest of all poor countries, including those in SSA, to argue for more flexibility in the application of *de minimis* support, such as reducing its level to take into account special and differential treatment (UNCTAD 2004); and/or presenting a case for a 5 per cent 'aggregate' *de minimis* support instead of the current 10 per cent product-specific *de minimis* (Josling and Tangerman 1999: 1389). This is because almost all developing countries (with the exception of twelve) have zero commitments for domestic support. That is, most have submitted a 'zero base' AMS.[29] In the case of poor developing countries, this implies that combined with the regulation of the current AMS not exceeding the base AMS, these countries can only provide product-specific support up to 10 per cent of the value of production; and non-product-specific support up to 10 per cent of the value of total agricultural production.

The ongoing agricultural negotiations are also considering the proposal to subject developing countries to a lower level of liberalization for designated 'special products' that would be based on a set of criteria reflecting food and livelihood security, and rural development. In this connection, a number of these countries have called for a special safeguard mechanism (SSM) that allows them sufficient policy flexibility with respect to food security, including the selection of special products, based on livelihood security and rural development criteria (UNCTAD 2004; see also WTO 2004: annex A, paras. 41–2).[30]

These specific proposals addressing the special needs of poor developing countries including SSA, may have to be situated in a broader context of a revised AoA. The objective of this review should be to tackle some of the shortcomings of the current agreement such as 'dirty tariffication', greater trade liberalization in products like sugar and meat, as well as reducing tariff escalation for a number of product chains. The special safeguards in place for products subject to tariffication should also be reviewed as they allow an additional duty to be imposed when imports of specific agricultural products exceed a trigger level, or when the import price falls below a trigger level.

Efforts have to be intensified to attain the main objectives of the Doha mandate in the agricultural negotiations. This would include substantial improvements in market access; reductions in all forms of export subsidies with a view to phase these out, and a substantial reduction in trade-distorting domestic support (UNCTAD 2004). Indeed, developing countries have to argue not only for larger reductions in domestic support, but also for tighter rules (or disciplines) to limit the distortions of the developed countries. A revision of Green Box policies or disciplines, including time limits and ceilings, may also be useful to speed up the agricultural liberalization

[29] That is a declaration of not providing any domestic support for agriculture in the baseyear, 1986–8.

[30] This proposal could be defended as part of the 'collective preferences' proposal of the former EU Trade Commissioner, Pascal Lamy, as an intellectual basis for accommodating non-trade concerns in the WTO framework to ensure that liberalization does not override domestic policy choices, which could enable countries to limit imports deemed as threatening to collective preferences in particular if there was, *inter alia*, 'a coherent underlying social demand' (available at: www.grictrade.cta.int/wto/).

process, particularly because of the reliance of the EU on such policies to delay liberalization.[31]

13.6 Concluding Remarks

Assessing the impact of trade liberalization measures highlights several complex conceptual and practical difficulties, not least in establishing cause and effect relationships in situations where the impact of many intervening variables cannot be ignored or adequately assessed. This assessment of the impact of AoA on the food security situation in SSA is no exception. It is, nevertheless, possible to make some general deductions based on the analysis of proxy variables such as daily per capita calorie intake, per capita food supplies, under-five mortality rates, food import capacity and dependence on food imports.

The analysis presented in this chapter suggests that the AoA has had little or no impact on food security in SSA to date. More important explanatory factors for the state of the Sub-Saharan food security situation between 1990 and 2002 include country-specific issues such as political instability and macroeconomic performance, especially the state of the countries' agricultural sector. This underscores the relevance of government policy or action in determining the state of food security in each country.

In this regard it has been noted that the AoA does not explicitly condemn any specific agricultural policy for all WTO members; the use of agricultural support measures has been regulated merely to forestall abuses, which could have production and trade-distorting impacts. Concessions, albeit limited, have been granted to poor developing countries, such as those in SSA, within the context of special and differential treatment incorporated into various agreements, as those included in the AoA, and reinforced in two specific ministerial decisions. The objective was to limit any food insecurity problems that these countries might encounter on account of the implementation of the Agreement. Without a doubt, the implementation of these decisions has been fraught with practical problems, and only limited progress has been made to date.

The surest guarantee to the attainment (or improvement) of food security in SSA would be for these governments to ensure that the poorest population sections have sustainable livelihoods or 'entitlements' (the discussion of which with regard to stable political systems falls outside the scope of this chapter).

[31] OECD policies have been designed to conform to blue and green boxes, with more than half of the total OECD domestic support notified to the WTO being exempted from reduction requirements. Green box support in OECD countries doubled between 1986–8 and 1995–8, and has been higher than AMS over the entire implementation period (OECD 2001: 4).

As discussed in the previous section, there is some policy leeway under the current AoA for SSA countries to develop their agricultural and rural sectors, and to enhance food security. Nonetheless, it does appear that SSA countries have yet to take advantage of the available policy options. This chapter advocates a self-sufficient food strategy to address food insecurity in SSA, particularly for those countries with a comparative advantage in agriculture in view of its multiplier effects of agriculture for the whole economy. Implementing such a policy would be rational, at least until such a time when international trade in agriculture is fully liberalized, particularly in view of the north's heavy agricultural protectionism that currently distorts price signals and thus opportunity costs of allocating factors of production in these economies. A reform of international commodity policy should also contribute to achieving food security objectives by reducing the vulnerability of SSA export revenues (entitlements) to sharp ToT decline or fluctuations.

For countries in the Sahel and in the Horn of Africa, public policies to enhance food security would have to incorporate programmes that impact directly on activities that underscore the entitlements of large sections of the population. Such programmes could cover control of locusts, control and eradication of livestock diseases, as well as improvements in animal husbandry, while striking a delicate balance between livestock numbers and the ecology of rangelands (FAO 2000b).

Food security could also be enhanced via intra-African trade, the huge potential of which has yet to be fully exploited, as the analysis by the UNCTAD secretariat reveals (UNCTAD 1998: 202–7; 2003: 54). This would, however, need to be encouraged by removing both physical (many check points and harassment at the borders, etc.) and non-physical barriers, the later, for example, through the harmonization of customs documentation and procedures.

In the final analysis, however, more research on how trade impacts on different households (rural and urban) would yield robust data on the patterns of poverty and levels of vulnerability to food insecurity. These could then form the basis of targeted policies to reduce the risk to, and improve, food security in both rural and urban areas of SSA.

That there is a case for enhanced liberalization in international trade in agriculture cannot be disputed. This is all the more evident when considering the huge inefficiencies in the current system, including huge resource transfers to a few rich farmers in the north, while their counterparts in the SSA struggle to make ends meet. It is in this context that the AoA has opened up the potential for the SSA countries with the comparative advantage in agriculture to increase their agricultural exports, even if the level of liberalization currently attained in international agricultural trade is limited. The major challenge now is to ensure that agricultural liberalization is extended to its logical conclusion by making the provisions of the AoA fully compatible with

WTO disciplines. This, and an objective application of WTO Agreements on SPS and TBT to reduce their unintended impact as NTB, should enable the SSA countries to utilize their huge agricultural potential, provided they implement the necessary domestic policy reforms.

While there may still be some role for food aid, particularly the emergency type food aid, this will have to be delivered more efficiently, using improved data (for more effective targeting of food-insecure groups), and improved management for reduced response times. Donors should also apply more flexibility by using, wherever the opportunity exists, triangular transactions and local purchases more often. This would not only encourage inter- and intra-regional trade, but also support regional agricultural production as well as provide food-aid recipients with local coarse staples (which could become the preferred choice instead of the foreign grains that could be detrimental to future demand for local staples).

References

Anderson, K. (2004). 'Agriculture, Trade Reforms and Poverty Reduction: Implications for Sub-Saharan Africa'. Policy Issues in International Trade and Commodities, Study Series, 22. Geneva: UNCTAD.

—— B. Hoekman, and A. Strutt (1999). 'Agriculture and the WTO: Next Steps. CIES Discussion Paper, 99/14. Adelaide: Centre for International Economic Studies, University of Adelaide.

Broca, S., and K. Stamoulis (2003). 'Micro- and Macroevidence on the Impact of Undernurishment', in K. Taniguchi and X. Wang (eds), *Nutrition and Economic Growth*. Rome: FAO.

Centre for International Trade, Economics and Environment (CUTS) (2002). 'Market Access Implications of SPS and TBT: Bangladesh Perspective'. Jaipur: CUTS.

Diao, X., E. Diaz-Bonilla, and S. Robinson (2003). 'How Much Does It Hurt? The Impact of Agricultural Trade Policies on Developing Countries'. Washington, DC: IFPRI.

Diaz-Bonilla, E., and A. Gulati (2003). 'Developing Countries and the WTO Negotiations', in *Trade Policies and Food Security*. Reprinted from IFPRI's 2002–3 Annual Report. Washington, DC: IFPRI.

Drèze, J. and A. Sen (1989). *Hunger and Public Action*. Oxford and New York: Oxford University Press for UNU-WIDER.

Fitter, R., and R. Kaplinsky (2001). 'Who Gains from Product Rents as the Coffee Market Becomes More Differentiated? A Value Chain Analysis'. *IDS Special Issue on The Value of Value Chains*, 32 (3): 69–82.

FAO (1995). 'Impact of the Uruguay Round on Agriculture'. Document CCP: 95/13. Rome: FAO.

—— (1996a). 'Food, Agriculture and Food Security: Developments since the World Food Conference and Prospects'. Technical Background Document 1 for the WFS. Rome: FAO.

—— (1996b). *The State of Food and Agriculture, 1996*. Rome: FAO.

—— (1996c). 'Socio-political and Economic Environment for Food Security'. Technical Background Document 3 for the WFS. Rome: FAO.

—— (1996d). 'Success Stories in Food Security'. Technical Background Document 2 for the WFS. Rome: FAO.

—— (1999). 'Assessment of the Impacts of the Uruguay Round on Agricultural Markets and Food Security'. Document CCP 99/12 Rev. Rome: FAO.

—— (2000). *The State of Food Insecurity in the World*, 2000. Rome: FAO.

—— (2003a). *The State of Food Insecurity in the World*, 2003. Rome: FAO.

—— (2003b). *Trade Reforms and Food Security: Conceptualizing the Linkages*. Rome: FAO.

—— (2004). *The State of Food and Agriculture*. Rome: FAO.

Fukasaku, K. (2000). 'Special and Differential Treatment for Developing Countries: Does it Help those who Help Themselves?'. WIDER Working Paper 197. Helsinki: UNU-WIDER.

Gayi, S. K. (1998). 'The Uruguay Round Agreement on Agriculture and Food Security in Least Developed Countries'. Working Paper 55. Manchester: Institute of Development Policy and Management, University of Manchester.

General Agreement on Tariffs and Trade (GATT) (1994). *Uruguay Round of Multilateral Trade negotiations, Legal Instruments Embodying the Results of the Uruguay Round of Multilateral Trade Negotiations Done at Marrakesh on April 15*. Geneva: GATT.

Greenfield, J., M. de Nigris, and P. Konandreas (1996). 'The Uruguay Round Agreement on Agriculture: Food Security Implications for Developing Countries'. *Food Policy*, 21 (4/5): 365–75.

Hamilton, C., and J. Whalley (1995). 'Evaluating the Impact of the Uruguay Round Results on Developing Countries'. *The World Economy*, 18 (1): 31–49.

Herrmann, M. (2003). 'Agricultural Support Measure of Advanced Countries and Agricultural Production in Least Developed Countries: Conceptualization of Transmission Effects'. Background Paper to the LDCs Report 2004. Geneva: UNCTAD. Mimeo.

Hoekman, B., F. Ng, and M. Olareaga (2002). 'Reducing Agricultural Tariffs versus Domestic Support: What's More Important for Developing Countries?'. Policy Research Working Paper 2918. Washington, DC: World Bank.

Husain, I. (1993). 'Trade, Aid and Investment in Sub-Saharan Africa'. Policy Research Working Paper 1214. Washington, DC: World Bank.

Josling, T., and S. Tangerman (1999). 'The Interests of Developing Countries in the Next Round of WTO Agricultural Negotiations'. Paper prepared for UNCTAD Workshop on Developing Proactive and Coherent Trade Agenda for Africa Counties, 29 June–2 July, Pretoria.

Kaplinsky, R. (2000). 'Spreading the Gains from Globalization: What can be Learned from the Value Chain Analysis?'. *Journal of Development Studies*, 37 (2): 117–46.

—— (2002). 'Competitions Policy and the Global Coffee and Cocoa Value Chains'. Report prepared for the Office of the Special Coordinator for Africa, UNCTAD, May. Geneva: UNCTAD.

Konandreas, P., and J. Greenfield (1996). 'Uruguay Round Commitments on domestic Support: Their Implications for Developing Countries'. *Food Policy*, 21 (4–5): 433–46.

Laird, S., R. Peters, and D. Vanzetti (2004). 'Southern Discomfort: Agricultural Policies, Trade and Poverty'. CREDIT Research Paper 04/02. Nottingham: Centre for Research in Economic Development and International Trade, University of Nottingham.

Lindland , J. (1997). 'The Impact of the Uruguay Round on Tariff Escalation in Agricultural Products'. Rome: Commodities and Trade Division, FAO.

Lewis, W. A. (1954). 'Economic Development with Unlimited Supplies of Labour'. *The Manchester School*, 22 (2): 139–91.

Maxwell, S. (1989). 'Food Insecurity in Northern Sudan'. IDS Discussion Paper 262. Sussex: Institute of Development Studies.

—— (1996). 'Food Security: A Post-Modern Perspective'. *Food Policy*, 21 (2): 149–70.

Mayer, J. (2002). 'The Fallacy of Composition: A Review of the Literature'. *The World Economy*, 26 (6): 875–94.

Messer, E., and M. J. Cohen (2004). 'Breaking the Links between Conflict and Hunger in Africa'. 2020 Africa Conference Brief 10. Washington, DC: IFPRI.

Michalopoulus, C. (1999). 'Developing Country Goals and Strategies for the Millennium Round'. Policy Research Working Paper 2147. Washington, DC: World Bank.

—— (2000). 'Trade and Development in the GATT and WTO: The Role of Special and Differential Treatment for Developing Countries'. Washington, DC: World Bank.

OECD (2001). 'Towards More Liberal Agricultural Trade'. OECD Policy Brief, November. Paris: Organization for Economic Cooperation and Development.

Page, S., and M. Davenport (1994). *World Trade Reform: Do Developing Countries Gain or Lose?* (ODI Special Report). London: Overseas Development Institute.

Panagariya, A. (2002). 'Trade and Food security: Conceptualizing the Linkages'. Paper presented at the conference on Trade, Agricultural Development and Food Security: The Impact of Recent Economic and Trade Policy Reform, 11–12 July. Rome: FAO.

Pingali P., and R. Stringer (2003). 'Food Security and Agriculture in the Low Income Food Deficit Countries: 10 Years after the Uruguay Round'. ESA Working Paper 03–18. Rome: Agriculture and Economics Division, FAO.

Ranis, G., and J. C. Fei (1961). 'A Theory of Economic Development', *American Economic Review*, 51 (4): 533–65.

Salih, S. A. (1994). 'Food Security in East and Southern Africa'. *Northern Journal of African Studies*, 3 (1): 3–28.

Schulthes, J. (1994). 'New Approaches to Food Security'. *Agriculture and Rural Development*, 1 (1): 41–5.

Sen, A. K. (1981). *Poverty and Famines: An Essay on Entitlement and Deprivation*. Oxford: Clarendon Press.

Sharma, R., P. Konandreas, and J. Greenfield (1996). 'An Overview of Assessments of the Impact of the Uruguay Round on Agricultural Prices and Incomes'. *Food Policy*, 21 (4/5): 351–63.

Summer, D. A. (2000). 'Food Security, Trade and Agricultural Commodity Policy'. Paper presented at the symposium on Challenging the Agricultural Economics Paradigm, 10 September, Columbus, OH.

Tyers, R., and K. Anderson (1992). *Disarray in World Food Markets: A Quantitative Assessment*. Cambridge: Cambridge University Press.

UNCTAD (1995a). 'Translating Uruguay Round Special Provisions for Least Developed Countries into Concrete Action: Issues and Policy Requirements'. Document TD/B/WG.8. Geneva: UNCTAD.

—— (1995b). 'The Uruguay Round and International Commodity Trade and Prices'. Document TD/B/CN.1/30. Geneva: UNCTAD.

—— (1995c). 'Report on Evaluating the Outcome of the Uruguay Round Agriculture Agreement using the Agricultural Trade Policy Simulation Model' Report prepared by Odd Gulbrandsen for the UNCTAD Secretariat. Geneva: UNCTAD.

—— (1996). *The Least Developed Countries 1996 Report*. Document TD/B/42/(2)/11. New York: United Nations, and Geneva: UNCTAD.

—— (1997). *The Least Developed Countries 1997 Report* (Sales No. E.97.II.D.6). New York: United Nations, and Geneva: UNCTAD.

—— (1998). *Trade and Development Report, 1998* (Sales No. E.98.II.D.11). New York: United Nations, and Geneva: UNCTAD.

—— (1999). *Trade and Development Report, 1999* (Sales No. E.99.II.D.1). New York: United Nations, and Geneva: UNCTAD.

—— (2003). *Economic Development in Africa: Trade Performance and Commodity Dependence*. Document UNCTAD/GDS/AFRICA/2003/1. New York: United Nations, and Geneva: UNCTAD.

—— (2004). 'Review of the Developments and Issues in the post-Doha Work Programme of Particular Concern to Developing Countries: A Post-UNCTAD XI Perspective'. Document TD/B/51/4. Geneva: UNCTAD.

Valdés, A., and A. McCalla (1999). 'Issues, Interests and Options of Developing Countries'. Paper presented at the conference on Agriculture and the New Trade Agenda from a Development Perspective: Interests and Options in the WTO 2000 Negotiations, 1–2 October. Geneva.

Watkins, K., and J. von Braun (2003). 'Time to Stop Dumping on the World's Poor'. *2002–2003 IFPRI Annual Report Essay*. Washington, DC: IFPRI.

Whalley, J. (1999). 'Special and Differential Treatment in the Millennium Round'. *World Economy*, 22 (8): 1065–93.

Winters, L. A. (2000). 'Trade, Trade Policy and Poverty: What are the Links?'. CEPR Research Paper 2382. London: CEPR.

Wilson, J. S., and T. Otsuki (2001). 'Global Trade and Food Safety: Winners and Losers in a Fragmented System'. Working Paper 2689. Washington, DC: World Bank.

World Bank (1986). *Poverty and Hunger: Issues and Options for Food Security in Developing Countries*, World Bank Policy Study. Washington, DC: World Bank.

—— (2001). 'Response to the Proposal of the WTO Net-Food Importing Countries'. Report prepared for WTO's High-Level Roundtable Discussion, 18 June. Geneva: WTO.

—— (various years). *World Development Indicators*. Washington, DC: World Bank.

WTO (1995). *The Results of the Uruguay Round of Multilateral Trade Negotiations, The Legal Texts*. Geneva: WTO.

—— (2004). 'Doha Work Programme: Decision Adopted by the General Council on 1 August 2004'. Document WT/L/579. Geneva: WTO.

14

Food Retailing, Supermarkets, and Food Security: Highlights from Latin America

Mehmet Arda

14.1 Introduction

As defined in the *Plan of Action 1996* of the World Food Summit, 'Food security exists when all people, at all times, have physical and economic access to sufficient, safe and nutritious food to meet their dietary needs and food preferences for an active and healthy life' (FAO 1996). Food security can be discussed at the level of households, regions or the nation. The focus of this chapter is households and, mainly, their access to food. The nutritional aspects of available food is mentioned only briefly, as is food quality, which is a major aspect of food safety, 'closely linked with sanitation, water supply, food preparation and marketing', and which is 'the result of many different actions in the food supply chain' (Unnevehr 2003: 1).

Poverty being the main cause of food insecurity, access to food is examined from the perspective of purchasing power, determined by prices and incomes. With a given the level of income, the prices paid for the food is the key element of food security for the urban population that is, by definition, a net food purchasing group—the lower the prices for a given quality of food, the easier is access to food. The impact of changes in the retail end of the food supply chain, particularly with the advent of supermarkets, on access to food by urban consumers is one of the main concerns of the chapter; the other being the impact on food producers.

For the rural population, the situation is more complex. Food producers supplying urban markets have better incomes and better means to purchase

This version of the study has benefited considerably from the comments of Benjamin Davis and Madelon Meijer, but it was impossible to do justice to all their comments within the confines of this chapter. The views expressed are those of the author and not necessarily those of the United Nations Conference on Trade and Development (UNCTAD) of which the author was a staff member at the time of writing.

the food items that they do not produce themselves (as is the case of producers integrated to markets but not subsistence farmers) when they receive higher prices for their products. Therefore, supermarkets appear to be a new element in the conflict of interest between urban consumers and rural food producers. The former are interested in low food prices that supermarkets may bring about, and the latter, so far as they are net sellers, in high prices which supermarkets suppress. However, large parts of the rural population are net food purchasers and their access to food and food security is also heavily affected by the prices of the food they purchase. They are interested in higher prices for the items they sell, but lower prices for those which they purchase. Moreover, incomes of the food suppliers are determined not only by prices but also by the quantities sold, and from this point of view, their ability to participate in the supply chain is crucially important. The challenges to securing access to these chains are herein addressed.

The variables mentioned, which crucially affect food security—namely, prices, incomes of producers, quantities, and qualities—are determined in the food system that comprises the activities carried out in a complex chain (or web[1]—in the light of the complexity of relationships among global and local firms engaged in this sector) starting from supplying of inputs to agriculture, through farming, food processing and wholesale operations to the retail sector and consumers. In this chapter, the focus is on the retailing stage of the food system and, especially on how the recent rapid growth of supermarkets affects the consumers (principally urban) and the farming sector (principally rural). A related question is whether the recent changes in food markets add a new dimension to the conflict of interest between and within the rural and urban areas.

The basic questions are relevant for all parts of the world, but the main examples used in this study come from Latin America. The role of supermarkets in the food system, particularly their impact on the suppliers, has been the subject of considerable recent research. The intention of this chapter is to highlight the food security aspect while summarizing some of the relevant literature, rather than adding original information to the extensive documentation already available. Moreover, much of the discussion is rather 'speculative'. It may serve to point out some areas of research that would be useful for reaching conclusive results.

14.2 The Advent of Supermarkets

The word 'supermarket' is used to denote a large self-service store, selling groceries, dairy products, and household goods. Supermarkets are owned and

[1] For a discussion of the food economy as a web with food consumption at its centre, see Kinsey (2003).

operated by a wide variety of business concerns, from wealthy local individuals to giant, globally active, transnational companies. The operational modalities also differ but in this chapter the focus is more on 'modernity', particularly in procurement and selling practices, rather than size of the shops. The extent of concentration in the sector is an important determinant of these practices. The procurement practices become more complicated and restrictive for suppliers as concentration, and therefore the size of purchases, increases.

The emergence of supermarkets in developing countries is relatively recent. Their expansion, however, has been rapid. 'Supermarkets are now dominant players in most of the agrifood economy of Latin America, having moved from a rough-estimate population-weighted average of 10–20 per cent in 1990 to 50–60 per cent of the retail sector in 2000.' The corresponding change in the US retail sector took fifty years (Reardon and Berdegué 2002: 371). According to available data, a plateau seems to have been reached. The share of supermarkets in the food retail sector of principal Latin American countries is now similar to those in developed countries.

Urbanization and the increasing participation of women in the workforce have been important factors behind the rise of supermarkets. As the time spent in shopping for food has become more valuable, transportation facilities, access to cars, and refrigeration at home have allowed more bulk shopping and a preference for shopping at one place. These are the basic elements of the demand side for supermarket services. As Table 14.1 shows, the growth rate of urban population in Latin America and the Caribbean has been, and will continue to be, higher than in developed countries, although Africa and Asia display higher rates. In Latin America and the Caribbean, the percentage of urban population has been the highest among developing regions and surpassed that of Europe by 2000.

Some examples are given later on the impacts of the advent of supermarkets on the structure of employment in the farming sector. However, rising supermarket domination also has an impact on employment in urban

Table 14.1. Urbanization indicators by regions

	Urban population as % of total				Urban population growth % per year	
	1950	1975	2000	2030	1950–2000	2000–2030
North America	63.9	73.8	77.4	84.5	1.21	0.77
Latin America & the Caribbean	41.9	61.4	75.4	84.0	2.27	1.11
Oceania	61.6	72.2	74.1	77.3	1.77	1.05
Europe	52.4	67.3	73.4	80.5	0.57	−0.27
Asia	17.4	24.7	37.5	54.1	1.93	0.99
Africa	14.7	25.2	37.2	52.9	2.56	2.10

Source: UN (2001: table 3).

areas. It is reported that in Argentina the number of retail stores, in general, dropped between 1984 and 1993 by 30 per cent, accompanied by a drop of 26 per cent in employment in food retail. While sales were being taken over by supermarkets, because of lower labour intensity per peso sold in them, employment was reduced. As supermarkets took over larger parts of the food retail business, 125,000 jobs were lost in the traditional shops, as against an increase in jobs in supermarkets of 22,500 (Gutman 2002: 419).

A rough correlation can be detected between the prevalence of supermarkets and the level of income as well as the rate of urbanization in the figures in Table 14.2. The dynamics of supermarkets, however, are such that after emerging in large cities and concentrating on wealthy consumer segments, they 'spread quickly from their "niche" in capital cities to intermediate cities, and then to medium-sized and small towns in the 1990s'. At the same time, they started to address the special needs of poorer consumers. They 'moved out of their "niche" in upper-income neighbourhoods where the few of them were located pre-1990, to spill into middle-class neighbourhoods in the mid-1990s... and then into working-class neighbourhoods from the late 1990s'. The latter development comes with an emphasis on low prices and austere

Table 14.2. Modern sector shares in food retail, income, and urbanization: Latin American countries (sorted by urbanization)

	Modern sector share in food retail		Per capita income US$1,000 (2001)	Urban population % of total (2001)
	(1)	(2)	(3)	(4)
Uruguay	59		5,545	92.1
Argentina	54	57	7,158	88.3
Venezuela	54		5,048	87.2
Chile	58	50	4,310	86.1
Brazil	45	75	2,888	81.7
Colombia	40	38	1,924	75.5
Mexico	66		6,150	74.6
Peru	44		2,050	73.1
Bolivia	32		940	62.9
El Salvador		37	2,176	61.5
Costa Rica		50	4,014	59.5
Paraguay	36		1,286	56.7
Panama		54	3,383	56.5
Honduras		42	965	53.7
Guatemala		35	1,748	39.9

Notes: Columns 1 and 2: The figures from the two sources (M + M Planet Retail—data covering the 'modern sector' for 2004, and Reardon and Berdequé—supermarkets circa 2000) are not comparable owing to definitional differences. Some of the 'supermarkets', mostly locally owned, do not appear in the 'modern' sector. Even figures given in the same source are not comparable. For example, in Brazil, ABRAS defines supermarkets as having two or more cash registers while most other countries define them as having three or more (Reardon and Berdegué: 2002: table 1, note f).

Sources: Column 1: M + M Planet Retail; Column 2: Reardon and Berdequé (2002: table 1); Column 3: UNCTAD (2003); Column 4: UN (2004).

presentation, and the opening of chains of hard discount stores (Reardon and Berdegué 2002: 376). Similar developments occur all over the world. The strategy includes small shops in the densely populated areas, which avoids transportation needs for consumers, narrower choice, and packaging in small quantities to allow poorer consumers to afford the products. Although it can be argued that the expansion of the supermarket network into poorer parts of cities is the outcome of an unequal power struggle between large supermarkets and small shops, it also reflects an effective demand for their services.

The entry of global supermarket chains into developing countries, including Latin American countries, has been an important factor behind the expansion of the supermarket network and the increased presence of supermarkets in food markets.[2] In Latin America, Chile is the only country that has been spared this trend of foreign dominance, possibly because 'in the 1990s foreign firms prioritized their entry into . . . much larger markets. In addition during that decade Chilean companies were themselves at their peak' (Faiguenbaum *et al.* 2002: 462). Deregulation of domestic markets in the context of structural adjustment programmes as well as trade liberalization that allows imports and leads to economies of scope (in addition to economies of scale) have facilitated and encouraged the entry of global supermarket chains into these countries. Large-scale food manufacturers have also increased their importance in the food system driven by similar factors as supermarkets, and have 'similar and indeed related impacts "upstream" in the food system' (Reardon and Berdegué 2002: 372).

14.3 The Impact of Supermarkets on the Food Chain

14.3.1 *Consumers*

The impact of supermarkets on the consumers (urban population) manifests itself in two levels. The most visible, and probably the most important variable from the point of view of the consumer, is the prices paid for food in supermarkets compared with those in traditional markets. So long as supermarkets help reduce food prices, they contribute to improving food security for those who have access to them.

There is an interesting dichotomy between the developed and developing countries as regards the comparative prices for food in supermarkets and small shops or wet markets. In developed countries, food prices in neighbourhood markets are considerably higher than in supermarkets. In the United States, the difference can reach 76 per cent and agricultural produce and other foods offered in smaller stores are of lower quality (Prevention Institute) and 'inadequate access to supermarkets elevates the rate of diet-linked disease'

[2] Appendix Table 14A.1 gives the largest supermarkets in several Latin American countries.

(Clairmont 2004). Hence, the lack of supermarkets in low-income areas (where consumers' possession of cars is also lower) is often associated with disadvantages in access to food. In developing countries, however, especially for fresh fruit and vegetables (FFV), the situation is the opposite. In Nairobi, supermarkets charge on average 50–60 per cent more than do roadside kiosks and market stall vendors. While the wealthiest 20 per cent of consumers make 25 per cent of their fresh fruit and vegetable purchases at supermarkets, the corresponding share is barely 1 per cent for the lower 80 per cent of consumers (Tschirley *et al.* 2004: 2). The situation in Latin America seems to be somewhere in the middle. In Mexico, 21 per cent of the consumers preferred to buy FFV in the supermarkets (Schwentesius and Gomez 2002: 493). In Argentina, 21 per cent of FFV was bought in supermarkets (Ghezán *et al.* 2002: 391) Thus, cross-country experience indicates that as a country's level of development increases, the role of the supermarkets in food consumption becomes more important. In poorer countries, policies to improve the efficiency and cleanliness of the traditional marketing systems appear as the priority for food security.

The second variable affected by supermarkets which impacts on food security is the quality and safety of the food bought in supermarkets. So long as progress is achieved in this realm, food security can be considered to have improved. In fact, supermarkets follow much stricter quality requirements than traditional markets, and this is one attraction for consumers. As a result of the recognition of this fact, there has been a positive impact in general. 'A certain amount of mimicry' has been observed in the hygiene practices of 'wetmarkets' in Chile (Reardon *et al.* 2003: 8).

Surveys among urban consumers,[3] including in Latin America, have confirmed that price is the primary concern of lower-income consumers in making a choice regarding where to shop. As income levels rise, dietary changes take place and the importance of quality, the richness of available varieties, food safety, and convenience increases. Results of surveys are not conclusive on whether the first two concerns are better satisfied by supermarkets or small shops. Supermarkets, however, appear to satisfy the latter two concerns better.

Supermarkets' impact on prices of different types of foodstuffs follows roughly their predominance in the sale of these different types. In the initial phases of their increasing participation in food retail, supermarkets are particularly focused on the sale of dried and prepared foods, such as dried beans, rice, spaghetti, and canned products. These products are easier to procure in large quantities and to store for longer periods of time than fresh items such as fruit and vegetables. Thus, their prices in supermarkets tend to be lower than in traditional channels from an early stage. Prepared foods are becoming more

[3] For example, as reflected in Faiguenbaum *et al.* (2002); Alvorado and Charmel (2002); and Rodriguez *et al.* (2002).

significant in the food basket of the urban population, because the increased participation of women in the labour force reduces the time allocated to food preparation at home, and it can be said that this has contributed to easier access to food. This is all the more so as supermarkets continue to extend their coverage to the lower-income areas of the cities and change the nature of their stores, opening hard discount chains with a narrower product choice with less fancy items.

Extending the range of relatively cheaper 'private brands' (alternatively called 'own brands') of the supermarket chains themselves at the expense of better-known trademarks contributes to bringing down prices. It is reported that in Costa Rica private labels—which started with the staples, that is, the products that are probably most important from a food security point of view and where the Costa Rican consumers (*vis-à-vis* those in other places) exhibit highest price sensitivity—are typically priced 10 per cent below national brands (Alvorado and Charmel 2002: 479). One of the reasons that private brands are cheaper is the ability of supermarkets to purchase more cheaply than others. The UK Competition Commission's 2000 report on supermarkets shows that the largest supermarket (Tesco in the UK) can consistently obtain discounts from its suppliers and pays 4 per cent below the industry average, while smaller players pay above the odds (DFID 2004: 12). There is no reason to believe that a comparative situation is not at least as favourable to Latin American supermarkets as those in the UK. Not only do the supermarkets sell products they package and process themselves under their private labels, but also use products obtained from the suppliers of regular brands, with whom their private brands normally compete. In Costa Rica, for example, Parmalat in a joint venture with a medium-sized firm supplies milk under a private label to a major chain, CSU (Alvorado and Charmel 2002: 480).

An added advantage of supermarket chains in this connection is their ability to import products from cheaper sources globally. While import liberalization would allow this to be done by anyone, access to information through global sourcing networks of international supermarket chains, access to finance at international rates which are generally better than local conditions, and the possibility to import in large quantities provide significant advantages to supermarkets for selling bulk products more cheaply than traditional markets. The impact on producers of products such as dried beans has not been extensively studied, but since they are in any case traded in bulk, the local trading channels are not likely to change much, apart from the emergence of competition from abroad.

Fresh fruit and vegetables (FFV) is another principal food group that enters into the consumption basket. In general, supermarkets are less prevalent in the supply of FFV to consumers than in the other types of food. In Argentina and Mexico, while supermarkets' share in food retailing is about 50 per cent, the corresponding share in FFV is less than 30 per cent. In Chile, the disparity

Table 14.3. Differences in average prices between traditional small shops and supermarkets in Argentina, 1992 and 1997

	Supermarkets (S)		Traditional shops (T)		Price difference (T/S %)	
	1992	1997	1992	1997	1992	1997
Fruit	100	87	91	85	−9.0	−2.3
Vegetables	100	115	87	99	−13.0	−14.0
All food and beverages	100	117	108	122	+8.0	+4.3

Source: Ghezán *et al.* (2002: table 2).

between these shares is even greater. They are, respectively, 62 per cent and 3–8 per cent (Reardon and Berdegué 2002: 379). It has been observed in Argentina that there is a higher probability that consumers will buy meat, vegetables, fruit and bread from small shops (Rodriguez *et al.* 2002: 437). This is a result of the choice of consumers' whose perceptions of freshness favour traditional markets. In Chile, consumers do not consider refrigerated FFV to be fresh (Faiguenbaum *et al.* 2002: 466). In Mexico, FFV prices in supermarkets are relatively high, and supermarkets have less diversity of produce (Schwentesius and Gomez 2002: 494).

Table 14.3 provides evidence from Argentina, showing that while fruit and vegetables are more expensive in the supermarkets (although the difference has declined in the case of fruit), the overall average of prices of all foods and beverages is lower in the supermarkets. Thus, the price differential for staple foods is larger than indicated in the table: they were more than four per cent cheaper in the supermarkets than in traditional shops. In Nicaragua, potato and tomato prices drop by about 10 per cent, at each stage as one moves from the upper to the middle segment to the discount supermarket to the plaza market (Reardon and Berdegué 2002: 379). While supermarkets may not have much impact on the availability of FFV from the point of view of food security, the impact on suppliers is very significant, reflecting the fundamental difference between the procurement practices of the supermarkets and traditional retailers.

It can thus be said that from a nutritional point of view, particularly if one associates nutritional improvement with increasing the consumption of fruit and vegetables, supermarkets are not contributing much in poorer countries. However, for the poorer segments of the society in developing countries, nutritional upgrading involves increased consumption of basic foods such as pulses, sugar, and vegetable oils, and these appear to be cheaper in the supermarkets, especially in their discount varieties, in developing countries as well as developed ones.

A significant contribution to food security is made by the new developments in food retailing in the area of processed foods. For example, supermarkets have had a considerable impact on increasing the availability of safe milk to consumers. Their role in widening the availability of safe milk and dairy products to a significant portion of urban areas has been supported by the expanding use of ultra-high temperature (UHT) technology. It was only through this means that large quantities could be obtained and stored. The offtake of large quantities for distribution in extended markets must have contributed to making investments viable in the relatively large plants utilizing UHT technology. The share of UHT milk in Brazil's liquid milk market went up from 5 per cent to 60 per cent (85 per cent in urban areas) during the decade of the 1990s. The possibilities for easy transport across long distances and storage (no need to refrigerate) allowed local, and at best regional, milk markets to become national. Thus, milk was produced and processed in low-cost areas of the country for distribution over a large area. Prices dropped and production as well as processing increased by 2.5 per cent each year from 1997 to 2000. Consumers benefited from this development while the situation of producers changed for the better or worse, depending on whether or not they could participate in the new structure of the supply chain.

One negative impact of supermarkets on food consumption patterns and the quality of nutrition is the increased and easier availability of highly processed 'unhealthy' foods.[4] Although there is no hard evidence, a rapid rise in the consumption of total energy, saturated fats, and refined sugars—the latter being mostly from consumption of sodas and other sweetened drinks—may have been facilitated by a change in food retail systems. Changes in dietary patterns are associated with a rise in obesity diabetes and cardiovascular diseases. A similar, and possibly more directly attributable, change in dietary transition has been the result not of supermarkets but of the expansion of fast food chains. While these have made eating out a cheaper option for the middle-income group, they have also changed the characteristics of at least part of the supply chains for the principal items served in these outlets, such as fried potatoes (French fries) and meat, and induced significant impacts on suppliers.[5]

14.3.2 *Producers*

Bringing cheaper food to consumers is achieved through two principal avenues, both of which reduce costs to the supermarkets. The first is the

[4] Thanks to an anonymous referee for signalling this point.

[5] There has been considerable press coverage of the unhealthy nature of food consumed in these outlets with, in particular the relationship with obesity, but this is not a particularity of modern fast food. 'Data from an Accra-wide survey show that the poorest income quintile consumed more of its calories (31.4 per cent) away from home than any other income group. Food from away from home sources tends to be higher in fat, often refried many times over' (Haddad 2003: 4).

increased efficiency in procurement practices, and logistics have become much more efficient in the case of supermarkets. The second is the ability to procure products more cheaply. Therefore, only the producers who can meet very stringent conditions with regard to qualities, quantities and, most importantly, prices, can participate in the supply chains. We now have economic actors engaging in transactions rather than anonymous firms selling their homogeneous products on the market. Commodities are turning into distinguishable special food items (Kirsten and Sartorius 2002) with traceability characteristics.

Regarding the producers, the procurement practices of supermarkets are the key factor that affects their working conditions, employment and income and thus, their own food security. Wages of landless workers in agriculture and food processing are also very important. For the landless and wage labourers in rural areas, any impact generated by the supermarkets' activities on the price of food that they buy needs to be taken into account in discussing food security. For this group, the impact would be the result of local products being channelled to the supermarket rather than the local market, and the subsequent effects on availability and prices. The net effect of the changing nature of supply chains on employment and poverty cannot be predicted, but depends on factors such as *ex-ante* spatial and sectoral distribution of the poor and the food insecure, the nature of technologies introduced and the indirect effects of new patterns of income generation (Reardon and Barrett 2000: 197) as well as the distribution of assets such as land. The nature of new institutional arrangements also has a crucial impact on employment and poverty. For example, the development of the FFV industry and processing activities, the extra care needed to meet the stringent requirements, preparation of products for sale, including packaging and barcoding, generate employment opportunities, principally for women (e.g. in Chile, Barrientos *et al.* 1999). Nevertheless, the increasing pressure to cut costs leads to permanent workers being replaced by lower-waged temporary workers and thus male workers by females.[6] Small producers who have to turn over their activities to the larger concerns become net additions to the local labour supply or are forced to migrate to urban areas in search for work. This group experiences a significant negative impact on their food security.

[6] There is a gender dimension with respect of the impact of increased incomes with, whether an increase in disposable income through lower prices on the part of consumers, or through increased production and sales on the part of producers. In Central American agriculture, it has been observed that when men control expenditures from increased income, money is spent on buying agricultural inputs, paying debts and purchasing land. When women earn their own wages *and* control expenditures, extra money is spent on food for their family (Thrupp 1995: 83).

The main change that takes place in procurement practices that has considerable impact on suppliers, is the replacement of traditional wholesale markets with alternative specialized channels and more direct contacts between supermarkets, food processors and producers. There is an increasing vertical integration of the supply chain. In terms of the 'value chain' literature (e.g. summarized in Dolan and Humphrey 2000), governance of the chain is with the supermarket (or large food processor). The following is a review of this phenomenon and its impact on producers in Latin America, focusing on two types of changes. The first is the FFV chain where the change and the impact can be directly attributed to supermarkets. The second type of change has been generated by food processors in the milk and potatoes sectors. Supermarkets have had a triggering role and an impact, albeit rather indirectly, with regard to milk. For potatoes, the instigator of the change has been the spreading of fast food chains. In spite of the differences in the dynamics of the process, the results have been similar in all instances. Changes have been favourable for large producers and unfavourable for small ones, particularly for those who have not been able to organize themselves into larger operational and organizational units. The cases of Purranque for vegetables in Chile and Hortifruti in Costa Rica have been cited as successful examples (Reardon and Berdegué 2002: 382), while the failure of the small growers into organizing themselves for selling to supermarkets is exemplified by the case of the Union of Lime and Tropical Fruit Growers in Mexico (Schwentesius and Gomez 2002: 498).

FRESH FRUIT AND VEGETABLES

Traditionally FFV producers, large or small, have operated in a system that allows them to decide what to produce and then to put their products on the market through various types of wholesale markets. Retailers procure supplies from these wholesale markets where the prices based on different qualities would also be established. Based on to these price signals, producers would decide on the produce to be planted. This is still the principal channel for the commercialization of FFV, but significant changes have occurred as a result of the increasing presence of supermarkets in FFV retailing.

At the initial stages of supermarket expansion in FFV retailing when the quantities involved are relatively small, supermarkets obtain supplies from the traditional wholesale markets. However, supermarkets quickly realize that the traditional wholesalers provide inadequate service since they lack standards, mix different grades, and have significant bargaining power in the wholesale markets (Reardon and Berdegué 2002: 380), thus reducing the relative power of the supermarkets. As the quantities involved become larger, alternative procurement methods become more attractive, and supermarkets tend to look for ways to eliminate the intermediaries. As a first step, when adequate storage facilities are built up and the volume of sales at specific stores becomes sufficiently enough to handle, for example, produce by the truckloads producers who have the capacity to offer such quantities become preferred suppliers. As long as the desired quantities and qualities are obtained through direct procurement, these producers have a direct access to supermarkets, bypassing the wholesale markets. In Mexico, direct procurement is estimated to offer 10 per cent savings on costs (Schwentesius and Gomez 2002: 496). This is the first phase of small producers facing major difficulties in accessing supermarket supply chains.

In the second stage, when the supermarket chain handles even larger volumes and a centralized distribution system is established, the volume and quality requirements become more numerous and stringent. At this stage, specialized, dedicated wholesalers also appear to serve the supermarkets. These are 'generally agroexporters and agroindustrial firms which are used to dealing in volume and meeting safety and quality standards.... Some chains even use their distribution centres, sourcing networks and/or joint venture operations to both supply their local stores and export produce between Latin American countries and from Latin America to the global market' (Reardon and Berdegué 2002: 380–1). Three examples cited in this context are Costa Rica's Hortifruti; Brazil's Carrefour which supplies from the country's contracted melon producers 67 stores in Brazil as well as Carrefour distribution centres in 21 countries, and the Argentinian-based Ahold's regional sourcing network, sourcing apples from Chile for its distribution centre in Peru (Reardon and Berdegué 2002: 381).

It is also at this phase that contracts are drawn between suppliers and supermarkets regarding volumes, qualities, and timing of supplies. Obviously, transaction costs for the supermarkets are lowered as the number of suppliers they deal with diminishes. This generates the dynamics that lead to the exclusion of produce from the supermarket shelves of the individual small producers precisely at a time these channels are becoming increasingly important for getting products to consumers. Exclusion can be avoided only if small producers organize themselves into cooperatives in order eliminate the need for supermarkets to deal with a large number of individual small producers. It is reported that farmers' economic organizations in Chile are having a hard time meeting the demands of the supermarkets, but in comparison to traditional markets still generating higher incomes for their members. In several successful organizations, public or private assistance to help the growers with technical assistance and suppliers' input credit has been provided (Reardon and Berdegué 2002: 381–2). Excluded suppliers face greater challenges in having to compete in the shrinking (traditional) market, while those that are linked to supermarkets have access to an expanding one. Larger farms appear to be at an advantage. In one locality in Argentina, total horticultural area doubled between 1978 and 1994 but the number of farms increased by only 12 per cent (Ghezán *et al.* 2002: 398). The takeover of small production units by larger ones is a common phenomenon, threatening the livelihoods of the former.

Meeting the standards set by supermarkets is a major challenge as these are almost always more stringent than general food safety requirements, including hazard analysis critical control point (HACCP) levels. Some are private standards without third-party certification, some involve third-party certification, and some are hybrid private–public standards. The latter are common for processed FFV products. There is a convergence between national and international supermarket standards and with export standards. For example, CSU-Supermarkets and Hortifruti in Costa Rica have indicated a plan to adopt the EUREPGAP standard applicable in European supermarkets (Reardon *et al.* 2003: 22–3). This means that producers who are able to supply local supermarkets are also qualified to enter international markets, while those who cannot meet the standards are quickly 'delisted' and lose their option to sell to supermarket chains. As international supermarket chains usually employ similar criteria for all their international procurement systems, suppliers complying with the standards also have the chance to access international supply channels, thus a much larger market.

Supplying FFV under contract (generally by large producers) brings with it new challenges and opportunities. The importance of prices in deciding resource allocation practically disappears. In fact, some researchers argue that there is a tendency for the emergence of a 'seamless system' as a fully integrated food system from seed to supermarket shelf. 'Within this emerging system there will be no markets and thus no price discovery... the first time the price of any input in the food system will be public information will be at the supermarket... The farmer becomes a grower, providing labour and often some capital, but never having clear title to the product as it moves through the food system and never making major decisions' once he is integrated into this system (Heffernan 1999: 6).

Nevertheless, the coordination of the supply chain through contract farming, which is an intermediate form of industrial organization between spot markets and full vertical integration, remedies such market failures as information asymmetry between the buyer and the seller. Contract farming in its different varieties is relevant not only for FFV but for farming of most products. As noted by Kirsten and Sartorius (2002 11–4):

> Farmers usually enter into contract production in order to reduce costs and gain access to information, technology, marketing channels, managerial skills, technical expertise, access to plant and equipment and patented production procedures. Contracting can also improve access to capital and credit. Reduction of marketing risks and greater stability of income are other attractive features of contract farming. Farmers are prepared to relinquish their autonomy, accept greater production risk for the sake of being able

to produce. Contracts can be of different types, the control of the buyer varying in proportion to the provision of resources and inputs to the grower.

In some cases, supermarkets charge the supplier a fee for the benefit of having access to a particular market. This fee, known as *rapel* in Chile, amounts to 3–8 per cent of the value of the produce (Faiguenbaum *et al.* 2002: 466).

Apart from the challenge of meeting the contract-stipulated requirements, one important aspect of supplying supermarkets is the practice of supermarkets generally paying suppliers with significant delay. In fact, supermarkets are known to make significant earnings from financial operations made possible by using funds generated through spot payments from consumers but delayed payments to suppliers that can extend to several months. 'On a worldwide scale, Carrefour's cash-flow cycle (from selling the product to the consumer to paying the suppliers, including days in stock) was 55 days'. In Argentina, 'by the end of 1990s, the average supermarket payment period was 90 days, varying between 60 and 100 days, while consumers provide immediate payment in cash or at most 25 days on consumer credit cards (Gutman 2002: 421).[7] In Chile, the 30–90 day waiting period implies that suppliers not only finance the net value of the produce but also the value-added tax paid by the supermarket each month (Faiguenbaum *et al.* 2002: 466). In Mexico, based on reports from the Union of Lime and Tropical Fruit Growers, supermarkets pay the highest price, but the Union also incurs extra costs for refrigeration and for providing credit to the supermarkets. Limes sold to wholesale markets were priced 10–20 per cent less than those sold to supermarkets but payment was immediate, or with a delay maximum of 15 days (Schwentesius and Gomez 2002: 499). Legislation has been enacted in some countries to reduce this delay on payment to suppliers. For example, in March 2002, the government of Argentina imposed a 30-day limit in connection with suppliers of perishable goods (Gutman 2002: 421).

Supermarkets provide certain opportunities. Apart from the enlarged markets, supermarket chains are known to assist their suppliers with technical support regarding production processes and with financing for fixed investments, such as cold storage, to improve quality and to ensure its maintenance. These are beneficial for the suppliers who can participate in these arrangements and they improve their earnings. The food insecure, however, are normally not among this group. Long-term contracts also reduce the marketing risks associated with production by ensuring a market and relatively stable prices. These prices may be somewhat lower in the long run than what could have been obtained if a perfect selling strategy taking advantage of all possible optimal prices would have been followed (a rather unlikely outcome), but the reduction of risks is a positive factor improving business performance. The fact

[7] Information on Carrefour as quoted by Gutman (2002).

that there is a secure income under contractual arrangements should enable farmers to obtain credit at relatively favourable terms through structured financing channels where they exist.[8]

Large concerns supplying supermarkets may also provide opportunities for value adding operations (packaging, bar-coding) and simple processing activities that can be handled on the producer farm (washing, preparing ready-to-eat salads). Other, more sophisticated processing operations (freezing, producing ready-to-eat meals) require different operations. In any case, all of these open up possibilities for employment, particularly for female workers, in the rural areas and can be perceived as positive from the point of view of food security, as they improve the earnings of the relatively poor segments of society.

MILK

The recent changes in the milk sector have also affected producers significantly. Also in the case of milk, small producers have been disadvantaged owing to similar factors as seen in the FFV sector. During 1997 to 2000, the number of farmers delivering milk to the top twelve companies in Brazil dropped by 60,000 (35 per cent) and there was a 55 per cent increase in the average size of the supplier (Farina 2002: 452–5). Nestlé alone removed 26,000 farmers from its supply list, a drop of 75 per cent (Farina 2003: 9). In Argentina, between 1988 and 1996, the number of dairy farms dropped by 30 per cent, while the number of cows increased by 17 per cent. The daily production of milk per farm doubled and total output increased 44 per cent (Gutman 2002: 425). The establishment of large-scale milk processing plants, however, may have contributed to some employment generation in these plants.

POTATOES

While the impact of fast food chains on food security and safety is debatable, these chains have brought new dynamics to Latin American agriculture, particularly to producers of essential ingredients, namely meat and potatoes. Changes in the potato industry have been well documented (Ghezán *et al.* 2002). Argentina's potato industry was basically targeted for consumption in the unprocessed state. The proliferation of fast food, in particular the McDonald's chain in Argentina, generated a change in the potato industry. As the number of fast food outlets increased, the chain's international potato suppliers took over from local producers. Business methods changed, but potatoes continued to be procured locally in Argentina. As a result, the import operations of principally McCain of Canada for frozen pre-fried potatoes

[8] For a discussion of structured finance in the commodity sector, including farming, see UNCTAD (2004).

were replaced by locally processed and frozen supplies, targeted not only to the Argentinean but also to the regional markets. Argentina now supplies 90 per cent of Latin America's exports, including 50 per cent coverage of the Brazilian market.

Given that restaurants submit orders to the distribution centre only 48 hours in advance of delivery, very sophisticated infrastructure and logistics are required. With this development, written contracts between processors and farmers became widespread. This requirement for sophisticated infrastructure and logistics, as in other cases of contract farming, promotes concentration. Nearly half of the produce supplied to the processors comes from 15 per cent of the farmers. Given the very specific quality requirements, new varieties of seeds were provided to the suppliers by the processing plants, who also imported harvesting machines (valued at about half a million dollars each), providing credit to three major farmers purchasing the machines. These firms also offer financing for operational expenses. This has spillover effects for production other than processing, and is found to be useful by the farmers. The opportunities created by McDonald's need for frozen French fries led to the emergence of a whole new industry. It has special requirements with regard to potatoes, resulting in a significant upheaval, repositioning, and consolidation among producers. For entrepreneurs in the processing industry, the market became much wider than the earlier domestic market, and extended to neighbouring countries.

14.4 Conclusion

The increasing importance of the supermarkets is one of the several changes taking place in the food chain. Supermarkets have not only changed the retail end of the food chain, but also generated very significant changes in the organization of production and delivery of food to the point of sale.

In the urban areas, food safety of those with access to supermarkets appears to have improved in line with the greater emphasis on cleanliness by supermarkets. For some food commodities, particularly bulk products, a drop in prices is observed, thus improving access to food, again for those who shop in supermarkets, particularly discount chains. There does not seem to be an impact on the food security of the poorer strata in middle-income counties, or even in the middle-income groups in poorer countries.

The advent of supermarkets in the rural communities has opened up unprecedented opportunities for a considerable number of (mostly large) farmers, albeit generating negative impact on small producers unable to meet the stringent requirements of supermarket chains and other modern food supply channels. Inevitably, the food security of this latter group is impaired. It is therefore imperative that development policies and national as well as international assistance programmes take this factor into account and include actions that will enable this disadvantaged group to benefit from the new opportunities opening up in the food trading system. Such action primarily needs to address the financing of the transition needed to comply with modern supply chain requirements. While financing by donor assistance is an option, dealing with the financing of small and relatively risky concerns within a value chain approach, namely using the stronger parts of the chain as a security for financing the weaker links, offers interesting opportunities (UNCTAD 2004). The supermarkets' corporate social responsibility also calls for closer ties with small producers with a view of assisting in the transformation of their production and business practices, and avoiding social problems. Although initiatives by small producers to organize themselves into viable cooperatives to deal with supermarkets have had mixed results, this still seems to be an area requiring attention and support. Legal and institutional improvements aimed at promoting 'good business practices that optimize retailer supplier relations, protecting both sides' (Reardon and Berdegué 2002: 386) are also required, particularly as contractual relations become prominent. Finally, competition policy actions that would prevent the abuse of market power and promote a competitive retail sector would help the producers get a better share of the final value of their products.

Appendix 14.1

Table 14A.1 Main supermarkets in Latin American countries

Rank		1998			2004		
		Food sales, US$	Market share in modern sales (%)	Market share in total food sales (%)	Food sales, US$	Market share in modern sales (%)	Market share in total food sales (%)
ARGENTINA							
1	Carrefour	3,297	11.0	7.7	1,272	11.5	6.2
2	Coto	1,321	4.4	3.1	734	6.6	3.6
3	Ahold	1,825	6.1	4.3	654	5.9	3.2
4	La Anónima	509	1.7	1.2	385	3.5	1.9
5	Cencosud	463	1.5	1.1	309	2.8	1.5
6	Wal-Mart	273	0.9	0.6	298	2.7	1.4
7	SHV Makro	420	1.4	1.0	202	1.8	1.0
8	Casino	311	1.0	0.7	159	1.4	0.8
9	Supermercados Toledo	323	1.1	0.8	154	1.4	0.7
10	Cooperativa Obrera	251	0.8	0.6	99	0.9	0.5
11	Auchan	45	0.2	0.1	22	0.2	0.1
	Subtotal	9,038	30.0	21.1	4,288	39.0	20.8
	Other	20,933	70.0	49.0	6,760	61.0	32.8
	Total modern food sales	29,971	100.0	70.1	11,048	100.0	53.6
	Total food sales	42,756		100.0	20,614		100.0

(cont.)

Table 14A.1 (*Continued*)

Rank		1998			2004		
		Food sales, US$	Market share in modern sales (%)	Market share in total food sales (%)	Food sales, US$	Market share in modern sales (%)	Market share in total food sales (%)
BOLIVIA							
1	Hipermaxi in Bolivia	15	1.8	0.6	39	5.0	1.6
2	Ketal in Bolivia	10	1.2	0.4	35	4.5	1.4
	Subtotal	25	3.0	0.9	74	9.0	3.0
	Other	804	97.0	30.5	705	91.0	28.9
	Total modern food sales	829	100.0	31.4	779	100.0	32.0
	Total food sales	2,639		100.0	2,437		100.0
BRAZIL							
1	Casino	3,297	6.7	3.1	3,877	7.9	3.6
2	Carrefour	3,950	8.1	3.7	2,985	6.1	2.8
3	Wal-Mart	172	0.4	0.2	1,063	2.2	1.0
4	Modelo Continente	1,013	2.1	1.0	965	2.0	0.9
5	Atacadao	771	1.6	0.7	912	1.9	0.8
6	SHV Makro	819	1.7	0.8	890	1.8	0.8
7	Zaffari	281	0.6	0.3	325	0.7	0.3
8	Coop Cooperativa de Consumo	243	0.5	0.2	312	0.6	0.3
9	Ahold	1,037	2.1	1.0	289	0.6	0.3
10	ExxonMobil	45	0.1	0.0	65	0.1	0.1
11	Ipiranga	41	0.1	0.0	51	0.1	0.0
	Subtotal	11,669	24.0	11.0	11,734	24.0	10.8
	Other	37,201	76.0	35.1	37,233	76.0	34.4
	Total modern food sales	48,870	100.0	46.1	48,967	100.0	45.2
	Total food sales	106,103		100.0	108,225		100.0
CHILE							
1	D&S (Distribución y Servicio)	1,289	18.3	10.1	1,329	16.2	9.5
2	Cencosud	250	3.6	2.0	900	11.0	6.4
3	Unimarc	389	5.5	3.1	232	2.8	1.7
4	Montserrat	140	2.0	1.1	211	2.6	1.5
5	Falabella	19	0.3	0.1	121	1.5	0.9
6	COPEC	79	1.1	0.6	71	0.9	0.5
	Subtotal	2,166	31.0	17.0	2,864	35.0	20.4
	Other	4,872	69.0	38.3	5,333	65.0	38.0
	Total modern food sales	7,038	100.0	55.3	8,197	100.0	58.4
	Total food sales	12,722		100.0	14,026		100.0
COLOMBIA							
1	Casino	1,140	14.6	5.8	1,241	14.0	5.6
2	Carulla Vivero	328	4.2	1.7	616	6.9	2.8
3	Olimpica	389	5.0	2.0	456	5.1	2.1
4	Carrefour	75	1.0	0.4	362	4.1	1.6
5	SHV Makro	149	1.9	0.8	180	2.0	0.8
6	CAFAM	198	2.5	1.0	152	1.7	0.7
	Subtotal	2,279	29.0	11.6	3,007	34.0	13.6
	Other	5,538	71.0	28.1	5,861	66.0	26.4
	Total modern food sales	7,817	100.0	39.6	8,868	100.0	40.0
	Total food sales	19,729		100.0	22,176		100.0

(*cont.*)

Table 14A.1 (*Continued*)

Rank		1998			2004		
		Food sales, US$	Market share in modern sales (%)	Market share in total food sales (%)	Food sales, US$	Market share in modern sales (%)	Market share in total food sales (%)
ECUADOR							
1	Supermercados La Favorita	143	11.8	4.1	397	18.2	6.5
2	Tia	53	4.4	1.5	85	3.9	1.4
	Subtotal	196	16.0	5.6	482	22.0	7.8
	Other	1,016	84.0	29.1	1,698	78.0	27.7
	Total modern food sales	1,212	100.0	34.8	2,180	100.0	35.5
	Total food sales	3,486		100.0	6,141		100.0
MEXICO							
1	Wal-Mart	3,267	6.8	4.3	5,248	8.1	5.4
2	Soriana	1,702	3.5	2.3	2,110	3.3	2.2
3	Comercial Mexicana	2,211	4.6	2.9	2,056	3.2	2.1
4	Gigante	1,872	3.9	2.5	2,083	3.2	2.1
5	OXXO	486	1.0	0.6	1,142	1.8	1.2
6	Safeway (USA)	725	1.5	1.0	845	1.3	0.9
7	Costco	243	0.5	0.3	812	1.3	0.8
8	Chedraui	537	1.1	0.7	609	0.9	0.6
10	Carrefour	440	0.9	0.6	548	0.8	0.6
11	H.E. Butt	167	0.3	0.2	576	0.9	0.6
	Subtotal	11,650	24.0	15.4	16,029	25.0	16.5
	Other	36,389	76.0	48.2	48,508	75.0	49.9
	Total modern food sales	48,039	100.0	63.7	64,537	100.0	66.4
	Total food sales	75,465		100.0	97,161		100.0
PARAGUAY							
1	Superseis	25	2.8	1.1	29	3.8	1.4
2	Supermercados Stock	50	5.7	2.1	14	1.8	0.7
	Subtotal	75	9.0	3.2	43	6.0	2.0
	Other	804	91.0	34.4	723	94.0	34.0
	Total modern food sales	879	100.0	37.6	766	100.0	36.0
	Total food sales	2,336		100.0	2,128		100.0
PERU							
1	E. Wong	329	6.3	2.7	504	7.1	3.1
2	Santa Isabel (formerly Ahold)	184	3.5	1.5	300	4.2	1.8
3	Falabella	5	0.1	0.0	51	0.7	0.3
	Subtotal	518	10.0	4.3	855	12.0	5.2
	Other	4,700	90.0	38.9	6,282	88.0	38.2
	Total modern food sales	5,218	100.0	43.2	7,137	100.0	43.5
	Total food sales	12,084		100.0	16,424		100.0
URUGUAY							
1	Casino	213	9.2	6.0	187	14.2	8.4
2	Tienda Inglesa	144	6.2	4.1	48	3.6	2.2
3	Multi Ahorro	112	4.8	3.2	43	3.3	1.9
4	Ta-Ta	77	3.3	2.2	29	2.2	1.3
	Subtotal	546	24.0	15.4	307	23.0	13.8
	Other	1,769	76.0	49.8	1,009	77.0	45.5
	Total modern food sales	2,315	100.0	65.2	1,316	100.0	59.3
	Total food sales	3,551		100.0	2,220		100.0

(*cont.*)

Table 14A.1 (*Continued*)

Rank		1998			2004		
		Food sales, US$	Market share in modern sales (%)	Market share in total food sales (%)	Food sales, US$	Market share in modern sales (%)	Market share in total food sales (%)
VENEZUELA							
1	Casino (Started in 2000)	0	0.0	0.0	320	4.0	2.2
2	SHV Makro	399	3.8	2.2	264	3.3	1.8
3	Central Madeirense	571	5.4	3.1	238	3.0	1.6
4	Unicasa	230	2.2	1.3	91	1.1	0.6
5	Automercados Plaza's	137	1.3	0.7	85	1.1	0.6
6	Excelsior Gama	86	0.8	0.5	51	0.6	0.3
	Subtotal	1,423	13.0	7.8	1,049	13.0	7.1
	Other	9,187	87.0	50.1	6,887	87.0	46.5
	Total modern food sales	10,610	100.0	57.9	7,936	100.0	53.6
	Total food sales	18,320		100.0	14,797		100.0

Source: Data from M + M Planet Retail, compiled by Mr Anar Mammadov, Commodities Branch, UNCTAD.

References

Alvorado, I., and K. Charmel (2002). 'The Rapid Rise of Supermarkets in Costa Rica: Impact on Horticultural Markets'. *Development Policy Review*, 20 (4): 473–85.

Barrientos, S., A. Bee, A. Matear, and I. Vogel (1999). *Women and Agribusiness: Working Miracles in the Chilean Fruit Export Sector*. Basingstoke: Macmillan.

Barrientos, S., S. McClenaghan, and L. Orton (1999). 'Gender and Codes of Conduct: A Case Study from Horticulture in South Africa'. In-Depth Report. London: Christian Aid. Available at: www.christian-aid.org.uk/indepth/9908grap/grapes2.htm

Clairmont, M. (2004). 'Taking Steps towards Adequate Supermarket Access'. *Today's Dietitian*, 6 (5): 38.

DFID (2004) 'Concentration in Food Supply and Retail Chains'. DFID Working Paper 13. London: Department for International Development.

Dolan, C., and J. Humphrey (2000). 'Governance and Trade in Fresh Vegetables: the Impact of UK Supermarkets on the African Horticulture Industry'. *Journal of Development Studies*, 37 (2): 147–76.

Faiguenbaum, S., J. Berdegué, and T. Reardon (2002). The Rapid Rise of Supermarkets in Chile: Effects on Dairy, Vegetable and Beef Chains'. *Development Policy Review*, 20 (4): 459–71.

Farina, E. (2002). 'Consolidation, Multinationalization and Competition in Brazil: Impacts on Horticulture and Dairy Products Systems'. *Development Policy Review*, 20 (4): 441–57.

—— (2003). 'The Latin American Perspective on the Impacts of the Global Food Economy: The Case of Brazil'. Paper presented at the Conference on Changing Dimensions of the Food Economy: Exploring the Policy Issues, 6–7 February. The Hague.

FAO (1996). *World Food Summit*. 13–17 November. Rome: FAO. Available: www.fao.org/wfs/index_en.htm.

Ghezán, G., M. Mateos, and L. Viteri (2002). 'Impact of Supermarkets and Fast-Food Chains on Horticulture Supply Chains in Argentina'. *Development Policy Review*, 20 (4): 389–408.

Gutman, G. (2002). 'Impact of the Rapid Rise of Supermarkets on Dairy Products System in Argentina'. *Development Policy Review*, 20 (4): 409–27.

Haddad, L. (2003). 'Redirecting the Diet Transition: What Can Food Policy Do?'. Paper presented at Conference on Changing Dimensions of the Food Economy: Exploring the Policy Issues, 6–7 February. The Hague.

Heffernan, W. (1999). 'The Influence of the Big Three: ADM, Cargil and ConAgra'. Paper presented at the conference Farmer Cooperatives in the 21st Century, 9–11 June. Des Moins.

Kinsey, J. (2003). 'Emerging Trends in the New Food Economy: Consumers, Firms and Science'. Paper presented at the conference on Changing Dimensions of the Food Economy: Exploring the Policy Issues, 6–7 February. The Hague.

Kirsten, J., and K. Sartorius (2002). 'Linking Agribusiness and Small Scale Farmers in Developing Countries: Is there a New Role for Contract Farming?'. *Development Southern Africa*, 19 (4): 503–29, Reprinted as Working Paper 2002–13. Pretoria: Department of Agricultural Economics, Extension and Rural Development, University of Pretoria (textual references refer to the pagination in the reprint).

M + M Planet Retail. Available at: www.planetretail.net. Accessed numerously during 2005.

Prevention Institute (nd). 'Supermarket Access in Low-Income Communities'. Oakland, CA: Prevention Institute. Available at: www.preventioninstitute.org/pdf/CHI Supermarkets.pdf#search='supermarket%20access.

Reardon, T., and C. Barrett. (2000). 'Agroindustrialization, Globalization, and International Development: An Overview of Issues, Patterns, and Determinants'. *Agricultural Economics*, 23 (3): 195–205.

—— J. Berdegué (2002). 'The Rapid Rise of Supermarkets in Latin America: Challenges and Opportunities for Development'. *Development Policy Review*, 20 (4): 371–88.

—— P. Timmer, and J. Berdegué (2003). 'The Rise of Supermarkets and Private Standards in Developing Countries: Illustrations from the Produce Sector and Hypothesized Implications for Trade'. Paper presented at the international conference on Agricultural Policy Reform and the WTO: Where Are We Heading?, 23–6 June. Capri.

Rodriguez, E., M. Berges, K. Casellas, R. di Paola, B. Lupin, L. Grrido, and N. Gentile (2002). 'Consumer Behaviour and Supermarkets in Argentina'. *Development Policy Review*, 20 (4): 429–39.

Schwentesius, R., and M. Gomez (2002). 'Supermarkets in Mexico: Impacts on Horticulture System'. *Development Policy Review*, 20 (4): 487–502.

Thrupp, L. A., with G. Gbergeron and W. Waters. (1995). *Bittersweet Harvests for Global Supermarkets: Challenges in Latin America's Agricultural Export Boom.* Washington, DC: World Resources Institute.

Tschirley, D., M. Ayieko, M. Mathenge, and M. Weber (2004). 'Where Do Consumers in Nairobi Purchase their Food and Why Does This Matter? The Need for Investment to Improve Kenya's "Traditional" Food Marketing System'. Policy Brief 3. Available at: www.tegemeo.org/publications.asp?title= and Subject ID= and Year= and form post=1 and document typeid=3 and languageid=.

UNCTAD (2003). 'Handbook of Statistics 2003'. Document TD/STAT.28. New York and Geneva: United Nations.

—— (2004). 'Financing Commodity-Based Trade and Development: Innovative Agriculture Financing Mechanisms'. Document TD/B/COM.1/EM.24/2. Geneva: United Nations.

United Nations (2001). 'World Urbanization Prospects: The 2001 Revision'. Document ST/ESA/SER.A/216. New York: United Nations.

Unnevehr, L. (2003). 'Food Safety in Food Security and Food Trade; Overview'. Brief 1, in L. Unnevehr (ed.), *Food Safety in Food Security and Food Trade*. 2020 Vision Focus 10. Washington, DC: IFPRI.

Index

Index

Index

Index